The Information Retrieval Series   Volume 33

T0181320

Massimo Melucci · Ricardo Baeza-Yates

Editors

Advanced Topics in Information Retrieval

 Springer

Editors
Massimo Melucci
Department of Information Engineering
University of Padua
Via G. Gradenigo, 6
Padua 35131
Italy
massimo.melucci@dei.unipd.it

Ricardo Baeza-Yates
Yahoo! Research Barcelona
Diagonal 177 p9
Barcelona 08018
Spain
rbaeza@acm.org

ISSN 1387-5264
ISBN 978-3-642-26863-2   ISBN 978-3-642-20946-8 (eBook)
DOI 10.1007/978-3-642-20946-8
Springer Heidelberg Dordrecht London New York

ACM Computing Classification (1998): H.3

Cover design: deblik, Berlin

Printed on acid-free paper

Springer is part of Springer Science+Business Media (www.springer.com)

Preface

This book presents a wide-spectrum illustration of what research in Information Retrieval has produced or will produce in the next years. The book content includes chapters on Aggregated Search, Digital Advertising, Digital Libraries, Discovery of Spam and Opinions in the Web, Evaluation, Information Retrieval in Context, Multimedia Resource Discovery, Quantum Mechanics applied to Information Retrieval, Scalability Challenges in Web Search Engines, and Users in Interactive Information Retrieval Evaluation. Every chapter is authored by well-known researchers, with an integrated bibliography and subject index. In the following paragraphs we describe briefly the content of each of these chapters, which are sorted in lexicographical order by first author.

We start with a chapter on Digital Libraries by Maristella Agosti from the University of Padova, Italy. Here she gives some historical background to then introduce the main concepts of present digital library systems. After that, the chapter covers usability, interoperability and evaluation issues.

The second chapter is Scalability Challenges in Web Search Engines by Berkant Barla Cambazoglu and Ricardo Baeza-Yates from Yahoo! Research Barcelona, Spain. This chapters looks at current search engine architectures, from a single search server to search clusters. The chapter ends in a hypothetical geographically distributed multi-site search system, focusing on scalability issues and current open problems.

Chapter three is entitled Spam, Opinions, and other Relationships: Towards a Comprehensive View of the Web by Bettina Berendt from Leuven University, Belgium. This chapter proposes an integrating model of learning cycles involving data, information and knowledge, which includes Information Retrieval and Knowledge Discovery in the Web as particular cases. This is illustrated by applying the model to spam detection, opinion mining and relation mining.

The fourth chapter is The User in Interactive Information Retrieval Evaluation by Peter Ingwersen from the Royal School of Library and Information Science, Denmark. This chapter explores interactive information retrieval by using a laboratory research framework for IR. This involves the definition of request types, ultra-light experiments, interactive-light studies and naturalistic field investigations.

Chapter five is entitled Aggregated Search by Mounia Lalmas from Yahoo! Research Barcelona, Spain. This chapter overviews the state of the art in the aggregation of different information sources to achieve diversity for broad or ambiguous queries, exploring the different challenges that arise in this problem.

The sixth chapter is Quantum Mechanics and Information Retrieval by Massimo Melucci and Keith van Rijsbergen, from University of Padova, Italy, and University of Cambridge, UK, respectively. This chapter provides a survey on quantum mechanics applied to IR, with an emphasis on the notation and probability aspects of this new field, which was started by the second author.

Chapter seven is entitled Multimedia Resource Discovery by Stefan Rüger from the Open University, UK. This chapter examines the challenges and opportunities of Multimedia Information Retrieval and its applications. In the case of image search, current techniques covered included piggy-backing text search, automated annotation of visual components, content-based retrieval and fingerprinting to match near duplicates.

The eighth chapter is Information Retrieval in Context by Ian Ruthven from the University of Strathclyde, UK. Here context refers to a complex set of variables describing the intentions and personal characteristics behind the person searching, the data and systems available, and the physical, social and organizational environments. This chapter studies why differences in context can affect how search systems can operate and ways that contextual information can be used to help search systems behave more intelligently to our changing context.

The last chapter is entitled Digital Advertising: An Information Scientists Perspective by James G. Shanahan and Goutham Kurra, USA. In this chapter, a major Internet industry is exposed, providing a detailed overview of the technologies and business models that are transforming the field of online advertising primarily from statistical machine learning and information science perspectives, including the IR problems behind it.

There are many important areas that are covered by more than one chapter. The most significant is evaluation, which is mentioned in every chapter, but in different ways. Despite the long tradition of evaluation in Information Retrieval, the advent of new problems and technologies requires new evaluation methodologies. Personalization and user interfaces are other two common topics, thus highlighting that the interaction between an Information Retrieval system and its users is more crucial than ever. Machine learning and relevance feedback are two other significant topics across the book and complete the general architecture of a system where the interaction between the user's side and the system's side always needs evaluation.

The book is intended to a wide audience of people interested in Information Retrieval: undergraduate and graduate students, post-doctoral researchers, teachers, scholars, as well as industrial researchers.

The Editors thank the authors for their intellectual generosity in writing the chapters of the book. Massimo Melucci thanks his colleagues of the Information Management Systems research group of the Department of Information Engineering at the University of Padova, while Ricardo Baeza-Yates would like to acknowledge the support of Yahoo! Research. Finally, we would like to thanks Springer, in particular Ralf Gerstner, for publishing this book.

Massimo Melucci
Ricardo Baeza-Yates

About ESSIR

The book originates in part from the Seventh European Summer School in Information Retrieval (ESSIR) which was held at the University of Padua, Italy, from August 31 to September 3, 2009 (http://essir2009.dei.unipd.it). ESSIR is the earliest international school in Information Retrieval and gathers lectures and satellite meetings for exchange and dissemination in the modeling, design and implementation of advanced systems for the representation, storage, search and retrieval of information.

The ESSIR series was the result of the successful experience of the Summer School in IR (SSIR) conceived and designed in 1989 by Nick Belkin (Rutgers University, USA) and Maristella Agosti (University of Padua, Italy) for an Italian audience. SSIR was organized by the Special Interest Group in IR (GLIR) of the Italian Computer Society (AICA) in July 1989 and was held at the Department of Electronics and Informatics (DEI, now Department of Information Engineering) of the University of Padua, Italy.

ESSIR was organized in: Bressanone, Italy (Maristella Agosti 1990); Glasgow, Scotland (Keith van Rijsbergen 1995); Varenna (Maristella Agosti, Fabio Crestani, and Gabriella Pasi 2000); Aussois, France (Catherine Berrut and Yves Chiaramella 2003); Dublin, Ireland (Alan Smeaton 2005); Glasgow, Scotland (Iadh Ounis and Keith van Rijsbergen 2007); Padua, Italy (Massimo Melucci and Ricardo Baeza-Yates 2009).

Contents

Contributors

Maristella Agosti Department of Information Engineering, University of Padua, Via Gradenigo, 6/a, 35131 Padova, Italy, maristella.agosti@unipd.it

Maristella Agosti is a Full Professor in Computer Science, with a main focus on databases, digital libraries and information retrieval, at the Faculty of Humanities and at the Department of Information Engineering of the University of Padua, Italy. Her research interests are in information infrastructures, digital library systems, information retrieval, search engines, analysis of log data in digital libraries and search engines, annotation of digital contents, design and development of advanced services and infrastructures for archives and libraries. She is one of the founding members and the coordinator of the Information Management Systems research group of the department. She coordinates a number of national and international research projects, and she has been the organizer of national and international conferences. Program Co-Chair of the 13th European Conference on Research and Advanced Technology for Digital Libraries—ECDL 2009, Corfu, Greece. Program Co-Chair of IRCDL 2010 the 6th Italian Research Conference on Digital Library Systems. General Co-Chair of CLEF 2010 Conference on Multilingual and Multimodal Information Access Evaluation 20–23 September 2010, Padua, Italy. Chair from 2009 of the Steering Committee of "Theory and Practice of Digital Libraries" (the new name of the European Conference on Digital Libraries). Member of the Steering Committee of the European Summer School of Information Retrieval (ESSIR). Editor of "Access through Search Engines and Digital Libraries". Springer-Verlag, Heidelberg, Germany, 2008. Member of the Editorial Board of the International Journal on Digital Libraries.

Ricardo Baeza-Yates Yahoo! Research, Diagonal 177, p9, 08018 Barcelona, Spain, rbaeza@acm.org

Ricardo Baeza-Yates is Vice-President of Yahoo! Research for Europe, Middle East and Latin America, leading the labs at Barcelona, Spain and Santiago, Chile, as well as supervising the newer lab in Haifa, Israel. Until 2005 he was the director of the Center for Web Research at the Department of Computer Science of the Engineering School of the University of Chile; and ICREA Professor at the Department of

Technology of the Pompeu Fabra University in Barcelona, Spain. He is co-author of the best-seller book Modern Information Retrieval, published in 1999 by Addison-Wesley with a second edition published in 2010, as well as co-author of the 2nd edition of the Handbook of Algorithms and Data Structures, Addison-Wesley, 1991; and co-editor of Information Retrieval: Algorithms and Data Structures, Prentice-Hall, 1992, among more than 200 other publications. He has received the Organization of American States award for young researchers in exact sciences (1993) and with two Brazilian colleagues obtained the COMPAQ prize for the best CS Brazilian research article (1997). In 2003 he was the first computer scientist to be elected to the Chilean Academy of Sciences. During 2007 he was awarded the Graham Medal for innovation in computing, given by the University of Waterloo to distinguished ex-alumni. In 2009 he was awarded the Latin American distinction for contributions to CS in the region and became an ACM Fellow.

Bettina Berendt Department of Computer Science, K.U. Leuven, Celestijnenlaan 200A, 3001 Heverlee, Belgium, bettina.berendt@cs.kuleuven.be

Bettina Berendt is a Professor in the Department of Computer Science at Katholieke Universiteit Leuven, Belgium. She obtained her habilitation in information systems from Humboldt University Berlin, Germany, and her PhD in computer science/cognitive science from the University of Hamburg. Her research interests include Web and Social-Web mining, digital libraries, personalization and privacy, and information visualization. Her work has been published in the VLDB Journal, Communications of the ACM, INFORMS Journal on Computing, and Data Mining and Knowledge Discovery.

Berkant Barla Cambazoglu Yahoo! Research, Diagonal 177, p9, 08018 Barcelona, Spain, barla@yahoo-inc.com

Berkant Barla Cambazoglu received his BS, MS, and PhD degrees, all in computer engineering, from the Computer Engineering Department of Bilkent University, Turkey, in 1997, 2000, and 2006, respectively. He has then worked as a postdoctoral researcher in the Biomedical Informatics Department of the Ohio State University. In 2007, he received the Embodying the Vision award as a developer in the caBIG project. He is currently employed as a researcher in Yahoo! Research. He has worked in several research projects, funded by the Scientific and Technological Research Council of Turkey, the European Union Sixth and Seventh Framework Programs, and the National Cancer Institute. His research interests mainly include information retrieval, web search, and distributed computing. He has papers published in prestigious journals (including IEEE TPDS, JPDC, Information Systems, IP&M) and conferences (including SIGIR, WWW, KDD, WSDM, CIKM).

Peter Ingwersen Royal School of Library and Information Science, Birketinget 6, 2300 Copenhagen S, Denmark, pi@iva.dk; Oslo University College, Oslo, Norway

Peter Ingwersen, Full Professor, Royal School of LIS, Denmark. PhD in 1991 from Copenhagen Business School. Visiting scholar at the European Space Agency, Italy, 1980–84. Affiliate Professor at Rutgers University, USA, 1987, the Dept. of Information Studies, Tampere University, Finland, 1999–2002, and Abo Academy, Finland, 1998–. Professor II at Oslo University College, 2010. Research areas: Interactive IR; IR in Context; Evaluation methods for IR; Informetrics–Scientometrics and Webometrics. He organized the 1992 ACM-SIGIR Conference in Denmark and served as PC Chair 1995 and 2000. He co-initiated the CoLIS conferences and chaired its 2nd meeting (1996) and organized with Kalervo Jarvelin the SIGIR Workshop IR in Context (2004 and 2005), which extended into the 1st International Symposium on Information Interaction in Context (IiiX), co-Chaired by Peter Ingwersen in 2006. He has served as invited lecturer and key-note at many doctoral fora, including ISSI, LIDA and CoLIS conferences, as well as ESSIR and NORSLIS research schools 1998–2009. He has published several highly cited research monographs, and more than 100 journal articles and conference papers, in addition to editing work. Among his academic awards are the ASIST Distinguished Research Award in 2003 and the Derek de Solla Price Medal for his informetric and webometric research awarded 2005 by the International Society of Scientometrics and Informetrics. In 2007 he received the ASIST Best Teacher Award of Information Science and in 2009 the Los Angeles ASIST Chapter's CISTA Award for continued contributions to Information Science. He is member of the International Advisory Board of ICALIS, Wuhan University, China, and the editorial boards of the international journals JASIST, IP&M, Scientometrics, and Journal of Informetrics as well as national journals in several countries.

Goutham Kurra Turn Inc., 186 Liberty St., San Francisco, CA 94110, USA, gkurra@gmail.com

Goutham Kurra is Director of technology at Turn, Inc., USA, where he focuses on research and development of cutting-edge technology for digital advertising including large-scale machine learning, predictive real-time bid and budget optimization, and contextual and behavioral/audience targeting among others. Over the last decade, Goutham has built innovative products and technology in diverse areas such as online advertising, enterprise search and e-discovery, distributed systems, computational biology, computer vision, and robotics. Prior to Turn, he was the first employee and an architect at the e-discovery pioneer Kazeon Systems (acquired by EMC); before that he was a founding member of the technical team at Adeosoft, where he built the world's first distributed common-language-runtime virtual computer. Goutham holds an MS degree in Computer Science from the University of Cincinnati, an MS degree in Physics and a BS degree in Engineering from the Birla Institute of Technology and Science, Pilani.

Mounia Lalmas Yahoo! Research, Diagonal 177, p9, 08018 Barcelona, Spain, mounia@acm.org

Mounia Lalmas joined in January 2011 Yahoo! Research in Barcelona as a Visiting Principal Scientist. Prior to this she held a Microsoft Research/RAEng Research Chair at the School of Computing Science, University of Glasgow. Before that, she was Professor of Information Retrieval, at the Department of Computer Science at Queen Mary, University of London, which she joined in 1999 as a lecturer. She is a Chartered IT Professional (CITP) and a Fellow of the British Computer Society (FBCS). She was also the (elected) vice chair, and before this the Information Director of ACM SIGIR. She is an editorial board member for ACM TOIS, IR (Springer) and IP&M (Elsevier). Her research focuses on the development and evaluation of intelligent access to interactive heterogeneous and complex information repositories. From 2002 until 2007, she co-led the Evaluation Initiative for XML Retrieval (INEX), a large-scale project with over 80 participating organisations worldwide, which was responsible for defining the nature of XML retrieval, and how it should be evaluated. She is now working on technologies for aggregated search and bridging the digital divide and applying quantum theory to model interactive information retrieval. In Barcelona, she will start a new research agenda, that of measuring user engagement. Her goal is to combine her experience in information retrieval evaluation and information science, to develop models of user engagements and associated user engagement metrics.

Massimo Melucci Department of Information Engineering, University of Padua, Via G. Gradenigo, 6, 35131 Padova, Italy, massimo.melucci@unipd.it

Massimo Melucci completed a PhD in Computer Science in 1996. Since 2001 he is associate professor in Computer Science at the Department of Information Engineering and Faculty of Statistics of the University of Padua, Italy. He has been the Chair of the 7th European Summer School in Information Retrieval (with Ricardo Baeza-Yates). He is on the Editorial Board of the Journal of Information Retrieval and is member of a number of Programme Committees. He chaired the Programme Committee of the 11th Symposium on String Processing and Information Retrieval (with Alberto Apostolico) and organised some research workshops, the 2004 Algorithmic Learning Theory conference, the 2004 Symposium on String Processing and Information Retrieval, and the 2004 Discovery Science conference. He has been General Chair of the 1st Italian Information Retrieval workshop in 2010 and Program co-Chair of the 2nd Italian Information Retrieval workshop in 2011. He has been Program Chair of the 5th Quantum Interaction symposium in 2011. His research interests are in information retrieval modeling and contextual search. He is also currently looking at the use of some theoretical instruments of quantum mechanics in information retrieval modeling. Besides the coordination of the EU Marie Curie IRSES project QONTEXT, he has been involved in EU and national research projects.

Stefan Rüger Knowledge Media Institute, The Open University, Milton Keynes, MK7 6AA, United Kingdom, s.rueger@open.ac.uk

Stefan Rüger read Physics at Freie Universität Berlin and gained his PhD (Dr rer nat) at Technische Universität Berlin (1996). He carved out his academic career at Imperial College London from PostDoc (1997) to a Readership in Multimedia and Information Systems (2005). During this period he was awarded an EPSRC Advanced Research Fellowship (1999 to 2004). In 2006 he became a full Professor of Knowledge Media when he joined The Open University's Knowledge Media Institute to head a research group on Multimedia and Information Systems. He also holds an Honorary Professorship (2009–2014) from the University of Waikato, New Zealand, where he collaborates with the Greenstone Digital Library group on Multimedia Digital Libraries.

Rüger has published widely in the area of Multimedia Information Retrieval. He has been Principal Investigator in the EPSRC-funded Multimedia Knowledge Management Network and Principal Investigator for The Open University in the FP6-ICT project PHAROS. He completed a joint 3-year NSF-EU project on Cultural Heritage Language Technologies in 2005, collaborated with BT in an industry-sponsored research project on Multimedia Libraries and executed a joint project with Waikato University on Video Digital Libraries. At this point he has served the academic community in various roles as conference co-chair, programme co-chair, associate editor of journals, guest editor for special journal issues, and as referee for wide range of Computing journals, international conferences and UK and overseas research funders, in particular the European Commission and the European Research Council. Rüger is a member of the EPSRC College, the ACM, the BCS, the BCS committee for Information Retrieval and a fellow of the Higher Education Academy. See http://kmi.open.ac.uk/people/stefan for details.

Ian Ruthven Department of Computer and Information Sciences, University of Strathclyde, 26 Richmond Street, Glasgow, G1 1XH, UK, ir@cis.strath.ac.uk

Ian Ruthven is a Professor of Information Seeking and Retrieval in the Department of Computer and Information Sciences at the University of Strathclyde. He graduated from the University of Glasgow with a Bachelor's degree in Computing Science, before completing a Masters degree in Cognitive Science at the University of Birmingham and a PhD in Interactive Information Retrieval at Glasgow. He works across the areas of information seeking and retrieval; understanding how (and why) people search for information and how electronic systems might help them search more successfully. This brings in a wide range of research including theoretical research on the design and modelling of information access systems, empirical research on interfaces and user interaction and research on the methodology of evaluating information access systems. Currently, he is particularly interested in interactive information retrieval for children through the development of novel search interfaces and evaluation measures for use in understanding children's interaction with search systems and on decision-making within searching by examining how people decide on what information is useful within interactive searches.

James G. Shanahan Independent Consultant, 541 Duncan Street, San Francisco, CA 94131, USA, James.Shanahan@gmail.com

James G. Shanahan has spent the last 20 years developing and researching cutting-edge information management systems to harness information retrieval, linguistics and machine learning. During the summer of 2007, he started a boutique consultancy, Church and Duncan Group Inc. (CaDGi), in San Francisco. CaDGi's major goal is to help companies leverage their vast repositories of data using statistics, machine learning, optimization theory and data mining for applications in areas such as web search, and online advertising. Church and Duncan Group's clients include AT&T Interactive, Digg.com, eBay, SearchMe.com, Ancestry.com, MyOfferPal.com, and SkyGrid.com. In addition, since January 2008, James G. Shanahan is affiliated with the University of California at Santa Cruz. He advises several high-tech startups in the Silicon Valley Area.

Prior to starting Church and Duncan Group Inc., James G. Shanahan was Chief Scientist and executive team member at Turn Inc. (an online ad network and demand side platform). Prior to joining Turn, James G. Shanahan was Principal Research Scientist at Clairvoyance Corporation where he led the "Knowledge Discovery from Text" Group. Before that he was a Research Scientist at Xerox Research Center Europe (XRCE). In the early 90s, he worked on the AI Team within the Mitsubishi Group in Tokyo.

He has published six books, over 50 research publications, and 15 patents in the areas of machine learning and information processing. James G. Shanahan was General Chair for CIKM 2008. He will co-chair the International Conference in Weblog and Social Media (ICWSM) 2011 in Barcelona. Previously he has co-organized workshops on online advertising at SIGIR and NIPS. He is a regularly invited to give talks at international conferences and universities around the world. James G. Shanahan received his PhD in engineering mathematics from the University of Bristol, UK and holds a bachelor of science degree from the University of Limerick, Ireland. He is a Marie Curie fellow and member of IEEE and ACM.

Keith van Rijsbergen Computer Laboratory, University of Cambridge, 14 Park Parade, Cambridge CB5 8AL, England, keith@dcs.gla.ac.uk

Keith van Rijsbergen was born in Holland in 1943. He was educated in Holland, Indonesia, Namibia and Australia. He took a degree in mathematics at the University of Western Australia. As a graduate he spent two years tutoring in mathematics while studying computer science. In 1972 he completed a PhD in computer science at Cambridge University. After almost three years of lecturing in information retrieval and artificial intelligence at Monash University he returned to the Cambridge Computer Laboratory to hold a Royal Society Information Research Fellowship. In 1980 he was appointed to the chair of computer science at University College Dublin; from there he moved in 1986 to the Glasgow University. In 2008 he retired to a Visiting Professorship in the Computer Laboratory in Cambridge.

Since about 1969 his research has been devoted to information retrieval, covering both theoretical and experimental aspects. He has specified several theoretical models for IR and seen some of them from the specification and prototype stage through to production. His current research is concerned with the design of appropriate logics to model the flow of information. He has been involved in a number of EU projects and working groups on IR, including Fermi, Miro, Mira, Idomeneus, and more recently K-space. He is a fellow of the Royal Academy of Engineering, Royal Society of Edinburgh, BCS, and ACM. In 1993 he was appointed Editor-in-Chief of The Computer Journal, an appointment he held until 2000. He has served as a

programme committee member and editorial board member of the major IR conferences and journals. He is the author of a well-known book Information Retrieval,
Butterworths, 1979. In 1999, together with Crestani and Lalmas, he published a
book entitled "Information Retrieval: Uncertainty and Logics". His most recent
book is The Geometry of Information Retrieval, CUP, 2004. Some of his research
papers can be accessed at http://www.dcs.gla.ac.uk/~keith/.

Abbreviations

ACM	Association for Computing Machinery
ADMV	*Archivio Digitale della Musica Veneta*
AIRW	Adversarial Information Retrieval on the Web
AJAX	Asynchronous JavaScript and XML
AOL	America On Line
API	Application Programming Interface
ARIST	Annual Review of Information Science and Technology
BBC	British Broadcasting Corporation
CIVR	Conference on Video and Image Retrieval
CLEF	Cross-Language Evaluation Forum
CPA	Cost Per Action
CPC	Cost Per Click
CPM	Cost Per Mille
CRF	Conditional Random Field
CRISP-DM	CRoss Industry Standard Process for Data Mining
CSS	Cascading Style Sheet
CTR	Click-Through Rate
DAAT	Document-At-A-Time
DCG	Discounted Cumulative Gain
DIRECT	Distributed Information Retrieval Evaluation Campaign Tool
DL	Digital Library
DLMS	Digital Library Management System
DLS	Digital Library System
DM	Data Mining
DNS	Domain Name System
DOM	Document Object Model
DSP	Demand Side Platform
DVD	Digital Versatile Disc
EC	European Commission
ECIR	European Conference on Information Retrieval
ECPM	Expected Cost Per Mille

EDL	European Digital Library
ESSIR	European Summer School in Information Retrieval
FAST	Flexible Annotation Service Tool
GATE	General Architecture for Text Processing
GPS	Global Positioning System
GSP	Generalized Second Price
HARD	High Accuracy Retrieval from Documents
HCI	Human Computer Interaction
HMM	Hidden Markov Model
HTML	HyperText Markup Language
HTTP	HyperText Transfer Protocol
IAB	Interactive Advertising Bureau
IBM	International Business Machines
IDF	Inverse Document Frequency
IEC	International Electrotechnical Commission
IFLA	International Federation of Library Associations and Institutions
IIR	Interactive Information Retrieval
INEX	INitiative for the Evaluation of XML Retrieval
IR	Information Retrieval
IRIX	Information Retrieval In conteXt
ISMIR	International Symposium on Music Information Retrieval
ISO	International Organization for Standardization
ISP	Internet Service Provider
KD	Knowledge Discovery
KDD	Knowledge Discovery in Databases
LDA	Latent Dirichlet Allocation
LINGEB	*LINguaggio GEstione Biblioteche*
LSA	Latent Semantic Analysis
LSI	Latent Semantic Indexing
MAP	Mean Average Precision
MIDI	Musical Instrument Digital Interface
MIR	Music Information Retrieval
MLR	Machine-Learned Ranking
MM	MultiMedia
MPEG	Moving Picture Experts Group
MSE	Mean Squared Error
NII	National Institute of Informatics
NIST	National Institute of Standards and Technology
NLP	Natural Language Processing
NSF	National Science Foundation
NTCIR	NII Test Collection for IR Systems
OAI-PMH	Open Archives Initiative Protocol for Metadata Harvesting
OCLC	Online Computer Library Center
OPAC	Online Public Access Catalogue
OWL	Web Ontology Language

PMI	Pointwise Mutual Information
PMML	Predictive Model Markup Language
PPA	Pay Per Action
PPC	Pay Per Click
PRP	Probability Ranking Principle
QA	Question Answering
QM	Quantum Mechanics
QPS	Queries Per Second
RDF	Resource Description Framework
RF	Relevance Feedback
ROI	Return On Investment
ROUGE	Recall-Oriented Understudy for Gisting Evaluation
SEM	Search Engine Marketer
SERP	Search Engine Result Page
SIGIR	Special Interest Group on IR
SIGKDD	Special Interest Group on Knowledge Discovery and Data Mining
SQL	Structured Query Language
SRU	Search/Retrieve via URL
SVD	Singular Value Decomposition
SVM	Support Vector Machine
TCP/IP	Transfer Control Protocol/Internet Protocol
TED	Transductive Experimental Design
TEL	The European Library
TF	Term Frequency
TFIDF	TF.IDF
TREC	Text Retrieval Conference
TRECVid	TREC Video track
URI	Uniform Resource Identifier
URL	Uniform Resource Locator
VCG	Vickrey Clarke Groves
WAND	Weighted AND
WWW	World Wide Web
XML	eXtensible Markup Language
YP	Yellow Pages

List of Figures

List of Tables

Chapter 1
Digital Libraries

Maristella Agosti

Abstract The Digital Libraries area is initially introduced with a report on initial approaches of designing library automation systems that can be considered "ancestors" of present days systems. After having presented the background to the area, the main concepts that underline present digital library systems are introduced together with a report on the efforts of defining the Digital Library Manifesto and the DELOS Digital Library Reference Model. Considerations on a possible way of improving present digital library systems to make them more user-centered are subsequently given. Finally, interoperability and evaluation issues are faced. The presentation ends with a concluding remark.

1.1 Introduction

In the beginning, Digital Libraries were almost monolithic systems, each one built for a specific kind of information resources—e.g. images or videos—and with very specialized functions developed ad-hoc for those contents. This approach caused a flourishing of systems where the very same functions were developed and re-developed many times from scratch. Moreover, these systems were confined to the realm of traditional libraries, since they were the digital counterpart of the latter, and they had a kind of static view of their role, which was data-centric rather than user-centric.

Afterwards, Digital Libraries moved from being monolithic systems to becoming component and service-based systems, where easily configurable and deployable services can be plugged together and re-used to create a Digital Library. Moreover, Digital Libraries started to be seen as increasingly user-centered systems, where the original content management task is partnered with new communication and cooperation tasks, so that Digital Libraries become a vehicle by which everyone can access, discuss, and enhance information of different forms. Finally, Digital Libraries are no longer perceived as isolated systems but, on the contrary, as systems

M. Agosti (✉)
Department of Information Engineering, University of Padua, Via Gradenigo, 6/a, 35131 Padova, Italy
e-mail: maristella.agosti@unipd.it

M. Melucci, R. Baeza-Yates (eds.), *Advanced Topics in Information Retrieval*, The Information Retrieval Series 33, DOI 10.1007/978-3-642-20946-8_1, © Springer-Verlag Berlin Heidelberg 2011

that need to cooperate with each other to improve the user experience and give personalized services.

The Digital Libraries area has attracted much attention in recent years both from academics and professionals interested in envisaging new tools and systems able to manage diversified collections of documents, artifacts, and data in digital form in a consistent and coherent way. The area can be still considered a relatively young area since it is only fifteen/twenty years old, with its origins in the "Digital Library Initiative" in USA.[1] and the constellation of the DELOS initiatives in Europe.[2]

In this evolving scenario, the design and development of effective services which foster cooperation among users and the integration of heterogeneous information resources becomes a key factor. Relevant examples of this kind are given together with examples that make digital libraries interoperable services.

The presentation is organized as follows: Section 1.2 introduces the Digital Libraries area and reports on the initial approaches of designing library automation systems that can be considered "ancestors" of present day systems; Section 1.3 presents the main concepts underlining present digital library systems; Section 1.4 reports on the efforts of defining the Digital Library Manifesto and the DELOS Digital Library Reference Model; Section 1.5 gives some clues on possible ways of improving present digital library systems to make them more user-centered systems; Section 1.6 addresses the concept of interoperability in the context of digital library systems; Section 1.7 sets the scene for an evaluation framework to be adopted for evaluating digital library systems; finally, Section 1.8 puts forward some final remarks.

1.2 Digital Libraries in the Beginning

Initial application systems able to manage the permanent data of interest to libraries were named *library automation systems* and they first appeared world-wide in the 1970s.

In general those systems were able to manage only the *catalog data* representing physical library objects—such as books, journals, and reports—that were held in a real and physical library, i.e. a physical place external to the application system, and were only able to refer to the physical library objects through the managed catalog data. The functions available through those systems were limited in

---

[1] See http://dli.grainger.uiuc.edu/national.htm.

[2] The initial European initiative for dealing with digital libraries was the DELOS Working Group, active from January 1996 to December 1999, which was funded by the ESPRIT Long Term Research Programme within the Fourth Framework Programme of the Commission of the European Union, URL: http://delos-noe.isti.cnr.it/home/background.html. Due to the success of the DELOS Working Group in terms of acting as a focal point for the European as well as the world-wide digital library community, the Commission approved funding for an initial DELOS Network of Excellence on Digital Libraries, from January 2000 to December 2002, and later on the DELOS Network of Excellence on Digital Libraries, from January 2004 to December 2007, URL: http://www.delos.info/.

particular because of limited space available on non-volatile random access memory; an example of a system that was impaired by a design approach that was limiting the possible management functions due to limitation in the availability of non-volatile memory was LINGEB, a system able to manage and retrieve documents only in classes instead of single items (Agosti et al. 1975), and the system named DOC-5 derived from it several years later (Agosti and Ronchi 1979; Agosti 1980).

Catalog data are now usually referred to as *metadata*, since they are data that represent other data (Metadata-IFLA-WG 2005). Each library or each group of cooperating libraries normally adopt a metadata scheme to make its metadata of general use for its users or for other libraries, institutions, and systems. At that time, catalog data represented only physical objects held in real and physical libraries, so objects held in archives and museums were not represented and managed in software application systems for library automation. Only book collections of archives and museums were managed at that time through library automation systems.

In the 1980s the most advanced library automation systems were designed to include procedures able to collect log data. Log data were collected to manage the system itself, and especially to monitor the usage of system search facilities by users, where the search facility which was designed for user search and access to catalog data was named *Online Public Access Catalog (OPAC)* (Hildreth 1985, 1989) and this name is still in use today.

An OPAC is a sophisticated software system designed to provide final users with direct access to the catalog data without the intervention of a professional user and to make available to final users all the data in the catalog database managed by the software system. The catalog database was and still is constructed by professional librarians who use *authority control* rules in describing author, place names and other relevant catalog data (Guerrini and Sardo 2003); over time the librarians have constructed many *authority files* where the software system stores all lists of preferred or accepted forms of names and other relevant headings (Baldacci and Sprugnoli 1983). Figure 1.1 shows an extract from an authority file of names which are stored in alphabetical order; the first depicted accepted form is "CARTESANA, MARISA"; the last depicted form is "CARTHARIUS, CAROLUS", which is not the accepted form, so a cross-reference to "CARTARI, CARLO", which is the accepted form, is made.

Termine	Occorr.
CARTESEGNA, MARISA	1
CARTESIANA 2000 <CAGLIARI>	1
CARTESIO --> DESCARTES, RENE	1088
CARTESIO <PSEUD.>	1
CARTESIO, PIETRO <M. 1650>	1
CARTESIO, RENATO	4
CARTESIO, RENATO --> DESCARTES, RENE	1080
CARTESIO, STEFANO	1
CARTESIUS <GALLERIA D'ARTE ; TRIESTE>	13
CARTEY, WILFRED	2
CARTEY, WILFRED G.	1
CARTHAGE FILM FESTIVAL <TUNISI ; 2002>	1
CARTHAGE, PHILIP I.	1
CARTHARIUS, CAROLUS --> CARTARI, CARLO	14

Fig. 1.1 An extract from an authority file of names which are stored in alphabetical order

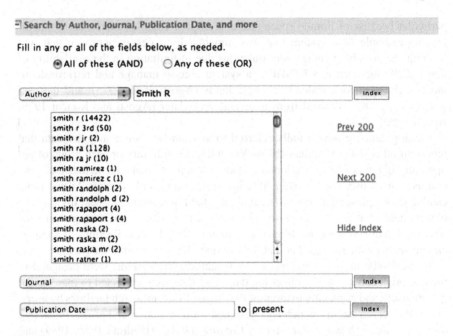

Fig. 1.2 A screen shot of the interface of a tool that gives access to authority files

Figure 1.2 shows a screen shot of the interface of a tool that gives access to authority files; the user has requested to see the list of authors that have works inserted in the catalog record database managed by the library automation system where the word "Smith" is a surname, and the letter "R" is the initial of the first name. The software tool is reporting all the variations of the string "Smith R" in alphabetical order together with the occurrences of each form present in the managed database.

The complex database which is managed by a library automation system is a coherent collection of catalog data and authority files which can be searched by the OPAC system to give a more professional and reliable answer to the final user.

Traditional OPAC systems were accessible by registered users and through public login procedures. In both cases it was possible to trace each user/system interaction and each user session was identifiable, because at this level of development of software systems, each application system, even in a distributed environment, was reached using a system dependent interface. We call this type of access *pre-Web access*, because only since the introduction of the web Internet application and the web clients, that is the "browsers",[3] have library automation system become reachable in a distributed environment through a standard software interface (Tanenbaum 1996). Figure 1.3 shows a screen dump of the interface of the DUO OPAC system which was in use at the University of Padua in early 1990s (Agosti and Masotti 1992a, 1992b); this constitutes an example of the type of interaction which was available to the user through a character oriented interface before the introduction of the Web.

---

[3] See http://www.w3.org/People/Berners-Lee/WorldWideWeb.

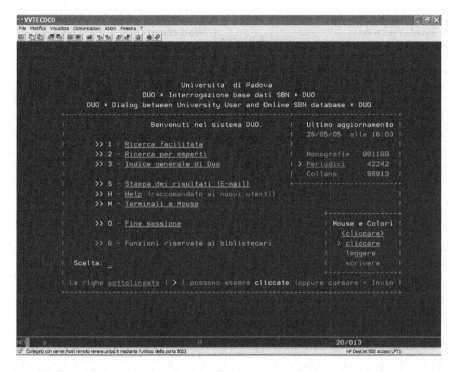

Fig. 1.3 Screen dump of DUO system: the OPAC system available at the University of Padua before the Web was invented

Fig. 1.4 Architecture of a
library automation system
before the Web

Figure 1.4 sketches the architecture of a library automation system before the Web was invented; this sort of library automation system can be considered a sort of ancestor of a present-day digital library system.

Figure 1.5 represents the architecture of the most common way of accessing a library automation system nowadays where the software system is made accessible through a web interface making the system itself interoperable with a web server. Figure 1.6 shows the view a final user has of the access through the web interface to the library automation system.

Fig. 1.5 Architecture of the different systems that interoperate to permit the user to access a library automation system through the Web

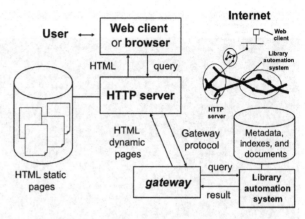

Fig. 1.6 Web user interface to the library automation system of the University of Padua

Due to the experience gained in the management of operating systems and the many other application systems that manage permanent data, log procedures are commonly put in place to collect and store data on the usage of application systems by its users. Since over time it became apparent that log data could also be used to study the usage of the application by its users, and to better adapt and personalize the system to the objectives the users were expecting to reach, log data started to be collected and analysed well before the library automation systems were accessible through the Web. Information on the use of the interaction between the system and the user was also stored at the beginning of the development of library automation systems in log files where information on the specific queries made by final users referring to the specific authority files from which the data were extracted were made. From that time the information on OPAC queries were used to better understand the effective use by the final user of the data stored by the library automation system.

Towards the end of the 1980s/beginning of 1990s it became apparent that a library automation system could not only manage catalog data or metadata describing physical objects, but also digital files representing physical objects, such as a digital file representing all the content of a book in digital form or a digital file representing an illuminated manuscript. Later on some objects started to appear in digital form—so called born-digital—so the collection of types of descriptions of physical objects and of digital objects themselves was becoming increasingly diversified and complex. Former library automation systems appeared to be limited in managing data related to such a diversified situation so the need to envisage and design a new generation of systems able to face the new reality of interest was evident.

The new collections of interest were those managed in book libraries, film libraries, music libraries, archives, museums, and so on. The new type of systems able to manage such diversified collections were named *Digital Library Systems* to highlight that the objects comprising the collection of interest were the many different types of objects that can be maintained in a library together with born-digital objects. Maintaining the term *library* was later considered misleading by some, but it still remains as the name for identifying this type of system, since no better name has been proposed and widely adopted by the reference community.

1.3 Digital Library Systems

Current digital library systems are complex software systems, often based on a service-oriented architecture, able to manage complex and diversified collections of digital objects. One significant aspect that relates current systems to the old ones is that the representation of the content of the digital objects that constitute the collection of interest is done by professionals. This means that the management of metadata can still be based on the use of *authority control* rules in describing author, place names and other relevant catalog data.

A digital library system can exploit *authority data* that keep lists of preferred or accepted forms of names and all other relevant headings, and it can also use more advanced systems of knowledge organization specifically envisaged for digital libraries, thus overcoming the shortcomings that derive from the use of authority files only in a traditional way (Hodge 2000). A more active and new way of using the principles of authority files can make a dramatic difference between digital library systems and search engines in terms of quality of information retrieval and access for the final users; by the way, this aspect is usually overcome with the analysis of log data. In fact a *search engine* often becomes a specific component of a digital library system, when the digital library system faces the management and search of digital objects by content, much the same way as information retrieval systems and search engines do (Salton and McGill 1983; Baeza-Yates and Ribeiro-Neto 1999; Agosti 2008). In all other types of searches, either the digital library system makes use of authority data to respond to final users in a more consistent and coherent way through a search system that is a sort of a new generation OPAC system, or the system supports the full content search with a service that gives the final users the facilities of a search engine.

If we consider the information space where a digital library system operates, as depicted in Fig. 1.7, it becomes evident that a digital library system operates on contents that require knowledge of user tasks and that are semi-structured. In fact, a digital library system operates at a sort of cross-roads between the structured data managed by catalog and database management systems, and the un-structured data managed in information retrieval systems/search engines and the Web.

The contents a digital library system is able to manage correspond to the diversified collections of media that can be represented in a digital form. This means that together with traditional textual documents, digital library systems are able to manage images, musical documents, and in general complex objects in the form of video, as shown in Fig. 1.8 where the spread of different types of media is reported. Each media can require specific services to be supported by the digital library system to match specific user requirements and tasks.

Fig. 1.7 Digital library information space

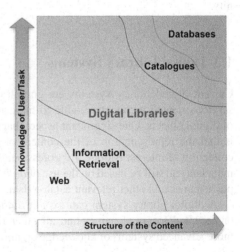

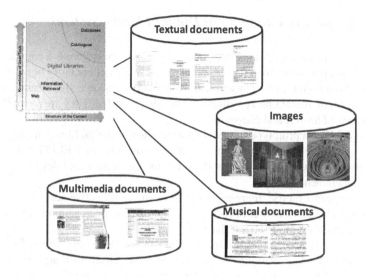

Fig. 1.8 Contents of digital libraries

1.3.1 User Interface to Digital Library Systems

It is worth underlining that the access to each service a digital library system provides is usually supplied through a web browser, and not through a specifically designed interface. This means that the analysis of user interaction with systems that have a Web-based interface requires the forecasting of ways that support the reconstruction of sessions in a setting, like the Web, where sessions are not naturally identified and kept (Berendt et al. 2002).

The use of a web interface is advantageous as it requires less effort by the final user accustomed to the use of a web browser to access and use many Web-based applications. The disadvantage is that through a Web-based interface the specific and rich semantics specifically related to the digital library application in use cannot be expressed. Often the digital library software system developer is forced to structure the user interface to the browser characteristics instead of structuring the interaction in a more natural way for the application under development. Another negative effect of a Web-based interface is that the user is accustomed to frequently interacting with search engines expects to find the functions a search engine supplies without having to open his mind towards a system that can give a richer interaction and browsing experience. All those different effects of having to interact with a Web-based interface to use a digital library system need to be taken into account when designing the log system of the digital library application to make possible the later study of user interaction data to improve the use of the digital library system of interest (Agosti et al. 2009).

1.3.2 Significative Examples of Digital Library Systems

The previous discussion demonstrates that a digital library system is a complex system able to support diversified functions and services. To better clarify how complex and powerful a digital library system can be, recently available significant and distinct examples of digital library systems are briefly presented. They are *DelosDLMS*, *The European Library*, and *Europeana*.

DelosDLMS is a prototype for the next generation of digital library management systems, and is the result of the joint effort of partners in the DELOS Network of Excellence[4] representing the state of the art in the conception and design of digital library management systems.

The European Library[5] represents a state of the art effective service providing access to the catalogs and digital collections of most European national libraries via one central multi-lingual web interface.

The idea for Europeana[6] came from a letter to the Presidency of the European Council and to the Commission on 28 April 2005: six Heads of State and Government suggested the creation of a virtual European library, aiming to make Europe's cultural and scientific resources accessible for all. In late 2005 the European Commission started to promote and support the creation of a European digital library, as a strategic goal within the European Information Society i2010 Initiative, which aims to foster growth and jobs in the information society and media industries.

1.3.2.1 DelosDLMS

DelosDLMS, the prototype Digital Library Management System developed in the context of the DELOS Network of Excellence,[7] is a relevant example of the new generation of service-oriented digital library systems. DelosDLMS combines a rich set of features in a combination unavailable in any existing system (Schek and Schuldt 2006). It combines text and audio-visual searching, offers personalized browsing using new information visualization and relevance feedback tools, provides novel interfaces, allows retrieved information to be annotated and processed, and integrates and processes sensor data streams. The system is built over OSIRIS (Weber et al. 2003), an environment initially developed at ETH Zurich and then expanded and maintained at the University of Basel.[8] OSIRIS is a middleware for

---

[4] See http://www.delos.info/.

[5] See http://www.theeuropeanlibrary.org/.

[6] See http://www.europeana.eu/portal/index.html.

[7] DELOS, the Network of Excellence on Digital Libraries which operated from 2004 to 2007 in the context of the Information Society Technologies (IST) Program of the European Commission (Contract G038-507618).

[8] The Databases and Information Systems (DBIS) Group of the University of Basel is taking care of the development of OSIRIS in the context of "OSIRIS next", a peer-to-peer based open service infrastructure aiming to implement and demonstrate a vision of modern service oriented information systems, URL: http://on.cs.unibas.ch/.

Fig. 1.9 An example of a service-oriented digital library system

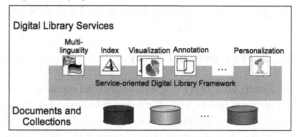

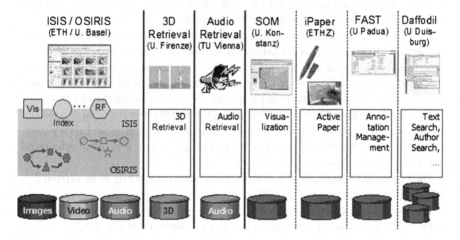

Fig. 1.10 DelosDLMS: Overview of the service-oriented digital library management system architecture

distributed and decentralized process execution that allows the building of process-based digital library applications starting from services (and already existing processes alike), and executes them in a distributed fashion.

The philosophy behind DelosDLMS is that digital library applications can be easily built starting from specialized services produced independently from each other. The basic architecture of DelosDLMS and, in general, of a service-oriented digital library system is depicted in Fig. 1.9.

DelosDLMS was developed in two different integration phases, with the results of the first integration phase being reported by Agosti et al. (2007), and the result of the second phase being reported by Binding et al. (2007); the overview of all the services which have been integrated is given in Fig. 1.10.[9]

The subsequent and present status of development of DelosDLMS has been reported in (Ioannidis et al. 2008) where the DelosDLMS digital library management

---

[9]An overall presentation of the DelosDLMS prototype is available at the URL: http://dbis.cs.unibas.ch/.

system is presented together with its components developed by the research groups that operated in a coordinated way in the DELOS Network of Excellence.

1.3.2.2 The European Library

The European Library is a noncommercial organization which provides the services of a physical library and offers search facilities for the resources of many of the European national libraries. Available resources can be both digital or bibliographical, e.g. books, posters, maps, sound recordings, and videos. The European Library is a service of the "Conference of European National Librarians" (CENL)[10] and it is hosted by the Koninklijke Bibliotheek, The Netherlands.[11]

The European Library initiative aims at providing a "low barrier of entry" so that the national libraries can join the federation with only minimal changes to their systems (van Veen and Oldroyd 2004). This means that The European Library exists to open up the universe of knowledge, information and culture of all European national libraries, where a national library is the library specifically established by a country to store its information database. National libraries usually host the legal deposit and the bibliographic control centre of a nation. Currently The European Library gives access to more than 150 million entries across Europe, and the amount of referenced digital collections is constantly increasing.[12]

The European Library portal[13] is an evolving service currently in its version 2.3. Its home page is reported in Fig. 1.11.

The European Library provides three protocols to access the collections in the portal.[14] The portal has corresponding components depicted in Fig. 1.12:

- a web server: this provides users with access to the services;
- a central index: this harvests catalog records from the national libraries, supports the "Open Archives Initiative Protocol for Metadata Harvesting" (OAI-PMH),[15] and provides integrated access to them via "Search/Retrieve via URL" (SRU);
- a gateway between SRU and Z39.50: this provides access through SRU to national libraries which would otherwise only be accessible through Z39.50.[16]

---

[10]See http://www.cenl.org/, since 2006 the Conference of European National Librarians has been added to the list of International Non-Governmental Organizations (INGO) enjoying participatory status with the Council of Europe.

[11]See http://www.kb.nl/index-en.html.

[12]At present 48 national libraries of Europe are collaborating with The European Library, an update map of the participating national libraries and information on them are available at the URL: http://search.theeuropeanlibrary.org/portal/en/libraries.html.

[13]See http://www.theeuropeanlibrary.org/portal/.

[14]Useful information on the way a partner has to adapt to the technical infrastructure of The European Library environment can be found in the Handbook available at the URL: http://www.theeuropeanlibrary.org/portal/organisation/handbook/.

[15]See http://www.openarchives.org/OAI/openarchivesprotocol.html.

[16]See http://www.loc.gov/z3950/agency/.

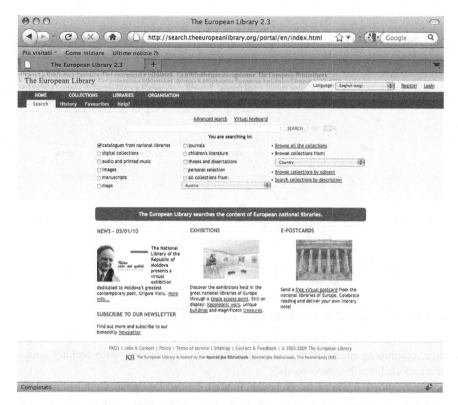

Fig. 1.11   The European Library portal home page

In addition, the interaction between the portal, the federated libraries, and the user mainly happens on the client side by means of an extensive use of Javascript and AJAX (Asynchronous JavaScript Technology and XML).[17]

Once the client, which is a standard web browser, accesses the service and downloads all the necessary information from the web server, all the subsequent requests are managed locally by the client. The client interacts directly with each federated library and the central index, according to the SRU protocol, makes separate AJAX calls towards each federated library or the central index, and manages the responses to such calls in order to present the results to the user and to organize user interaction.

1.3.2.3 Europeana

The European Commission's goal for Europeana is to make European information resources easier to use in an online environment. It will build on Europe's rich her-

---

[17]See http://www.w3.org/TR/XMLHttpRequest/.

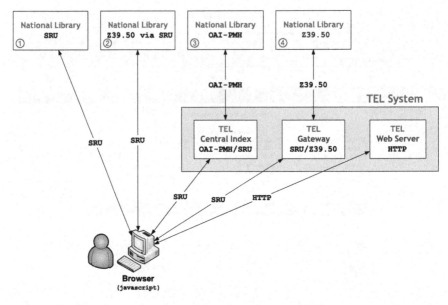

Fig. 1.12 Architecture of the European Library portal

itage, combining multicultural and multilingual environments with technological advances and new business models.

Europeana is a Thematic Network funded by the European Commission under the eContentplus programme, as part of the i2010 policy. Originally known as the European digital library network—EDLnet—it is a partnership of 100 representatives of heritage and knowledge organizations and IT experts from throughout Europe. The partners of the thematic network are contributing to the work of solving technical and usability issues. The project is run by a core team based in the national library of the Netherlands, the Koninklijke Bibliotheek. It builds on the project management and technical expertise developed by The European Library.

The development route, site architecture and technical specifications are all published as deliverable outcomes of the project. After the launch of the Europeana prototype, the project's final task is to recommend a business model that will ensure the sustainability of the website. It will also report on the further research and implementation needed to make Europe's cultural heritage fully interoperable and accessible through a truly multilingual service. A number of satellite projects have been designed and are under development to reach the different and ambitious aims of Europeana. Among those "Europeana version 1.0"[18] is a project that is operating to bring the Europeana prototype to full service; during 2010, a new version of the service was made available giving access to over 10 million digital objects, and in 2011 a fully-operational service with improved multilingual-

---

[18] See http://version1.europeana.eu/web/europeana-project/home.

Fig. 1.13   Web home page of Europeana

ity and semantic web features is released. The contents are coming from libraries, museums, archives and audio-visual collections. The software solutions under development are mostly open source. The effort sees the co-operation among many different institutions, including universities, ministries and heritage strategy bodies.

The Europeana effort is still under development. Figure 1.13 shows the Web home page of the Europeana portal, and Fig. 1.14 shows the screen shot of Europeana version 1.0.

1.4 The Digital Library Manifesto and the DELOS Digital Library Reference Model

Given the absence of reference tools or guidelines for the scientists and professionals approaching the field, some scientists operating in the context of the DELOS Network of Excellence decided to work to fill this gap. They conceived the "Digital Library Manifesto" and the "Digital Library Reference Model". The aim of the former has been to set the foundations and identify the cornerstone concepts within the universe of Digital Libraries to facilitate the integration of research and propose better ways of developing appropriate systems (Candela et al. 2006). The aim of

Fig. 1.14 Screen shot of Europeana version 1.0

the latter has been to unify and organize the overall body of knowledge gathered together in the sector in a coherent and systematic way (Candela et al. 2007).

Digital Libraries represent the meeting point of a large number of disciplines and fields, i.e. data management, information retrieval, library sciences, document management, information systems, the web, image processing, artificial intelligence, human-computer interaction, and others. It was only natural that these first fifteen years were mostly spent on bridging some of the gaps between the disciplines (and the scientists serving each one), improvising on what Digital Library functionality is supposed to be, and integrating solutions from each separate field into systems to support such functionality, sometimes with the solutions being induced by novel requirements of Digital Libraries. These have been achieved through much exploratory work, primarily in the context of focused efforts devising specialized approaches to address particular aspects of Digital Library functionality.

For example, one of the earliest projects was the Jukebox project which was launched in 1991, approved and supported by the European Commission in 1992[19] which proposed to create a new library service based on acces to large sound collections via the network. The final aim was to enlarge library services by making available sound documents which represent relevant products of twentieth century culture, since it was evident from then that sound documents play a relevant role

---

[19]See http://ifla.queenslibrary.org/IV/ifla61/61-sotc.htm.

in historical, anthropological and musical research. However, public access to these collections had previously been restricted to a small user community. The Jukebox service was innovative because it represented one of the first opportunities to offer library users easy access to new information resources at the same place. Another interesting example of research activities that were preceding effective digital libraries is the feasibility study named ADMV ("Archivio Digitale della Musica Veneta"— digital archive of Venetian music), for the creation of a digital archive of images of manuscripts of musical scores, digitized versions in MIDI format, and recordings of performances of musical works by Venetian composers, such as Marcello and Pellestrina (Agosti et al. 1998). Following the feasibility study, the ADMV system was developed and made available.[20]

In spite of its short life, the Digital Library Manifesto introduced the entities of discourse of the digital library universe by introducing the relationships between three types of relevant "system" in the area: Digital Library, Digital Library System, and Digital Library Management System. Then it presented the main concepts characterizing the three types of systems: content, user, functionality, quality, policy, and architecture. The Manifesto also introduced the main roles that actors may play within a Digital Library, i.e. end-user, designer, administrator and application developer.

While the reader is referred to (Candela et al. 2006) for a complete presentation of the Manifesto, it seems useful to extract from it and report here two figures that sketch the three relevant systems contributing to the constitution of an effective digital library, and the main concepts of the digital libraries universe. Figure 1.15 represents the three layers of the digital libraries universe, where:

- A Digital Library (DL) is an organization, which might be virtual, that comprehensively collects, manages and preserves for the long term rich digital content, and offers to its user communities specialized functionality on that content, of measurable quality and according to codified policies.

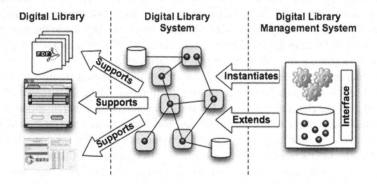

Fig. 1.15 Digital Library (DL), Digital Library System (DLS), and Digital Library Management System (DLMS)

---

[20] See http://marciana.venezia.sbn.it/catalogazione.php?sst=46.

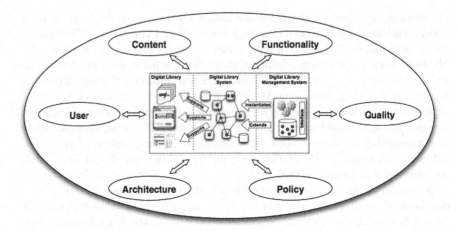

Fig. 1.16 The digital library universe

- A Digital Library System (DLS) is a software system that is based on a defined (possibly distributed) architecture and provides all functionality required by a particular Digital Library. Users interact with a Digital Library through the corresponding Digital Library System.
- A Digital Library Management System (DLMS) is a generic software system that provides the appropriate software infrastructure both to produce and administer a Digital Library System incorporating the suite of functionality considered fundamental for Digital Libraries and to integrate additional software offering more refined, specialized or advanced functionality.

Figure 1.16 introduces the general concepts of the area (Candela et al. 2006, p. 11).

The DELOS Digital Library Reference Model is a first step towards the development of a foundational theory and the result of the "collective understanding" matured by the community of scholars who have been contributing to the growth of the sector. The DELOS Digital Library Reference Model identifies a set of notions and relations that are typical of the Digital Libraries area.

The reference model is a conceptual framework for capturing significant entities and their relationships in the universe of digital libraries. The goal is to use current knowledge of the characteristics of a DLMS to develop more concrete models of it. Conceptual maps of the reference model domains are presented and described, providing a brief overview of the concepts of each domain, the relations that bind them as well as the interaction between concepts of different domains. Lastly, the reference model presents concepts and relations in a hierarchical fashion, thus providing an overview of the specialization relations between them. Concept and relation definitions are provided for each of the concepts and relations of the concept maps. Each concept definition contains a brief definition of the concept, its relations to other concepts, the rationale behind the addition of the concept and an example. Each relation, accordingly, is described by a definition, a rationale and an example.

Thus, this model represents the only published reference guide both for scientists and professionals interested in the development and use of digital library systems.

1.5 Digital Library Systems Become User-Centered Systems: Adding Advanced Annotation Functions to Digital Library Systems

Digital library systems are in a state of fast evolution. Although they are still places where information resources can be stored and made available to end users, present design and development efforts are moving in the direction of transforming them into systems able to support the user in different information centric activities. This evolution is depicted in Fig. 1.17 where digital library systems focused on specific and specialized data are depicted on the left, and systems that can be used in a concurrent way by the users are depicted on the right.

Annotations are an effective means of enabling interaction between users and one or more digital library systems, since their use is a diffuse and very well-established practice. Annotations are not only a way of explaining and enriching an information resource with personal observations, they are also a means of transmitting and sharing ideas to improve collaborative work practices. Furthermore, annotations allow users to naturally merge and link personal contents with the information resources provided by one or more digital library systems so that a common context unifying all of these contents can be created (Agosti and Ferro 2008b).

Furthermore, annotations cover a very broad spectrum, because they range from explaining and enriching an information resource with personal observations to transmitting and sharing ideas and knowledge on a subject. Moreover, they may cover different scopes and have different kinds of annotative context: they can be private, shared or public, according to the type of intellectual work that is being

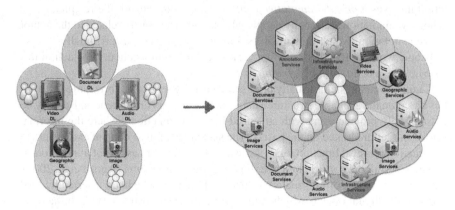

Fig. 1.17 Evolution of digital library systems: from a data centric system (*left*) to a user centric one (*right*)

carried out. In addition, the boundaries between these scopes are not fixed, rather they may vary and evolve with time. Finally, annotations call for active involvement, the degree of which varies according to the aim of the annotation: private annotations require the involvement of the authors, whereas shared or public annotations involve the participation of a whole community. Therefore, annotations are suitable for improving collaboration and co-operation among users.

Annotations allow the creation of new relationships among existing contents, by means of links that connect annotations together and with existing content. In this sense we can consider that existing content and annotations constitute a hypertext, according to the definition of hypertext provided in (Agosti 1996). This hypertext can be exploited not only for providing alternative navigation and browsing capabilities, but also for offering advanced search functionalities (Agosti and Melucci 2001). Furthermore, Marshall (1998) considers annotations as a natural way of creating and growing hypertexts that connect information resources in a digital library system by actively engaging users. Finally, the hypertext existing between information resources and annotations enables different annotation configurations, such as *threads of annotations*, i.e. an annotation made in response to another annotation, and *sets of annotation*, i.e. a bundle of annotations on the same passage of text (Agosti and Ferro 2003; Agosti et al. 2004).

Thus, annotations introduce a new content layer aimed at elucidating the meaning of underlying documents, so that annotations can make hidden facets of the annotated documents more explicit. In conclusion, we can consider that annotations constitute a special kind of context, that we call *annotative context*, for the documents of a digital library, because they provide additional content concerned with the annotated documents. This viewpoint about annotations covers a wide range of annotation kinds, ranging from personal jottings in the margin of a page to scholarly comments made by an expert to explain a passage of a text. Thus, these different kinds of annotations involve different scopes for the annotation itself and, consequently, different kinds of annotative context. If we deal with a personal jotting, the recipient of the annotation is usually the author himself and so this kind of annotation involves a *private annotative context*; on the other hand, the recipients of a scholarly annotation are usually people who are not necessarily related to the author of the annotation, which thus involves a *public annotative context*; finally, a team of people working together on a topic can share annotations about it, which in this case involve a *collaborative annotative context*.

Digital library systems usually offer some basic hypertext and browsing capabilities based on the available structured data, such as authors or references. But they do not normally provide users with advanced hypertext functions, where the information resources are linked on the basis of the semantics of their content and hypertext information retrieval functionalities are available. A relevant aspect of annotations is that they permit the construction over time of a useful hypertext (Agosti et al. 2004), which relates pieces of information of personal interest, which are inserted by final users, to the digital objects which are managed by the software system. In fact, the user annotations allow the creation of new relationships among existing digital objects by means of links that connect annotations together with existing objects. In addition, the hypertext between annotations and annotated objects can be exploited not only for providing alternative navigation and browsing capabilities, but also for offering advanced search functions, able to retrieve more and better ranked objects in response to a user query by also exploiting the annotations linked to them (Agosti and Ferro 2005a, 2006).

Therefore, annotations can turn out to be an effective way of associating this kind of hypertext to a digital library system to enable the active and dynamic use of information resources. In addition, this hypertext can span and cross the boundaries of the single digital library system, if users need to interact with the information resources managed by multiple digital library systems (Agosti and Ferro 2008a). This latter possibility is quite innovative, because it offers the means for interconnecting various digital library systems in a personalized and meaningful way for the end-user, and, as it has been highlighted by Ioannidis et al. (2005), this is a relevant challenge for the digital library systems of the next generation.

An annotation service with these characteristics has been designed and developed at the University of Padua. This service is named "Flexible Annotation Service Tool" (FAST) (Agosti and Ferro 2003, 2005b; Ferro 2005) because it is able to represent and manage annotations which range from metadata to full content. Its flexible and modular architecture makes it suitable for annotating general web resources as well as digital objects managed by different digital library systems, as depicted in Fig. 1.18, which shows that the FAST annotation service can be used as

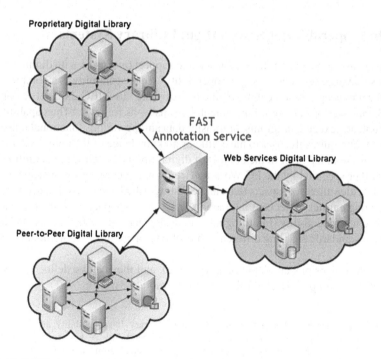

Fig. 1.18 FAST: A user annotation service for many digital library systems

Fig. 1.19 Users annotations managed by FAST and digital libraries of annotated documents managed by different systems

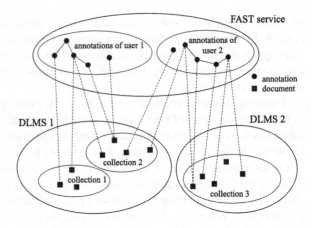

a tool for keeping user memory of thoughts integrating and relating them to information resources managed by different digital library systems.

The annotations themselves can be complex multimedia compound objects, with varying degree of visibility which range from private to shared and public annotations and different access rights. Figure 1.19 illustrates the situation in which FAST manages the annotations that have been produced by two users and that are on documents managed by two different digital library management systems.

1.6 Interoperability between Digital Library Systems

A relevant aspect that needs to be addressed to support final users with digital library systems that are user-centric is "interoperability". Interoperability is a complex and multiform concept, which can be defined—as by the "ISO/IEC 2382-01, Information Technology Vocabulary, Fundamental Terms"—as follows: "The capability to communicate, execute programs, or transfer data among various functional units in a manner that requires the user to have little or no knowledge of the unique characteristics of those units". But in the context of digital library systems, the definition has been further specified by the EC Working Group on Digital Library Interoperability which has identified six aspects that can be distinguished and taken into account: interoperating entities, objects of interaction, functional perspective of interoperation, linguistic interoperability (multilingualism), design and user perspectives, and technological standards enabling different kinds of interoperability[21] (Gradmann 2007).

The six dimensions are depicted in Fig. 1.20, and they can be defined as by the EC Working Group on Digital Library Interoperability as:

---

[21]The results of the EC Working Group on Digital Library Interoperability are reported in the briefing paper by Stefan Gradman, entitled "Interoperability. A key concept for large scale, persistent digital libraries" which can be downloaded from the URL: http://www.digitalpreservationeurope.eu/publications/briefs/interoperability.pdf.

Fig. 1.20 Dimensions of interoperability in the context of digital libraries

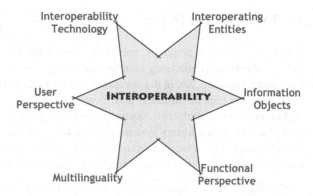

- Interoperating entities: These can be assumed to be the traditional cultural heritage institutions, such as libraries, museums, archives, and other institutions in charge of preservation of artifacts, that offer digital services, or again the digital repositories (institutional or not), eScience and/or eLearning platforms or simply web services.
- Information objects: The entities that actually need to be processed in interoperability scenarios. Choices range from the full content of digital information objects (analogue/digitized or born digital) to mere representations of such objects—and these in turn are often conceived as librarian metadata attribute sets, but are sometimes also conceived as "surrogates".
- Functional perspective: This may simply be the exchange and/or propagation of digital content. Other functional goals are aggregating digital objects into a common content layer. Another approach is to enable users and/or software applications to interact with multiple digital library systems via unified interfaces or to facilitate operations across federated autonomous digital library systems.
- Multilinguality-multilingualism: Linguistic interoperability can be thought of in two different ways: as multilingual user interfaces to digital library systems or as dynamic multilingual techniques for exploring the digital library systems object space. Three types of approaches can be distinguished in the second respect: dynamic query translation for addressing digital library systems that manage different languages, dynamic translation of metadata responding to queries in different languages or dynamic localization of digital content.
- User perspective: Interoperability concepts of a digital library system manager differ substantially from those of a content consuming end user. A technical administrator will have a very different view from an end user providing content as an author.
- Interoperability technology: Enabling different kinds of interoperability constitutes a major dimension with more traditional approaches geared towards librarian metadata interoperability such as Z39.50, SRU or the harvesting methods based on OAI-PMH or web service-based approaches.

1.7 Evaluation of Digital Libraries

Although evaluation activities started soon after the first digital library systems
were available, the underlying assumptions and goals of the evaluation approaches
were quite disparate. So, in the context of the DELOS activities, efforts were made
to analyse the general situation and to propose a framework for evaluating digital library systems with the objective of providing a set of flexible and adaptable
guidelines for digital library systems evaluation (Fuhr et al. 2007); a number of recommendations have emerged from the proposed framework, and those of specific
interest when setting up a digital library evaluation activity are here recalled:

- Flexible evaluation frameworks: For complex entities such as digital library systems, the evaluation framework should be flexible, allowing for multi-level evaluations (e.g. by following the six levels proposed by Saracevic (2004), including
  user and social). Furthermore any evaluation framework should undergo a period
  of discussion, revision and validation by the digital libraries community before
  being widely adopted. Flexibility would help researchers to avoid obsolete studies based on rigid frameworks, and to use models that can "expand" or "collapse"
  at their project's requirements and conditions.
- Involvement of practitioners and real users: Practitioners have a wealth of experience and domain-related knowledge that is often neglected. Better communication and definition of common terminology, aims and objectives could establish a
  framework of co-operation and boost this research area.
- Build on past experiences of large evaluation initiatives: Initiatives of evaluation, such as TREC,[22] CLEF,[23] INEX,[24] and NTCIR[25] have collected a wealth of
  knowledge about evaluation methodology, which needs be effectively deployed.

In order to foster evaluation research in general, the following issues should be
addressed:

- Community building in evaluation research: The lack of globally accepted abstract evaluation models and methodologies can be counter-balanced by collecting, publishing and analyzing current research activities. Maintaining an updated
  inventory of evaluation activities and their interrelations can help to define good
  practice in the field and to help the research community to reach a consensus.
- Establishment of primary data repositories: The provision of open access to primary evaluation data (e.g. transaction logs, surveys, monitored events), as is common in other research fields, should be a goal. In this respect, methods to render
  anonymous the primary data must be adopted, as privacy is a strong concern.
  Common repositories and infrastructures for storing primary and pre-processed

---

[22]Text REtrieval Conference, URL: http://trec.nist.gov/.

[23]Cross-Language Evaluation Forum, URL: http://www.clef-campaign.org/.

[24]INitiative for the Evaluation of XML Retrieval, from 2002 to 2007 at the URL: http://inex.is.
informatik.uni-duisburg.de/, onwards at the URL: http://www.inex.otago.ac.nz/.

[25]NII Test Collection for IR Systems Project, URL: http://research.nii.ac.jp/ntcir/.

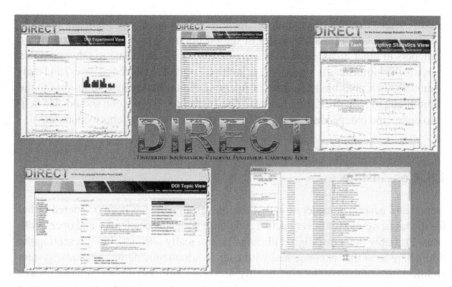

Fig. 1.21 DIRECT: Examples of supported activities in CLEF campaigns

data are proposed along with the collaborative formation of evaluation best practices, and modular building blocks to be used in evaluation activities. An exem-
plary model of such a primary data repository is DIRECT, a digital library which
manages scientific data to be used during the evaluation campaign of multilingual
search and access systems (Di Nunzio and Ferro 2005; Dussin and Ferro 2009;
Agosti and Ferro 2009). Figure 1.21 illustrates some examples of the activities
that are supported by the DIRECT system during the CLEF evaluation campaigns.[26]

- Standardized logging format: Further use and dissemination of common logging
  standards is also considered useful (Klas et al. 2006). Logging could be extended to include user behavior and system internal activity and to support the
  personalization and intelligent user interface design processes.
- Evaluation of user behavior in-the-large: Currently, evaluation is focused too
  much on user interface and system issues. User satisfaction with respect to how
  far the user information needs have been satisfied (i.e. information access) must
  be investigated, independently of the methods used to fulfill these needs. The de-
  termination of user strategies and tactics is also recommended (such as search
  strategies, and browsing behaviors). This relates to evaluation in context, and to
  the question of identifying dependencies in various contexts (e.g. sociological,
  business, institutional). Collecting user behavior as implicit rating information
  can also be used to establish collaborative filtering services in digital library environments.

---

[26]More information on the DIRECT system and on the data collections managed by it can be found
at the URL: http://direct.dei.unipd.it/.

- Differences that are specific of the domain of evaluation: An important problem is how to relate a possible model of digital library system to other overlapping models in other areas. How does a digital library system relate to other complex networked information systems (e.g. archives, portals, knowledge bases) and their models? Is it possible to connect or integrate digital library system models to the multitude of related existing models? The answer to this question should also help to define the independent research area of digital library systems evaluation.

1.8 Conclusions

A final and general consideration that emerges from what has been presented is that the digital libraries area is very active and dense with new challenges and open problems. Probably the term "digital libraries" is not really adequate in representing the flourishing area that is concerned with user requirements, digital contents, system architectures, functions, policies, quality, and evaluation, but it is a token that evokes the fascinating world of representing and managing the knowledge that humankind has been able to produce and make collectively available.

Acknowledgements The paper reports on work which originated in the context of the DELOS Network of Excellence on Digital Libraries. The author thanks Costantino Thanos, coordinator of DELOS, for his continuous support and advice.

The reported work has been partially supported by the TELplus Targeted Project for digital libraries, as part of the eContent*plus* Programme of the European Commission (Contract ECP-2006-DILI-510003) and by EuropeanaConnect Best Practice Network funded by the European Commission within the area of Digital Libraries of the eContent*plus* Programme (Contract ECP-2008-DILI-52800).

Chapter 2
Scalability Challenges in Web Search Engines

Berkant Barla Cambazoglu and Ricardo Baeza-Yates

Abstract Continuous growth of the Web and user bases forces web search engine companies to make costly investments on very large compute infrastructures. The scalability of these infrastructures requires careful performance optimizations in every major component of the search engine. Herein, we try to provide a fairly comprehensive coverage of the literature on scalability challenges in large-scale web search engines. We present the identified challenges through an architectural classification, starting from a simple single-node search system and moving towards a hypothetical multi-site web search architecture. We also discuss a number of open research problems and provide recommendations to researchers in the field.

2.1 Introduction

Large-scale search engines are the primary means to access the content in the Web. As of February 2011, the indexed Web is estimated to contain *at least* 16.3 billion pages.[1] The actual size of the Web is estimated to be much larger due to the presence of dynamically generated pages. The main duty of web search engines is to fetch this vast amount of content and store it in an efficiently searchable form. Commercial search engines are estimated to process hundreds of millions of queries daily on their index of the Web.

---

[1]The size of the indexed Web (visited on February 1, 2010), http://www.worldwidewebsize.com/.

B.B. Cambazoglu (✉) · R. Baeza-Yates
Yahoo! Research, Diagonal 177, p9, 08018 Barcelona, Spain
e-mail: barla@yahoo-inc.com

R. Baeza-Yates
e-mail: rbaeza@acm.org

B.B. Cambazoglu
url: http://research.yahoo.com/Berkant_Barla_Cambazoglu

R. Baeza-Yates
url: http://www.baeza.cl

M. Melucci, R. Baeza-Yates (eds.), *Advanced Topics in Information Retrieval*,
The Information Retrieval Series 33,
DOI 10.1007/978-3-642-20946-8_2, © Springer-Verlag Berlin Heidelberg 2011

Given the very high rate of growth in the number of web pages and the number of issued queries, the scalability of large-scale search engines becomes a real challenge. Increasing the investment on hardware in order to cope with this growth has certain financial implications for search engine companies. Therefore, designing efficient and scalable search systems is crucial to reduce the running cost of web search engines.

In this chapter, we provide a survey of the scalability challenges in designing a large-scale web search engine. We specifically focus on software design and algorithmic aspects of scalability. For a hardware perspective, interested readers may refer to (Barroso et al. 2003; Barroso and Hölzle 2009).

In Sect. 2.2, we first provide a very brief overview of the main components in a web search engine. We then, in Sect. 2.3, summarize the quality and efficiency objectives that must be considered during the design of these components. A number of parameters that affect the scalability of search engines are discussed in Sect. 2.4. In Sect. 2.5, we provide a detailed survey of research issues in search engines, going into detail only on scalability-related issues. Finally, in Sect. 2.6, we discuss several open research problems in the field.

2.2 Components

A full-fledged web search engine contains three main components: a crawler, an indexer, and a query processor. In practice, commercial search engines include many other components as well (e.g., web graph builder, spam classifier, spelling corrector). However, we prefer to omit these supplementary components herein as they are too specific to a particular purpose or they do not have a significant impact on the scalability.

Figure 2.1 illustrates the functioning of the three components mentioned above. The main duty of the crawler is to locate the pages in the Web and download their content, which is stored on disk for further processing. This processing typically involves various parsing, extraction, and classification tasks. The indexer is responsible for extracting the textual content from the stored pages and building an inverted index to facilitate processing of user queries. It also extracts various features that will be used by the query processor in relevance estimations. The query processor

Fig. 2.1 A simplified view of the three major components in web search engines and their functioning

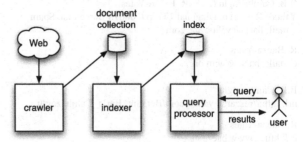

is responsible for receiving online user queries and evaluating them over the constructed index. It presents to the user a small set of best-matching results, typically links to ten pages selected from the indexed collection, together with their titles and short summaries (snippets). In general, the results are displayed in decreasing order of their estimated relevance to the query.

2.3 Objectives

All three components are designed to meet certain quality and efficiency objectives. Table 2.1 summarizes the main objectives we have identified. Despite their high number and variety, the ultimate goal in achieving all of these objectives is to maximize the satisfaction that users get from the service provided by the search engine.

The main quality objectives for the crawler are to achieve high web coverage (Dasgupta et al. 2007), high page freshness (Cho and Garcia-Molina 2000, 2003), and high content quality (Cho et al. 1998; Najork and Wiener 2001). The crawler aims to locate and fetch as many pages as possible from the Web. In this way, it increases the likelihood that more pages useful to users will be indexed by the search engine. In the meantime, the crawler tries to keep the pages that are already discovered as fresh as possible by selectively refetching them, as an effort towards providing pages' up-to-date versions in the Web, rather than their stale versions in the repository. Finally, the crawler tries to prioritize fetching of pages in such a way that relatively more important pages are downloaded earlier (Cho et al. 1998) or are fetched more often, keeping them more fresh compared to less important pages (Cho and Garcia-Molina 2000).

Achieving the above-mentioned quality objectives requires sustaining high page download rates, which is the most important efficiency objective for the crawler. This is simply because, as the crawler downloads pages faster, it can cope better with the growth and evolution of the Web. Hence, it can achieve a higher web coverage

Table 2.1 The main quality and efficiency objectives in crawling, indexing, and query processing

Component	Quality objectives	Efficiency objectives
Crawling	High web coverage High page freshness High content quality	High download rate
Indexing	Rich features	Short deployment cycle High compactness Fast index updates
Query processing	High precision High recall Result diversity High snippet quality	Low average response time Bounded response time

and page freshness, perhaps with some positive impact on search result quality as well (Cambazoglu et al. 2009).

The most important quality objective for the indexer is to extract a rich set of features from the downloaded document collection and potentially from other sources of information. The extracted features are used by the query processor to estimate relevance of documents to queries. Therefore, it is vital to identify a fairly high number of features that are good indicators of relevance and to precompute them as accurately as possible. In current search engines, the commonly computed features include corpus statistics, e.g., term frequencies, document lengths (Baeza-Yates and Ribeiro-Neto 2010), various link analysis metrics (Page et al. 1999), click features (Joachims 2002), and features computed by means of query log analysis and session analysis (Boldi et al. 2008).

The efficiency objectives in indexing involve reducing the length of index deployment cycles, speeding up index update operations, and creating highly compact indexes. The first objective is meaningful for search engines where the index is constructed and deployed periodically. Reducing the length of the deployment cycle is important because the search queries are continued to be evaluated over an old copy of the index until the new index is deployed. This may harm the user experience as some search results may involve stale results (Lewandowskii 2008). The second objective is meaningful for search engines where the index updates are incremental and performed on the copy of the index that is actively used in query processing. In this case, optimizing these update operations becomes important as they share the same computing resources with the query processor (Büttcher and Clarke 2005). Independently of the strategy used to construct the index, the created web index needs to be compact, i.e., the memory requirement for storing the index should be low (Zhang et al. 2008). This is because a large fraction of the index has to be cached in main memory to prevent costly disk accesses during query processing.

The success of a search engine typically correlates with the fraction of relevant results in the generated search results (i.e., precision) and the fraction of relevant results that are returned to the user in all relevant results that are available in the index (i.e., recall) (Baeza-Yates and Ribeiro-Neto 2010). Achieving high precision and high recall are the two main quality objectives for the query processor as they are highly related to user satisfaction (in practice, precision is more important as users view only the first few result pages). Another quality objective that has recently become popular is to achieve high result diversity, where the goal is to minimize the overlap in the information provided to the user and to cover as many different intents of the query as possible in the presented search results (Agrawal et al. 2009; Rafiei et al. 2010). Finally, providing descriptive summaries of documents, i.e., high quality snippets (Varadarajan and Hristidis 2006), is important as this increases the likelihood of users to click on search results (Clarke et al. 2007).

The response time to a query is determined by the query processing time and the network latency between the user and the search site. The main efficiency objective for the query processor is to evaluate the queries in a fast manner (Cambazoglu and Aykanat 2006) and return the results to the user typically under one second.

This goal is perhaps one of the most challenging among all efficiency objectives mentioned before. In addition, it has been recently shown that high query response times may have a negative impact on user satisfaction and hence the revenues of the search engine (Schurman and Brutlag 2009). Therefore, a bounded response time is a must.

2.4 Parameters

There are a number of parameters that may affect the scalability of a search engine. These can be classified as internal and external parameters. Internal parameters are those on which the search engine has at least some control. External parameters are those that cannot be controlled by the search engine. Table 2.2 gives a summary of the parameters we identified.

Among the internal parameters, the amount of hardware is the most important for achieving scalability. Increasing the hardware processing and storage capacity greatly helps the efficiency objectives in both crawling, indexing, and query processing. However, adding more machines is not a long term solution for scalability due to high depreciation and maintenance costs. Besides hardware, an important parameter for crawling is the network bandwidth. Assuming that the backend text processing system is powerful enough and hence does not form a bottleneck, the network bandwidth available to the crawler determines the page download rate. For scaling the query processing component, it is vital to increase the hit rate of the result cache (Cambazoglu et al. 2010c). This significantly helps reducing the query traffic reaching the query processor. Another important parameter is the peak query processing throughput that can be sustained by the query processor (Chowdhury and Pass 2003). This is mainly determined by the amount of available hardware and the efficiency of the data structures used by the query processor.

There are three main external parameters that affect the scalability of the crawling component: web growth (Ntoulas et al. 2004), Web change (Fetterly et al. 2004), and malicious intent (Gyöngyi and Garcia-Molina 2005b). Finding and surfacing

Table 2.2 The parameters that affect the scalability of a search engine

Component	Internal parameters	External parameters
Crawling	Amount of hardware Available network bandwidth	Rate of web growth Rate of web change Amount of malicious intent
Indexing	Amount of hardware	Amount of spam content Amount of duplicate content
Query processing	Amount of hardware Cache hit rate Peak query processing throughput	Peak query traffic

the content in the Web becomes the most important challenge as it continues to grow (Lawrence and Giles 2000). In the mean time, modifications on web pages affect freshness of indexed collections and force the crawlers to refresh previously downloaded content by refetching their potentially new versions on the Web (Cho and Garcia-Molina 2000). Moreover, malicious intent of Internet users may have a negative impact on crawling performance. This mainly involves spider traps (Heydon and Najork 1999) and link farms (Gyöngyi and Garcia-Molina 2005a), both of which lead to useless work for the crawler. Similarly, spam or duplicate pages lead to useless work for the indexer as these pages need to be identified to exclude them from the index. Otherwise, both the quality of search results and the efficiency of the query processor is negatively affected by the presence of such pages. Finally, the distribution of the query traffic is an important parameter for scaling the query processing component. If the peak query traffic exceeds the maximum query processing throughput that can be sustained by the query processor, queries are dropped without any processing or processed in degradation mode, yielding partial, less relevant results (Cambazoglu et al. 2010c).

2.5 Scalability Issues

A large body of work exists on the scalability issues in search engines (see (Arasu et al. 2001) and (Baeza-Yates et al. 2007c) for related but older surveys). Herein, we provide a detailed survey on these issues in two different dimensions. First, we classify the issues according to the component associated with them, i.e., crawling, indexing, and query processing. Second, we consider the complexity of the search architecture. More specifically, we consider four search architectures at different granularities: a single-node system, a multi-node cluster, a multi-cluster site, and a multi-site engine, listed in increasing order of design complexity.

Figure 2.2 shows our classification of scalability issues. We note that all of the issues that fall under a simpler architecture are also issues in more complex architectures, but not the other way around. For example, index partitioning, which appears under multi-node cluster, is also an issue in multi-cluster and multi-site architectures, but not in single-node systems. In Fig. 2.3, we summarize the symbols used by the figures in the rest of the paper.

2.5.1 Single-Node System

This is a very simple architecture in which a single computer is dedicated to each component (Fig. 2.4). In this minimalist approach, the Web is crawled by a single computer (potentially, through multiple crawling threads (Heydon and Najork 1999)), and a common document repository is formed. This repository is converted into an index by another computer that runs an indexer (Zobel and Moffat 2006).

	Single node	Multi-node cluster	Multi-cluster site	Multi-site engine
Crawling	DNS caching multi-threading data structures politeness mirror detection link farm detection spider trap detection	link exchange web partitioning web repartitioning	focused crawling	web partitioning crawler placement
Indexing	index creation index maintenance index compression document id reassignment duplicate elimination	index partitioning load balancing document clustering	full index replication index pruning tiering	partial index replication
Query processing	caching early termination query degradation personalization search bot detection	collection selection	tier selection	query routing query forwarding search site placement

Fig. 2.2 Issues that have an impact on scalability

Fig. 2.3 The legend for the symbols used in the rest of the figures

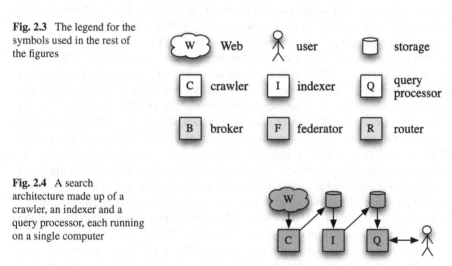

Fig. 2.4 A search architecture made up of a crawler, an indexer and a query processor, each running on a single computer

The query processor evaluates a query sequentially over the constructed web index (Cambazoglu and Aykanat 2006). In this architecture, users issue their queries directly to the query processing node and receive the search results from this node.

2.5.1.1 Single-Node Crawling

A standard sequential crawler works as follows. It starts with a given set of seed URLs and iteratively fetches these URLs from the Web by establishing HTTP connections with their web servers. Downloaded pages are stored in a repository (see

(Hirai et al. 2000) for repository management issues). In the mean time, they are parsed and the extracted new links are added into the crawler's frontier, i.e., the set of URLs that are discovered but not yet downloaded. Typically, the frontier is implemented as a queue. Hash values of discovered URLs are stored in a large hash table so that the existence of a URL in the repository or the frontier can be easily checked. Different techniques for efficient in-memory caching of seen URLs is discussed by Broder et al. (2003b). The crawler also maintains a repository of the encountered robots.txt files and a cache for DNS entries of hosts. DNS caching and multi-threading are vital to reduce the overhead of DNS resolution, which needs to be performed at every HTTP request (Heydon and Najork 1999).

For the single-node crawling scenario, the network bandwidth is hardly a bottleneck. Therefore, the crawler makes use of multi-threading, i.e., Web pages are fetched and processed by many task-wise identical threads, each handling a different HTTP connection (Heydon and Najork 1999). The number of threads can be increased until the available download bandwidth saturates or the overhead of context switches in the operating system beats the purpose of multi-threading. Under multi-threading, disk accesses and memory form the main bottlenecks in crawling. Hence, efficient implementation of data structures used by the crawler is crucial. A very good discussion of data structure issues, together with a comparison of previous implementations can be found in (Lee et al. 2008).

Another important issue is to decide on the download order of URLs. Older techniques prioritize the URLs in the frontier according to a quality metric (e.g., the linkage between pages) (Cho et al. 1998; Najork and Wiener 2001) and recrawl the stored content based on the likelihood of modification (Cho and Garcia-Molina 2003; Edwards et al. 2001). More recent approaches prioritize URLs (Pandey and Olston 2008) and refresh the content (Fetterly et al. 2009; Pandey and Olston 2005; Wolf et al. 2002) to directly increase the benefit to search result quality. In this impact-based crawling approach, the pages that are expected to frequently appear in search results are crawled earlier or more often than the others. Similarly, web sites can be prioritized for crawling so that the sites that contribute more pages to search results are crawled deeper or more often. A recent work also takes into account the information longevity of pages (Olston and Pandey 2008).

Ideally, a crawler is expected not to overload the same web server (or even subnetworks) with repetitive connection requests in a short time span, i.e., it should be polite in its interaction with web servers (Eichmann 1995). In practice, web crawlers limit the number of concurrent connections they establish to a server or set an upperbound on the time between two successive requests in order to avoid complaints from web site owners or even long-term blocking of the crawler. As noted by Lee et al. (2008), which suggests using per-server time delays instead of per-host delays, achieving politeness may have an important impact on the performance of a crawler due to complications in data structures.

A number of obstacles arise for crawlers due to malicious intent of web site owners. An example of malicious intent is the delay attacks, where web servers introduce unnecessary delays in their responses to requests of the crawler. Perhaps, the most important hazard is spider traps, which try to keep the crawler busy by dynamically creating infinitely many useless links (Heydon and Najork 1999). A crawling thread caught in a spider trap can significantly degrade utilization of system resources. Another important hazard is link farms (Gyöngyi and Garcia-Molina 2005a), which are composed of spam sites linking to each other with the hope of increasing the popularity values assigned to them by search engines for ranking purposes. Although the main objective of link farms is search engine optimization by means of link spam, they also harm crawlers since a crawler may allocate a significant portion of its resources to download these spam pages. A well known technique to detect link spam, TrustRank, is proposed by Gyöngyi et al. (2004). Mirror sites form a similar threat even though they are not maliciously created (Bharat and Broder 1999; Bharat et al. 2000; Cho et al. 2000). Early detection of link farms and mirror sites is important for a good utilization of the network and computational resources of the crawler. A good discussion of other hazards is available in Heydon and Najork (1999).

2.5.1.2 Single-Node Indexing

A sequential indexer is responsible for creating an efficiently searchable representation of the collection. To this end, each document in the crawled collection is passed through a preprocessing pipeline, composed of a number of software modules. At each module in the pipeline, various tasks are performed. Typical tasks involve HTML parsing, link extraction, text extraction, spam filtering, soft 404 detection, text classification, entity recognition, and feature extraction.

After preprocessing, each document is represented by the terms appearing in it and also by some additional terms (e.g., the anchor text extracted from the links pointing to the document). The indexing component takes these cleansed forms of documents and converts them into an inverted index (Harman et al. 1992; Zobel and Moffat 2006), which consists of an inverted list for each term in the vocabulary of the collection and an index that keeps the starts of these lists. The inverted list of a term keeps a set of postings that represent the documents containing the term. A posting stores useful information, such as a document id and the frequency of the term in the document. This information is later used by the query processor in estimating relevance scores. In addition, for each term-document pair, a position list is maintained to record the positions that the term appears in the document. The position information is needed for computing relevance scores based on proximity of query terms in documents (Büttcher et al. 2006b; Rasolofo and Savoy 2003). Similarly, for each term in the document, the section information, i.e., different parts of the document that the term appears (e.g., title, header, body, footer), is also stored as this is used by the ranking system.

In principle, creating an inverted index is similar to computing the transpose of a sparse matrix. There are different approaches in research literature for index creation (Fox and Lee 1991; Harman and Candela 1990; Moffat and Bell 1995; Witten et al. 1999). One possible indexing strategy is based on in-memory inversion (Fox and Lee 1991; Moffat and Bell 1995). This strategy requires making two passes over the document collection. In the first phase, the storage requirement of every inverted list is determined and a skeleton is created for the index. In the second phase, the actual index content is computed in-memory. It is also possible to keep and update the skeleton on the disk. For large collections, making two passes over the collection is too costly and a one-phase indexing approach performs better (Heinz and Zobel 2003; Moffat and Bell 1995). In this approach, parts of the index are computed and flushed on the disk periodically as the memory becomes full. A disk-based merge algorithm is then used to combine these indexes into a single index.

To keep the index fresh, modifications over the document collection, i.e., document insertions, deletions, and updates, should be reflected to the index. In general, there are three ways to maintain an inverted index fresh (Lester et al. 2004). The simplest option is to rebuild the index from scratch, periodically, using one of the techniques mentioned above. This technique ignores all modifications over the collection and is the preferred technique for mostly static collections. Another option is to incrementally update the current index as new documents arrive (Cutting and Pedersen 1990; Shieh and Chung 2005). It is also possible to accumulate the updates in memory and perform them in batches (Clarke et al. 1994; Tomasic et al. 1994). Incremental indexing requires keeping additional unused space in inverted lists and the efficiency of update operations is important. This is the technique preferred in indexing time-sensitive collections (e.g., a crawl of news sites). A final option is to grow a separate index and periodically merge this index into the main index (Lester et al. 2008). A hybrid strategy that combines incremental updates with merging is proposed by Büttcher et al. (2006a).

For efficiency reasons, during query processing, the inverted index is tried to be kept in the main memory in a compressed form. When processing queries over the index, the relevant portions of the index are decompressed and used. The objective in index compression (Anh and Moffat 2004, 2006a; Moffat and Stuiver 2000; Scholer et al. 2002; Shieh et al. 2003) is to create the most compact index, with the least decompression overhead. In the research literature, different techniques are available for compressing different parts of the inverted index (e.g., document ids (Zhang et al. 2008), term frequencies (Yan et al. 2009b), and term positions (Yan et al. 2009a)). For an overview of inverted index compression techniques (Witten et al. 1999) can be referred to. An experimental evaluation of recent index compression techniques can be found in (Zhang et al. 2008).

The compressibility of document ids can be improved by reassigning document ids in such a way that the gaps between the ids are reduced (Blandford and Blelloch 2002; Blanco and Barreiro 2006; Silvestri 2007; Silvestri et al. 2004). In (Yan et al. 2009b), new algorithms are proposed for compressing term frequencies, under reassigned document ids. A scalable document id reassignment technique is given in (Ding et al. 2010).

A final issue in indexing is to eliminate exact duplicates and near duplicate documents. This helps reducing the index size and saves computing power. Detection of exact duplicates is an efficient and accurate task as comparison of document hashes is sufficient to identify duplicate documents. Near duplicate detection (Chowdhury et al. 2002; Cooper et al. 2002; Henzinger 2006), on the other hand, is a relatively more costly and inaccurate task as it typically involves computing a number of shingles (Broder et al. 1997) for every document and their comparison.

2.5.1.3 Single-Node Query Processing

After a user query is issued to the search node, it goes through a series of preprocessing steps. These steps involve basic cleansing procedures, such as case-folding, stemming and stopword elimination, as well as more complicated procedures, such as spell correction, phrase recognition, entity recognition, localization, query intent analysis, and various other processing techniques. After these steps, the user query is transformed into an internal representation, which may be substantially different from the original user query.

The internal representation of the query is looked up in a result cache to determine if the related search results are already computed for a previous submission of the query. In case of a hit, the results are immediately served by the cache. In the research literature, both static (Baeza-Yates and Saint-Jean 2003; Baeza-Yates et al. 2007b; Markatos 2001; Ozcan et al. 2008) and dynamic (Baeza-Yates et al. 2007b; Markatos 2001; Saraiva et al. 2001) caching of query results is considered. Static and dynamic caching is combined in (Fagni et al. 2006). So far, most works have focused on admission (Baeza-Yates et al. 2007a), eviction (Markatos 2001; Saraiva et al. 2001), and prefetching (Lempel and Moran 2003) policies trying to increase the hit rates of result caches. Some works proposed strategies that take into account the predicted processing costs of queries when making caching and eviction decisions (Altingovde et al. 2009; Gan and Suel 2009). A novel incremental result caching technique is proposed by Puppin et al. (2010). Two recent works argue that the main issue in current result cache architectures is freshness (Blanco et al. 2010; Cambazoglu et al. 2010c). In (Blanco et al. 2010), to achieve freshness, cache entries are invalidated as the index is updated due to modifications on the document collection. In (Cambazoglu et al. 2010c), the result cache is tried to be kept fresh by expiring cache entries via a simple time-to-live mechanism and proactively refreshing the entries during the idle cycles of the backend search system.

Queries whose results are not found in the cache are processed over the index. To speed up processing of queries, various optimization techniques are employed. An important technique is posting list caching, where most frequently or recently accessed posting lists are tried to be kept in the main memory (Baeza-Yates et al. 2007b; Jónsson et al. 1998; Tomasic and Garcia-Molina 1993). In (Zhang et al. 2008), the impact of inverted index compression on the performance of posting list caches is studied. The idea of caching intersections of frequently accessed posting lists and using these intersections for efficient query processing is proposed by Long and Suel (2005).

Perhaps, one of the most important optimization techniques in query processing is early termination, where processing of a query is tried to be terminated before all postings that are associated with the query are traversed. A large number of early termination optimizations are proposed for query processing algorithms that process queries in term order (Anh et al. 2001; Anh and Moffat 2006b; Buckley and Lewit 1985; Harman and Candela 1990; Moffat and Zobel 1996; Persin 1994; Wong and Lee 1993) or document order (Brown 1995; Broder et al. 2003a; Strohman et al. 2005; Turtle and Flood 1995). Some of these algorithms guarantee the correctness of results with respect to evaluation over the full index while some others do not. Interestingly, most algorithms proposed so far assume disjunctive mode of query processing, whereas search engines typically process their queries in conjunctive mode.

There are also other works that propose similar optimizations for term-proximity-aware scoring computations (Schenkel et al. 2007; Tonellotto et al. 2010). In large-scale search engines, a selected set of documents that are top-ranked over the index are further processed via more complex ranking techniques, such as machine-learned ranking. A recent work proposes early termination techniques for such an architecture (Cambazoglu et al. 2010a).

Another important issue is query degradation (Cambazoglu et al. 2010c). Due to tight constraints on response times, queries are processed with certain budgets. If the query processing time exceeds the allowed budget (e.g., because the query requires processing too many postings or a maximum processing time has been reached), the computation may need to be terminated and the search results computed so far are returned to the user. Under a heavy query traffic that exceeds the capacity of the query processor, queries are processed in query degradation mode, in which case search results are only partially computed. A related issue here is to detect and filter the traffic generated by search bots (Yu et al. 2010).

Most commercial search engines employ some form of personalization (Liu et al. 2002; Pitkow et al. 2002; Tan et al. 2006; Teevan et al. 2005; Sun et al. 2005). The objective in personalization is to augment the general search results to suit individual users' tastes. Although the main impact of personalization is on search quality, it can also affect the performance of the search system. This is because personalization of search results imply a huge decrease in result cache hit rates. Consequently, the query traffic processed over the index significantly increases, hindering the scalability. A side issue is efficient computation of personalized page importance vectors (Jeh and Widom 2003).

Once the documents best matching the query are determined, their snippets are generated, typically using the terms adjacent in the document to the query terms. These snippets are presented to the user together with links to the documents. An efficient snippet generation technique is proposed by Turpin et al. (2007).

2.5.2 Multi-Node Cluster

Obviously, it is not possible to achieve any of the objectives mentioned in Sect. 2.3 by means of a simple, low-cost search system, such as the one described in Sect. 2.5.1. Assuming more financial investment is made, execution of the three

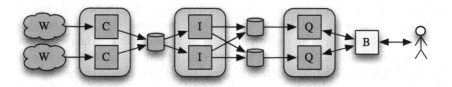

Fig. 2.5 An architecture with a separate multi-node cluster for crawling, indexing, and query processing

components can be parallelized over a multi-node cluster (Fig. 2.5), typically composed of off-the-shelf commodity computers (Barroso et al. 2003). In this architecture, parallel crawling offers increased page download rates as web pages can be concurrently crawled by many computers (assuming the network bandwidth is not saturated). In the mean time, index creation and deployment becomes a much faster process due to the availability of many indexing computers. Finally, query response times are reduced as the query processing task is parallelized over multiple computers. In this multi-node cluster architecture, a user query is issued to a broker node, which dispatches the query to the search nodes. This node is also responsible for merging the results retrieved from the search nodes and returning a final result set to the user.

2.5.2.1 Multi-Node Crawling

Given a robust crawler that runs on a single node, it is relatively easy to build a parallel crawler that runs on multiple nodes (Boldi et al. 2004; Heydon and Najork 1999; Shkapenyuk and Suel 2002; Zeinalipour-Yazti and Dikaiakos 2002). In practice, crawlers on different cluster nodes can run in a pretty much embarrassingly parallel mode and can crawl the Web independently. However, this approach results in high redundancy as the same web pages may be downloaded by different crawling nodes. A simple yet effective solution is to partition the Web across different crawling nodes. This approach guarantees that each page will be downloaded once, but another problem remains: because each crawling node has access to only its local data structures, it cannot decide, without coordinating with the other nodes, whether a newly found link is already fetched or not. In addition, having only local information implies that the crawling order cannot be optimized in a global manner.

In (Cho and Garcia-Molina 2002), three possible solutions are proposed to the above-mentioned coordination problem. The first solution is a naïve one, which simply ignores the newly discovered link if the current node is not responsible for fetching it. Obviously, this approach reduces the coverage of the crawler as some pages are never discovered. The second solution delays the download of non-local links until all local links are exhausted. This approach achieves full coverage, but the redundant crawling problem remains as the same page may be fetched by different nodes. The third and best solution is to communicate the discovered non-local links

to the nodes that are responsible for fetching them. Even though the total communication volume is not very high, communicating individual links right after they
are discovered incurs a significant overhead on the system as link exchanges require
traversing the entire TCP/IP stack at the sender and receiver nodes (Cho and Garcia-
Molina 2002). As a solution, links can be accumulated an exchanged in batch mode.
Delaying exchange of links is shown not to cause any loss in the quality of downloaded collections (Cho and Garcia-Molina 2002).

Partitioning of the Web, i.e., assignment of URLs to crawling nodes, can be performed in a straightforward manner by assigning fixed ranges of hash values to
the nodes (Heydon and Najork 1999). Given a uniform hashing function, download
workloads of nodes are expected to be balanced. In practice, it is better to assign
to crawling nodes the entire web sites rather than individual web pages. This helps
reducing the overhead of link exchanges. More importantly, this enables better politeness mechanisms as the load incurred on a web server can be tracked within the
same crawling node. Based on a similar observation, in (Chung and Clarke 2002),
a topical assignment approach is taken to improve duplicate content detection and
page quality computations.

If the URL assignment depends on the structure of the Web (e.g., the graph partitioning approach in (Cambazoglu et al. 2004)), the URL space may need to be
repartitioned among the crawling nodes. In this case, the URL assignment is periodically recomputed to maintain a load balance across crawling nodes. Achieving fault
tolerance is another reason for reassigning URLs to crawling nodes. As an example,
the URL space of a failed crawling node may have to be partitioned among the active nodes or a subset of existing URLs may have to be assigned to a newly added
crawling node. In (Boldi et al. 2004), consistent hashing is proposed as a feasible
solution to the URL reassignment problem.

2.5.2.2 Multi-Node Indexing

Since the created index will be stored in a multi-node search cluster, it is partitioned
into a number of disjoint subindexes. In general, an inverted index can be partitioned
based on the documents or terms. In document-based partitioning, each subindex
contains the postings of a disjoint set of documents. This technique is also referred
to as local index partitioning because each subindex can be locally built by a separate indexing node. In this technique, the assignment of documents to subindexes
is typically obtained by creating a mapping between hashes of document ids and
indexing nodes. Document-based partitioning leads to well-balanced partitions in
terms of storage. However, it requires collecting and replicating on all nodes the
global collection statistics (Melnik et al. 2001).

In term-based partitioning, which is also referred to as global index partitioning,
each part contains a set of posting lists associated with a disjoint set of terms. Due
to the large variation in sizes of posting lists and their access frequencies, the main
goal is to achieve a reasonable load balance during parallel query processing. In

the research literature, there are works focusing on load balancing in term-based-partitioned indexes, by taking into account sizes and access patterns of posting lists (Jeong and Omiecinski 1995; Lucchese et al. 2007).

Both term- and document-based indexes can be created by means of a parallel indexing system. In (Melnik et al. 2001), parallel index creation and statistics gathering strategies are proposed to create a document-based-partitioned index. A few papers discuss strategies for creation of term-based-partitioned indexes in parallel (Ribeiro-Neto et al. 1998, 1999). Because of the time complexity of indexing and updating a global term-based-partitioned index, commercial search engines use document partitioning and some of them rely on the MapReduce framework (Dean and Ghemawat 2008) to parallelize the indexing process.

In contrast to the aforementioned non-topical partitioning approaches, it is also possible to create subindexes specific to certain topics by clustering documents and assigning each document cluster to a different search node. As before, each subindex acts as a separate entity that can be individually queried. In the literature, most approaches adopt the k-means clustering algorithm to cluster documents (Kulkarni and Callan 2010; Larkey et al. 2000; Liu and Croft 2004). In (Kulkarni and Callan 2010), three document clustering algorithms are evaluated, and k-means clustering is found to be superior to random and URL-based clustering, in terms of both search efficiency and effectiveness. A novel query-driven clustering technique is presented by Puppin et al. (2010). In this technique, a document is represented by the terms appearing in queries that have requested the document in the past. The co-clustering of queries and documents is then used to select the appropriate collections for queries.

2.5.2.3 Multi-Node Query Processing

Query processing in a multi-node search cluster depends on the way the index is partitioned. In case of document-based partitioning (Cahoon et al. 2000; Hawking 1997), the broker issues the query to all search nodes in the cluster. Results are concurrently computed and returned to the broker. Assuming that the number of results requested by the user is k, it suffices to receive only the top k results from each node. As global collection statistics are made available to all search nodes, the relevance scores assigned to the documents are compatible. Hence, merging of the results at the broker is a trivial operation. In (Badue et al. 2007), it is shown that even though document-based partitioning leads to well-balanced partitions, processing times of a query on different nodes may be imbalanced due to the effect of disk caching.

In case of term-based partitioning (Lucchese et al. 2007; Moffat et al. 2007), the query is issued to only the search nodes that contain the posting lists associated with query terms. The contacted nodes compute result sets, where document scores are partial, by using their posting lists that are related to the query. These result sets are then transferred to the broker, which merges them into a global result set. In this case, entire result sets have to be transferred to the broker. A novel pipelined query processing technique is proposed by Moffat et al. (2007). In this technique, a query is sequentially processed over the nodes with intermediate results being pipelined between them. Unfortunately, the performance remained below that of document-based partitioning.

There are a high number of works that analyze the performance of distributed query processing systems (Cacheda et al. 2007; Chowdhury and Pass 2003) as well as works that compare query processing techniques on document-based- and term-based-partitioned indexes via simulations (Ribeiro-Neto and Barbosa 1998; Tomasic and Garcia-Molina 1993) and experimentation on real systems (Badue et al. 2001; MacFarlane et al. 2000). Although these studies are not very conclusive, in practice, document-based partitioning is superior to term-based partitioning as it achieves better load balancing and lower query processing times, despite the fact that term-based partitioning provides higher query throughput. Indeed, search engines are known to employ a document-based partitioning strategy as it also provides better fault tolerance in case of node failures (Barroso et al. 2003).

If documents are partitioned over the search nodes via topical document clustering, collection selection techniques are used to decide on the nodes where the query will be processed. In collection selection, the broker node maintains summaries of collections in each search node and issues a query to search nodes selectively, according to the relevance of collections to the query. The objective is to reduce the workload of search nodes by querying as few nodes (collections) as possible, without significantly degrading the search quality. There is a vast body of research on collection selection (Callan et al. 1995b; D'Souza et al. 2004; Gravano and Garcia-Molina 1995; de Kretser et al. 1998; Puppin et al. 2010; Si et al. 2002a; Tomasic et al. 1997; Xu and Callan 1998; Xu and Croft 1999; Yuwono and Lee 1997). A popular collection selection algorithm, based on inference networks, is presented by Callan et al. (1995b). This work is later adapted to handle partial replicas of the index (Lu and McKinley 1999) and compared with result caching (Lu and McKinley 2000). In a recent work (Puppin et al. 2010), load balancing techniques are proposed for collection selection on a search cluster.

2.5.3 Multi-Cluster Site

A financially more costly strategy is to build multiple clusters within a search site (Brin and Page 1998) to run many instances of the three components (Fig. 2.6). In fact, the issues discussed under this architecture, such as focused crawling, tiering, and index pruning, could have been discussed under the heading of the previous two architectures. However, we prefer to discuss these issues here as this better reflects what is done in practice. From the performance point of view, for the crawling and indexing components, there is no significant difference between constructing C clusters each with K computers or a single cluster with $C \times K$ computers because both crawling and indexing nodes work in an embarrassingly parallel fashion. However, for practical purposes, different crawling clusters are constructed. Each crawling cluster is specialized in fetching a certain type of content (e.g., news pages). For

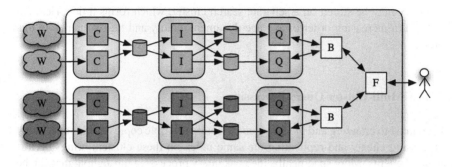

Fig. 2.6 A search architecture with a single site containing multiple clusters, specialized on different crawling, indexing, and query processing tasks

every crawled collection, an indexing cluster builds a corresponding index. These indexes are served by separate search clusters, each with its own broker. Queries are issued to a federator, which blends the results retrieved from different brokers and returns the final results to users.

2.5.3.1 Multi-Cluster Crawling

In practice, a search site contains multiple crawling clusters of varying sizes. Typically, there is a very large cluster that crawls the entire Web and there are other small-scale clusters that run focused web crawlers to harvest the Web selectively according to a selected theme (e.g., news pages, blogs, images, academic papers). Focused web crawling allows accessing high-quality content faster and is especially important for vertical search engines (Chakrabarti et al. 1999; Diligenti et al. 2000). As mentioned before, if the target is to crawl the entire Web, however, there is no significant difference between building a large crawling cluster or many small-sized clusters in terms of crawling performance.

2.5.3.2 Multi-Cluster Indexing

In addition to creating replicas of the same index on multiple search clusters, index pruning and tiering techniques can be employed to reduce the workload incurred by queries. In index pruning, the objective is to create a small web index containing the postings of documents that are more likely to appear in future search results and process the queries only over this index (Carmel et al. 2001). It is also possible to create a two-level index architecture, where the queries are first processed over the pruned index and optionally on the full index (Ntoulas and Cho 2007).

In principle, tiering is similar to pruning. In case of tiering (Risvik et al. 2003), however, the index is disjointly partitioned into multiple tiers based on the quality of documents, i.e., the full web index is not maintained in a single cluster. Each subindex may be stored on a separate search cluster, which forms a tier. Tiers are ordered in increasing order of average document quality and hit by queries in this order.

2.5.3.3 Multi-Cluster Query Processing

In contrast to crawling and indexing, constructing multiple copies of the same query processing cluster and replicating the same index on these clusters brings performance benefits. More specifically, the peak query processing throughput that can be sustained by the query processor is increased (Barroso et al. 2003). We note that the optimum query processing throughput is achieved with a certain C and K value pair, which depends on the size of the document collection and hardware parameters.

A two-tier index pruning architecture that guarantees correctness of results (relative to the results obtained over the full index) is proposed by Ntoulas and Cho (2007). In this architecture, a pruned index is placed in a separate search cluster in front of the main cluster that contains the full web index.

Queries are first processed over the pruned index in the small cluster. If obtained results are found to be unsatisfactory based on a certain criterion, the query is processed over the full web index in the main search cluster. This approach is shown to result in significant savings in query processing workload. The impact of result caching on the above-mentioned architecture is investigated by Skobeltsyn et al. (2008), showing that pruning is not really effective.

In case of tiering, a query is sequentially processed over the tiers, in increasing quality order of the tiers (Risvik et al. 2003). The challenge in tiering is to identify the optimum number of tiers to be hit in query processing. Naïve approaches may decide on the stopping condition based on the number of retrieved results from tiers (Risvik et al. 2003). For example, if a sufficiently large result set is obtained, further tiers may not be hit. More complicated approaches employ machine learning strategies to predict to which tiers a query should be submitted and then increase the parallelism of the system and decrease the response time (Baeza-Yates et al. 2009b). Similar to static index pruning, the main benefit of tiering is the reduced workload.

2.5.4 Multi-Site Engine

The final and most sophisticated architecture we now discuss distributes all three components over multiple, geographically distant sites (Baeza-Yates et al. 2009a; Cambazoglu et al. 2009) (Fig. 2.7). In this architecture, sites crawl the web pages in their geographical neighborhood. Indexes are built over local document collections and certain documents are replicated on multiple sites. Each user query is routed to an initial local search site, based on geographical proximity. Queries are selectively processed on a subset of search sites via effective query forwarding mechanisms.

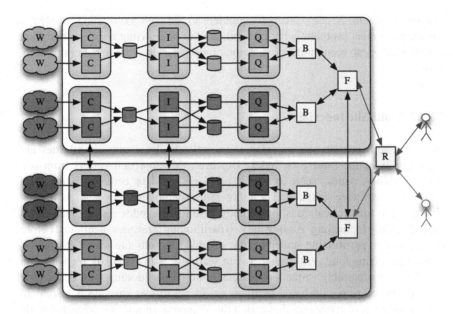

Fig. 2.7 A multi-site search engine with geographically distributed crawling, indexing, and query processing

We note that the techniques discussed herein are taken from the research litera-ture. They do not necessarily exist in current multi-site web search engines. How-ever, commercial search engines are known to span multiple sites, where the full web index and search clusters are replicated.

2.5.4.1 Multi-Site Crawling

In most search engines, crawling is performed by a single site. However, a single-site crawler suffers from the standard scalability issues in centralized systems. More-over, since the network topology cannot be efficiently utilized, achieved download rates are limited. A feasible alternative is to crawl the Web from multiple, geograph-ically distributed sites. Multi-site crawlers can increase the page download rate rel-ative to a centralized system as the network latency between crawlers and web sites is lower. Feasibility of multi-site crawlers and associated performance issues are discussed by Cambazoglu et al. (2008).

In case of multi-site crawlers, web partitioning and repartitioning problems take a different shape as hash-based assignment is no longer meaningful. A successful partitioning function tries to maximize the download rate while keeping the load imbalance across sites under a satisfactory level. In (Exposto et al. 2005) and (Ex-posto et al. 2008), a multi-objective graph partitioning approach is employed to partition the Web, taking into account the geodesic distances between web sites. In (Gao et al. 2006), the problem is formulated as a geographically focused web crawling problem. A complementary problem to the web partitioning problem is the site placement problem, where a fixed number of crawling sites are tried to be placed, taking into account the distribution of web sites, in order to better utilize the network.

2.5.4.2 Multi-Site Indexing

One approach in multi-site indexing is to replicate documents on all sites and build copies of the same web index. However, this approach suffers from several scalability issues, such as space problems in data centers, maintenance overheads, hardware costs, and lengthy index deployment cycles. A feasible alternative to full replication is to disjointly partition the index across data centers, instead of fully replicating. Among the two partitioning strategies mentioned before, the term-based partitioning strategy is not suitable for multi-site search engines because transferring long result sets between search sites is too costly for wide area networks. Two possible variants of document-based partitioning may be feasible: language-based or region-based partitioning. In the former case, each search site is assigned a set of languages that match the languages of queries submitted to the search site. Documents are partitioned and indexed across the search sites according to their languages. In the latter case, each site is given a geographical region, preferably close to its location. All documents obtained from a region are indexed by the site corresponding to the region. So far, all works investigated the region-based partitioning strategy (Baeza-Yates et al. 2009a; Cambazoglu et al. 2009, 2010b).

The partitioning strategies mentioned above can be coupled with partial replication of documents across the search sites. A naïve replication approach is to sort documents according to their popularity, which can be estimated using their past access frequencies, and replicate a small fraction of most popular documents on all sites (Baeza-Yates et al. 2009a). A similar approach is taken by Cambazoglu et al. (2010b), but also taking into account the storage costs of documents. In (Kayaaslan et al. 2010), more advanced partial document replication techniques are proposed for geographically distributed web search engines.

2.5.4.3 Multi-Site Query Processing

One motivation behind building multiple data centers and processing queries over replicated indexes is to provide fault tolerance. Moreover, this approach brings gains in query response times as network latencies between users and search sites become shorter. In case the web index is partitioned across the sites, reduction in workload and some other scalability benefits can also be achieved (Cambazoglu et al. 2009).

In multi-site query processing on partitioned indexes, assuming the user space is partitioned among the sites (e.g., according to the geographical proximity of sites to users), each search site acts as a local site for queries originating from a specific region. Queries are first processed in the local site to generate a set of local results.

Due to the partitioned nature of the web index, achieving good search quality requires evaluating queries on non-local sites as well. Therefore, some queries are selectively forwarded to non-local sites for further evaluation. Contacted non-local sites return the results they computed over their local indexes to the initial local site, which merges all retrieved results and return them to the user.

The main problem in multi-site query processing is to accurately identify non-local search sites that can contribute good results into the final result set. As a solution, in (Baeza-Yates et al. 2009a), a threshold-based query forwarding strategy is proposed. In an offline phase, this strategy computes the maximum possible score that each term in the vocabulary can receive from a search site. In the online phase, these score thresholds are used to set upper-bounds on potential query scores that can be produced by non-local sites. Queries are forwarded to only the sites with a threshold larger than the locally computed top kth score. One of the main results of this work is that a distributed search engine can achieve the same quality of a centralized search engine at a similar cost. In (Cambazoglu et al. 2010b), a linear-programming-based thresholding solution is proposed to further improve this algorithm, as well as several other optimizations. The impact of index updates on freshness of computed thresholds is studied in (Sarigiannis et al. 2009).

In this architecture, a side issue is the placement of search sites. In practice, locations of search sites are selected based on various characteristics of the host country, such as tax rates, climate, and even political issues. It is possible to enhance these decisions by taking into account distribution of web sites and users. This problem can be seen as an instance of the facility location problem. In the research literature, replica placement algorithms are proposed for distributed web servers and CDNs (Radoslavov et al. 2002).

We note that, herein, we assume that the assignment of users to search sites is static. That is, queries are simply routed to their local data centers by means of a router. If the assignment of users is dynamic (e.g., depends on the workloads of search sites at the query time), the router may act like a load balancer or more generally, like a scheduler.

2.6 Open Problems

We provide a number of open problems that are related to the scalability issues in search engines. We should note that the list we provide is not exhaustive. Moreover, this list might be biased toward our current research interests.

2.6.1 Crawling

An open problem is the so-called push-based crawling. In this technique, web pages are discovered and pushed to the crawler by external agents, instead of being discovered by the crawler itself through the link structure of pages (see for example Castillo 2003). The external agents can be ISPs, toolbars installed on users' browsers, mail servers, and other software or hardware agents where URLs may be collected. Push-based crawling enables discovery of content, which is not easy to discover by a regular crawler (e.g., hidden web sites Raghavan and Garcia-Molina 2001), and rare or newly created content.

Another problem that requires further research attention is effective partitioning of the Web to improve the scalability of multi-site web crawlers (Cambazoglu et al. 2008). The main challenge in this problem is to come up with techniques to accurately identify locations of web sites and map them to the closest crawling sites (Exposto et al. 2005; Gao et al. 2006, 2008). Although the primary objectives in a successful partitioning are minimization of the crawling time and load balancing across the sites, the partitioning should also take into account the potential overheads in distributed indexing.

2.6.2 Indexing

A challenge for the search engines is to present in their result pages the content created in real-time. With wide-spread use of blogging sites and social networking sites (e.g., Twitter and Facebook), indexing such content becomes important. An open research problem is to develop scalable techniques for processing and indexing vast amounts of real-time streaming text data (e.g., tweets).

Static pruning architectures have already taken some research attention, but more research is needed on tiering. It is still unclear how the number of tiers and sizes of individual tiers can be selected in an optimum manner. Furthermore, better measures are needed to decide on the placement of documents in the tiers.

Some works have considered region-based index partitioning for query processing on multi-site search engine architectures. However, language-based partitioning has not taken much attention so far. Hence, a pros and cons analysis of these two partitioning techniques may be valuable. Another possibility here is hybrid partitioning, which mixes language and region-based partitioning. Hybrid partitioning can also mix document and term based partitioning.

A final open problem that has not taken any research attention so far is multi-site distributed indexing. Although there are works on parallel index creation, it is not clear how these works can be extended to multi-site architectures, which are connected by wide-area networks. The performance overheads of distributed indexing in such architectures need further study.

2.6.3 Query Processing

A recently introduced problem is the freshness issue in result caches of web search engines (Blanco et al. 2010; Cambazoglu et al. 2010c). The problem here is to identify stale cache entries and refresh them before they are requested by queries. Refreshing stale entries is not a trivial problem as this should be done without incurring too much computational overhead to other parts of the search engine (e.g., the back-end search system).

Most research so far has focused on efficiency of ranking over inverted indexes. In addition to this type of ranking, however, commercial search engines employ complex ranking mechanisms, based on machine learning, over a small set of filtered documents (Cambazoglu et al. 2010a). Efficiency of these mechanisms is important to satisfy query processing time constraints. Moreover, given more time for ranking, search result qualities can be improved (Cambazoglu et al. 2009). The research problems here is to find effective early termination algorithms (Cambazoglu et al. 2010a) and learning algorithms that take into account the efficiency of the generated models (Wang et al. 2010).

In web search engines, queries are processed with certain fixed time budgets. Queries that cannot be processed within their budget lead to degraded result quality. An interesting problem is to identify these time budgets on a per-query basis, rather using fixed thresholds. The budgets can be shrunk based on the geographical proximity of users and extended based on predicted query difficulties or obtained partial result qualities.

For multi-site search engines, better replication strategies can be developed. Current strategies assume that documents are statically assigned and periodically partitioned. One possible improvement could be to replicate documents as the need arises and queries are processed.

Another important issue is to minimize the energy spendings of the search engine. Typically, electricity prices show variation across countries and also during the day within a country. Query processing and forwarding algorithms that are aware of this variation need to be developed to reduce the electricity bill of the search engine.

2.7 Conclusions

We have presented the current scalability challenges in large-scale web search engines. We also discussed a number of open research problems in the field. We envision that the scalability of web search engines will continue to be a research challenge for some time.

We feel that, unlike the past research, the current scalability research is mainly driven by the needs of commercial search engine companies. We must admit that the lack of large hardware infrastructures and datasets make conducting scalability research quite difficult, especially for the researchers in the academia. However, we still find it appropriate to make the following recommendations to those who work in the field:

- The trends in the Web, user bases, and hardware parameters should be closely followed to identify the real bottlenecks in scalability.
- The newly emerging techniques whose primary target is to improve the search quality should be followed and their implications on efficiency should be well understood.

- In solving scalability problems, rather than reinventing the wheel, solutions should be adapted from previously solved problems in related, more mature research fields, such as databases, computer networks, and distributed computing.
- Evaluating new solutions may imply simulating large systems and using synthetic data, as the cost of using real distributed systems is quite large.

Chapter 3
Spam, Opinions, and Other Relationships: Towards a Comprehensive View of the Web Knowledge Discovery

Bettina Berendt

Abstract "Web mining" or "Web Knowledge Discovery" is the analysis of web resources with data-mining techniques such as classification, clustering, association-
rule or graph-structure methods. Its applications pervade much of the software web
users interact with on a daily basis: search engines' indexing and ranking choices,
recommender systems' recommendations, targeted advertising, and many others.
An understanding of this fast-moving field is therefore a key component of digital
information literacy for everyone and a useful and fascinating extension of knowledge and skills for Information Retrieval researchers and practitioners. This chapter
proposes an integrating model of learning cycles involving data, information and
knowledge, explains how this model subsumes Information Retrieval and Knowledge Discovery and relates them to one another. We illustrate the usefulness of this
model in an introduction to web content/text mining, using the model to structure the
activities in this form of Knowledge Discovery. We focus on spam detection, opinion mining and relation mining. The chapter aims at complementing other books
and articles that focus on the computational aspects of web mining, by emphasizing
the often-neglected context in which these computational analyses take place: the
full cycle of Knowledge Discovery, which ranges from application understanding
via data understanding, data preparation, modeling and evaluation to deployment.

3.1 Introduction

Most web users are in daily contact with web mining: They profit from search
engines' analyses of web pages' texts and multimedia materials for indexing and
ranking these resources with respect to their relevance for users. They also see
the results of these search engines taking link structure into account to determine
which sites are more "authoritative" than others as evidenced by what incoming
links they receive. Users receive (and often follow) buying and viewing recommendations for books, music, films, and many other items based on an analysis of their

B. Berendt (✉)
Department of Computer Science, K.U. Leuven, Celestijnenlaan 200A, 3001 Heverlee, Belgium
e-mail: bettina.berendt@cs.kuleuven.be
url: http://people.cs.kuleuven.be/~bettina.berendt/

M. Melucci, R. Baeza-Yates (eds.), *Advanced Topics in Information Retrieval*,
The Information Retrieval Series 33,
DOI 10.1007/978-3-642-20946-8_3, © Springer-Verlag Berlin Heidelberg 2011

own and other people's web-viewing, rating, tagging and buying behaviors. They receive "targeted advertising" based on their own and their friends' behaviors, search queries, or mail contents.

Thus, the scope of web mining—the analysis of web resources with data-mining techniques such as classification, clustering, association-rule or graph-structure methods—has by now become vast. Web mining is a fascinating approach to making sense of the Web and how people use and build it, and the results of web mining in turn shape the Web and its usage. Therefore, a basic understanding of this field is a key component of digital information literacy for everyone, and a deeper understanding is a recommendable extension to the knowledge and skills for Information Retrieval researchers and practitioners. The purpose of this chapter is to provide an introduction to the field, especially but not exclusively for readers with (some) background in Information Retrieval.

Very good textbooks now exist on various aspects of web mining. For excellent general overviews of web mining, see (Liu 2007; Baldi et al. 2003). Highly recommendable overviews of its three key subfields, content, structure and usage mining, are, respectively (Feldman and Sanger 2007; Chakrabarti 2003; Mobasher 2007).

The present chapter aims to complement these texts, which focus on the computational aspects of web mining, by emphasizing the oft-neglected context in which these computational analyses take place: the full cycle of Knowledge Discovery. Thus, we attempt to pay as much attention to the phases of application and data understanding, evaluation and deployment, as to the more technical ones of data preparation and modeling. The purpose of this chapter is to show general lines of current developments in web mining in a restricted space; we therefore strove for a choice of literature that exemplifies these well, rather than for a comprehensive survey. (Yet, we have aimed at pointing to classical papers, overviews, and other good starting points for further reading.) For reasons of space, we restrict attention to web mining that operates on texts found on the Web ("web content/text mining").

Within web content/text mining, we focus again on three application areas: spam detection, opinion mining and the extraction of relational information. These were chosen because they (a) represent important current foci of research and real-world tools and (b) illustrate the use of and design choices in key mining techniques. In addition, (c) spam detection is one of the areas of today's web mining where the three subareas meet and complement each other in innovative ways: The content of a site is obviously an important cue as to whether this site is spam or not. In addition, link structures can reveal auxiliary structures designed specifically to boost a spam site's ranking in search engines, and therefore the effective visibility of this site to the target groups. Last but not least, whether and how people query and use sites gives rich information about sites' value; for example, the large majority of people immediately recognize something as spam when they see it and do not explore such sites further.[1]

---

[1]Two other application areas of web mining that have received a lot of attention recently are the mining of news and the mining of social media such as blogs; for overviews of their specifics,

The chapter is structured as follows: Section 3.2 explains why we use "Knowledge Discovery" (KD) and "data mining" synonymously (but prefer the former term). It situates the field in relation to Information Retrieval and proposes an integrating model of learning cycles involving data, information and knowledge. It also gives an overview of KD phases, of modeling tasks and structures, and of the three areas of web mining: content, structure and usage mining. Section 3.3 illustrates the phases of web content mining with reference to the three example application areas. Section 3.4 focuses on a currently heavily discussed challenge to web mining (and in fact web activities as a whole): the dangers to privacy inherent in the large-scale collection, dissemination and analysis of data relating to people. Section 3.5 closes with an outlook on four specific challenges for web mining as viewed from the big-picture perspective of this chapter: context, the pervasiveness of learning cycles and prior knowledge, the question of definitional power and viewpoints, and the importance of accessible tools.

3.2 Basics and Terminology

3.2.1 From Information Retrieval to Knowledge Discovery

The classical notion of Information Retrieval (IR) assumes a person with an—often underspecified—information need, a query this person (or a helper) formulates to express this information need, and a document store towards which an IR system issues this query. The IR system is good to the extent that it returns a selection of these documents: those that are *relevant* to the information need. We shall refer to documents as *information*.[2] Thus, IR systems take as input information and the process data of the query (which is today generally expressed in free text), perform IR, and return information. This mode of interacting with human users is today extremely popular and powerful, as witnessed by the huge success of search engines.

Knowledge Discovery (KD), also known as data mining, attempts to go a step further. The aim is not to return (existing) documents and therefore information, but new *knowledge*: *valid* and *interesting* statements about the domain being described.[3] This is a semi-automatic process, in which humans interpret the *patterns* that the KD process has generated from its inputs. The inputs are typically data from (e.g., relational) databases, but also semi-structured and unstructured data/information including documents as used in IR, or knowledge as stored in knowledge bases. Patterns

---

see for example the proceedings of the International Conference on Weblogs and Social Media at http://www.icwsm.org and Berendt (2010).

[2]There are various concepts of "data vs. information vs. knowledge". The notions we use are designed to be maximally consistent with the uses of the term in the databases, Information Retrieval, and Knowledge Discovery literatures. For a summary, see Fig. 3.1 for details.

[3]The classical definition is "the nontrivial process of identifying valid, previously unknown, and potentially useful patterns" (Fayyad et al. 1996).

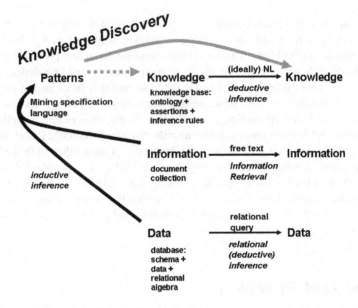

Fig. 3.1 From information retrieval to knowledge discovery

may be global over the whole investigated dataset (e.g. clusterings or classifiers) or local (e.g. association rules). In line with KD's focus on *new* patterns, it relies on *inductive* inference as opposed to data and knowledge bases whose inference is deductive.[4]

IR and KD are compared and related to each other as well as to the more fundamental database retrieval in Fig. 3.1.[5] In the interest of clarity, typical forms and terms were chosen (relational databases, ontologies, …). Querying the stores in the middle and their content (data, information or knowledge) yields the corresponding type of output. Captions above arrows show the process-data type, captions below arrows show the retrieval/inference type. NL stands for "Natural Language". *Knowledge Discovery* is the process depicted by thick arrows at the left and top of the figure. Input are typically data or information plus the mining specification as process data. These process data are generally specified interactively and therefore often ephemeral; emerging standards aim at machine-readable, declarative, interoperable and re-usable specifications.[6] From the output patterns, people produce knowledge; this semi-automatic step is shown in grey. Often, they only produce it for one-off use; more rarely, and therefore shown by a dotted line, do they feed it directly into a knowledge base.

---

[4]The association of induction/abduction with new knowledge goes back to Peirce, cf. the collection of relevant text passages at http://www.helsinki.fi/science/commens/terms/abduction.html.

[5]Thanks to Ricardo Baeza-Yates for the ideas and discussions that led to this figure.

[6]See http://www.ecmlpkdd2007.org/CD/tutorials/KDUbiq/kdubiq_print.pdf, retrieved on 2010-04-07.

Today, many confluences exist between IR and KD. For example, IR systems like web search engines use KD methods such as PageRank in order to find knowledge about which web pages or sites are more "authoritative" than others (see Chakrabarti 2003 for an overview and details). The intuition is that the more authoritative pages hyperlink to a page, the more authority this page gets. This recursive notion can be assessed by a graph algorithm that returns a score for each page (the authority score, a new piece of knowledge). This score can then be used as an input to the ranking function on the pages' system-computed relevance, and this ranking function determines which pages (information) the search engine returns and in which order. Conversely, the fundamental vector-space model of text known from IR is often used to derive the word features that represent a text and from which, for example, a spam classifier is learned whose output is the new knowledge that a given document is probably spam (or not). Some analysis techniques support a range of analyses from IR to KD. For example, clustering documents may be considered mainly an interface-presentation question for IR results (cf. www.clusty.com), it may be used for extracting keyword patterns that characterize clusters (Fortuna et al. 2005), or even for semi-automatically learning a new descriptive model ("ontology") of the domain described in the documents (Fortuna et al. 2006; Berendt et al. 2010). The increasing closeness of the two areas can, for example, be seen in the contents of publications at major IR and KD conferences such as SIGIR, ECIR, SIGKDD or PKDD.

Due to these differences and commonalities, KD is an inspiring and relevant topic for everyone interested in IR, and *web mining*, i.e., KD applied to web resources, is relevant for those interested in web IR.

3.2.2 Knowledge Discovery Phases

KD rests on the application of automated methods from areas such as statistics, machine learning, graph/network theory, and visualization. For example, the applications discussed at the end of the previous section utilize clustering, classifier learning, the solving of an eigenvalue problem, and multidimensional scaling. However, KD is not a blackbox into which data, texts, etc. can be fed such that knowledge automatically emerges. Rather, it is a process which requires extensive human intellectual effort, especially in the first phases that can be described as "application, context and question understanding" and "input understanding", and in the last phases that can be described as "evaluating the results" and "acting on them, for example by deploying changes in business processes, software, and/or actions towards users/customers".

In between are phases whose problems are more well-defined and whose solution approaches therefore more formalized, such that these phases are wholly or mostly automatic: "data preparation" and "modeling". It is also by now established that the evaluation of patterns that leads to the selection of the *interesting* patterns can rely on subjective, but also on many objective criteria, which makes the "evaluation"

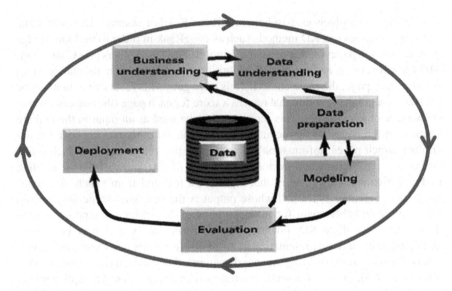

Fig. 3.2 The CRISP-DM process model

phase partially automatic (McGarry 2005). These objective interestingness criteria include extensions of the criterion of statistical significance of a result.

This common structure of the typical KD process has given rise to a process model that is widely used in the KD community: CRISP-DM (Cross-Industry Standard Process for Data Mining) (Shearer 2000), whose standard graphical summary is shown in Fig. 3.2. The phase names reflect the business focus of the authors; they may be adapted/generalized to reflect other application contexts, such as done in the previous paragraph. The diagram shows the central role of the analysed material (due to the roots of KD in the database community and the original term "knowledge discovery in databases/KDD", all input is considered as "data"). It also shows the iterative nature of the task; typically, the feedback loops ensure that several iterations of the whole process are needed to fully profit from one's data and the implicit knowledge in it.

The inner loop of the diagram corresponds to the depiction of KD in Fig. 3.1: the arrows pointing to the left there correspond to the phases from business understanding through modeling; the arrows pointing to the right correspond to the phases evaluation and increased business understanding. The pragmatic phase of deployment is abstracted away. Conversely, in Fig. 3.2, the discovered "knowledge" remains implicit in actions taken (deployment) and understanding gained.[7]

The reason is probably the business rather than knowledge-base focus of CRISP-DM. The gained and not necessarily formalized understanding may also be thought of as "knowledge that resides only in a person's head"; we will return to this in Sect. 3.2.4. This comprehensive view of KD is important because results and their

---

[7]Diagram adapted from http://www.crisp-dm.org/Process/index.htm.

interpretation will always depend on the context created by decisions made in all of these phases. For example, concentrating too much on methodological details of the modeling phase may lead to oversights regarding the consequences of data preparation choices.

Some people use the term "data mining" to refer only to the modeling phase, and in addition identify it with certain tasks and methods (such as association-rule discovery) used for modeling, but not others (such as classifier learning). We do not follow this terminological usage here and instead regards "data mining" as synonymous with "KD". This ensures that activities such as "web mining" or "news mining" or "multimedia mining" are understood as intended: encompassing also specific activities of data understanding, data preparation, etc. A standard book on data preparation is (Pyle 1999); specifics of data preparation for web materials will be described below. Overviews of issues in evaluating patterns by interestingness can be found in (McGarry 2005). Business understanding and deployment issues tend to be much more strongly covered in business science, e.g. (Berry and Linoff 2002, 2004), and (generally non-published) company practices—after all, KD is a core part of the business model of companies building search engines or offering personalization.

3.2.3 Modeling Tasks and Model/Pattern Structures

There are many classifications of the tasks and the methods of the modeling phase. We follow the classification proposed by Hand et al. (2001, pp. 9–15), with minor modifications.

The first distinction is that between the *kinds of representations* sought during modeling. These representations may be *global models* or *local patterns*. A *model structure* is a global summary of a data set; it makes statements about any point in the full measurement space. In contrast, *pattern structures* make statements only about restricted region of the space spanned by the variables. This structure consists of constraints on the values of the variables. Thus, in contrast to global models, a local pattern describes a structure relating to a relatively small part of the data or the space in which data could occur. Both global models and local patterns need to be fitted with the help of parameters.

The following *data-mining tasks* and associated *model or pattern structures* can be distinguished:

- exploratory data analysis with interactive, often visual methods;[8]
- descriptive modeling (density estimation, cluster analysis and segmentation, dependency modeling);

---

[8]While the exploration of data is often considered but one and the first step of data-mining modeling, it is also common to regard the whole of data mining (modeling) as exploratory data analysis. The reason is that in contrast to confirmatory methods, one usually does not test a previously specified hypothesis, does not collect data only for this purpose, and performs an open-ended number of statistical tests.

- predictive modeling (classification and regression): the aim is to build a model with which the value of one variable can be predicted from the known values of other variables. In classification, the predicted variable is categorical; in regression, it is quantitative;
- discovering (local) patterns and rules: typical examples are frequent patterns such as sets, sequences or subgraphs, and rules derived from them (e.g., association rules).

Finally, the data mining algorithms have *components*:

- model or pattern structure;
- score function(s) for judging the quality of a fitted model;
- optimization and search methods, to optimize the score function and search over different model and pattern structures;
- a data management strategy.

3.2.4 Learning Cycles and Knowledge Discovery

The input materials for activities such as IR or KD have no independent existence. Data, information and knowledge are typically created by people. They create this from the 'knowledge in their heads', which is the meaning of the term "knowledge" outside of Computer Science (e.g. in Psychology). To differentiate this from the CS term that denotes externalized knowledge, we refer to it as Knowledge$_P$. Knowledge$_P$ is needed to create (most) data, information or knowledge; it is needed when people embark on querying activities, and it is created or (re)shaped from the results of these information-related behaviors. These activities form a cycle that has been described by many theories of learning from Psychology, the Social Sciences, and— within computer science—knowledge management theory (Nonaka and Takeuchi 1995).

In Fig. 3.3a, this cycle is embedded into our basic model from Fig. 3.1. Note that many knowledge production and consumption activities are social, thus Figs. 3.3a and 3.3b make no commitment to an agent or bearer of Knowledge$_P$. Social aspects of knowledge creation are discussed in depth in knowledge management theory and other fields; they have entered web mining through the increasing relevance of social media as a source of data and an application type.

New human knowledge shows itself not only in the production of new manifestations of knowledge (such as documents) or new ways of dealing with it (such as queries), but also in new ways of creating it. As but one example of this, the left-pointing arrow at the bottom of Fig. 3.3a shows how new knowledge may change knowledge-discovery processes. This arrow completes the correspondence between our basic model and CRISP-DM: it closes the feedback loop of KD. Graphically, the outer cycles of Figs. 3.2 and 3.3a correspond to each other. Learning cycles are also at the heart of many machine learning methods within the CRISP-DM modeling phase (not shown in the figure). For example, supervised neural network training by back-propagation (Hand et al. 2001) tries one mapping from inputs to outputs, obtains corrections from the teacher, tries the next mapping, and so on.

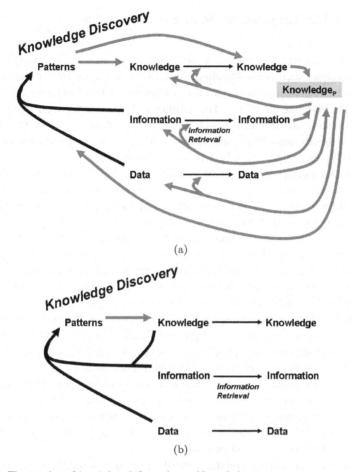

Fig. 3.3 The creation of (new) data, information and knowledge

Another learning cycle is behind the vision of *Semantic (Web) Mining* (Stumme et al. 2006), shown in Fig. 3.3b: The basic (human) knowledge creation and consumption cycle (a), Semantic Web Mining (b). All captions from Fig. 3.1 still apply, but have been omitted for clarity. Here, the left side of Fig. 3.1 is closed into a loop (rather than the right side that describes human learning). Semantic Web Mining "aims at combining the two areas Semantic Web and Web Mining. This vision follows our observation that trends converge in both areas: Increasing numbers of researchers work on improving the results of Web Mining by exploiting (the new) semantic structures in the Web, and make use of Web Mining techniques for building the Semantic Web. Last but not least, these techniques can be used for mining the Semantic Web itself" (Stumme et al. 2006, p. 124). Some current forms of Semantic Web Mining are described below, see in particular Sect. 3.3.3 on relation mining.

3.2.5 Web Mining: Content, Structure and Usage

As mentioned above, web mining is the analysis of web resources with data-mining techniques such as classification, clustering, association-rule or graph-structure methods. Technically, this means that all kinds of data/information/knowledge related to the Web may be mined. The traditional distinction between web content mining, web structure mining and web usage mining (Zaïane 1998) is based on a typology of these inputs. The distinction is still applicable today, even if the data investigated by these three areas have become more diverse.

Web content mining operates on all 'content' of the Web, i.e., that which any web user (or authorized user in the case of restricted-access resources) can access. The resources are web pages, the analysed content is the text, the multimedia elements, the metadata (such as the URL) and/or the layout of these resources. These pages can be of very different genres, which has given rise to new subfields such as blog mining or news mining. Web content mining has seen a large surge in activity in recent years, partially because rich data sources are available for everyone—often, corpora are generated by downloading a dump (e.g. of Wikipedia), crawling, or querying an archive such as news.google.com or www.digg.com.

Web structure mining operates on 'structures' found on the Web. The classic structures were those between pages (hyperlinks) and within pages (DOM tree). Increasingly, structures between people are now also being analysed. One research direction derives networks between people from transformations on (usually bipartite) graphs; an example is co-authorship analysis on the co-author links derived from author-paper links in literature databases. Another research direction utilizes the relational self-profiling of the users of social-network sites, expressed for example in "friend links". To the extent that these structures are generally visible, data are as easy to procure as for content mining.

Web usage mining operates on data describing 'usage' of the Web. The research focus changed with the design of typical sites: from click data on generally static pages, through the selection or specification of a choice from a menu on form-generated pages and sites for ranking movies etc., to free-form textual queries in an era dominated by Web-wide and internal search engines. In addition, the action type of a click is no longer only that of moving through a space of given options ("navigation"), but is indicative of a range of actions concerning the creation of content (e.g. the upload of a new or edited page in Wikipedia) and the use of content (querying it, downloading it, printing it, tagging it, . . .). Data describing usage are typically recorded in web server logs, application-server logs, or program-specific logs (an example of the latter is the "history" functionality of Wikipedia). This also means that most usage data are not open; in fact, many businesses regard this as sensitive business knowledge about reactions to their Web offers. In addition, research and practice have shown that usage data such as queries or ratings cannot effectively be anonymized and therefore remain *personal data* that may threaten privacy. As a consequence, only aggregate data (if any) tend to be made public. Examples of aggregations are http://www.google.com/trends or http://buzz.yahoo.com/ for search queries, visited sites, or search queries and resources associated with them and discussed by users in various forms. (Wikipedia content creation rests on an entirely different 'business model' than search-engine usage; it can therefore afford to be an exception).

Content mining draws on text-analysis models of IR, on (computational) linguistics, and on fields such as image analysis where non-textual content is concerned. Structure and content mining (can) draw on bibliometrics for methods of analyzing the graphs induced by people authoring papers and citing other papers, and to some extent on the textual analysis of those papers. Increasingly, methods for social network analysis from other areas such as sociology or complex-systems theory, are becoming relevant too. Usage mining analyses behavioral data and therefore draws on HCI, business studies, user research in digital libraries, and similar fields. Conversely, mining methods feed back into those disciplines and research areas.

3.3 A Short Overview of Web Content Mining on Text

The typical content to be mined is the textual content of web pages. This includes classical material such as academic or commercial web pages, pages created in social media such as fora, blogs, or social networks, and all other content that is distributed over the Web such as scientific publications in online digital libraries. The generic KD steps are adapted to the characteristics that texts in general have (text mining), to the characteristics that texts on web pages have (web text mining) and optionally to further specific characteristics induced by the material and/or questions (e.g., in blog mining).

3.3.1 Application and Data Understanding

Application understanding requires that one considers the environment(s) in which authors and readers operate, the intentions they harbor when authoring or reading, and how they produce and consume content in response to these. This can best be understood with reference to our three examples.

3.3.1.1 Spam

Spam was originally a phenomenon of email, but soon spread on the Web. Spammers want to convince gullible people to buy something.[9] They operate in an environment that is wary of spammers and that has mechanisms in place to counter

---

[9]Other spammers want to convince gullible people to disclose their passwords (phishing). For reasons of space, we do not investigate this further here.

the spamming methods identified so far. They face readers who in principle want to buy things, but who oppose to being defrauded (= to the intentions of the spammers) and also generally oppose to spamming in general. Thus, the problem to be solved is that of *spam detection*: determine whether something is spam or not. However, one person's spam may be another person's appreciated recommendation, cf. the continuing debate over web advertisements personalised based on someone's mailbox (Gmail), social network (Facebook Beacon), etc.

These characteristics of the application have effects on the data: Spam data on the Web tend to be (a) similar in topics and wording to non-spam commercial content, (b) appealing directly to popular instincts of bargain hunting, (c) sites that in fact are non-popular or even unknown to a general public, but that trick search engines into believing they are, in order to be found by users. Strategies for achieving (c) depend on, and change with, overarching search-engine strategies.

In the early Web, the reliance on textual content led spammers to embed popular search terms (e.g., "free") that were unrelated to the real content invisibly in the HTML body (e.g., with textcolor = backgroundcolor) or in the HTML head (<meta> tags). In the social web with its reliance on linkage-induced authority, a popular spamming strategy uses program-generated "link farms" (large numbers of fake, identical pages all pointing to the spam site) and, often also program-generated, incongruous contributions to fora containing these links. Further strategies are explained with reference to technical details in Sect. 3.3.3. Due to the adversarial setting, an 'arms race' has developed: continuously changing spamming and spam-detection methods.

3.3.1.2 Opinions

Opinions of web users concern, for example, movies or other products, and they are most often voiced in dedicated sites such as movielens.umn.edu or www.ciao.com or in generic social-media sites such as blogging sites, which are then indexed by systems such as www.technorati.com. Opinions are voiced in different ways, including "positive" or "negative" (or 1–5 out of five stars) concerning a product, binary or graded judgments of features/aspects of a product (such as price vs. energy efficiency), several dimensions such as "polarity" and "strength" of the opinion, or even unforeseen groupings of utterances. Opinion-giving users operate in an environment that is generally welcoming: other users are grateful for helpful opinions, for recommendations based on them, and companies view reviews and ratings as a fast and cheap way of doing market research. For various reasons, including a wish to help other users, many authors of reviews write understandably, use standard terminology and straightforward language. On the other hand, voiced opinions may not be representative due to a self-selection of authors and an often stronger tendency to write something when angry or particularly happy. Many authors are not particularly good writers, write in a hurry, or for other reasons use non-standard language. Depending on their literary abilities and preferences as well as on their opinion, authors may use irony and other stylistic means.

These characteristics of the application lead to a broad range of mining tasks, which are described in Sect. 3.3.3.

3.3.1.3 Relations

Relational assertions like "Paris is a city", "cameras are a type of consumer electronics", or "antibiotics kill bacteria" capture 'what the web community thinks about the world' or, with some liberty of generalization, 'what mankind knows'. The idea of *open information extraction from the Web* (as Banko et al. 2007 called it) is to extract all such assertions from the Web, weigh them by plausibility of being true, and from the reliable ones construct a huge and comprehensive knowledge base. The application, its setting and the approach to text data share many characteristics with opinion mining: generally well-intentioned authors and readers, the locus of information generally being at sentence rather than document level, operands of the statements that are not known a priori ("Paris", "camera", "antibiotics", "bacteria" all need to be extracted from the data), and aggregation problems. Due to the much wider semantic and conceivably also syntactic range of utterances, as well as the much more open-ended problems of aggregating inconsistencies, the problem is however more difficult.

3.3.1.4 Web Documents in General

Most web resources are published in the setting of an attention economy (Davenport and Beck 2001) and a specific aesthetics. This means that web documents are not only marked up in HTML, but that they are also designed with a view to retrievability and indexing by current-day search engines, that they present themselves not as stand-alone documents but parts of a bigger system (company pages, information space, community, ...), that they often contain advertising that finances the production of the core content, and that core content, navigation and search elements as well as advertising may be closely intertwined in graphically determined DOM-tree encodings. All these characteristics have implications on data preparation (e.g., the need to remove advertisement noise) and modeling.

3.3.2 Data Preparation

The goal of data preparation is to produce records for the chosen data model. The basic model in text mining is one in which the instances are documents, the features are terms (= words or multiword compounds), and a matrix with numerical weights that characterize each instance in terms of these features. This is the traditional vector-space model also used in IR.

To produce such a database of records, the following steps need to be taken. First, HTML and other markup as well as embedded non-textual content such as pictures needs to be removed, and the content-bearing parts need to be selected with the help of a template. Often, HTML markup gives valuable clues as to where the content-bearing parts are. A simple heuristic for such template recognition is that given a site, the part of the DOM tree that varies across pages is content-bearing, while the parts of the DOM tree that are identical or similar across pages contain navigation bars, banner ads, etc. and can therefore be ignored. Alternatively, templates can be learned from annotated examples ("wrapper induction").

In some applications, HTML markup can be useful input for weighting or otherwise interpreting features. For example, the words of a title (marked by an HTML heading) may be given more weight for describing the topical content than other words, and text rendered invisible by HTML markup may be an indicator of spam. Table markup may be interpreted as listing relations (one row = one tuple), with the attribute names given by the column headings and the attribute values given by the table cells.

After this data cleaning, further steps are applied to obtain processable lexical/syntactical units that can be interpreted as features, and to concentrate on the relevant ones and create features that are more 'semantic' than mere word tokens that vary strongly with surface features of the text. Typical steps include the following; they are not always all performed, and they typically require some others to be completed previously.

Tokenisation consists of separating strings by word boundaries (such as spaces in Western languages). *Stopword removal* deletes words that are frequent but generally not content-bearing, such as articles and conjunctions or terms that are meaningless in the given application (for example, "Java" in a corpus of documents all dealing with this programming language). *Lemmatization* and *stemming* reduce words to a base form, eliminating differences in number, case, tense or even word class (e.g. noun vs. verb). Various forms of (usually shallow) parsing classify words into word classes (*part-of-speech tagging*: nouns, verbs, adjectives, ...) or perform *semantic role labeling* (roles include Agent, Patient or Instrument; they are labelled along with their adjuncts, such as Locative, Temporal or Manner). *Named-entity recognition* unifies occurrences with different names for the same person, place, company, etc. *Word-sense disambiguation* is one method for resolving synonymy and homonymy. This requires a lexical resource such as WordNet (Fellbaum 1998) that models that the term "key" has senses key#1 (metal device shaped in such a way that when it is inserted into the appropriate lock the lock's mechanism can be rotated) and key#4 (any of 24 major or minor diatonic scales that provide the tonal framework for a piece of music), and that the term "tonality", in its first (and only) sense. tonality#1, is synonymous with key#4.

All these steps may be used for further filtering (e.g., only nouns, and of these, only lemmata). Many steps are language-dependent, and the coverage of languages other than English varies widely. Free and/or open-source tools or web APIs exist for most steps. The result is then processed to obtain the feature weights; where a typical weight is TF.IDF: term frequency multiplied by inverse document frequency. In the basic vector-space model, a text is regarded as a bag of words, i.e., without regard to the order in which the terms occur. This lends itself most easily to the standard relational-table model of data.

Popular variations of the basic model include (i) a different unit for instances, for example, a site (instead of a document/web page) may be a spam site, or a sentence (instead of a document) may contain an opinion about a product feature, or a blog (> document) or blogpost (< document) may be the appropriate unit for content classification; (ii) structure on terms, such as sequential order; (iii) transformed features, such as the latent "topics" of word co-occurrence in LSI (Deerwester et al. 1990), LDA (Blei et al. 2003) and similar methods; and (iv) additional features, such as linkage. The basic idea of latent topic models is to use the statistics of word co-occurrences in a corpus to detect latent "topics" that are indicated by the presence of various words without necessarily requiring the presence of each of them. Depending on the goal of the analysis, topic modeling may be used for pre-processing or modeling. Linkage as the basis of additional features also leads to a different data model: instances become nodes in a graph model.

A more extended overview and further reading on preprocessing for text mining can be found in (Feldman and Sanger 2007).

3.3.3 Modeling

In this section, several solutions to the problems introduced in Sect. 3.3.1 are described briefly.

3.3.3.1 Classification

The task of classification consists of deciding, on the basis of a description of an *instance* (e.g., a document), to which *class* (e.g., "documents about nature") it belongs. The description is in terms of *features* (e.g., the words in the English language) and the *value* of each feature for an instance (e.g., the TF.IDF weight of this word in the document). The classifier is therefore a function mapping from the space of features (e.g., the vector space spanned by the words and populated by document vectors) into the set of classes. This function is learned from a training set of instances, often in *supervised* fashion (the class value of all training-set instances is known and input/fed back to the learner). The goodness-of-fit is measured by metrics such as accuracy (percent correct) on a test set. The function is then applied to new instances, under the assumption that they have the same patterns of features and feature-class relationships. The classifier thus *predicts* the most likely class for each unseen instance. It is important that the classifier is able to generalize beyond the instances seen during training and to avoid overfitting to them. The quality of a classifier therefore hinges critically on (a) the right choice of features, (b) the type of function that the classifier can learn to separate between the classes, and (c) the set of assumptions that the learner uses to predict outputs given inputs that it has not encountered. Here, we will show three examples of (b) that have a straightforward geometrical interpretation and mention typical choices of (a) for the problem of spam detection. For a discussion of (c), the "inductive bias", we refer the reader to (Gordon and des Jardins 1995).

Three prominent types of web content mining applications classify by topical content, by opinion (~ emotional content), or by a higher-level classification such

B. Berendt

Fig. 3.4 Classification:
geometric interpretation and
the importance of feature and
learning-algorithm choice

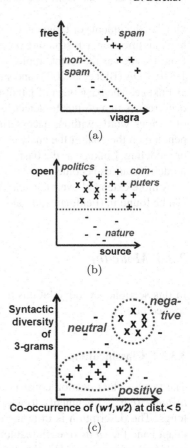

as "spam or not". The third is a two-class problem and can therefore be used to explain the simplest form of classifiers. In Fig. 3.4a, the fictitious feature space of a spam detector consists of the TF.IDF weights of two typical spam words; all spam instances in the training set have high values on one or both of the dimension; while all non-spam instances have lower values. The former are shown by "+" tick marks; the latter, by "−" tick marks. Thus, the function "all instances to the right of the dotted grey line are spam, all instances to the left of it are not" perfectly classifies the training instances. This type of function, a separating hyperplane, can be learned by one of the simplest learning techniques, a perceptron classifier.

Topical content classifiers (Mladenic 1998) map documents to a keyword or class name from a set or hierarchy of classes, which are often disjoint (as in the example shown in the figure), but may also overlap (this is better addressed with probabilistic learning schemes, which we do not discuss here). The fictitious feature space of a content classifier in Fig. 3.4b again consists of the TF.IDF weights of two words with good discriminatory power for the three classes of interest, but here, high values on both dimensions indicate one class, while high values on only one dimension indicate other classes. A decision-tree learner like C4.5 can learn an arbitrary tiling of the feature space into (hyper)rectangular areas each mapped to one class. The figure also shows an example of a document misclassification incurred by restricting the boundaries to be parallel to one of the axes.

Opinion-mining classifiers of whole documents generally map documents to a small number of classes such as "positive" (opinion about the common topic, previously identified for example by topic classification), "negative" (opinion) and "neutral" (all other documents). Figure 3.4c shows a fictitious space of complex features whose values are computed from documents and auxiliary resources such as large corpora for language statistics and grammatical parsers for assigning syntactical categories to words in a sentence. These are inter-term features computed not per word/term, but on larger parts of the texts; examples of other features are given in the application examples below. In the fictitious example, instances of one class occur in the bounds of more complex geometrical shapes such as ellipses; such bounds can be learned by techniques such as Support Vector Machines.

Note that classification illustrates an interesting meeting point of Information Retrieval and Knowledge Discovery: viewed from the latter perspective, classification/classifier learning finds a global model of a space of items and a function mapping these items' features into one of n classes. The application of this classifier enables a program such as a search engine to retrieve/return only those documents that belong to the class considered "relevant" to the current user or query, which is a basic decision of an Information Retrieval process.

3.3.3.2 Spam-Detection Modeling

Spam detection is a two-class classification problem. Classifiers are trained in a supervised-learning setting that uses pages that were manually labelled as spam or non-spam as a training set. These techniques may be enhanced by semi-supervised learning (which requires fewer manually labelled examples), e.g. (Tian et al. 2007), or active learning, e.g. (Katayama et al. 2009). Content-based features have been shown to work well for detecting web spam (and also email spam). Early spam pages simply repeated attractive keywords that are not frequent in general documents ("free", "viagra", etc.) to respond to the weighting by TF.IDF that was applied by early search engines. Classifiers could therefore rely on words-as-features, or later features based on checksums and more sophisticated word-weighting techniques (Drost and Scheffer 2005). Many standard classifier-learning techniques like C4.5, Naïve Bayes or Support Vector Machines have been applied.

However, search engines soon increased the sophistication of their spam filtering, identifying statistical properties of natural human text such as individual or bigram word frequencies, and singling out outliers as possible spam. Spammers increased their linguistic sophistication by techniques such as weaving (copying an existing body of text and inserting various terms to be spammed throughout the text) or phrase stitching (gluing together individual phrases or sentences from a large corpus and inserting the spam terms). The results comply with general language statistics and therefore escape basic detection schemes.

Figure 3.5 shows an example, which combines phrase stitching (to generate content that fooled the search engine, see Fig. 3.5a); corruption of a legitimate URL

(a)   (b)

Fig. 3.5 Web spam example (page excerpts)

(the URL indexed by the search engine is the domain of a food cooperative in North America plus a script request, with the script presumable placed there by hackers); and redirection to another script-generated page that at first sight resembles a legitimate online pharmacy, but upon closer inspection reveals suspicious elements such as machine-translated text (see Fig. 3.5b). The corrupted URL was ranked 10th of several millions of results to the search query highlighted in (a) by a major search engine on 10th April 2010; Figure 3.5 (a) shows parts of the cache contents and (b) shows the result of clicking on the search result link. Thus, presumably, (a) is what the search engine sees and (b) what the user sees.

In response, new features have been proposed and successfully applied to current corpora, including inter-term features such as the distributions of term co-occurrence at various distances (Attenberg and Suel 2008) or linguistic features like the diversity of grammatical categories (parts-of-speech) in n-grams (Piskorski et al. 2008). Text-mining techniques that transform words-as-features into fewer features to capture the "latent semantics" of a corpus of texts have also been applied for spam detection, e.g. (Bíró et al. 2008). Current research also investigates HTML features, e.g. (Urvoy et al. 2006), and link features such as link farms, e.g. (Wu and Davison 2005; Drost and Scheffer 2005).

The fundamental setting of spamming is at the same time a boon and a curse for spam detection techniques: Spam only works, economically, if *huge* volumes of messages (web pages/sites, emails) are being generated; therefore most spam is generated by programs. On the one hand, such programs are easier to reverse-engineer than the unfathomable processes that lead real humans to creative writing. A reverse-engineered spamming technique, in turn, is comparatively easy to transform into an accurate classifier. On the other hand, the "adversarial" setting of spam and the arms race between spammers and spam detectors requires an ever-changing and increasing sophistication of effective techniques.[10] Insight into a range of current

---

[10]"New web spam techniques are introduced every 2–3 days." (Liverani 2008).

approaches to spam detection can be obtained from the proceedings of the AIRWeb ("Adversarial information retrieval on the Web") workshops.[11]

3.3.3.3 Opinion-Mining Modeling

As discussed above with reference to Fig. 3.4, opinion mining may be just another example of learning how to assign whole documents to one of a set of classes. This has many applications and can deliver important application information, cf. the study of 'what makes bloggers happy' (Mihalcea and Liu 2006) that found that the word "shopping" was the best predictor of a blog labelled by the blogger with the information that s/he was in a happy mood.

However, more often, whole documents are not the right unit of analysis for opinion mining. A typical interest in opinions voiced on the Web is that of market research formerly (and still today) done with the help of focus groups: What do (potential) customers think about a given product? Typically, this will be differentiated judgements, for example, people may like the price but not the design or usability of a product. Often, interest then focuses not only on a retrieval of all users' fine-grained opinions on all possible aspects, but also on a summary of these. Opinion mining is therefore a prime application area of analysis at a level below full documents (often sentences) and of summarization techniques. To illustrate these ideas, we will concentrate on examples from "review mining" for opinions. The *extraction* of such information is a move from the global models of classification to local patterns. In the remainder of this section, we will concentrate on local patterns and methods for discovering them.

The extraction of users' opinions on specific aspects from sentences involves two parts: the extraction of aspects that are associated with an opinion (e.g., product features) and the extraction of the opinions on these aspects. Through part-of-speech tagging, a simple form of grammatical analysis of sentences, one can determine the word classes of the words in a sentence such as noun, verb or adjective. Candidates for aspects are generally nouns or noun phrases found by a simple grammatical analysis of the sentences (e.g., "the lens" of a camera) (Hu and Liu 2004) or with the help of typical natural-language phrases indicating that the noun phrase is indeed a part of the object under discussion (e.g., "of camera", "camera has", "camera comes with", etc. for the Camera class) (Popescu and Etzioni 2005). Opinions are often expressed by adjectives ("good"), but also by verbs ("like"/"hate"). Lower bounds for frequency are used to concentrate on more important/more likely candidates. To establish that an opinion relates to an aspect, one can rely on the co-occurrence of aspect candidates with opinion candidates close to each other (in a window of a few words) (Hu and Liu 2004) or on extraction patterns modeled on the syntactic dependencies in natural language. For example, "* product" can help extract "expensive" as an opinion word via texts containing "expensive camera"; "aspect has *" can yield "problems" via "lens has problems"; "I * this product" can yield

---

[11] See, e.g. AIRWeb 2009 at http://airweb.cse.lehigh.edu/2009.

The most helpful favorable review	The most helpful critical review
22 of 22 people found the following review helpful:	2 of 2 people found the following review helpful:
★★★★★ **Great value for the price**	★★☆☆☆ **DO NOT GET IF YOU WANT QUALITY VIDEO!**
I did a lot of research on digital cameras before settling on this one. I couldn't afford much more than $100, and yet I wanted 10mpx, low noise, long battery life, and good color reproduction and sharpness. This samsung kept recurring in all my queries, and after checking it out, I took a chance that low price didn't always mean low quality--and this time I was very... Read the full review >	When i got this camera, it was really easy to set up and use. The pictures are great but there is one MAJOR flaw with it that there is no info on anywhere i looked; When recording video, when you're zooming in and out, the audio (all sound) will be cut. It WILL NOT record any audio durring zooming on a video. I was very disapointed in this because when taping a... Read the full review >

(a) http://www.amazon.com/Samsung-SL420-Digital-Stabilized-Black/product-reviews/
B001PKTRA8

While other large manufacturers are starting to talk about launching mirrorless systems, Samsung has become the third manufacturer to actually to turn talk into tangible product. However, while Samsung is only the third party to enter the fray, enough time has passed for the other mirrorless makers to have moved on to their second-generation of cameras, including the newly-launched Panasonic G2 and G10. Between them these two cameras (which like the NX take many of their styling ideas from DSLR designs) are likely to make life pretty difficult for the Samsung. The G10 doesn't match the NX's spec but is aggressively priced while the G2 offers smarter video compression and touch-screen cleverness, which will be attractive to some. And they have the advantage of being second-generation products, with the enhanced level of refinement that this tends to bring.

(b) http://www.dpreview.com/reviews/samsungnx10/

McNally's dialogue provides clear motivation for most of the actions and sets up DAVID YAZBEK's punchy songs. Yazbek's pop score deserves closer examination. He wisely avoids the inanities of hard rock that has for the most part been rejected by theater-going audiences until now. His melodies are like pop jingles, light on tune. But his lyrics are gems, some with intricate and unexpected rhymes, as in the standout "Big-Ass Rock."

(c) http://www.theatrereviews.com/fullmonty.html

Fig. 3.6 Different reviews containing opinions (excerpts)

"hate" via "I hate this camera'. Extraction can also be helped by background knowledge about the topics (e.g., WordNet (Fellbaum 1998) assertions about properties vs. parts) (Popescu and Etzioni 2005). Further knowledge can be integrated into the process of mining via sentiment-related lexicons that list, for example, the polarities of words.

Neither the non-linguistic heuristics based on frequency and co-occurrence nor the linguistic heuristics based on parsing nor the use of lexical resources are straightforward and error-proof. Reasons include: (i) words mean different things in different contexts, which includes different polarities (e.g., "not bad", "terrific", "a ... to die for" may all be strongly positive); (ii) language choices may depend on the domain; (iii) grammatical constructions may be very complex (cf. the many ways of expressing negation); (iv) often, authors are very creative in utilizing the generativity of language. Figure 3.6 shows examples:[12] Figure 3.6a shows customer reviews of cameras at shopping site, enhanced by author global rating of product (stars) and reader rating of the helpfulness of the review. Figure 3.6b is a part of an expert review of a camera having a total length of 30 pages. Figure 3.6c is a part of a review of a theatre performance. (The choice of domains is inspired by Williams and Anand

---

[12] All retrieved on 2010-04-10.

(2009); the reader is encouraged to consider the likely success of various extraction rules on these texts.)

If polarities are associated with opinions, a summarization over different sentences and/or reviews may be done. Simple counting of positive vs. negative opinions may reveal that a given text is "more positive than negative" or that most of a set of texts (e.g. those that discuss some new camera model A) are positive concerning some aspect (the price) and more so than those about a competing product B, while concerning another aspect (the lens), they are more often negative than those of B.

The extractions that are involved in opinion mining of this type can each be regarded as classification tasks: a word or group of words is to be classified as a product aspect or not, an opinion word or not, etc. However, the identification of candidates follows typical unsupervised and local mining techniques such as association-rule/co-occurrence analysis. This type of mining also shows the advantages of mining with background knowledge (see Sect. 3.2.4 on Semantic Web Mining in general and (Popescu and Etzioni 2005) for a comparison of extraction quality between methods with and without background knowledge) such as grammatical and lexical knowledge about the natural language of the texts. Finally, the examples illustrate the importance of using heuristics because these knowledge sources can never be exhaustive and/or because deep processing would be computationally inefficient.

A comprehensive recent survey of opinion mining can be found in (Pang and Lee 2008).

3.3.3.4 Relation-Mining Modeling

In a linguistically comparatively circumscribed area such as review mining, certain relations play a key role. As the examples above have shown, products *have* aspects/product features, and these *are (assessed to be)* of a certain quality. This puts a focus on two relation types—meronymy and attribution of value—that occur frequently throughout conceptual (semantic) models as well as the syntax of natural language. Mining is successful to the extent that these relation types can be comprehensively and correctly extracted from language found on the Web.

This idea lends itself to straightforward generalization: Much of linguistically expressed human knowledge takes the form of assertions, and among these, binary relations are a very common form. Common forms of relations are the aforementioned meronymy (part-whole relation), hyponymy/hyperonymy (subclass-superclass relation), and various relations expressed by transitive verbs (e.g., "eats" relates living beings to food items). Such relations are also a key building block of knowledge models such as logics (e.g. predicate logic) or ontologies. Thus, forms of mining that successfully extract correct relational assertions from a wide range of (web) sources hold the promise of 'learning all the knowledge that the world has' and converting it to machine-readable and therefore highly generative knowledge structures.

Web sources from which such relational knowledge can be learned vary widely, and current research aims at leveraging as many different forms as possible. Before investigating free text as input, we need to step back and consider more structured sources. One form are relational databases.[13] Many schemas lend themselves to straightforward extraction: For example, assume that the review site referred to in Fig. 3.6b maintains a database with the schema CAMERA (NAME, MANUFAC-TURER, PRICE). From this, one can learn that cameras have-a name, have-a manufacturer, and are-sold-at a price. Moreover, one can learn that a specific camera has name NX10 and manufacturer Samsung. Here, "learning" is done by a direct mapping from schema to knowledge structure ("ontology") and from record contents to "instances" of the concepts in this ontology and their properties.

This approach is limited: It has to be done separately for each database, and many databases are neither open to such knowledge extraction nor interoperable with other sources. Also, it is unclear whether the entity called "Samsung" in database A is the same as that with the same name in database B, and whether these are different from the entity "Samsung Semiconductor Inc."? The *Linked Data* (also known as Linked Open Data on the Web) initiative (for an overview, see (Bizer et al. 2009)) goes one step further: (a) Each data source provides a set of relational statements (RDF triples); as the previous paragraph has suggested, mapping existing databases to this structure is feasible; (b) these statements are interoperable by the use of the "Semantic Web stack"; (c) disambiguation of entities is performed through globally unique identifiers (URIs), jointly used namespaces, and the assertion of `<sameAs>` relations between different identifiers for one entity.[14] In principle, this type of "knowledge learning" is as simple as that from individual databases: the "learning" consists only of the combination of knowledge from different sources and the deductive inferences afforded by this combination. Major open issues are data quality, conflict resolution, and the validity of de-contextualising and re-combining atomic pieces of knowledge (the RDF triples), see Sect. 3.5.

Much relational knowledge is not expressed, or not accessible, in one of these forms, but in their equivalent in text tables. (Lists work analogously; for clarity, in the following all explanations refer to tables.) The semi-structured nature of HTML gives clear cues for information extraction from tables. For example, `<th>` cells typically contain attribute names, `<td>` cells contain attribute values (in the same order), and a caption or title (marked as a heading, in bold font, etc.) immediately preceding or following the table the relation name or description. In real-world examples of HTML, not all tables represent relations, since tables are also used for formatting, and not all relations are represented in tables. Yet, as long as a sufficient

---

[13]These are typical examples of humans having fed their knowledge into machine-readable *data* as described by the left-pointing arrows at the bottom of Fig. 3.3.

[14]RDF triples (just like database content) do not need to be authored by technology-savvy users: Web forms are a convenient way to collect structured data from laypeople. Thus, for example, social networks generate and hold masses of personal data in table/RDF form and accessible over the Web. Examples are the FOAF export of Livejournal (http://www.livejournal.com/bots/) and exporter tools for Facebook (http://www.dcs.shef.ac.uk/~mrowe/foafgenerator.html), Twitter (http://sioc-project.org/node/262) or Flickr (http://apassant.net/home/2007/12/flickrdf).

number of pages follow the same conventions (this is the case for most content management systems pages), wrapper induction can learn a mapping from structuring (XML) or formatting (HTML/CSS) elements to relational structure (Kushmerick et al. 1997).

Tables tend to be produced when the author wants to express knowledge about a larger number of instances of one relation (e.g., the name, director, release date, etc. of a collection of films), but rarely when only one or a small number of instances are described. Particularly in the latter case, free text is the more common medium of expression.[15] Again, natural language shows many regularities, and text mining approaches for leveraging these can be grouped by the type of regularity.

The first is purely statistical and based on co-occurrence information. Thus, the observation that most sentences (or passages or documents) that mention "Samsung NX10" also contain "camera", while only a fraction of text units that mention "camera" also contain "Samsung NX10", and that the same pattern holds for "Canon EOS", can be used to infer that both Samsung NX10 and Canon EOS are a subclass or instance of camera.[16] Such *association rules* however need not express taxonomical information; they may also express other types of conceptual associations (such as "people who liked this also liked that").

A second type of regularity therefore leverages typical ways of expressing relations in a given natural language. Examples have been given in the section on opinion mining; probably the best-known of these lexico-syntactic patterns (or templates) are the "Hearst patterns": two noun-phrases A and B linked by "such A as B" or "B and other A" often signal that B is a kind of A (Hearst 1992). Patterns such as "A such as B, C and D" identify several relation instances at once.

Such patterns are *lexico*-syntactic, i.e., they rely on the lexicon of a given language and its meaning (i.e., special relations like hyponymy/hyperonymy). A third type of regularity rests only on the grammar of a given natural language and can therefore capture different types of relations. Thus, the above-mentioned parts-of-speech tagging label constituents of a sentence with (e.g.) noun1, verb and noun2, and a simple grammatical parser can identify that the sentence is in the active voice. This can be interpreted as asserting the relational information verb(noun1, noun2). An example is "[the] camera takes pictures".

Templates can be hand-crafted inputs to the mining process, or they can be learned from corpora in supervised fashion (if sentences are labelled) or with less than full supervision (see below). Statistical patterns and natural-language templates (with hand-crafted extraction patterns) are used in *ontology learning from text* (Maedche and Staab 2001; Buitelaar et al. 2005).

---

[15]These are typical examples of humans having fed their knowledge into machine-readable *information* as described by the left-pointing arrows in the middle of Fig. 3.3.

[16]The decision whether to treat something as a concept (standing in a subclass relation to another concept) or as an instance (standing in an instance-of relation) is not always straightforward, handled differently by different extraction methods, and even treated differently by different logics and ontology formalisms. For reasons of space, we will therefore not investigate this differentiation.

The transition from *text* to *text on the Web* implies a number of new challenges and new opportunities: First, corpora need to be created; for this, many
current approaches utilize general-purpose search engines queried with seed patterns. Second, the magnitude of the Web means that there will be redundant and
also conflicting information. The usual response to this is to rely on the massive redundancy of the Web and assume that frequently asserted statements are
correct and infrequent statements contradicting them can be ignored. The huge
size of the Web also means that extraction techniques can successfully operate
in a *self-supervised* fashion. For example, candidates for A, B, C and D standing in a hyponomy relation as stated above may be found by a search-engine
query with a seed Hearst pattern ("A such as B, C and D"). To (a) validate
these candidates as "true" examples and (b) obtain more extraction patterns, further steps of the process can investigate frequency statistics of the candidates and
use them in a new query (e.g. "+A +B +C +D": enforcing the presence of all
four in the results). Such self-supervised learning is the core of "open information extraction from the Web" as performed by, for example (Etzioni et al. 2004;
Banko et al. 2007). Two examples of live systems that learn arbitrary relations from
free texts (both currently displaying the results of pre-indexed fixed corpora) are
shown in Fig. 3.7.[17] In Fig. 3.7a, Textrunner (operating on a web corpus) is shown
with a query specifying the first argument and the relation, and results showing
different instantiations of the second argument and different forms of the relation.
Figure 3.7b shows Yahoo! Quest (operating on a corpus of questions and answers
by users), a query and resulting clustered entities. Clustered entities are associated as follows with the query: (i) kinds of the query class, (ii) verbs (relations) associated with it, or (iii) nouns (often the other argument of the relation) associated with
it. Yahoo! Quest is a good example of how a browsing-oriented display of various
extracted relations invites users to explore a corpus.

Mining the Web in this frequency- and feedback-driven way may be said to profit
from the *constraints* that each document implicitly defines on the others (since documents confirm or do not confirm others, and since some documents determine the
extraction patterns for others). Not only can different documents be combined such
that the knowledge mined from them is 'self-constraining', the same can also be
done with different formats (for example, (Cafarella 2009) combines mining hy-
ponymy relations (Etzioni et al. 2004), other relational triples (Banko et al. 2007)
and HTML tables, and a purely statistical association miner). Constraints can also
come from existing knowledge bases; for example, the knowledge that a digital
camera has exactly one "number of megapixels", but may have several lenses is
readily expressible in an OWL ontology and can help evaluate multiple findings
from free-text mining, and coupling the knowledge from different (parts of) ontologies may provide further constraints for consistency checking, cf. for example
(Matuszek et al. 2005; Carlson et al. 2010).[18] A promising idea is to leverage the

---

[17]Both retrieved on 2010-04-10.

[18]These are typical examples of humans having fed their knowledge into machine-readable *knowledge* as described by the left-pointing arrows at the top of Fig. 3.3a, and into the form that can be
used for automatic consistency checking in the sense of Fig. 3.3b.

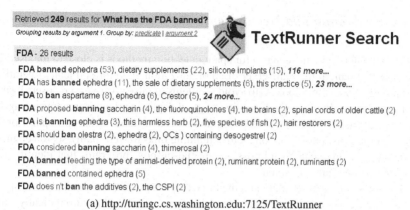

(a) http://turingc.cs.washington.edu:7125/TextRunner

(b) http://quest.sandbox.yahoo.net

Fig. 3.7 Interfaces for relation extraction (excerpts)

knowledge inherent in very large and highly quality-controlled resources such as Wikipedia[19] and Cyc[20] (whose modes of quality control are very different, with one relying on distributed editing and "the wisdom of the crowds" and the other on highly skilled knowledge engineers), e.g. (Sarjant et al. 2009).

In sum, current approaches that couple mining from different resources (data, information, knowledge) and that use different feedback loops for validity checking and evaluating, together are beginning to realize the vision of Semantic Web Mining (see Figs. 3.3a and 3.3b).

---

[19] See http://www.wikipedia.org.

[20] See http://www.cyc.com.

3.3.4 Evaluation and Deployment

The typical deployment scenario for spam detection methods is close to the user: in the case of email, at the mailserver of an organization and more typically operating on individual users' mailboxes (to avoid problems of false positives, i.e., users losing legitimate mail). In the case of web spam, good deployment environments are again mail programs (to warn of sites/pages announced in emails that are spam, or to classify emails as spam based on them containing links to web spam), search engines (to avoid indexing spam), and possibly special-purpose programs that identify, for example, online-banking spam.

The preponderance of spam and the large consensus over most instances of spam has led to filters in email readers and search-engine indexers that automatically classify something as a spam candidate. However, in the environment of email readers (which is more personal than that of indexers), the subjectivity of the notion of spam makes many spam filter developers include "active learning" elements into the spam classification: a checkbox that allows users to file, delete, and report something as spam (or not) and to remove automatically generated spam flags.

Yet, for all deployment scenarios, evaluation needs to ask "A key objective is to determine if there is some important business issue that has not been sufficiently considered [even if the model is of high quality from a data analysis perspective]."[21] A good example can again be found in the web spam domain. As mentioned above, including hidden or invisible text that is unrelated to the spam site's real content, but is judged as attractive for searchers, is a popular strategy for spammers. Text can be hidden in HTML code such as "no frame" or "no script" sections or ALT attributes. However, hidden text is not always a sign of spamming; it can also be used to enhance accessibility. In fact, ALT text equivalents for images, frames, scripts, etc. are *prescribed* by the W3C's accessibility guidelines (W3C 2000). Thus, a classifier that relies heavily on such attributes for detecting spam—whether it be prescribed as a heuristic or machine-learned—is likely to produce false positives, which may result in the non-indexing of legitimate, accessible sites. Such tradeoffs and their (financial, societal, etc.) costs have to be considered in order to evaluate whether and how learned models or patterns should be deployed.

The deployment of results may range from (annotated) trend meters such as those by www.blogpulse.com, where the mere mention of something, i.e., a topical analysis, is already interpreted as 'the opinion that something is interesting/hot', to detailed positive/negative opinions-on-product-features barometers. Opinion spam, designed to push or damage brand reputations, may be a severe problem whose frequency is only very partially known. Another problem may be privacy issues. For example, people may object to the re-purposing, for marketing purposes, of content that they wrote as a forum post designed to help other users. Similar issues may arise in the deployment of relation-mining results. In addition, the de-contextualisation and re-combination of atomic relational statements may endanger consistency and

---

[21] See http://www.crisp-dm.org/Process/index.htm, retrieved on 2010-04-10.

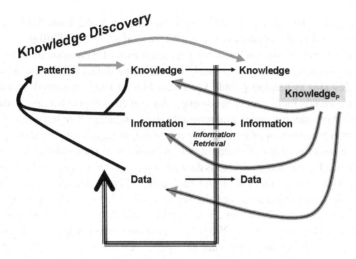

Fig. 3.8 Full web mining or "You're a document too" (Berendt 2008)

validity. Questions of privacy and context are further investigated in the following two sections.

3.4 New Challenges: Web Mining and Privacy

As Sect. 3.2.5 described in general form and Sect. 3.3 illustrated for specific examples, modern mining in general and web mining in particular operate not only on data/information/knowledge that have been put into some repository consciously and intentionally, often for the purpose of being findable/queryable. They also operate on documents that may not have been put online for the purpose of being analysed, on structural characteristics of these such as hyperlink structure between web documents, and on data arising from usage activities such as querying, browsing/navigating, or creating content. These are intellectual activities, of which measurable outcomes such as clicks, issued queries, uploads or edits can become input for KD. These intellectual activities and measurable outcomes are shown as grey and black arrows, respectively, in Fig. 3.8.

The main outcome of this is that the Web contains increasingly large amounts of "personal data", data that relate to an identified or identifiable individual. This concerns such things as behavior (which sites were visited, for how long, etc.), interests and questions (those sites' contents as well as queries posed, self-profiling on social networks, etc.), social relationships ("friendship" links in social networks, blogrolls, etc.), plus a wealth of self-reported or third-party-reported views, attitudes, etc. (all authored content). This is increasingly viewed as a threat to privacy, where privacy can refer to the interest in a protected sphere of personal and intimate life, the ability to keep different social identities separate and also to otherwise know and control what happens to data about oneself, and to (re-)negotiate the boundaries between these private and public spheres in social and societal processes (Phillips 2004).

Data protection legislation limits the permitted uses of data in an attempt to protect individuals and help them to control the use of their data, and privacy-enhancing technologies aim at helping people keep data hidden from unwanted accesses or uses. However, it is increasingly becoming clear that current provisions are reaching their limits. For example, many planning activities—whether it be for research, marketing, urban planning, or other uses—require data, in particular data about people. A common solution to avoid infringing on individuals' private spheres has been to anonymize such data, and anonymous data are not protected by data protection laws. However, with even a small amount of background knowledge from other sources, it is possible to de-anonymize people, for example with the help of basic demographic data (Sweeney 2002), queries (Barbaro and Zeller 2006), social-network relationships (Backstrom et al. 2007), self-profiling information in e-Commerce websites (Owad 2006) or ratings and user-generated content such as forum posts (Frankowski et al. 2006; Narayanan and Shmatikov 2008). Many such sources of background knowledge are freely accessible.

The data mining and security/privacy communities have addressed this issue by extensive research on "privacy-preserving data mining", "privacy-preserving data publishing", "private information retrieval" and similar families of techniques. However, a number of findings shed doubt on the effectiveness of these techniques in real-world scenarios. A first concern is that some of these techniques may protect the privacy of different groups of people (data subjects, data owners, or data users), but not of others (Domingo-Ferrer 2007). A second concern is that the full theoretical and practical consequences of the de-anonymization results mentioned are only beginning to become clear. A third concern is that current accounts of privacy in computer science and law are disregarding the issues arising from relational information (that pertains not only to one individual, but to several, like the "friendship" links in social networks) and the many external effects that one person's dealings with their data have on others (Gürses and Berendt 2010; Berendt 2007).

A fourth concern is the focus of data protection laws and current privacy-enhancing technologies on the individual. This disregards the privacy-relevant effects of social categorizations (classifications). To understand this concern, one needs to consider the uses of classification in web mining for classifying people.

Classification is used for a wide range of personalisation services. The goal is to predict what the current user may find most interesting, attractive, etc., based on what the service knows about this user and what regularities have been observed in the past between these features and "liked items". These regularities may have been observed in this particular user's behavior or, more often, in larger populations of all users. Features may be the words (or other text-derived attributes) of previously read and therefore presumably liked texts; the prediction may be the degree of personal relevance of a new search result. Outcomes may range from recommendations via filtering, re-ranking, to a denial of service because the current user is classified as "belonging to an undesirable group" (such as a group of people with a high risk of defaulting on a loan). The function learned may map directly from the user-describing feature space into the space of items; this however often suffers from the sparseness of typical datasets used as the training-set universe.

Often, therefore, there is a modeling step in the middle: First, the current user is mapped into a previously defined set of classes of users; second, the new item to be evaluated is scored with respect to this user class. These classes include such criteria as gender or age bracket (Liu and Mihalcea 2007; Hu et al. 2007), and socioeco-nomic or other categories deemed important by the provider of the personalisation service. For example, many marketing people in Germany work with the category of *DDR-Nostalgiker*, people who are "nostalgic for the former East German State", because their consumption patterns and attitudes differ from those of other target groups.[22] Marketing also has a tradition of classifying by ethnicity, skin colour, or sexual orientation (Wardlow 1996). Criticism of such classes is being voiced es-pecially in the literature on social sorting from surveillance studies,[23] and it is also being discussed in the privacy literature at the interface between surveillance studies and privacy-enhancing technologies (Phillips 2004).

At the moment, it appears that in addition to adapting privacy legislation and legal practice to the changing realities of today's Web and other data spaces, in addition to educational and computational initiatives with various goals (confi-dentiality, data control, etc.), new methods for structured negotiations between data subjects and service providers on the one hand and between data sub-jects among themselves on the other will need to be developed (Preibusch 2006; Gürses 2010). These are likely to have major impacts on business models and re-lated high-level application strategies, and therefore also on mining phases like busi-ness/application understanding.

3.5 Conclusions

In this article, we have touched upon several current application areas of web (con-tent/text) mining. It has become clear that while much progress has been made, problems remain hard[24]—because the "target" keeps moving (spammers and their strategies for fooling search engines and users), because the target is, even in a non-adversarial setting, intrinsically changing (natural language evolves continu-ally), because the target is not fully automatable (natural language understanding), or because pursued goals are contradictory (data analysis needs data with a high

---

[22] See http://www.sociovision.de/loesungen/sinus-milieus.html, retrieved on 2010-04-10.

[23] A cross-disciplinary initiative to understand the ways in which personal details are collected, stored, transmitted, checked, and used as means of influencing and managing people and popula-tions; for an overview, see Lyon (2007).

[24] We have deliberately not discussed any accuracies, F measure values, or other absolute numbers here, in order to concentrate on the big picture. However, the reader is encouraged to consult original articles, investigate the reported quality values closely, and consider what for example a 20% misclassification rate or an unknown recall rate may mean in practice.

signal-to-noise ratio, privacy is about restricting data or their information content). This implies a wide range of research challenges on both computational and wider information-systems-related questions.

As an outlook, we want to point to some specific lessons learned and their implications for future research.

3.5.1 Context

The first challenge is the increasing realization that *context* is highly important for intelligent behavior (including inferences) of all kinds. This has been discussed (not only) in the privacy literature for some time. As pointed out above, one important part of many notions of privacy is the ability and right to keep different social identities apart. This means that a given piece of data/information/knowledge may not be taken out of its "context" and re-used somewhere else. For example, photographs may be meant for one's circle of friends or family, but not for one's employer. "Contextual integrity" (Nissenbaum 2004) ties adequate protection for privacy to norms of specific contexts, demanding that information gathering and dissemination be appropriate to that context and obey the governing norms of distribution within it. A formal model of contextual integrity has been proposed by Barth et al. (2006).

Context may affect not only the legitimacy, but also the validity of data-processing operations. Asserting that two social roles of one "physical individual" refer to "the same" individual and can therefore be combined ad lib may be wrong in a similar way as asserting that two URIs are <sameAs>, refer to the same entity, and that therefore all statements about them may be atomized and recombined ad lib. An example of the latter is provided by Hayes (2009): Two pieces of knowledge about sodium, one referring to the 3D model of this chemical, the other to the 4D model. Combining statements from these two universes of discourse is bound to lead to incorrect conclusions. Some logics provide for such contexts of conceptualizations (Cycorp 2001); applications in Linked Data and web mining are a promising application area and testing ground for such constructs.

3.5.2 Learning Cycles

The second lesson learned is the basic observation that all learning rests on iterations of a basic cycle such as that shown in Fig. 3.3b: All new knowledge is obtained on the basis of some previous knowledge and conceptualizations. This does not mean that such existing knowledge cannot also lead the learner astray. The argument between those who argue for the importance of background knowledge for reasoning and other intelligent activities, and those who regard it as cumbersome, misleading, etc. is at least as old as Artificial-Intelligence research as such. In mining, one strategy for avoiding background knowledge is to search for "domain-independent" and/or "language-independent" techniques. However, such independence may be illusory. The critical reader should always closely examine all heuristics, extraction patterns, enumerations of classes, data preparation choices, etc. in order to find possibly hidden assumptions that do hinge on language, domain, or other properties of the mined materials.

3.5.3 Definitional Power and Viewpoints

The example of a multitude of contexts raises another question: Who may decide on contexts, and is this agent in possession of an absolute truth? The pragmatic answer to the second part is obviously "no", and results from semiotics and informatics suggest that it is not even possible to find such an agent or even a complete and expressive system of assertions. A structuralist approach in which people are enabled to dig deeper when they so desire appears to be superior. This makes *sourcing* a key element of knowledge processing: the indication of where a statement comes from—and thus what the inferences based on it rest on. The Cyc inference engine, for example, allows for such source-enhanced chains of reasoning (Baxter et al. 2005). In web/text mining, the search for viewpoints or biases in news reporting, user-generated content, etc. has recently received a lot of attention and new techniques for identifying common elements (to identify a common 'story') and differentiating elements (to identify diversity and bias), e.g. (Fortuna et al. 2009; Lin et al. 2008; Nakasaki et al. 2009). Sourcing is related to the modeling and processing of data *provenance*, which has been researched so far especially with a view to data quality and trustworthiness, cf. (Hartig 2009) for references and the relation to Linked Data.

3.5.4 Tools and Access

Finally, all these ideas will only be able to live up to their full potential if they are deployed in tools that are being used, tools for end users and not only skilled mining experts. More and more tools that marry data-analysis functionality with user-friendly interfaces are becoming available, see for example the development sections of major search engines, research-led initiatives like MovieLens,[25] or other tools like the Wikiscanner.[26] However, most tools are rather fixed in their functionality and/or data sources; thus, they support generativity (Zittrain 2008) at most at a content level, while generativity at a program level remains reserved for informatics-savvy elites. It is an open question whether this is the most we can get, whether we can and want to raise information-literacy levels to enable everyone to be a web miner, and what compromises this would entail.

---

[25] See http://movielens.umn.edu.

[26] See http://wikiscanner.virgil.gr.

Acknowledgements   I thank my students and colleagues from various Web Mining classes for many valuable discussions and ideas. In particular, I thank the members of the European Summer School in Information Retrieval ESSIR 2007, the members of the Information Retrieval and Data Mining course at Universitat Pompeu Fabra in Barcelona 2010, and the members of the Advanced Databases and Current Trends in Databases courses at K.U. Leuven/U. Antwerp/U. Hasselt.

Chapter 4
The User in Interactive Information Retrieval Evaluation

Peter Ingwersen

Abstract This chapter initially defines what characterizes and distinguishes research frameworks from research models. The Laboratory Research Framework for IR illustrates the case. We define briefly what is meant by the concept of research design, including research questions, and what this chapter regards as central IIR evaluation research settings and variables. This is followed by a description of IIR components, pointing to the elements of the Integrated Cognitive Research Framework for IR that incorporates the Laboratory Framework in a contextual manner. The following sections describe and exemplify: (1) Request types, test persons, task-based simulations of search situations and relevance or performance measures in IIR; (2) Ultra-Light Interactive IR experiments; (3) Interactive-Light IR studies; and (4) Naturalistic field investigations of IIR. The chapter concludes with a summary section, a reference list and a thematically classified bibliography.

4.1 Introduction

Since the dawn of Information Retrieval (IR) experimentation and IR evaluation two approaches have been predominant. The mainstream laboratory-based IR research and evaluation framework, also named the Cranfield Model or Laboratory IR Research Framework (Baeza-Yates and Ribeiro-Neto 1999; Belew 2000; Ingwersen and Järvelin 2005), and the user-oriented perspectives on interactive IR (IIR) (Belkin and Vickery 1985; Järvelin 2007). The latter matured somewhat later, are commonly not adhering to one single research framework, but display variations between models and methodologies (Ingwersen and Järvelin 2005).

This chapter puts forward an integrated and contextual perspective on IR experimentation and evaluation, founded upon a cognitive approach to IR (Ingwersen

P. Ingwersen (✉)
Royal School of Library and Information Science, Birketinget 6, 2300 Copenhagen S, Denmark
e-mail: pi@iva.dk
url: http://www.iva.dk/pi

P. Ingwersen
Oslo University College, Oslo, Norway

M. Melucci, R. Baeza-Yates (eds.), *Advanced Topics in Information Retrieval*,   83
The Information Retrieval Series 33,
DOI 10.1007/978-3-642-20946-8_4, © Springer-Verlag Berlin Heidelberg 2011

and Järvelin 2005), as an alternative to the Laboratory IR Research Framework. Hence, this perspective is regarded an attempt to create an Integrated Cognitive Research Framework that may cover a variety of interactive IR models as an umbrella and provide a range of workable research methodologies. The framework integrates human actors, like searchers or authors of information, with their socio-cultural-organizational *and* systemic contexts. The motivation behind is twofold: (1) it is not sufficient to postulate an alternative epistemological perspective to IR (viz. the integrated cognitive approach) *without also* providing the consequential research design tools and methodologies; (2) in recent years laboratory researchers have increasingly asked for the provision of such tools and methodologies, so that they might address user-IR system interaction from a more contextual perspective.

This chapter initially defines what we believe characterizes and distinguishes research frameworks from research models. The Laboratory IR Research Framework illustrates the case. We define briefly what is meant by the concept of research design, including research questions, and what this chapter regards as central IIR evaluation research settings and variables. This is followed by a description of IIR components, pointing to the central elements of the Integrated Cognitive Research Framework for IR that incorporates the Laboratory Research Framework in a contextual manner.

The following sections describe and exemplify (1) Request types, test persons, task-based simulations of search situations and relevance or performance measures in IIR; (2) Ultra-light Interactive IR experiments; (3) Interactive-Light IR studies; and (4) Naturalistic field investigations of IIR. The chapter concludes with a summary section and a double-purpose reference section. References are listed as in the text. Then follows a more comprehensive bibliography categorized according to the structure of the chapter, including many additional bibliographic entries.

4.2 Research Frameworks, Models and Other Central Concepts

A *research framework* for IR describes and models the central objects to study, their relationships as well as changes in objects and in their relationships that (may) affect the functioning of the IR system and interactive processes. Further, it outlines promising goals and methods of research (Ingwersen and Järvelin 2005, pp. 11–13). Research frameworks typically contain (tacit) knowledge and shared assumptions on its ontological, conceptual, factual, epistemological and methodological elements. *Models* are precise (often formal) representations of objects and relationships or processes within a research framework.

Examples of formal models in IR are probabilistic, vector space, language, logical, quantum-theoretical, etc. models that compete under the umbrella of the Laboratory Research Framework for IR. IR Models may indeed also be graphic and in principle encompass human actors and organizations. Figure 4.1 depicts graphically

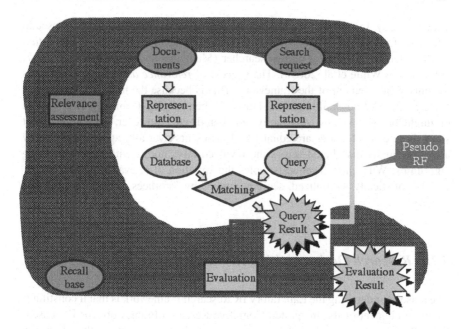

Fig. 4.1 The Laboratory Research Framework for IR; revision of Ingwersen and Järvelin (2005, p. 115)

the Laboratory Research Framework for IR with the generalized Cranfield model at its centre.

The framework displays its central variables (objects located in the laboratory cave as seen in a vertical cut, with the entry of the cave to the right), relationships and processes to be carried out or/and studied. It holds at its centre the *Cranfield Model of IR* containing a set of requests (topics in TREC) represented (indexed) as queries, a collection of documents, their representation (indexing) in a database (nowadays including the full documents), and a matching algorithm. Obviously, if the same sets of queries and documents are applied for all experiments, whereby they are controlled or variations are statistically neutralized, one may simply stick to one indexing algorithm during experimentation (then also controlled) and solely vary the matching algorithms. Or do the opposite. This is the robust natural science-like research design philosophy behind the Laboratory Research Framework for IR that makes it so successful: only one independent variable is in play at a time in each experiment.

The Laboratory Research Framework in addition contains the process of *relevance assessment* made by human assessors, one for each request/topic, commonly based on a pooling principle of the retrieved documents per query. For the total set of requests/topics the relevant documents are stored in a *recall base* and compared to the *query results* for each retrieval run in the experiment. The *evaluation result* can then be calculated in terms of performance measures of various kinds (Baeza-Yates and Ribeiro-Neto 1999; Belew 2000). Commonly, the relevance assessment scale is binary. In addition, the Laboratory Research Framework allows for pseudo relevance feedback (pseudo RF) to be studied. Pseudo RF works as a *simulation* of RF behavior made by a human searcher (Magennis and van Rijsbergen 1997; White 2006; White et al. 2005b). The process of *relevance assessment* constitutes the only weak element of the framework. This is because the human assessor is— *human*—i.e., he/she would become saturated when judging documents after a while or might become sloppy, non-motivated, bored, etc.; however, it is argued that since these characteristics are equal for all assessors over all requests/topics, they are also equally distributed across the involved laboratories with their competing algorithms. With enough requests/topics the variation of relevance judgments becomes statistically neutralized, see e.g. studies by Voorhees (1998) over the last decade.

4.2.1 Research Design and IIR Research Setting Types

The reason for detailing the Laboratory IR Research Framework is that it constitutes a central element of the Integrated Cognitive Research Framework for IR. Essentially, the latter framework pushes the experimental situation outside the laboratory cave into the context of reality. The Integrated Research Framework for IR is called 'cognitive' because it adheres to the epistemological cognitive viewpoint, in which the contextual (social and systemic) elements of an actor influence and become influenced by that actor during interaction. IR systems are seen as systems supporting human cognition (Ingwersen and Järvelin 2005, pp. 23–31). The problem when setting up a laboratory experiment that involves users is to keep the experimental situation under *control* and, at the same time, allow the test persons to have *cognitive freedom*. Whilst control relates to something artificial and static, the latter associates to realism and situational dynamism.

A solid *research design* generates the research problem—*what* is to be studied? It consists of research questions—*why?*—and the decisions concerning the degree of human involvement in experiments—the *control* issue. Research design deals with setting up the data collection and deciding the methodological approach—*how* and *when*. This includes the range of research outcomes and thus the data analysis method. We should always remember that the aim of IR is twofold: designing and evaluating IR systems *and/or* understanding searcher behavior in context. The Laboratory Research Framework is isolated to deal with the former whilst the Integrated Cognitive Research Framework seeks to circumscribe both aims.

Research questions should ideally be answered by the investigation at hand. They must be concise and meaningful statements of the research goal(s), i.e. the research outcomes. Hypotheses are closely related to the research questions by serving as their precursors or motivation. They form beliefs or predictions about relationships of objects that arises in accordance with the research framework, model(s) or theory. An example of a hypothesis could be '[knowledge of] multi-evidence of a searcher's information situation may improve retrieval performance through query expansion, compared to initial searcher request formulation and use of pseudo-relevance feedback' (Kelly and Fu 2007).

In the remaining of this chapter the following types of IR *research settings* are used as investigations:

- Laboratory experiments: no test persons participate. Investigations deal with performance tests of kinds of algorithms, simulations of searcher behavior or log analyses (not treated in this chapter);
- Laboratory study: test persons participate:
  - Ultra-light IR study: investigations of short-term IR interaction of 1–2 retrieval runs;
  - Light IR study: investigations of session-based multi-run IR interaction;
- Field experiment: experimental situation tested in natural setting with test persons;
- Field study: investigation of system performance or human behavior in natural setting with test persons;
- Longitudinal studies.

In IR investigations the common tradition is that experiments and studies are carried out in a rigorous statistical manner, i.e., a sufficient number of test persons and/or search jobs are applied to the setting in order to produce statistically valid results (within its data limits). This tradition adheres to the performance measurement history of the Cranfield investigations, dating back to the 1960s. Case studies, although accepted in most social science fields, are not really accepted in the Laboratory Research Framework, but acceptable in the Integrated Cognitive Research Framework, in particular concerning behavioral investigations of IR phenomena. We may here observe a link to Human-Computer Interaction (HCI), which by nature commonly do *not* operate with large groups of test persons or search jobs (Hornbaek 2006).

Regardless the research setting and research frameworks applied to IR investigations the following variables are at play (Ingwersen and Järvelin 2005; Fidel and Soergel 1983):

- Independent variables: the cause, e.g., different IR models; interface functionality; searcher knowledge level;
- Dependent variables: the effect, e.g., as measured by some performance measure of retrieval result (MAP; DCG) or usability measures (search time; clicks);
- Controlled variables: variables held constant, statistically neutralized or randomized, e.g., document collection; retrieval model; assigned topics or simulated task situations (the search jobs); test persons;
- Hidden variables: moderating or intervening (may create bias), e.g., variations of searcher domain knowledge levels; de-motivation of test persons; no up-to-date collection.

As stated above in the Laboratory Research Framework the number of variables is limited and although each may take many values, the setting is fairly easy to control. In TREC this may be the case also because each TREC track feeds on its own document collection and applying tailored search jobs. The experimental situation would be more loose if the one and same collection was applied to a mixture of research goals (tracks), e.g., mixing different kinds of requests and document types. The chance of hidden variables and lack of control would definitively increase in such rather naturalistic scenarios, simulating a digital library or integrated searching.

4.2.2 Central IIR Components

Figure 4.2 displays the six central components of IIR, with the Laboratory Research Framework (dotted figure) to the left, covering Information Objects, the IT component and the interaction them in between. The Interface, the Cognitive Actor and the Socio-cultural and Organizational context—and the remaining portion of the Interaction processes—are outside the framework, and outside the cave stipulated in Fig. 4.1. The one-way arrows signify influence and transformation, e.g., from the communities of actors (the socio-cultural and organizational context) towards the documents or the IT components over time (dotted arrows), or the direct act of creation of objects or IT elements (straight arrows). The interaction processes consist of *IR Interaction* between Cognitive Actor and Interface component (request formulations and other statements from searcher) and further into the IT-Information-Object interaction, via query formulations. This is where the access to IR systems takes place. The interaction between actor and socio-cultural and organizational context constitutes *Social Interaction*.

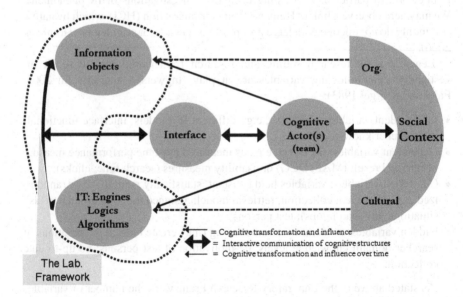

Fig. 4.2 Central components of interactive IR—the basis of the Integrated Cognitive Research Framework for IR. Revised version of Ingwersen and Järvelin (2005, p. 261)

4.2.3 The Integrated Cognitive Research Framework for IR

The six central components, Fig. 4.2, constitute the nine dimensions of the Integrated Cognitive Research Framework. Each dimension holds a number of variables, each with two or more values (Ingwersen and Järvelin 2005, 2007):

- Natural work task variables, from the socio-cultural and organizational context;
- Natural search task variables, from the socio-cultural and organizational context;
- Actor characteristics variables, actor's personal characteristics;
- Perceived work task variables, actor's perception of natural work task;
- Perceived search task variables, actor's perception of natural search task;
- Document variables, dealing with all information object features and representations;
- Algorithmic search engine variables, concerned with features of the IT component;
- Algorithmic interface variables, dealing with interface functionalities;
- Access and interaction variables, concerning all features of IR and social interaction.

The work task is viewed as the underlying motivation for searchers to have an information need and the search task as the instrumental activity that may lead to solving the work task. Work tasks may be job-related or associated with non-job but daily-life situations (Ingwersen and Järvelin 2005, 2007). Work and search tasks can be natural, i.e. really existing in the world—or they may become perceived and interpreted by actors. Manuals or Good Laboratory Practice (or like documentation) are examples of natural work tasks described in the real world. There exists of course a difference between such *natural* work or search tasks and the range of *assigned* ones IR research makes use of. This range of assignments goes from semantically open simulated work task situations (cover stories) (Borlund 2003b) over semantically closed situations to TREC topics with description and narrative or simply to one-line or two-term assigned requests.

The contents of the nine dimensions relies on empirical or analytic investigations carried out over the last three decades on IIR and laboratory IR. For instance, the variables and values constituting the Interface dimension derives from a mixture of the MONSTRAT and MEDIATOR models generated by Belkin et al. (1983) and Ingwersen (1992), respectively.

The lists of variables forming up the Integrated Cognitive Research Framework originates from Ingwersen and Järvelin (2005, pp. 356–357) and are discussed by Ingwersen and Järvelin (2007), in particular associated with relevance and interaction. Tables 4.1 and 4.2 display the original multi-dimensional array of dimensions and variables.

The framework is intended to operate with a maximum of three independent variables, each containing binary values. The variables must be treated in pairs and can be illustrated by the following typical IIR variables:

Table 4.1 Five dimensions of variables of the Integrated Cognitive Research Framework (Ingwersen and Järvelin 2005, p. 356)

Natural Work Tasks (WT) & Org	Natural Search Tasks (ST)	Actor	Perceived Work Tasks	Perceived Search Tasks
WT Structure	ST Structure	Domain Knowledge	Perceived WT Structure	Perceived Information Need Content
WT Strategies & Practices	ST Strategies & Practices	IS&R Knowledge	Perceived WT Strategies & Practices	Perceived ST Structure/ Type
WT Granularity, Size & Complexity	ST Granularity, Size & Complexity	Experience on Work Task	Perceived WT Granularity, Size & Complexity	Perceived ST Strategies & Practices
WT Dependencies	ST Dependencies	Experience on Search Task	Perceived WT Dependencies	Perceived ST Specificity & Complexity
WT Requirements	ST Requirements	Stage in Work Task Execution	Perceived WT Requirements	Perceived ST Dependencies
WT Domain & Context	ST Domain & Context	Perception of Socio-Org Context	Perceived WT Domain & Context	Perceived ST Stability
		Sources of Difficulty		Perceived ST Domain & Context
		Motivation & Emotional State		

- Interface function X, value a/b—e.g. response generation (presentation form): Yahoo snippet vs. bibliographic record;
- IS&R knowledge—search expertise, having values none/much;
- Natural/assigned work task type—e.g. size: richly vs. poorly defined.

The array of dimensions, Tables 4.1, 4.2, is later used to mark up the specific variables involved in the three research design examples outlined below according to the Integrated Cognitive Research Framework for IR.

4.3 IR Interaction—Research Designs with Test Persons

Regardless how IR interaction laboratory studies or field experiments are developed the research designs must deal with request types used in the setting, number of test persons and search jobs involved, and the application of appropriate relevance,

Table 4.2 Four dimensions of variables of the Integrated Cognitive Research Framework (Ingwersen and Järvelin 2005, p. 357)

Document and Source	IR Engines IT Component	IR Interfaces	Access and Interaction
Document Structure	Exact Match Models	Domain Model Attributes	Interaction Duration
Document Types	Best Match Models	System Model Features	Actors or Components
Document Genres	Degree of Document Structure and Content Used	User Model Features	Kind of Interaction and Access
Information Type in Document	Use of NLP to Document Indexing	System Model Adaption	Strategies and Tactics
Communication Function	Document Metadata Representation	User Model Building	Purpose of Human Communication
Temporal Aspects	Use of Weights in Document Indexing	Request Model Builder	Purpose of System Communication
Document Sign Language	Degree of Request Structure and Content Used	Retrieval Strategy	Interaction Mode
Layout and Style	Use of NLP to Request Indexing	Response Generation	Least Effort Factors
Document Isness	Request Metadata Representation	Feedback Generation	
Document Content	Use of Weights in Requests	Mapping ST History	
Contextual Hyperlink Structure		Explanation Features	
Human Source (see Actor)		Transformation of Messages Scheduler	

usability and evaluation measures. Section 4.3.1 discusses such issues of interactive research design. Sections 4.3.2, 4.3.3 and 4.3.4 outline, discuss and exemplify, respectively, IR interaction ultra-light, interactive-light and naturalistic research scenarios.

4.3.1 Search Job Design, Simulated Task Situations, Test Persons and Evaluation Measures

Search Job Design   The choice of appropriate request types to form the search jobs in IR interaction is important and depends on the research questions. Originally the Laboratory Research Framework applied assigned and quite rich *topical* information need formulations (here regarded 'requests'), mainly owing to the best match retrieval models' preference of a substantial number of search keys in order to function well. This issue has been softened in recent years, predominantly due to the scarcity of search keys applied in natural Web searching; see e.g. the TREC developments (Harman 1996).

First of all, in IIR the 'query' is the retrieval mechanism's translation of the 'request formulation', according to its logic (Ingwersen and Järvelin 2005). In command-driven IR systems like Thomson-Reuter's Dialog online Service, Medline and all web retrieval engines, the searcher is responsible for this translation in advanced search mode. The central request types applied in interactive IR investigations belong to three sets of characteristics: (1) whether they are *natural* or *assigned*; (2) whether they are content-*rich* or *poor*; (3) depending on input features and outcome, i.e., whether they are *topical* (in the TREC sense), *factual*, *known-item* like, or concerned with other *metadata*.

Assigned requests may take the form as: (a) *simplistic* request formulations that commonly are context-free, as in TREC 'topics', in which the title, description and narrative do not explain why the request is posed or exists—the TREC 'topic' title alone may form the shortest or most simplistic assigned request type; (b) *'query by example'* where an information object (a photo, a publication, a tune . . .) function as request formulation and a goal may be to retrieve something similar to that (Campbell 2000)—commonly, such request types are quite contextual; (c) *simulated work task situation* or cover story (Borlund 2003b)—see below. By assigning requests (a), (b), (c) the researcher attempts to keep the investigation under control—in contrast to allowing natural information need situations to occur in the experiments or study, which entail less control of the research situation.

Natural information need situations should be applied to the adequate context, i.e., the document collection characteristics and themes must be known to the test persons in order for them to generate appropriate requests for information. One should note that it is quite difficult to make searchers generate more that one-two different natural information needs each (i.e. per week or so in the same document environment). If forced, the same person often produces several information needs that look alike or are facets of the same core. Obviously, the researcher does not really know the retrieval outcome of natural requests before they have been searched in the given system.

Simulated Search Jobs   Simulated work task situations (Borlund 2003b) consist of a 'story' that explains the search job the test person is supposed to do and why, e.g. a description of a job-related work task or a daily-life associated task situation, see Fig. 4.3. The idea is that when given to the test person the story provides the underlying reason or context for potential *interpretations* made by the person, thus posing an information request to the system. By giving the same simulated situation to all the test persons the research design is to a certain extent controlled. If the situation or cover story is content-rich and specific the potential for interpretation is more limited (increased control) than if the story is formulated in general and few terms. This issue deals with degree of *semantic openness*—Case of Fig. 4.3a is more closed than Case of Fig. 4.3b.

Beijing is hosting in 2008 (8th–24th August) the Olympic Games. A friend of yours, who is a big fan of the Olympic Games, wants to attend the events and asks you to join in this trip. You find this invitation interesting. You are not a big fan of the games but you always wanted to visit China, therefore you want to find information about the sightseeing in the city and the activities that the Chinese will offer during the games. Find for instance places you could visit, activities you could do in relation to the Chinese culture or in the spirit of the games.	After your graduation you will be looking for a job in industry. You want information to help you focus your future job seeking. You know it pays to know the market. You would like to find some information about employment patterns in industry and what kind of qualifications employers will be looking for from future employees.
(a)	(b)

Fig. 4.3 Two examples of simulated work task situations

The Borlund evaluation package for IIR (Borlund 2003b) contains recommendations as to data collection, in particular involving simulated work task situations, their styles and designs, and performance analysis applying alternative measures of performance. An essential feature of such situations is the degree of motivation they provide the test persons. They must be tailored to realistic and motivating scenarios in order to be carried out successfully. Because of their nature the subjects' perceptions and interpretations tend to promote targeted searching behavior (for facts, topical and known item retrieval) rather than exploratory searching behavior. One may profit from mixing simulated works task situations with natural ones, as shown by Kelly et al. (2005); see also below, Sect. 3.5.

Number of Test Persons and Search Jobs   The number depends on the research questions; but foremost it depends on the number of variables involved in the investigation. There are some rules of thumb to be applied (Ingwersen and Järvelin 2005, p. 367). The central point is always to have at least 30 analysis entities in each cell of the result matrix.

If the study concerns *behavioral issues* many test persons are required in order to control potential human variation. At least 30 persons would be preferable, performing 2–3 search jobs each, if we are dealing with one variable with two values or two single value variables. Additional variables or values would entail additional search jobs per person.

If one investigates *retrieval performance*, involving test persons in IR interaction studies as done below, many search jobs per person, assigned or natural, are required but the number of test persons may be less than 30. The issue here is to control search job variations; but at the same time the knowledge characteristics of the test persons must be known and preferably similar across the subjects. Otherwise the end result can be biased because some persons stick out from the average—turning into hidden variables instead of being controlled or neutralized. 30 entities are still the magic number in the result matrix, in order to be statistically significant. As an example one might deal with two independent variables in a study: two different groups of test persons (say medical doctors and nurses) vs. two different retrieval models (probabilistic and PageRank). The result matrix holds four cells, each with

Fig. 4.4 Latin Square design
with test persons (1–6) and
search jobs (A-F)
investigating two systems
(X and Y) (Ingwersen and
Järvelin 2005, pp. 253–254)

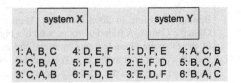

system X		system Y	
1: A, B, C	4: D, E, F	1: D, F, E	4: A, C, B
2: C, B, A	5: F, E, D	2: E, F, D	5: B, C, A
3: C, A, B	6: F, D, E	3: E, D, F	6: B, A, C

30 analysis entities, thus providing 120 entities in total. To do this research design with 10 medical doctors and 10 nurses as test persons $2 \times 3 = 6$ search jobs per person are required. 5 nurses will carry out search jobs 1–3 on the probabilistic machine and jobs 4–6 on the PageRank machine; the other 5 nurses do the search jobs in opposite order, see Fig. 4.4 for typical Latin Square design illustration. The same execution pattern is applied to the medical doctors and the 2×3 search jobs. In addition the search job sequence is permuted; see Fig. 4.4. No repetition has taken place (Ingwersen and Järvelin 2005, pp. 253–254) and each analysis cell in the matrix will hold 30 events.

This design is workable and statistically valid but may not satisfy the TREC research scenarios because of TREC's *competitive* nature. With 30 analysis entities only, the final rank order of the competing systems will not be stable. In TREC terms at least 50 entities must be present in each analysis cell in order to satisfy the competition principle (Voorhees 1998); indeed it has been shown that if performance measures are done by MAP at quite *shallow ranking levels*, e.g., at the realistic ranks of top-10 or top-15 documents, more than 60 search jobs are required to maintain result sequence stability (Sanderson and Zobel 2005). In the medical case above that implies that either (a) each test person must perform 12 search jobs, or (b) the number of test persons must be doubled to 2×20 subjects. The former is doable over a series of search sessions whilst the latter alternative often is cumbersome to fulfill owing to difficulty in getting enough persons with similar training and knowledge levels.

Performance Measures In IIR one may apply the traditional performance measures like precision, precision @ n, recall, Mean Average Precision (MAP), etc. They are commonly based on *binary* relevance assessments. Alternatively and more realistically *graded relevance* measures can be applied, as proposed, tested and generalized by Kekäläinen (2005) and Kekäläinen and Järvelin (2002b). Similarly, novel measures are applicable, like the DCG family of performance indicators that observe the degree of success by the retrieval engine of pushing up the relevant documents on the retrieval ranking compared to an ideal ranking sequence (Järvelin and Kekäläinen 2002). The graded relevance issue and the degree of liberal assessment of relevance made in TREC scenarios have been tested by Sormunen (2002).

Figure 4.5 demonstrates the Integrated Cognitive Research Framework for IR with the Laboratory Research Framework to the left and the extension into an increasing degree of context from centre to right-hand side. In this model Laboratory IR is regarded in context of information seeking activities and work task processes. Simultaneous with the contextualization different novel performance indicators and

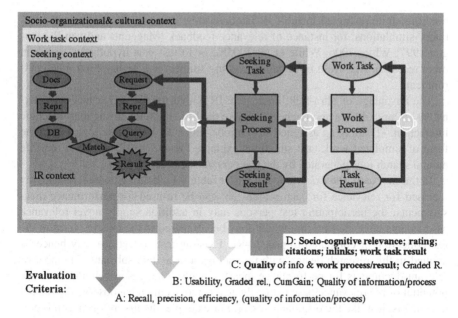

Fig. 4.5 The Integrated Cognitive Research Framework; relevance criteria, revision of Ingwersen and Järvelin (2005, p. 322)

other relevance/usefulness measures come into play. For instance, *usability* measures (Hornbaek 2006) and the DCG family appear in association with IR interaction ultra-light and light investigations that in principle involve information seeking activities. Associated with usability measures, such as: display time; hovering over objects; amount of views and clicks; number of objects assessed; selection patterns; perception of ease; satisfaction; would be relevant dependent variables in interactive IR investigations.

Moving into the work task activity realm or even into the social and organizational context, i.e., into natural field experiments or studies, the *work task result* as well as several *socio-cognitive* (Cosijn and Ingwersen 2000) or *social utility indicators* become useful measures of retrieval and system performance: peer reviewing results (e.g. in conference reviewing scores); density of social tagging; rating; citation counts; inlink volume; visits, search and download events; work task result; etc. Which measures to apply depend on the actual research questions and the nature of the independent variables in the actual research design.

4.3.2 IR Interaction Ultra-Light Studies

Ultra-light IR studies are *laboratory* investigations of short-term IR interaction that consists of 1–2 retrieval runs with participation of test persons. The motivation be-

hind this quite restricted form of IR interaction is to test results made from laboratory simulations, for instance of relevance feedback (Magennis and van Rijsbergen 1997; White 2006; White et al. 2005b), or to test new hypotheses based on
other research, e.g., from information seeking studies, in a highly controlled environment.

The advantage of ultra-light interactive IR is that the researcher has two alternative research design approaches, owing to the little iteration during man-machine
interaction: (1) applying assigned search jobs, either as TREC-like topics or in the
form of simulated work task situations explained above; or (2) applying real-life
natural search jobs generated by the test persons themselves.

In the first case, the *existing* recall base (Table 4.1), holding documents already
assessed for relevance for each search job, can be re-used for performance measurements; the participating test persons may in addition supply novel relevance
assessments after the first run, which may be compared to the existing ones in the
test collection or compared to pseudo-RF. Existing test collections may hence be
applied in this research design with the inclusion of a quite substantial number of
relevant documents for performance measurements. The reason behind the re-use
potential of the relevance base is that the test persons only *once* observe the ranked
documents, just like the original assessor. For example, the first retrieval run is carried out by the searcher (or done automatically), followed by a relevance feedback
(RF) process done by the person, followed by the second run from which the results
can be compared to the recall base, see Fig. 4.6. The test person has suffered from
similar learning effects as the original test collection assessor. However, if ensuing
human RF activities and retrieval runs should be made, learning effects *will* surface

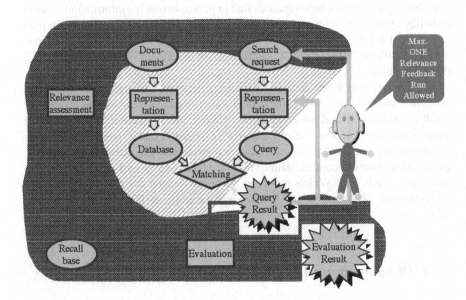

Fig. 4.6 IR interaction Ultra-light—short-term IR—revision of Ingwersen and Järvelin (2005,
p. 5)

and the research scenario makes the original assessments totally out of tune with the current test person's relevance perception. The research design then moves into an IR Interaction-light scenario.

The second alternative does not allow for re-use of the recall base in a test collection. With natural information needs/task situations all relevance assessments must be made by the test persons themselves from scratch. This research design is more realistic, although still containing a maximum of two runs under the ultra-light label. The advantage is that collections tailored to the research questions may be applied in the research design. Graded relevance can be applied by the test persons (Kekäläinen 2005; Kekäläinen and Järvelin 2002b).

In both research designs several pseudo RF runs may be applied prior to the single human RF run, thus allowing for more elaborate automatic/algorithmic experiments, but still involving searchers.

The disadvantages of IR interaction Ultra-light studies are: (1) the research design is *limited in realism* with only one run with human perception and interpretation involved; context features are hardly at play—interestingly, this scenario corresponds to that of the probabilistic retrieval model (Ingwersen and Järvelin 2007) in order to get the model to function properly; (2) the second alternative with natural search jobs replacing assigned ones may only produce a *small number of assessments* owing to *assessor saturation* (Ingwersen and Järvelin 2005; Borlund 2003b). This saturation facet of retrieval evaluation is less discussed in the Cranfield-based Laboratory Research Framework for IR. Realistically one may expect between 20–40 assessments done (Borlund 2000), out of which some are highly, fairly or marginally relevant (Sormunen 2002). The naturalistic judgment might thus result in quite few relevant documents that are available for evaluation purposes per search job. However, as Sanderson and Zobel pointed out above one may go for a shallow layer of documents to be measured, if there are enough of search jobs performed (Sanderson and Zobel 2005), i.e., greater than 60 jobs from a statistical point of view.

4.3.2.1 Example Illustrating IR Interaction Ultra-Light Studies

We have chosen the Kelly and Fu (2007) and Kelly et al. (2005) laboratory study of query expansion made from data extracted from the searcher's situational context. Kelly et al.'s hypothesis is outlined above, Sect. 2.1, as an example of such; the central IR components are displayed in Fig. 4.7.

Kelly et al.'s hypothesis was that if evidence from his/her knowledge state or/and work task description could be extracted from the searcher's task situation that evidence may improve retrieval performance, compared to the application of the request formulation only, *and* compared to various kinds of pseudo RF. Figure 4.7 demonstrates the three variables in focus (in *italics*): (1) The IT component with pseudo RF algorithms and the searching actor component, in particular the variables of the (2) Work task perception and (3) Information need situation.

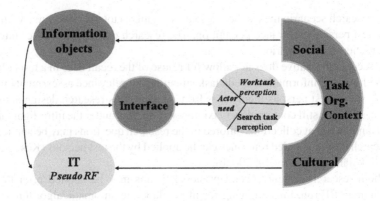

Fig. 4.7 Focus elements (in *italics*) of IR Interaction Ultra-light Laboratory study made by Kelly and Fu (2007), Kelly et al. (2005)

The research setting consisted of 13 test persons supplying 45 natural topics to HARD TREC, that is, topic title and description. The same persons also made the relevance assessments for their own topics as TREC assessors. The HARD TREC collection (Buckland and Voorhees 2005) and the Lemur system with the BM25 probabilistic retrieval model was used to run a bag-of-words retrieval run for each topic based on topic title and description terms. That served as the baseline of the study. Then a number of pseudo RF models were run on top of the baseline (using top-5; top-10 ... documents for pseudo RF).

In addition the 13 test persons were asked 4 questions via an online form:

- Q1: state the times in the past you have searched that topic;
- Q2: describe what you *already know* about the topic (knowledge state);
- Q3: state *why* you want to know about the topic; and
- Q4: add any *keywords* that further describe the topic.

The BM25, the HARD collection and the 45 topics served as controlled and neutralized variables. *Pseudo RF* variations as well as Q2–Q4 terms—on top of the baseline—served as independent variables. MAP with statistical significance test was used as dependent variable.

The results are statistically significant (t-test) and very promising from retrieval performance as well as cognitive framework points of view. The different Q2–Q4 and the baseline request yield quite different volumes of keys:

1. Baseline request: 9,33 keys
2. Q2, knowledge state: 16,18 keys
3. Q3, work task: 10,67 keys
4. Q4, added keys: 3,3 keys.

The keys repeated in the various Q-forms were weighted when they were combined. Single query forms, based on the individual Q-versions, outperformed the request-based baseline. Pseudo-RF outperformed the baseline and single Q-forms.

However, Q2+Q3 (and Q2–Q4 combined) outperformed any pseudo-RF on top of the baseline. This result implies that by involving the searcher situational *context* one may indeed improve retrieval performance in best match environments. The study also showed that performance increases with query length.

4.3.3 IR Interaction Light

When the IR interaction Ultra-light retrieval scenario is extended into more than one run, in which the test persons may observe the documents (or representations), it turns into an IR interaction Light laboratory study or field experiment.

In IR interaction light investigations (Fig. 4.8), the test persons themselves must carry out the relevance assessments. The scenario thus has a similar disadvantage as the ultra-light research design, in that the test persons may become saturated and produce a limited number of assessed (and relevant) documents. But the 'light' scenario is more realistic in terms of runs over a retrieval session and other behavioral patterns (including the saturation issue).

Again there are two basic research design scenarios. One is to execute a laboratory study, taking into the laboratory the test persons, as in the ultra-light studies. The assigned search jobs could be all the variations discussed above, but the original test collection assessments cannot be used. *New relevance assessments* must be applied to the search situations in a posteriori manner.

The second scenario moves the setting out into the field, e.g. into an organization, but introduces some experimental component, for instance, a novel search engine or

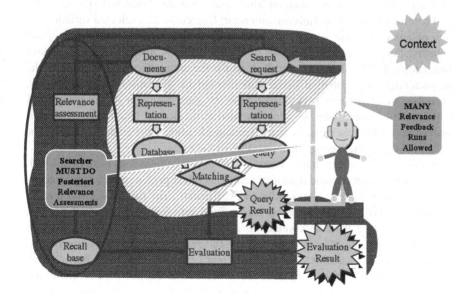

Fig. 4.8 IR Interaction 'light'—revision of Ingwersen and Järvelin (2005, p. 5)

interface configuration. This scenario is named Field Experiment in the Integrated Cognitive IR Research Framework. Obviously, the documents (database) and the context is the local one; but one wishes to try out some novel feature in that natural environment. Again, the relevance assessments must be done by the test persons themselves. In common to both alternative research designs both natural as well as assigned search jobs may be used.

4.3.3.1 Example Illustrating IR Interaction Light Studies

To illustrate a laboratory study of IR interaction light the Borlund investigation concerned with testing the ability of simulated work task situations to substitute natural information needs in evaluation of interactive IR systems (Borlund 2000) was chosen. Her original research question was: Can simulated information needs substitute real information needs? And if yes: What makes a 'good' simulated situation? The experimental setting included the historical Financial Times collection (TREC) supplemented by an *up-to-date collection* of the Glasgow news paper The Herald. The test system was based on a probabilistic retrieval model. The design included 24 university students, graduates and undergraduates from different departments and each test person provided one real need plus was assigned 4 simulated work task situations (cover stories). The research design thus included 24 natural need situations and 96 simulated ones, which were searched by the test persons in the system located in the computing laboratory of Glasgow University. An example of one of the simulated situations from the study is given in Fig. 4.3.

Among the study's independent variables were Natural Work/Search Task—i.e., the test persons' own need situation which may have many (unknown) values; and the Perceived Search Task (information need) Contents—i.e., selected variations in kind of contents of the cover stories, such as, local topical vs. historical topical contexts, Table 4.3. All the variables in the Interface, IR algorithms, and Database dimensions, Table 4.2, were controlled, whilst the entire Access & Interaction dimension might hold potential hidden variables outside the control of the researcher, since the interaction was performed by the test persons. Latin square design and permutation of search jobs were incorporated in the design. One notices that each analysis cell in the result matrix would contain 24 entities, just on the borderline for the application of strong significance tests like the t-test.

Both pre and post-search interviews as well as transactions logs were performed, the retrieval system became demonstrated to each test person and each person executed one training search task prior to experiments. The results showed that no difference could be found between real, natural information need situations and assigned simulated work task situations as to search runs; average use of search terms; application of different search terms; full-text-based relevance assessments; and title-based assessments. The only difference was in search time between the two kinds of search jobs. In 87% of the search events the test persons found the simulated task situations realistic. The conclusion is that simulated work task situations (cover stories) indeed *can* substitute natural information needs. It was also

Table 4.3 Independent variables in the Borlund IR Interaction Light laboratory study (Borlund 2000) mapped on to the Integrated Cognitive Research Framework dimensions

Natural Work Tasks (WT) & Org	Natural Search Tasks (ST)	Actor	Perceived Work Tasks	Perceived Search Tasks
WT Structure	*ST Structure*	Domain Knowledge	Perceived WT Structure	*Perceived Information Need Content*
WT Strategies & Practices	*ST Strategies & Practices*	IS&R Knowledge	Perceived WT Strategies & Practices	Perceived ST Structure/Type
WT Granularity, Size & Complexity	*ST Granularity, Size & Complexity*	Experience on Work Task	Perceived WT Granularity, Size & Complexity	Perceived ST Strategies & Practices
WT Dependencies	*ST Dependencies*	Experience on Search Task	Perceived WT Dependencies	Perceived ST Specificity & Complexity
WT Requirements	*ST Requirements*	Stage in Work Task Execution	Perceived WT Requirements	Perceived ST Dependencies
WT Domain & Context	*ST Domain & Context*	Perception of Socio-Org Context	Perceived WT Domain & Context	Perceived ST Stability
		Sources of Difficulty		Perceived ST Domain & Context
		Motivation & Emotional State	*Independent Variables*	

found that a mixture of simulated and real task situations is applicable. The study by Borlund (2000) outlines and recommends characteristics as to what signifies 'good' simulated task situations (Borlund 2003b), for instance, that the database must be up-to-date and the assignments realistic. Test persons are less motivated by 'historical' assignments, implying that some TREC test collections hold too 'old' materials to be used directly in IR interaction light or ultra-light studies.

Increasingly IR interaction light investigations take place world-wide, either in order to test results from laboratory simulations of real life searching behavior or to obtain novel insight into natural IR interaction processes and behavior—carried out in a controlled and realistic manner—see examples in the classified bibliography at the end of this chapter. Essentially the researcher should isolate very few independent variables, since natural IR interaction is complex, and attempt a robust research design. If mixed with real information situations the simulated ones may be checked for realism in their execution. The test persons must always provide the relevance assessments, which are feasible according to a grading scheme.

4.3.4 Naturalistic Field Investigations of IR
Interaction—Exemplified

Naturalistic field investigations of IR interaction take two forms. They are made as *field experiments* in a natural setting, e.g. in an organizational or cultural social context, testing a novel retrieval feature or they are *field studies* that investigate searcher behavior, satisfaction with the retrieval context or overall performance of systems. Usability or performance measures are applicable, like in IR interaction light studies.

The example of naturalistic IR interaction refers to the Marianne Lykke Nielsen (now Marianne Lykke) investigation made in an international pharmaceutical company (Lykke 2004). Her *research goal* was to observe whether a company thesaurus (local ontology) based on human conceptual associations affects searching behavior, retrieval performance, and searcher satisfaction different from a domain-based thesaurus. Already a few years previously she had developed the *associative thesaurus* by means of association tests made by 35 research and marketing employees from the company (Lykke 2001). The test persons provided synonyms, narrow and broader concepts founded in the 'company vocabulary'. The associative thesaurus was slightly larger in number of entries (379 entries more) than the *domain thesaurus*, made by domain experts and based on a 'scientific vocabulary'. The latter ontology served as the control mechanism in the later experiments.

Creating the associative thesaurus was a kind of field study, whilst the investigation of its effects on searcher behavior and IR performance became a *field experiment*. 20 test persons from the basic and clinical researchers, including marketing staff also with pharmaceutical background, were each assigned three simulated work task situations. They all had the same task structure and level of complexity, and were based on real work tasks observed via recently logged requests to the company retrieval system, see Fig. 4.9.

Blind testing was used in the research design: The test persons were told that the investigations were part of the system design process. They did not know which thesaurus type they were actually interacting with—only the research team knew that. Latin square design to avoid learning effects was used with permuted sequences of search jobs given the subjects. The 20 test persons would consequently in total make 30 searches in each thesaurus system. Relevance assessments were made via a three-grade scale: Highly, partially, and not relevant. Recall and precision served as performance measures—aside from the use of satisfaction measures and other behavioral observations.

You are product manager working for Lundbeck Pharma. A physician, who wants to know if the combination of Citalopram and Lithium leads to approve therapeutic effect on bipolar disorders, has consulted you. You need to find reports or articles investigating interaction and effect of the two drugs.

Fig. 4.9 Simulated work task situation assigned the test persons by Lykke (2004)

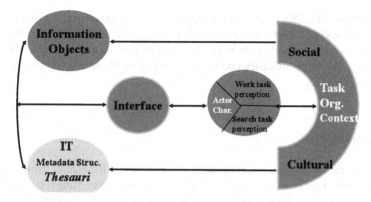

Fig. 4.10 Independent variables (*italics*) and potential influential variables (white characters)

There were some constraints usual for research designs in commercial environments. Only two working hours per test person was allowed by the employer. This
time slot covered capture of search skills (actually done via e-mail prior to the allocated period); explanation of the research setting; pre-search interview of searcher's
mental model of each search job plus capture of expectations; search session of
the three search jobs with relevance assessments of retrieved documents; and post-
search interview of motivations and satisfaction for each search job.

Figure 4.10 displays the independent variable, Thesauri, with two values: the associative thesaurus (ASSO) and the domain-based one (DOMAIN). With reference
to Tables 4.1–4.2, the controlled variables were the Natural Work/Search Task dimensions (the organizational context of Lundbeck Pharma); Perceived Work Task
Structure, Complexity (high); Perceived Search Task, Information Need content;
Documents and Sources; Retrieval Engine; and Interface dimensions. Hidden (or
influential/modifying) variables could adhere to the Access & Interactions dimension, but also to the Actor characteristics.

Among the interesting results were: both thesauri demonstrate quite the same performance in recall & precision (ASSO: .14 & .32; DOMAIN: .11 & .37). Both thesauri were applied to query formulation and modifications and did provide lead-in
terms to searching. The time using ASSO was slightly longer than using DOMAIN,
the latter was more used in the pre-search stage. Quite interestingly the test persons assessed the same documents quite differently. This (unexpected) phenomenon
owed to the fact that the two major staff groups (basic vs. clinical/marketing researchers) used the two thesauri very differently. This difference in Actors was
found to be a *hidden (influential) variable* in the study. Fortunately, the distribution of the two group members over the research execution was equal and did not
interfere with the results. Basic researchers appreciated ASSO because they could
easier explore new drugs and use local and novel vocabulary; clinical staff preferred DOMAIN for their rigorous clinical and standard scientific drug testing purposes.

The naturalistic IR interaction example demonstrates how complex the research
design may become when the control of the context is slackened, although as many

dimensions of variables as possible actually are either neutralized statistically (the simulated tasks) or directly under control. Both IR interaction light and the naturalistic investigations *per se* allow for freedom of the Access & Interaction variables; they cannot be so easily controlled in experiments directly aiming at those processes.

4.4 Conclusions

In pure laboratory experiments following the Laboratory Research Framework for IR only *simulations* of searcher behavior can be executed. If existing test collections with sets of assigned 'topic' and corresponding relevance assessments are used in interactive IR investigations only *IR interaction ultra-light* studies are feasible. In such short term IR investigations the single encounter between the test person and retrieved documents assures the avoidance of learning effects—in line with the conditions of human test collection assessors. If non-test collections are applied in the investigations, i.e., that assigned as well as natural search jobs are feasible, one may chose between ultra-light studies or the session-based *IR interaction light* research design. In both research settings the test persons *must* perform the relevance assessments and other usability measures.

IR interaction ultra-light experiments are tightly controlled, but less realistic owing to the short term interaction. The interaction light studies are less controlled but more realistic, although both takes place in the laboratory. The ultra-light laboratory experiments in particular are highly effective in tightly controlled IIR investigations, as demonstrated by Kelly and Fu (2007) and Kelly et al. (2005). Ultra-light IR interaction investigations are thus recommendable for computer scientists who wish to try out a first step of IR interaction. Meanwhile, the number of test persons, search jobs and set-ups are the same for the two research designs, as well as for the third step into context: the IIR *field experiments* and studies. The advantages of interaction (ultra)-light and field experiments are the freedom of choice between assigned requests, assigned simulated work task situations and/or natural or real tasks. The search jobs may be associated with particular working or organizational contexts or with daily-life situations. Another advantage is of methodological nature. In all IR interaction studies several *data collection* methods are applicable simultaneously. Recall base evaluation, client logs, observation (including eye-tracking) and interviewing provide in combination valuable information on the interaction phenomena and performance.

Another central feature of IR interactive investigations concerns the relevance scaling, which have moved beyond the binary one into more realistic 3–4 graded relevance scales (Kekäläinen 2005; Kekäläinen and Järvelin 2002b; Sormunen 2002), at the same time as novel performance measures have been defined and tested, such as the DCG family (Järvelin and Kekäläinen 2002; Ingwersen and Järvelin 2005).

The *disadvantage* of the IR interaction (ultra)-light studies and field experiments lies in the relatively small number of assessed documents in realistic settings in which the test persons are allowed to perform 'natural', on their own terms and are

becoming saturated. The balance between having control of the research setting and, at the same time, allowing for a certain degree of realism is vital for the validity of interactive investigations. Thus, when realism dictates that the research designs operate with relative few relevant documents and that performance hence should be measured at a shallow depth of the ranked result lists, novel measures are called for. One way would be the suggestion made by Sanderson and Zobel (2005) among others to allow for shallow-level measures but then to measure over more IR interaction events.

When stepping into context outside the laboratory the number and complexity of variables increase. The Laboratory Research Framework for IR, Fig. 4.1, does not display many variables. With the exception of the assessor they are all rather tightly controlled. The Integrated Cognitive Research Framework for IR offers nine dimensions of variables including those of the former framework. Although the number and complexity of variables has increased in the Integrated Cognitive Research Framework it also offers methodological tools for handling the higher level of complexity and suggestions to explore a long range of IR phenomena involving searchers. In particular, the strength of the Integrated Cognitive Research Framework lies in its capacity of pointing to potentially hidden or influential variables in investigations, and how to neutralize them in research designs.

4.5 Classified Bibliography

IR Interaction 'Light'

- Beaulieu (1997)
- Beaulieu (2000)
- Beaulieu and Jones (1998)
- Belkin et al. (1993)
- Belkin et al. (1996b)
- Belkin et al. (1996a)
- Belkin et al. (2003)
- Bilal (2000)
- Borlund (2000)
- Byström and Järvelin (1995)
- Borlund and Ingwersen (1998)
- Campbell (2000)
- Cothey (2002)
- Efthimiadis (1993)
- Joachims et al. (2005a)
- Koenemann and Belkin (1996)
- Maglaughlin and Sonnenwald (2002)
- Palmquist and Kim (2000)
- Petrelli et al. (2004)
- Puolamäki et al. (2005)

- Ruthven et al. (2002)
- Ruthven et al. (2003)
- Tombros et al. (2003)
- White et al. (2003)

IR Interaction 'Ultra-Light'

- Belkin et al. (1982)
- Harper et al. (2004)
- Hsieh-Yee (1998)
- Kelly and Fu (2007)
- Papaeconomou et al. (2008)
- Kelly et al. (2005)
- White et al. (2005a)
- White et al. (2006)

Laboratory Experiments IR simulations

- Croft and Thompson (1987)
- Dennis et al. (2002)
- Magennis and van Rijsbergen (1997)
- White (2006)
- White et al. (2005b)

Methdological Issues Research Design

- Baeza-Yates and Ribeiro-Neto (1999)
- Belew (2000)
- Efron (2009)
- Ericsson and Simon (1996)
- Fidel (1993)
- Fidel and Soergel (1983)
- Frankfort-Nachmias and Nachmias (2000)
- Hawking et al. (2000)
- Hersh et al. (1996)
- Ingwersen and Järvelin (2005)
- Järvelin (2007)
- Ingwersen and Järvelin (2007)
- Borlund (2003b)
- Belkin et al. (1983)
- Harman (1996)
- Ingwersen and Willett (1995)
- Kekäläinen and Järvelin (2002a)
- Saracevic et al. (1988)
- Tague and Schultz (1988)
- Teevan et al. (2004)

Naturalistic IR Interaction

- Anick (2003)
- Barry (1994)
- Bellotti et al. (2003)
- Bilal (2002)
- Dumais et al. (2003)
- Fidel et al. (1999)
- Ford et al. (2001)
- Hirsh (1999)
- Lykke (2004)
- Lykke (2001)
- Kelly and Belkin (2004)
- Saracevic and Kantor (1988a)
- Saracevic and Kantor (1988b)
- Vakkari (2001)
- Vakkari and Hakala (2000)
- Wang et al. (2000)
- Wang (1997)

Relevance and Performance Measures Issues in Interactive IR

- Barry and Schamber (1998)
- Borlund (2003a)
- Cosijn and Ingwersen (2000)
- Czerwinski et al. (2001)
- Frokjaer et al. (2000)
- Hornbaek (2006)
- Kekäläinen (2005)
- Kekäläinen and Järvelin (2002b)
- Käki (2004)
- Järvelin and Kekäläinen (2002)
- Järvelin and Kekäläinen (2000)
- Larsen and Tombros (2006)
- Lun (2001)
- Nielsen (2003)
- Salojärvi et al. (2003)
- Sanderson and Zobel (2005)
- Spink et al. (1998)
- Vakkari and Sormunen (2004)
- Voorhees (1998)

Chapter 5
Aggregated Search

Mounia Lalmas

Abstract To support broad queries or ambiguous information needs, providing diverse search results to users has become increasingly necessary. Aggregated search attempts to achieve diversity by presenting search results from different information sources, so-called verticals (image, video, blog, news, etc.), in addition to the standard web results, on one result page. This comes in contrast with the common search paradigm, where users are provided with a list of information sources, which they have to examine in turn to find relevant content. All major search engines are now performing some levels of aggregated search. This chapter provides an overview of the current developments in aggregated search.

5.1 Introduction

A main goal of a web search engine is to display links to relevant web pages for each issued user query. In recent years, search engines have extended their services to include search, so-called *vertical search*, on specialized collections of documents, so-called *verticals*, focused on specific domains (e.g., news, travel, shopping) or media/genre types (e.g., image, video, blog). Users believing that relevant content exists in a vertical may submit their queries directly to a vertical search engine. Users unaware of a relevant vertical, or simply not wishing or willing to search a specific vertical, would submit their queries directly to the "general" web search engine. However, even when doing so, users who type certain queries, for instance, "red cars", may actually be interested in seeing images of red cars even if they did not submit this query to an image vertical search. To address this, search engines include, when appropriate, results from relevant vertical within the "standard" web results. This is referred to as *aggregated search* and has now been implemented by major search engines.

Aggregated search addresses the task of searching and assembling information from a variety of information sources on the Web (i.e., the verticals) and placing it in a single interface. There are differences between "standard" web search and

M. Lalmas (✉)
Yahoo! Research, Diagonal 177, p9, 08018 Barcelona, Spain
e-mail: mounia@acm.org

M. Melucci, R. Baeza-Yates (eds.), *Advanced Topics in Information Retrieval*,
The Information Retrieval Series 33,
DOI 10.1007/978-3-642-20946-8_5, © Springer-Verlag Berlin Heidelberg 2011

aggregated search.[1] With the former, documents of the same nature are compared (e.g., web pages or images) and ranked according to their estimated relevance to the query. With the latter, documents of a different nature are compared (e.g., web pages against images) and their relevance estimated with respect to each other. These heterogeneous information items have different features, and therefore cannot be ranked using the same algorithms. Also, for some queries (e.g., "red car"), it may make more sense to return, in addition to standard web results, documents from one vertical (e.g., image vertical) than from another (e.g., news vertical). In other words, the relevance of verticals differ with queries. The main challenge in aggregated search is how to identify and integrate relevant heterogeneous results for each given query into a single result page.

Aggregated search has three main components: (1) *vertical representation*, concerned with how to represent verticals so that the documents contained within and their type are identifiable, (2) *vertical selection*, concerned with how to select the verticals from which relevant documents can be retrieved, and (3) *result presentation*, concerned with how to assemble results from selected verticals so as to best layout the result page with the most relevant information. These components are described in Sects. 5.3, 5.4 and 5.5, respectively. We also provide some background about aggregated search and related paradigms in Sect. 5.2, and discuss evaluation of aggregated search in Sect. 5.6. This chapter finishes with some conclusions.

5.2 Background and Motivation

Aggregated search seeks relevant content across heterogenous information sources, the verticals. Searching diverse information sources is not new. Federated search (also referred to as distributed information retrieval (Callan 2000)) and metasearch are techniques that aim to search and provide results from various sources.

In federated search, a user submits a query, and then may select a number of sources, referred to as resources, to search. These resources are often standalone systems (e.g., corporate intranets, fee-based databases, library catalogs, internet resources, user-specific digital storage). The federated search system, when not explicitly stated by the user, has to identify the most relevant resources (those with the highest number of relevant documents) to search given a query (resource selection). It then sends the query to those (one or several) selected resources. These resources return results for that query to the federated search system, which then decides which and how many results to retain. These selected results are presented to the user. The results are often returned merged within one single ranked list, but can also be separated, for example, grouped per resource where they originate. In some cases, resources may return duplicate results, which should be removed. Examples

---

[1] Although now standard web search is mostly aggregated search. Standard here refers to the pre-aggregated search era.

of federated search systems include Funnelback,[2] Westlaw,[3] FedStats.[4] We refer the reader to (Shokouhi and Si 2011) for an extensive survey on federated search and the Federated Search Blog at http://federatedsearchblog.com/ for latest developments in the federated search industry.

Bringing federated search to the Web led to two different paradigms, metasearch and aggregated search (Shokouhi and Si 2011). A metasearch engine is a search engine that queries several different search engines, and combine results from them or display them separately. A metasearch engine operates on the premise that the Web is too large for any one search engine to index, and that more comprehensive search results can be obtained by combining results from several search engines. This also saves the user from having to use multiple search engines separately. Metasearch engines were more popular 10–15 years ago as now the partial coverage of the web space seems less of an issue with current major search engines (Google, Yahoo!, Bing[5]) compared to earlier ones (Altavista, Lycos, etc.). In addition, unless some agreements are in place, current search engines usually do not provide unlimited access of their search results to third party applications, such as a metasearch engine, because of incurred traffic loads and business models. Examples of existing metasearch engines include Dogpile,[6] Metacrawler,[7] and Search.Com.[8]

An aggregated search system also provides information from different sources. However, in aggregated search, the information sources are powered by dedicated vertical search engines, all mostly within the remit of the general web search engine, and not several and independent search engines, as is the case with metasearch. In addition, the individual information sources in aggregated search retrieve from very different collections of documents (e.g., images, videos, news). A typical example of an aggregated search system is shown in Fig. 5.1. Here is the result page for the query "world cup" issued just after the final world cup football game in July 2010 to Google. We can see a mixture of structured data (editorial content), news, homepage, wikipedia, real-time results, videos and tweets.

The idea of aggregated search was explicitly introduced as universal search in 2007 by Google:[9]

> "[...] search across all its content sources, compare and rank all the information in real time, and deliver a single, integrated set of search results [...] will incorporate information from a variety of previously separate sources including videos, images, news, maps, books, and websites—into a single set of results."

---

[2] See http://www.funnelback.com/.

[3] See http://www.westlaw.co.uk/.

[4] See http://www.fedstats.gov/.

[5] Note that since August 2010, Yahoo! search engine is powered by Bing.

[6] See http://www.dogpile.com/.

[7] See http://www.metacrawler.com/.

[8] See http://www.search.com/.

[9] See http://www.google.com/intl/en/press/pressrel/universalsearch_20070516.html.

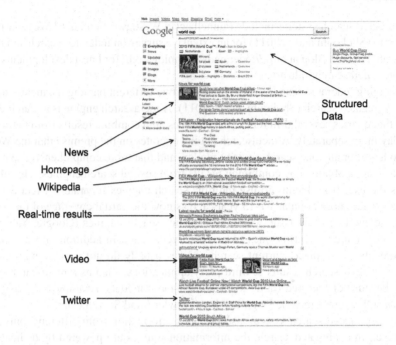

Fig. 5.1 Example of aggregated search (blended design)—Google

The goal behind aggregated search is to remedy the fact, that overall, vertical search is not prevalently used by users. Indeed, JupiterResearch (iProspect 2008) carried out a survey in 2007–2008 that indicates that 35% of users do not use vertical search. This does not mean that users do not have queries with one or more vertical intents. The fact that queries can be answered from various verticals was shown, for instance, in (Arguello et al. 2009), who looked at 25,195 unique queries obtained from a commercial search engine query log. Human editors were instructed to assign between zero and six relevant verticals per query based on their best guess of the user vertical intent. About 26% of queries, mostly navigational, were assigned no relevant vertical and 44% were assigned a single relevant vertical. The rest of the queries were assigned multiple relevant verticals, as they were ambiguous in terms of vertical intent (e.g., the query "hairspray" was assigned the verticals movies, video, and shopping (Arguello et al. 2009)). Query logs from a different commercial search engine analysed in (Liu et al. 2009b) showed that 12.3% of the queries have an image search intent, 8.5% have a video search intent and so on (the total number of analysed queries was 2,153). Similar observations were reached by Sushmita et al. (2010a), who analysed query log click-through in terms of vertical intents. Thus, a vertical search intent is often present within web search queries.

Within one year of major search engines providing users with aggregated search results, a greater percentage of users clicked on vertical search result types within the general search results, compared to when the verticals were searched directly (iProspect 2008). For example, news results were the most clicked vertical results within aggregated search, and users click them more than twice as much within aggregated search than they do when they use the vertical news search directly. More recent statistics showing similar trends can be found in a ComScore report (Goodman and Feldblum 2010). Thus, despite users limited use of vertical search engines, it is important for search engines to ensure that their relevant vertical contents are being shown.

5.3 Vertical Representation

To select the relevant vertical(s) for each submitted query (described in Sect. 5.4), an aggregated search engine needs to know about the content of each vertical (e.g., term statistics, size, etc.). This is to ensure that, for example, the query "tennis" is passed to a sport vertical, whereas the query "Madonna" is sent to a music vertical and eventually a celebrity vertical. For this purpose, the aggregated search system keeps a representation of each of its verticals.

Vertical representation can be compared to resource representation in federated search, in which a number of techniques have been proposed (Shokouhi and Si 2011). In federated search, a resource representation can be generated manually by providing a short description of the documents contained in that resource, e.g., (Gravano et al. 1997). However, these representations are likely to be brief, thus providing only a limited coverage of the documents contained in the resource, and more importantly, quickly become stale for dynamic resources, where new documents are often added, and in large number. In practice, automatically generated representations are more common.

In aggregated search, various statistics about the documents (e.g., term frequency, vertical size) contained in the vertical are available—for those verticals operated by the same body—and are used to generate the vertical representation. Therefore, a vertical representation can be built using techniques from federated search working with cooperative resources.[10] A technique reported in the literature is the generation of vertical representations from a subset of documents, so-called sampled documents. Two main sampling approaches have been reported in the literature (Arguello et al. 2009), one where the documents are sampled directly from the vertical, and another using external resources.

To directly sample from a vertical, query-based sampling is used. In the context of federated search (Callan and Connell 2001), this works as follows. An initial query is used to retrieve documents from the resource, which are then used to generate an initial representation of the resource (or update the current representation if the aim is to refresh the representation to account for newly added documents). Then, a so-called new sampling query is selected from the representation. As documents are retrieved for each sampling query, the evolving resource representation

---

[10]The resources provide to the federated search system comprehensive statistics about their documents (e.g., term frequency, size).

and sampling queries are derived from the retrieved documents. It was, however, shown (Shokouhi et al. 2007) that better performance were obtained when high-frequency queries were used for sampling the documents, than when derived from the sampled documents themselves. Similarly, in the context of aggregated search, high-frequency queries, extracted from vertical query logs, have been used for sampling documents (Arguello et al. 2009). Indeed, queries issued directly to a vertical represent explicit vertical intent, and therefore constitute good candidates to sample documents for that vertical.

Although initially introduced to deal with un-cooperative resources, and even though that (most) verticals can be viewed as cooperative resources, the sampling approach is particularly appropriate for aggregated search. Indeed, using high-frequency vertical queries leads to sampled documents that are biased towards those that are more likely to be useful to users, and thus more likely to be seen by these users (Arguello et al. 2009). This is important because it is likely that a significant part of the vertical is of no interest to users, and thus should not be represented. In addition, using high-frequency vertical queries on a regular basis (how regularly depends on the vertical), is a way to ensure that vertical representations are up-to-date, in particular for verticals with a highly dynamic content, such as news. For this type of verticals, users are mostly interested in the most recent content.

An alternative, or in addition to sampling directly from the verticals, is to sample documents from external sources, if documents can be mapped to verticals. This approach was investigated in (Arguello et al. 2009) who sampled documents from Wikipedia, making use of Wikipedia categories (one or several) assigned to documents to map documents to verticals. For instance, a sample of documents representative of the "car" vertical can be gathered from documents assigned a Wikipedia category containing any of the terms "auto", "automobile", "car", and "vehicle". Wikipedia is rich in text, so sampling from it can help in providing better representations of text-impoverished verticals such as image and video verticals. In addition, Wikipedia articles have a consistent format, are semantically coherent and on topic. This means that a better coverage of the vertical content can be achieved, as well as a more uniform representation across verticals. The latter can also make comparing rankings across verticals easier.

Overall, using high-frequency vertical queries to sample the vertical directly, together with sampling from external sources such as Wikipedia, can ensure that the most relevant and recent vertical content can be retrieved (popular and/or peak queries), while still providing a good coverage of the vertical content (useful for tail queries), and that text-impoverished verticals can be properly represented (image and video verticals).

5.4 Vertical Selection

Vertical selection is the task of selecting the relevant verticals (none, one or several) in response to a user query. Vertical selection is related to resource selection in federated search, where the most common approach is to rank resources based on the similarity between the query and the resource representation. Some approaches (Callan et al. 1995a; Si et al. 2002b) treat resources, i.e. their representations, as "large documents" and adapt ranking functions from IR to score resources. More effective techniques, such as ReDDE (Si and Callan 2003), consider the distribution of relevant documents across resources to score them.

Vertical selection also makes use of the vertical representations, in a way similar to federated search, but has access to additional sources of evidence. Indeed, verticals focus on specific types of documents (in terms of domain, media, or genre). Users searching for a particular type of document (e.g., "images of red cars") may issue domain/genre/media specific words in the query (e.g., "picture"). The query string therefore constitutes a source of evidence for vertical selection. Second, vertical search engines are being used explicitly by users, so associated query logs may be available, which can be exploited for vertical selection. These two sources of evidence can be used to provide directly to the aggregated search engine a so-called "vertical relevance value", by the vertical search engine, reflecting how relevant the vertical content might be to the query.

How these two sources of evidence, and the vertical representations, are used to select verticals has been reported in a series of papers (Arguello et al. 2009; Diaz and Arguello 2009; Arguello et al. 2010). Machine learning techniques are used to build models of verticals based on features extracted from vertical representations, query strings and vertical query logs. More precisely (Arguello et al. 2009), features from the vertical representations include vertical ranking scores such as those produced by ReDDE in federated search (Si and Callan 2003). Features for the query string features were based on rules triggered by word occurrences in the query. These rules mapped words to verticals (e.g., "car" to the autos vertical). Geographical words were also used; for example, queries with the words "continent", "country", "county", "point of interest" were mapped to verticals related to local, travel and maps. Finally, features for the vertical query logs correspond to the query likelihood built from a unigram language model constructed from the vertical query logs.

The findings showed that ranking verticals by the query likelihood estimated from the vertical query log language model was the best single-evidence to select a vertical. It was also shown that using rules mapping query strings to verticals led to significant improvement in vertical selection. This is particularly useful in situations where no training data is available for a vertical. With respect to the latter, research reported in (Arguello et al. 2010) looked at how models learned for a vertical with training data could be "ported" to other verticals for which there is no training data. The technique of machine adaptation, from machine learning, was employed, which consists of using training data from one or more source domains to learn a predictive model for a target domain, typically associated with little or no training data.

5.5 Result Presentation

For a large percentage of queries, relevant results mostly come from the conventional Web. However, for an increasing number of queries, results from other sources (verticals) are relevant, and thus should be added to the standard web re-sults. Research reported in (Diaz 2009) showed the positive effect (in relevance ranking) of properly integrating news within web results, and Sushmita et al. (2009) demonstrated through a user study the effectiveness of aggregated search for non-navigational queries. Thus, in aggregated search, a main challenge is to identify the best positions to place items retrieved from relevant verticals on the result page to e.g., maximizing click-through rate.

There are two main types of result page design in aggregated search, one where results from the different verticals are blended into a single list, referred to as *blended*, and another, where results from each vertical are presented in a separate panel, referred to as *non-blended*.

A blended integration as applied by Google universal search and many other search engines presents results from the different verticals within a single ranked list. It should be pointed out that blending is not the same as inter-leaving. In the blended design of aggregated search, results from the same vertical are usually "slot-ted" together in the ranking, as can been seen in Fig. 5.1. The blended design seems the most common way to present results in aggregated search.

With the blended design, relevance remains the main ranking criteria within ver-ticals and across verticals. Results from the same vertical are slotted together (e.g., 4 news, 6 images, etc., each ranked with respect to their estimated relevance to the query), but the entire slot is ranked with respect to other slots, including standard web search results. Other ranking criteria may be used, for example, newsworthiness for results coming from a news vertical. For example, in our example in Fig. 5.1, the newsworthiness of the query "world cup" just after the final game in July 2010 was very high, and as such, news were placed towards the top of the result page (in addition to editorial content). Today, submitting the same query to Google returns a completely different result page (the top result is the official FIFA site).

Two approaches for blended aggregated search have been reported in the litera-ture. In (Liu et al. 2009a), using machine learning techniques, probabilities such as a document in a vertical being relevant, a vertical being relevant, etc., to a query, were estimated, and used in a probabilistic model. The resulting probabilistic document scores were used to rank all documents, from the standard web and vertical results, into one single list. Although an increase in performance is observed, the quality of the blended search results is not really evaluated. Indeed, it is not clear whether the returned results are optimal in terms of aggregated search (i.e. the right combination of web search results and vertical results, and at the right position). It should also be added that results were inter-leaved (as given by the calculated probabilistic scores), and not blended as above described.

A recent work (Ponnuswami et al. 2011) investigates blended aggregated search, where the relationship between results from the web and verticals is accounted for. The focus of their work is that given multiple already known to be relevant verticals, how to place results from them relative to web results. Machine learning techniques are used on training data based on elicited pairwise preferences between groups of results, i.e. a group of standard web results and a group of vertical results. When ranking, what is being compared is a group of web results and a group of vertical

http://au.alpha.yahoo.com

Fig. 5.2 Example of aggregated search (non-blended design)—Yahoo! Alpha

results. For the final composition of the blended result page, a group of vertical results is placed at a slot if the score is higher than some threshold employed to guarantee specific coverage for verticals at each slot. Features used include query log-based features, vertical-based features (provided by the vertical partner), and query string-based features. They show that using pairwise preferences judgements for training increases user interaction with results. This the first work publishing detailed account on how blended result pages are composed.

The non-blended integration presents results from each vertical in a separate panel. In search engine terminology, the panel is also referred to as a "tile". Alpha Yahoo![11] shown in Fig. 5.2 is an example of such a design. Other examples include Kosmix,[12] Naver[13] and the discontinued Google Searchmash.[14] Whenever a minimal amount of results from a vertical is available for a query, the various corresponding panels are filled and displayed. The main web search results are usually displayed on the left side and within the largest panel, conveying to users that most results still come from the general Web. There is no relationships between results from the different panels. The placement of the various panels is also mostly predefined.

---

[11] See http://au.alpha.yahoo.com/.

[12] See http://www.kosmix.com/.

[13] See http://www.naver.com/.

[14] See http://techcrunch.com/2008/11/24/why-did-google-discontinue-searchmash/.

Fig. 5.3 Eye-tracking study comparing Google universal search to "standard" search—Taken from Hotchkiss (2007)

Although a large number of studies devoted to the design and evaluation of conventional web search interfaces have been reported in the literature, less is known about aggregated search interfaces, apart for maybe three studies, two eye-tracking and one within-subject task-based experiments.

An eye-tracking experiment on Google Universal search soon after its launch has been reported (Hotchkiss 2007). Screenshots of the eye-tracking outcomes (users visual attention on the result page) are shown in Figs. 5.3 and 5.4, where the main difference is the addition of image results (thumbnails) in the result page. In the pre-aggregated search interface (right screenshot of Fig. 5.3), the common trend is to start in the upper left corner (indicated by A) and to scan results from there, first vertically (the down arrow) and then across—likely when a title catches the user attention. A distinct pattern is observed with the aggregated search interface (left screenshot of Fig. 5.3). While there is still some scanning in the very upper left (B), the scanning does not start there, but from around the image results (C). Scanning seems to be predominantly to the side and below of the thumbnail (D). Furthermore, the F pattern (Nielsen 2009) for scanning results in conventional web interface seems to change to an E pattern in an aggregated interface (Fig. 5.4).

However, another eye-tracking study reported by Google (Aula and Rodden 2009) observed that, returning results from verticals blended within typical web

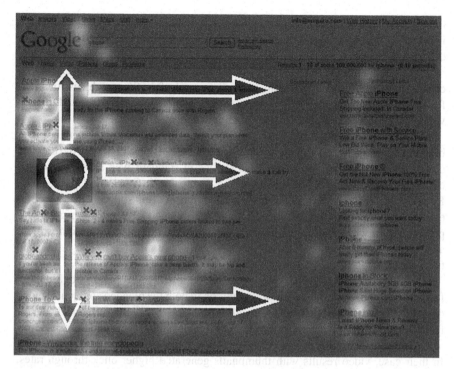

Fig. 5.4 Google universal search eye-tracking study: E scanning pattern—Taken from Hotchkiss (2007)

search results did not affect the order of scanning the results, neither did it disrupt the information seeking process of users. This study was carried in 2009 where users by then would have become more familiar with being returned results from verticals.

These studies provide insight into how users view results in an aggregated search interface. There is some understanding on where on the result page the user looks at or gives attention to, and where the user starts viewing results from verticals. However, whether and how results are presented affects user behavior (e.g., click-through rate, task completion, etc.) was not discussed in these studies, and to our knowledge, nothing has been reported about this in the literature. Therefore, to provide some insight into the latter, we carried out two within-subject task-based user studies (Sushmita et al. 2010b), one using a blended design and another using a non-blended design. Our objective was to investigate the impact of factors on user click-through behavior on these two types of aggregated search interface. The factors studied included position of search results, vertical types, and the strength of search task orientation towards a particular vertical.

Studies (e.g., log analysis and eye-tracking experiments) which look at the effect of result position in the context of conventional web search, are not new. For instance, Guan and Cutrell (2007) showed that when results were placed relatively low in the result page, people spent more time searching and were less successful in their search task. Similar behavior is likely to be observed with aggregated search interfaces. This has motivated us to investigate the position effect across results from different verticals.

Although, compared to in-house investigations carried out by commercial search engine companies, our experiment is small (a total of 1,296 search sessions performed by 48 participants were analysed, and 3 verticals were considered, image, video and news), we obtained interesting findings.

Our first finding is that the factors that affect user click-through behavior differ between the blended and non-blended designs. Behaviors observed with the blended design echoed the findings of previous studies in standard web search interfaces e.g., (Joachims et al. 2005b; Agichtein and Zheng 2006; Guan and Cutrell 2007; Keane et al. 2008), but not in the non-blended design. This suggests that a careful estimation of the relevance of verticals is needed when the blended design is employed. When we cannot measure their relevance, the non-blended design is more appropriate since users click-through behavior was not affected by the position in this type of aggregation.

The second finding is that videos resulted in a different click-through pattern from news and images. This trend was common in both the blended and non-blended designs. This suggests that, when deciding to retrieve videos, different behavior from other verticals may be observed. A different pattern with video results was also observed in (Goodman and Feldblum 2010), compared to standard web results. In their case, video results with thumbnails generated higher click-through rates, across all positions, and especially helped results in lower positions. More generally, the above suggests that click-through behavior can be different across verticals, and this should be accounted for by aggregated search systems.

The third finding was that a search task orientation towards a particular vertical can affect click-through behavior. This trend was common to both the blended and non-blended designs. Traditional information retrieval research has been focused on the modeling of thematic (or topical) relevance of documents. However, research in other areas has demonstrated that relevance can be multidimensional (Cosijn and Ingwersen 2000), e.g., in XML retrieval (Lalmas and Tombros 2007) and geographic information retrieval (Purves and Chris 2004). In a similar way, experiments on aggregated search should control the level of orientation towards a particular vertical, as this is an important factor to investigate, not only with respect to algorithms (e.g., vertical selection), but also result presentation. Ultimately, developing interaction design that can help aggregated search systems capture a user vertical preference of an information need would be welcome.

5.6 Evaluation

IR has a long evaluation history (Cleverdon 1991). Advances in IR research (in terms of effectiveness) have mostly been made through experimental evaluation on test collections. A test collection is created to allow experimentation with respect to a retrieval scenario (e.g., blog retrieval, XML retrieval). Given that scenario, a collection of items that are representative for this scenario is collected. Then, a set of topics is developed, reflecting information needs typical of the scenario. These topics are created by humans, who, when possible, are domain experts. Finally, using a pooling technique, a subset of items (the "pool" containing the items that are most likely to be relevant) is judged by humans to whom various incentives are given (e.g., monetary or access to data), and who, when possible, are the creators of the topics. The TREC evaluation initiative from NIST (Voorhees and Harman 2005) has been a major player in IR evaluation, and its methodology has been adopted by many other initiatives, such as CLEF (2010), INEX (Lalmas and Tombros 2007), and NTCIR (2010), to name a few.

The most time-consuming part of generating a test collection is the creation of relevance judgments. Indeed, for every topic, a large number of items (even though a "pool" is used) must be judged. Although methods to alleviate this problems have been proposed (e.g., formally selecting a subset of the most promising items to be judged (Carterette et al. 2006) or using crowd-sourcing techniques (Alonso et al. 2008)) judging a set of items (e.g., documents), and in particular, heterogeneous documents from a variety of sources, remains an extremely tedious task. Constructing such a test collection from scratch is very time-consuming. For example, INEX ran a heterogenous track (Frommholz and Larson 2007), that never really flourished due to the required effort of having to create topics with relevant documents across multiple heterogeneous XML repositories and the laborious task of providing relevance assessments for the topics.

A test collection for aggregated search requires verticals, each populated by items of that vertical type, a set of topics expressing information needs relating to one or more verticals, and relevance assessments, indicating the relevance of the items and their associated verticals to each topic. Although work on aggregated search has been conducted and experimental results reported (e.g., vertical selection (Arguello et al. 2009), result presentation (Ponnuswami et al. 2011)), no large-scale test collection for aggregated search is available.

Evaluation of aggregated search in terms of effectiveness so far reported in the literature has focused on vertical selection accuracy (Arguello et al. 2009), but also on the quality of the blended search results (Liu et al. 2009a; Ponnuswami et al. 2011). The data sets, aka the test collections, used for the evaluation are those typical to commercial search engines. They include a mixture of editorial data (e.g., labelers judged the relevance between queries and verticals, or pairwise preferences between groups of results), and behavioral data (e.g., query logs inferred from click data). Nonetheless these data sets are not widely accessible.

Following the spirit of TREC and similar initiatives, we recently proposed a methodology to build a test collection for aggregated search (Zhou et al. 2010). Our methodology makes use of existing test collections available from TREC, CLEF and INEX, where a vertical is simulated by one, part of, or several existing test collections. Reusing existing test collections to build new ones is not new. Indeed, because current test collections (e.g., ClueWeb, see (Callan 2009)) have become extremely large to reflect the much larger amount of information in many of today's retrieval scenarios, the idea of reusing test collections is very appealing. For example, Clarke et al. (2008) reused an existing Q&A test collection to generate a test collection to investigate diversity in IR, and Carterette et al. (2010a) developed means to quantify the reusability of a test collection for evaluating a different retrieval scenario than that originally built for. In federated search, test collections (e.g., trec4-kmeans (Si and Callan 2003)) have also been developed using existing test collections by partitioning different text-based TREC corpora into a number of sub-collections. However, these test collections cannot be applied to aggregated search as all sub-collections are of the same type. The main difference between these types of (federated vs. aggregated) search is the heterogeneous natures of the items, as each vertical comprises of items of a particular genre, domain, and/or media.

As stated earlier there are three parts to a test collection, the collection of items, the topics and the relevance assessments. Our first step was to decide which existing (or part) test collections could be used to simulate verticals. We used, for example, ImageCLEF to simulate an image vertical, INEX Wikipedia to simulate a wiki vertical, TREC blog to simulate a blog vertical, etc. We also used Clueweb09; however as this collection is made of text-based documents of different genres, we employed a classifier to assign documents to verticals related to genre (e.g., news, references). In total, we obtained a total of 80 million documents, with ten simulated verticals. General web documents were prevalent, thus mimicking aggregated search scenarios.

We selected topics (from all available topics coming from the used test collections) that we believed would reflect concrete search scenarios in aggregated search, i.e. topics for which only "general web" documents are relevant, and those for which documents from more than one vertical are relevant. For the former, we randomly chose web topics from e.g., Clueweb09, submitted their titles to a search engine, and retained only those that returned only standard web results. For the latter, various strategies were applied, depending on whether topics "co-exist" in several test collections, or topics for which relevant documents of different genres exist (e.g., all of which come from Clueweb09). At the end, 150 topics were collected, 67% with two vertical intents (i.e. contain relevant documents in two verticals) and 4% with three or more vertical intents. These statistics compare to those in (Arguello et al. 2009), coming from editorial data.

The relevance assessments were simply those coming from the chosen collections and selected topics. One main drawback with this approach, however, is that of incomplete relevance assessments with respect to a whole (simulated) vertical. Indeed, it can happen that a topic coming from test collection A is not a topic of a second test collection B, but B may actually contain documents relevant to that topic, where A and B have been used to simulate two different verticals. Initial experiments showed that this did not have too strong adversarial affect, but providing additional relevance assessments may be required. Nonetheless, performing these additional assessments remains less costly compared to building a test collection for aggregated search from scratch.

When evaluating retrieval effectiveness using a test collection, metrics are employed (e.g., precision/recall and variants of them). In the standard scenario, a ranked list of results is returned for each topic forming the test collection used for the evaluation. These rankings are individually evaluated using the metrics, and some average effectiveness value across topics is calculated afterwards (e.g., MAP). The returned items are usually considered separately, but not always, e.g., in XML retrieval (Kazai et al. 2004), and the earlier TREC web track (Hawking et al. 1999). In aggregated search, simply looking at the results individually is definitively not sufficient. For example, relations between the retrieved items may be important to deliver better rankings (as shown in Ponnuswami et al. 2011); this goes beyond relevance. Indeed, sometimes some items have to be shown before others even if less relevant (e.g., because of chronological order), or should be grouped together (similar content, similar type of content, alternative, A is a picture of B, etc.). Devising metrics that consider these relationships when evaluating retrieval effectiveness is challenging.

Finally, there has been a recent increased interest toward the notion of result diversification not only in web search, e.g., (Clarke et al. 2009), but also e.g., geographical (Tang and Sanderson 2010) and image search (Sanderson et al. 2009). Diversification is believed to maximize the likelihood for ambiguous queries returning at least one relevant result, while also showing the multiple aspects of queries. Although web search queries may often hide vertical intents, the impact of diversity, in the context of aggregated search, i.e. returning results from several verticals (vertical diversity) remains to be explicitly assessed.

5.7 Conclusions

For a large percentage of queries, relevant results mostly come from the conventional Web. However, for an increasing number of queries, results from other sources, the so-called verticals, are relevant, and thus should be added to the standard web results. Aggregated search aims to facilitate the access to the increasingly diverse content available from the verticals. It does so by searching and assembling relevant documents from a variety of verticals and placing them into a single result page, together with standard web search results. The goal is to best layout the result page with the most relevant information from the conventional web and verticals. Most current search engines perform some level of aggregated search. We have surveyed the state of the art in aggregated search. We expect this to be a rich and fertile research area for many years to come.

Acknowledgements   This chapter was written when Mounia Lalmas was a Microsoft Research/RAEng Research Professor of Information Retrieval at the University of Glasgow. Her work on aggregated search was carried out in the context of a project partly funded by a Yahoo! Research Alliance Gift. This chapter is inspired by a tutorial "From federated search to aggregated search" presented at the 33rd ACM SIGIR Conference on Research and Development in Information Retrieval, 19–23 July 2010, Geneva, Switzerland (Diaz et al. 2010). Special thanks go to Ke (Adam) Zhou and Ronnan Cummins for their feedbacks on earlier versions of this paper.

Chapter 6
Quantum Mechanics and Information Retrieval

Massimo Melucci and Keith van Rijsbergen

Abstract This chapter aims at providing a survey of the body of scientific literature relevant to Quantum Mechanics (QM) and Information Retrieval (IR). The survey is illustrated with a common notation to fully grasp the contribution of each paper. In particular, the probability aspects of IR and those of QM are emphasized because probability is one of the most important topics of both disciplines.

6.1 Introduction

The Geometry of Information Retrieval by van Rijsbergen (2004) introduced a formalism based on the Hilbert spaces for representing the Information Retrieval (IR) models within a uniform framework. As the Hilbert spaces have been used for formalizing Quantum Mechanics (QM), the book has also suggested the hypothesis that quantum phenomena have their analogues in IR.

Since the publication of van Rijsbergen (2004), a number of IR researchers have investigated the quantum phenomena and their analogues in IR, thus producing a body of scientific literature published in journals or conference proceedings and scientific initiatives such as the Quantum Interaction symposia, the UK-based EPSRC "Renaissance" project, or the European Union VII Framework Programme Marie Curie International Staff Exchange Scheme project called "QONTEXT".

This chapter aims at providing a survey of the body of scientific literature relevant to QM and IR. The survey is illustrated with a common notation to fully grasp the contribution of each paper. In particular, the probability aspects of IR and those of QM are emphasized because probability is one of the most important topics of both disciplines.

M. Melucci (✉)
Department of Information Engineering, University of Padua, Via G. Gradenigo, 6,
35131 Padova, Italy
e-mail: massimo.melucci@unipd.it

K. van Rijsbergen
Computer Laboratory, University of Cambridge, 14 Park Parade, Cambridge CB5 8AL, England
e-mail: keith@dcs.gla.ac.uk

M. Melucci, R. Baeza-Yates (eds.), *Advanced Topics in Information Retrieval*,   125
The Information Retrieval Series 33,
DOI 10.1007/978-3-642-20946-8_6, © Springer-Verlag Berlin Heidelberg 2011

To this end, Sect. 6.2 introduces the probability used in IR through the quantum formalism, Sect. 6.3 briefly explains some specific concepts of QM and Sect. 6.4 illustrates how the QM concepts have been exploited in IR or related disciplines.[1]

6.2 Another View of Probability

Sooner or later, many IR researchers have faced the problem of defining event sets, estimating probabilities and making predictions. For this reason, our starting point is probability and, in particular, a special view of probability distributions. This view applies to the theory obeying Kolmogorov's axiom, but it also helps introduce quantum probability, which is a non-classical theory, in the remainder of this chapter.

Let's recall some basic notions. A probability space is a set of mutually exclusive events such that each event is assigned a probability between 0 and 1 and the sum of the probabilities over the set of events is 1. The case of binary event sets (e.g., 0 and 1) is very common in IR: term occurrence and binary relevance are two famous examples. When the event set is the product of two binary sets, there are four possible events (e.g., 00, 01, 10, 11 where the first bit refers to the first event set and the second bit refers to the second event set). In general, the product of n binary sets is an event set of size 2^n. The mapping between the probabilities and the events is called a probability distribution.

To understand the relationship between classical probability and quantum probability, it is useful to represent the probability space in an algebraic form. The book by van Rijsbergen (2004) suggests that the Hilbert spaces can provide this algebraic form, that is, probability spaces can be represented as vectors, matrices and operators between them. The *density matrix* (or density operator), that is, a Hermitian matrix with trace 1 which encapsulates a probability space, is the key notion. In QM, a density operator represents the state of a system. However, note that "system" does not necessarily correspond to what it is meant in IR—it is rather a microscopic system, such as a particle, a photon, etc., that is, something for, which the structure is unknown and, on which one can only make measurements to obtain some information. These measurements are subject to errors and interferences between the system and the measurement apparatus. This is the reason why the density matrix is an implementation of the state of a system. In QM, "density operator" is preferred to "density matrix". In this chapter, for the sake of clarity, "matrix" is used instead under the assumption that, for a fixed basis, the matrices are isomorphic to the operators.

Let's explain how probability spaces are defined in terms of density matrices (a condensed illustration of the following and other notions are in Rieffel 2007). Suppose that there are two events. The probability distribution can be arranged along the diagonal of a two-dimensional matrix—the other matrix elements are zeros. For

---

[1] The reading of this chapter requires some knowledge of Probability and Linear Algebra.

example, the matrix corresponding to the probability distribution of two equally probable events is

$$\mu = \begin{pmatrix} \frac{1}{2} & 0 \\ 0 & \frac{1}{2} \end{pmatrix}$$

The density matrix corresponding to a classical probability distribution is always diagonal and has trace 1. A clear explanation of the matrix-based view of probability is given by Parthasarathy (1992).

A special case is the pure distribution. A distribution is pure when the probability is concentrated on a single event which is the certain event and has probability 1. For example, the matrix corresponding to a pure distribution of two events is

$$\begin{pmatrix} 1 & 0 \\ 0 & 0 \end{pmatrix}$$

The density matrix corresponding to a pure distribution is always a projector, that is, a matrix such that the product by itself is the same matrix. For example,

$$\begin{pmatrix} 1 & 0 \\ 0 & 0 \end{pmatrix} \begin{pmatrix} 1 & 0 \\ 0 & 0 \end{pmatrix} = \begin{pmatrix} 1 & 0 \\ 0 & 0 \end{pmatrix}$$

So far, how distributions are expressed in an algebraic form has been explained. While matrices represent distributions, the events correspond to vectors—vectors and matrices are defined over the complex field. There are two main instructions for defining the vectors corresponding to events:

- the vectors are mutually orthogonal in order to represent the mutual exclusiveness of the events, and
- the vectors have length 1 in order to make probability calculation consistent with probability axioms.

The Dirac notation is briefly introduced at this point and is used in this chapter. A complex vector x is represented as $|x\rangle$ and is called "ket". The conjugate transpose of x is represented as $\langle x|$ and is called "bra" (therefore, the Dirac notation is called the bra(c)ket notation). The inner product between x and y is represented as $\langle x|y\rangle$, which is a complex number. The outer product (or dyad) is $|x\rangle\langle y|$. If A is a matrix (or an operator), then $A|x\rangle$ is the vector resulting from the linear transformation represented by A. The properties have been illustrated by van Rijsbergen (2004).

The length of the vector is the norm defined as the square root of the sum of the squared vector elements. As matrices and vectors are defined in the complex field, a squared vector element is the squared modulus of a complex scalar; for example, the vectors corresponding to two mutually exclusive events may be

$$|1\rangle = \begin{pmatrix} 1 \\ 0 \end{pmatrix} \qquad |0\rangle = \begin{pmatrix} 0 \\ 1 \end{pmatrix}$$

but the following are also representing mutually exclusive events:

$$\begin{pmatrix} \frac{1}{\sqrt{2}} \\ \frac{1}{\sqrt{2}} \end{pmatrix} \quad \begin{pmatrix} \frac{1}{\sqrt{2}} \\ -\frac{1}{\sqrt{2}} \end{pmatrix}$$

The range of a linear transformation is the set of vectors assigned to the vectors of the space (i.e., it is the image of the transformation applied to the whole vector space). The *rank* of a linear transformation (i.e., a matrix) is the dimension of the range (Halmos 1987).

In QM, Hermitian (or self-adjoint) linear transformations (i.e., matrix) are crucial. A matrix is Hermitian when is equal to its conjugate transpose. Hermitian matrices are important because their eigenvalues are always real and thus represent the outcomes of a measurement.

Each vector corresponds to one and only one projector with rank one, namely, a dyad, defined as the product of the (column) vector by its conjugate transpose (i.e., the row vector). For example, the projector of the two events defined above are, respectively,

$$|1\rangle\langle 1| = \begin{pmatrix} 1 & 0 \\ 0 & 0 \end{pmatrix} \qquad |0\rangle\langle 0| = \begin{pmatrix} 0 & 0 \\ 0 & 1 \end{pmatrix}$$

A projector corresponds to a pure distribution when the event is certain. When a distribution is not pure, the spectral theorem helps find the underlying events and the related probabilities. Because of the importance of the spectral theorem, its definition is given below whereas the proof is in (Halmos 1987, p. 156).

Theorem 6.1 *To every Hermitian matrix A on a finite-dimensional complex inner product space there correspond real numbers $\alpha_1, \dots, \alpha_r$ and projectors $E_1, \dots, E_r$ so that*

- *the α_j's are pairwise distinct,*
- *the E_j are mutually orthogonal,*
- $\sum_{j=1}^{r} E_j = I$, *and*
- $\sum_{j=1}^{r} \alpha_j E_j = A$.

The spectral theorem says that any matrix corresponding to a distribution can be decomposed as a linear combination of projectors (i.e., pure distributions) where the eigenvalues are the probability values associated to the events represented by the projectors. Therefore, the eigenvalues are real, non-negative and sum to 1. For example, when the matrix corresponding to the distribution of two equally probable events is considered, the spectral theorem says that

$$\mu = \begin{pmatrix} \frac{1}{2} & 0 \\ 0 & \frac{1}{2} \end{pmatrix} = \frac{1}{2} \begin{pmatrix} 1 & 0 \\ 0 & 0 \end{pmatrix} + \frac{1}{2} \begin{pmatrix} 0 & 0 \\ 0 & 1 \end{pmatrix}$$

For this reason, one speaks of mixture or mixed distribution in contrast with pure distribution—a distribution is pure when the spectral decomposition is the distribution itself or equivalently when there is a single eigenvalue 1. When the distribution is mixed, the corresponding matrix has two or more eigenvalues (which sum to 1).

The power of the spectral theorem is that it provides a probability space starting from a density matrix (actually, a Hermitian matrix with trace 1). That is, the spectral theorem provides a distribution, which is the set of eigenvalues, and a representation of the events, which are the eigenvectors.

In classical probability, every pure distribution represented by a diagonal density matrix corresponds to a projector. However, in general, a density matrix is not necessarily diagonal, but the matrix is necessarily Hermitian (i.e., symmetric in the real field). It follows that the matrix representing a projector may not be diagonal. For example, consider the following density matrix:

$$\begin{pmatrix} \frac{1}{2} & \frac{1}{2} \\ \frac{1}{2} & \frac{1}{2} \end{pmatrix}$$

This is a projector and has trace 1. Indeed

$$\begin{pmatrix} \frac{1}{2} & \frac{1}{2} \\ \frac{1}{2} & \frac{1}{2} \end{pmatrix} = \begin{pmatrix} \frac{1}{2} & \frac{1}{2} \\ \frac{1}{2} & \frac{1}{2} \end{pmatrix}\begin{pmatrix} \frac{1}{2} & \frac{1}{2} \\ \frac{1}{2} & \frac{1}{2} \end{pmatrix}$$

Since it is a projector, it corresponds to a pure distribution. However, it is not diagonal. As this projector corresponds to a pure distribution, there is a certain event (with probability 1) and an impossible event (with probability 0, of course) corresponding to the distribution. Spectral theorem provides the representation of these two events:

$$\begin{pmatrix} \frac{1}{2} & \frac{1}{2} \\ \frac{1}{2} & \frac{1}{2} \end{pmatrix} \qquad \begin{pmatrix} \frac{1}{2} & -\frac{1}{2} \\ -\frac{1}{2} & \frac{1}{2} \end{pmatrix}$$

with eigenvalues 1 and 0, respectively. This means that the former represents the certain event and the latter the impossible event in that probability space. It follows that the density matrix is

$$\begin{pmatrix} \frac{1}{2} & \frac{1}{2} \\ \frac{1}{2} & \frac{1}{2} \end{pmatrix} = 1\begin{pmatrix} \frac{1}{2} & \frac{1}{2} \\ \frac{1}{2} & \frac{1}{2} \end{pmatrix} + 0\begin{pmatrix} \frac{1}{2} & -\frac{1}{2} \\ -\frac{1}{2} & \frac{1}{2} \end{pmatrix}$$

The extension of the algebraic form to the case of a two-dimensional event space ($n = 2$) is quite straightforward. In general, any pair of event sets can be considered. Suppose that both event sets are $\{0, 1\}$. When an event is observed from each set, there are four possibilities: 00, 01, 10, 11 where the first bit refers to the first event set and the second bit refers to the second event set. Hence, the probability distribution has four values $p_{00}, p_{01}, p_{10}, p_{11}$ arranged along the diagonal of a matrix (0 elsewhere) such that p_{ij} is the probability that the outcome from the first event set is i and that from the second event set is j. Consider, for example, two terms such that either they co-occur or do not with equal probability. The matrix corresponding to this distribution is

$$
\begin{pmatrix}
\frac{1}{2} & 0 & 0 & 0 \\
0 & 0 & 0 & 0 \\
0 & 0 & 0 & 0 \\
0 & 0 & 0 & \frac{1}{2}
\end{pmatrix}
\tag{6.1}
$$

where the top-left element (p_{00}) is the probability that neither term occurs and the bottom-right element is the probability that both terms occur (p_{11}); the probability that a term occurs and the other term does not is zero. In general, any pair of events can have the probability distribution arranged along the diagonal of (6.1). Other examples of pairs of events are: term occurrence and relevance, aboutness and relevance, document retention and term occurrence.

Suppose that the distribution of the product of two event sets is uncorrelated (i.e., the events are independent). It follows that $p_{ij} = f_i g_j$ for $i, j = 0, 1$ where f is the marginal distribution of the first event set and g is the marginal distribution of the second event set. A distribution p is uncorrelated when it can be written as a tensor product of f and g. If f and g can be written as diagonal matrices, the tensor product is

$$
\begin{pmatrix}
p_{00} & 0 & 0 & 0 \\
0 & p_{01} & 0 & 0 \\
0 & 0 & p_{10} & 0 \\
0 & 0 & 0 & p_{11}
\end{pmatrix}
=
\begin{pmatrix}
f_0 & 0 \\
0 & f_1
\end{pmatrix}
\otimes
\begin{pmatrix}
g_0 & 0 \\
0 & g_1
\end{pmatrix}
\tag{6.2}
$$

A correlated distribution cannot be written as tensor product, that is, the event sets are not independent. For example, $(\frac{1}{2}, 0, 0, \frac{1}{2})$ is correlated; indeed, both marginals are $(\frac{1}{2}, \frac{1}{2})$ and one can see that the tensor product of them is

$$
\begin{pmatrix}
\frac{1}{2} & 0 \\
0 & \frac{1}{2}
\end{pmatrix}
\otimes
\begin{pmatrix}
\frac{1}{2} & 0 \\
0 & \frac{1}{2}
\end{pmatrix}
=
\begin{pmatrix}
\frac{1}{4} & 0 & 0 & 0 \\
0 & \frac{1}{4} & 0 & 0 \\
0 & 0 & \frac{1}{4} & 0 \\
0 & 0 & 0 & \frac{1}{4}
\end{pmatrix}
\neq
\begin{pmatrix}
\frac{1}{2} & 0 & 0 & 0 \\
0 & 0 & 0 & 0 \\
0 & 0 & 0 & 0 \\
0 & 0 & 0 & \frac{1}{2}
\end{pmatrix}
$$

A bidimensional pure distribution is uncorrelated. Indeed there exists only one pair i, j such that $p_{ij} = 1$. It follows that $f_i = 1$ and $g_j = 1$ which are the only values such that $p_{ij} = f_i g_j$ for every i, j. This can be seen using tensor products, for example:

$$
\begin{pmatrix}
1 & 0 & 0 & 0 \\
0 & 0 & 0 & 0 \\
0 & 0 & 0 & 0 \\
0 & 0 & 0 & 0
\end{pmatrix}
=
\begin{pmatrix}
1 & 0 \\
0 & 0
\end{pmatrix}
\otimes
\begin{pmatrix}
1 & 0 \\
0 & 0
\end{pmatrix}
$$

When using this algebraic form to represent probability spaces, the function for computing a probability is the trace of the matrix obtained by multiplying the density matrix by the projector corresponding to the event. The usual notation for the probability of the event represented by projector E when the distribution is represented by density matrix ρ is

$$\text{tr}(\rho E) \tag{6.3}$$

For example, when $\rho = \mu$

$$\mu = \begin{pmatrix} \frac{1}{2} & 0 \\ 0 & \frac{1}{2} \end{pmatrix} \qquad E = \begin{pmatrix} 1 & 0 \\ 0 & 0 \end{pmatrix}$$

the probability is

$$\text{tr}(\mu E) = \frac{1}{2}$$

When the dyad $|x\rangle\langle x|$ is considered, the trace-based probability function can be written as

$$\text{tr}(\rho X) = \langle x|\rho|x\rangle$$

When ρ is a rank-one projector $|y\rangle\langle y|$, then

$$\text{tr}(\rho X) = |\langle x|y\rangle|^2$$

From the example, it may be odd to have to define a function that computes the probability of an event when this probability is already allocated in the diagonal of the density matrix. However, it has been shown that not all the density matrices corresponding to a distribution need to be diagonal matrices and that the diagonal elements do not necessarily correspond to probability values, although they do have to sum to 1, for example, the density matrix can be

$$\begin{pmatrix} \frac{1}{2} & \frac{1}{2} \\ \frac{1}{2} & \frac{1}{2} \end{pmatrix}$$

This means that the space of the density matrices is much larger than the space of the classical probability distribution and the trace-based function can also be applied when the density matrix is not diagonal. This also means that there exists a one-to-one correspondence between probability distributions and density matrices (Parthasarathy 1992, p. 51) and suggests that there exist more general theories of probability than the classical theory obeying Kolmogorov's axioms.

In Sect. 6.3, after introducing three key notions, it will be shown that quantum probability is one of these more general theories. It is this generality that has attracted the interest from that part of the IR community searching for a major breakthrough. This has been made possible by the fact that a density matrix encapsulates all the information about a probability space.

Why does a density matrix encapsulate all the information about a probability space? The answer is contained in Gleason's theorem whose proof is as complex as its impact—a full account is provided by Hughes (1989) and its importance in IR was pointed out by van Rijsbergen (2004).

Theorem 6.2 *To every probability distribution on the set of all projectors in a complex vector space with dimension greater than 2 there corresponds a unique density matrix ρ on the same vector space for which the probability of the event represented by a projector $|x\rangle\langle x|$ is $\mathrm{tr}(\rho|x\rangle\langle x|)$ for every unit vector x in the vector space.*

Basically, this theorem tells us that corresponding to every probability distribution is exactly one density matrix such that the probability of any event represented as a projector is calculated by the trace function. In other words, this theorem says that the density matrix is the natural way of computing a probability space when the events are represented by projectors and the distribution is represented by a matrix. The impact of this result within quantum probability is comparable to the impact within classical probability of the Bayes Theorem or the frequentist argument. Indeed, the Bayes Theorem gives a rule for updating probabilities after observing additional evidence (Kolmogorov 1956, p. 7). The frequentist argument says that if an experiment is repeated n times under certain conditions and an event occurs m times, the ratio m/n will differ very slightly from the probability of the event (Kolmogorov 1956, p. 4).

Before illustrating three key notions of quantum probability, it is useful to introduce how conditional probability deals with density matrices and projectors. Conditional probability is the probability of an event when another (or the same event) has occurred or is supposed to occur. The latter expression implies that, if an event has occurred, it is certain that it occurs again if the measurement is repeated. Conditional probability is written as $P(A|B)$ where A is the conditioned event and B is the conditioning event.

Suppose that the event $|1\rangle\langle 1|$ has occurred (for example, a relevant document has been found). It follows that the density matrix is $|1\rangle\langle 1|$, that is, it is certain that $|1\rangle\langle 1|$ has occurred. If

$$|v\rangle\langle v| = \begin{pmatrix} \frac{1}{2} & \frac{1}{2} \\ \frac{1}{2} & \frac{1}{2} \end{pmatrix}$$

represents term occurrence, where $|v\rangle = \frac{1}{\sqrt{2}}(|0\rangle + |1\rangle)$, the conditional probability that a term occurs when a document has been found is $\mathrm{tr}(|1\rangle\langle 1||v\rangle\langle v|) = \frac{1}{2}$. In general, i.e., when the conditioning event is supposed to occur, conditional probability $P(A|B)$ is implemented by Lüders' rule:

$$\frac{\mathrm{tr}(B\rho BA)}{\mathrm{tr}(\rho B)} = \mathrm{tr}(\rho'A) \quad \rho' = \frac{B\rho B}{\mathrm{tr}(\rho B)} \tag{6.4}$$

where A is the projector corresponding to the conditioned event, B is the projector corresponding to the conditioning event, ρ is the density matrix associated with the conditioning events and ρ' is the density matrix modified after the occurrence of B. For the details, see (Hughes 1989).

6.3 Three Notions of Quantum Probability

So far, an algebraic form of probability has been illustrated. Of course, this form is not required when using classical probability which can still be used in the usual way as in IR. In contrast, this algebraic form becomes very useful when quantum probability has to be introduced—indeed it has been the form adopted by those who introduced the quantum view of probability in IR.

Those who introduced the quantum view of probability in IR have supposed that at least one of three notions, i.e., superposition, interference and entanglement studied in Physics for a long time, may have their analogues in IR or can be leveraged to make a significant breakthrough at the theoretical level. In this section, these notions are briefly illustrated whereas their applications in IR or related disciplines are described in Sect. 6.4.

6.3.1 Superposition

The algebraic form used in Sect. 6.2 for representing probability spaces allows us to distinguish between superposition and mixture. An example can help understand the difference. The following matrix,

$$\mu = \begin{pmatrix} \frac{1}{2} & 0 \\ 0 & \frac{1}{2} \end{pmatrix} = \frac{1}{2}|0\rangle\langle0| + \frac{1}{2}|1\rangle\langle1| \qquad (6.5)$$

is a mixture of two projectors (i.e., pure distributions), but not a projector.

The following is a more general mixture:

$$\mu = \begin{pmatrix} |a_1|^2 & 0 \\ 0 & |a_0|^2 \end{pmatrix} = |a_0|^2|0\rangle\langle0| + |a_1|^2|1\rangle\langle1| \qquad (6.6)$$

which is a special case of a density matrix.

In contrast,

$$\rho = \begin{pmatrix} \frac{1}{2} & \frac{1}{2} \\ \frac{1}{2} & \frac{1}{2} \end{pmatrix} \qquad (6.7)$$

is a projector, but not a mixture. This is because $\rho = |v\rangle\langle v|$ where $|v\rangle$ is superposition of $|0\rangle$ and $|1\rangle$, that is,

$$|v\rangle = \frac{1}{\sqrt{2}}|0\rangle + \frac{1}{\sqrt{2}}|1\rangle \qquad (6.8)$$

The following is a more general superposition:

$$|v\rangle = a_0|0\rangle + b_0|1\rangle \quad \text{where } |v\rangle\langle v| = \begin{pmatrix} |a_1|^2 & a_1\bar{a}_0 \\ a_0\bar{a}_1 & |a_0|^2 \end{pmatrix} \tag{6.9}$$

The a_i's are called *probability amplitudes*—the relationship between probability amplitude and probability is that the latter is the square of the modulus of the former but the basic difference is that a probability amplitude is a complex number and a probability is a real number.

The mathematical difference between mixture and superposition is clear, but the conceptual difference is more subtle. To make things clearer, let's consider an example from IR. Suppose that the event $|1\rangle$ (i.e., $|1\rangle\langle 1|$) means that a document is relevant and $|0\rangle$ (i.e., $|0\rangle\langle 0|$) means that a document is not relevant. If a document is relevant half the time, a probability space will be given by (6.5).

Suppose that we wish to represent the event "it is uncertain that a document is relevant". Using a classical probability space, such an event is hard to represent because two concepts (relevance and uncertainty of relevance) are superposed in a single sentence. Actually, the probability space is already an expression of the uncertainty about the relevance of a document and the events of a classical probability space are either true or false. In contrast, QM tells us that such an event can be represented as the superposition (6.8) corresponding to the density matrix $|v\rangle\langle v|$. One can check that the probability of $|1\rangle\langle 1|$ and $|0\rangle\langle 0|$ are

$$\text{tr}(|v\rangle\langle v||1\rangle\langle 1|) = \frac{1}{2} \qquad \text{tr}(|v\rangle\langle v||0\rangle\langle 0|) = \frac{1}{2}$$

which are consistent with our expectations.[2]

Consider $|v\rangle$ and its opposite event defined as

$$|\bar{v}\rangle = \frac{1}{\sqrt{2}}|0\rangle - \frac{1}{\sqrt{2}}|1\rangle$$

or equivalently

$$|\bar{v}\rangle\langle\bar{v}| = \begin{pmatrix} \frac{1}{2} & -\frac{1}{2} \\ -\frac{1}{2} & \frac{1}{2} \end{pmatrix}$$

which is orthogonal to $|v\rangle\langle v|$. The inner product between $|v\rangle$ and $|\bar{v}\rangle$ is zero. Indeed, the classical negation operator translates into an orthogonal projector when quantum probability is used. One can check that

$$\text{tr}(|v\rangle\langle v||v\rangle\langle v|) = 1 \qquad \text{tr}(|v\rangle\langle v||\bar{v}\rangle\langle\bar{v}|) = 0$$

that is, the probability that it is uncertain that a document is relevant when this uncertainty is true, is 1. Similarly, the probability that it is certain that a document

---

[2]Note that $\text{tr}(|x\rangle\langle x||y\rangle\langle y|) = |\langle x|y\rangle|^2$, which is 1 when $x = y$.

is relevant when uncertainty is true, is 0. So far, everthing is consistent with our intuition.

Suppose, however, we want to compute the probability of the event $|1\rangle\langle 1|$ when it is certain that a document is relevant, that is, the probability distribution is provided by the pure distribution $|\bar{v}\rangle\langle\bar{v}|$. This probability is

$$\text{tr}(|\bar{v}\rangle\langle\bar{v}||1\rangle\langle 1|) = \frac{1}{2} \qquad \text{tr}(|\bar{v}\rangle\langle\bar{v}||0\rangle\langle 0|) = \frac{1}{2}$$

which is counter-intuitive because one would expect that the probability that a document is relevant when the relevance is certain, was 1.

Another IR example of superposition refers to relevance and aboutness (van Rijsbergen 2004, pp. 19–23). Suppose that $|1\rangle, |0\rangle$ (i.e., the corresponding projectors) represent relevance and non-relevance, respectively, whereas $|v\rangle, |\bar{v}\rangle$ represent aboutness and non-aboutness, respectively. The probability space for relevance can be defined using (6.6), that is, using a mixture. However, as $|v\rangle, |\bar{v}\rangle$ are vectors in the space spanned by $|1\rangle, |0\rangle$, that is, they are a superposition of $|1\rangle, |0\rangle$, an equivalent density matrix of relevance is (6.9). The latter is equivalent since

$$\text{tr}(\mu|i\rangle\langle i|) = \text{tr}(|v\rangle\langle v||i\rangle\langle i|) \quad i = 0, 1.$$

The superposition $|v\rangle$ is distinguished from the mixture μ not by the probabilities assigned to relevance, but by those assigned to aboutness. Indeed,

$$\text{tr}(\mu|v\rangle\langle v|) = \frac{1}{2} \qquad \text{tr}(|v\rangle\langle v||v\rangle\langle v|) = 1$$

The fact that different probabilities are assigned to aboutness by the mixture and the superposition is associated with the fact that the subspaces representing aboutness are geometrically obliquely inclined to those representing relevance (Hughes 1989, p. 110).

Two observables are compatible when the measurement of an observable does not disturb the system and does not alter the other observable value that shall be measured. For the sake of clarity, suppose we have an urn of balls. Every ball has a color and a weight. Thus, the observables are "color" and "weight". If the observables were incompatible, drawing a ball to observe "color" would alter the weight of ball and drawing a ball to observe "weight" would alter the color. Using the Hilbert spaces, if $R_0, \ldots, R_{k-1}$ are the k projectors corresponding to the possible events of an observable and $A_0, \ldots, A_{h-1}$ are the h projectors corresponding to the possible events of another observable, the observables are compatible when $R_i A_j = A_j R_i$ for every i, j.

If relevance and aboutness could be represented by mutually orthonormal basis vectors, then they are compatible. We show this fact using the Lüders rule in the following. Suppose that two observables, e.g., relevance and aboutness can be represented using a common set of one-dimensional subspaces where each one-dimensional subspace corresponds to a basis vector $|e_i\rangle$ (i.e., to a projector $|e_i\rangle\langle e_i|$).

Suppose also that relevance assumes one of the outcomes corresponding to the mutually orthogonal projectors $R_0, \ldots, R_{k-1}$ and that aboutness assumes one of the outcomes corresponding to the mutually orthogonal projectors $A_0, \ldots, A_{h-1}$; note that these projectors can not be one-dimensional.

There exists a density matrix ρ such that $\text{tr}(\rho X)$ is the probability that X is observed. Suppose that the measurement of relevance and aboutness is performed in such a way that, relevance is observed first and then aboutness, or aboutness is observed first and then relevance. We would expect that the probability that a conjoint event, e.g., (R_i, A_j) estimated when relevance is observed first and then aboutness is the same as that estimated when aboutness is observed first and then relevance (or, they differ due to a negligible difference). However, it can be argued that this commutability does not hold because of the mutual influence between the observables; when commutability does not hold, QM provides the formalism to model it. Indeed, the probability of the conjoint event R_i, A_j is

$$P(R_i, A_j) = P(R_i|A_j)P(A_j) = P(A_j|R_i)P(R_i)$$

if classical probability and the Bayes Theorem are assumed. If, however, $P(R_i|A_j)P(A_j) \neq P(A_j|R_i)P(R_i)$, classical probability and the Bayes Theorem cannot be assumed. Let's express the probability of the conjont event using the Lüders rule instead of the Bayes Theorem. We have that

$$P(R_i|A_j)P(A_j) = \text{tr}(A_j\rho A_j R_i)$$

and that

$$P(A_j|R_i)P(R_i) = \text{tr}(R_i\rho R_i A_j)$$

However, it is well known that matrix product is not commutative, thus $A_j R_i \neq R_i A_j$ and, therefore, the cyclic property of trace cannot be applied and $P(A_j|R_i)P(R_i) \neq P(R_i|A_j)P(A_j)$. When A_j, R_i are expressed using a common basis, they represent a common subspace, thus a subspace is included in the other. When inclusion holds, e.g., the subspace of A_j is included in the subspace of R_i, we have that $R_i A_j = A_j$. It follows that $A_j R_i = A_j$; indeed, if $R_i A_j = A_j$, then $A_j R_i A_j = A_j A_j$, that is, $A_j R_i = A_j$, that is, the observables are commutative.

We give the following interpretation. The common basis vectors represent mutually exclusive events common to both matrices. As the matrices are about two observables (i.e., relevance and aboutness), the existence of a common basis means that these two observables can be expressed by using the same set of events. As both matrices are diagonalizable using the same basis, the existence of a common basis also means that these matrices are diagonal with respect to that basis, that is, represent a classical probability space with respect to that basis.

6.3.2 Interference

The double-slit experiment is perhaps the best known and investigated case of interference—(Feynman et al. 1965) and (Hughes 1989) are two excellent descriptions of this phenomenon. There is a source E emitting photons which pass or do not

Fig. 6.1 The double-slit
experiment; curves show
distribution of hits in
experiment a, experiment b
and experiment c.
From (Feynman et al. 1965;
Hughes 1989)

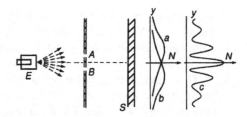

pass through a screen with two slits A, B; those passing are detected by screen S
(Fig. 6.1). When A is open and B is closed, the distribution of the photons detected
by S at point y is depicted by curve a. When A is closed and B is open, the distribution of the photons detected by S is depicted by curve b. One would expect that when
both slits were open, the distribution of the photons detected by S would be a mixture of distributions, that is, a sort of $pa + (1 - p)b$, where p is the probability that a
photon passed through A. In fact, the distribution observed when both slits are open
is N (far right) in which the proportion of photons may be either less than or greater
than $pa + (1 - p)b$—this was of course observed independently of p. Interference
occurs between the photons when both slits are open and it causes the difference
between the expected result from classical probability (i.e., the bell-shaped curve)
and the actual observation (i.e., the rollercoaster-shaped curve).

The difference can be mathematically described by a real number called *interference term*. Suppose also that the detection of a photon by S corresponds to the event
"the term occurs", the latter being represented by projector $S = |s\rangle\langle s|$. The vector
$|s\rangle$ is in the same space of $|0\rangle$ and $|1\rangle$, which are mutually orthogonal and then form
a basis, therefore

$$|s\rangle = b_0|0\rangle + b_1|1\rangle \qquad |b_0|^2 + |b_1|^2 = 1 \qquad |s\rangle\langle s| = \begin{pmatrix} |b_1|^2 & b_1\bar{b}_0 \\ b_0\bar{b}_1 & |b_0|^2 \end{pmatrix}$$

The problem is how to represent the probability space of the events "the particle
passes through A" (event $|1\rangle\langle 1|$) and "the particle passes through B" (event $|0\rangle\langle 0|$)
when both slits are open and it is uncertain where the photon passes.

The density matrix corresponding to this probability space can be either a mixed
distribution (i.e., a mixture) or a pure distribution. It can be shown that the probability of S when computed using a mixture differs from that computed using a
superposition, yet they share a common factor. The common factor is the "classical" probability whereas the difference is called *interference term*. Using a mixture,

$$\text{tr}(\mu|s\rangle\langle s|) = |a_0|^2|b_0|^2 + |a_1|^2|b_1|^2 \qquad \mu = \begin{pmatrix} |a_1|^2 & 0 \\ 0 & |a_0|^2 \end{pmatrix} \qquad (6.10)$$

Using superposition,

$$\text{tr}(\rho|s\rangle\langle s|) = |a_0|^2|b_0|^2 + |a_1|^2|b_1|^2 + 2|a_0||b_0||b_1||b_0|\cos\theta \qquad (6.11)$$

where $\rho = |v\rangle\langle v|$.[3]

---

[3] θ is the angle of the polar representation of the complex number $a_0\bar{b}_0 a_1\bar{b}_1$.

The common factor (6.10) is the sum of two probabilities: the probability that the document is not relevant ($|a_0|^2$) multiplied by the probability that the term occurs in a non-relevant document ($|b_0|^2$), and the probability that the document is relevant ($|a_1|^2$) multiplied by the probability that the term occurs in a relevant document ($|b_1|^2$). This sum is nothing but an application of the law of total probability.

The quantity $|a_0||b_0||b_1||b_0|\cos\theta$ is a real number and is the interference term. As it ranges between -1 and $+1$, it can make the probability of term occurrence computed when relevance is superposed with non-relevance very different from the common factor in which relevance and non-relevance are mutually exclusive and their probability distribution is described by a mixture. The interference term can be so large that the law of total probability is violated and any probability space obeying Kolmogorov's axioms cannot admit the probability values $|a_1|^2$ and $|b_1|^2$, thus requiring the adoption of a quantum probability space (Accardi and Fedullo 1982; Accardi 1997).

6.3.3 Entanglement

In Sect. 6.2 it was explained that there are two main types of density matrix, i.e., those representing pure distribution and those representing mixed distribution. Pure distributions correspond to rank one projectors and mixed distributions correspond to mixtures of projectors such that the mixture weights are the probabilities of the events represented by the projectors. In a four-dimensional Hilbert space, a density matrix associated with four mutually exclusive events is a mixed distribution when it is a mixture of four orthogonal projectors. In general, the mixture may involve any set of mutually orthogonal projectors which are not necessarily represented as diagonal matrices. It follows that

$$\rho = p_{00}P_{00} + p_{01}P_{01} + p_{10}P_{10} + p_{11}P_{11} \tag{6.12}$$

is a generic mixed density matrix in a four-dimensional Hilbert space such that $P_{ij}P_{i'j'} = 0$ when $i \neq i'$ or $j \neq j'$ and $P_{ij}P_{ij} = P_{ij}$ such that $i, i', j, j' \in \{0, 1\}$. Starting from this generic mixed density matrix, separability, correlation and entanglement can be introduced.

A mixed density matrix is *separable* if every P_{ij} can be written as the tensor product of two projectors, one projector for each event set. It follows that a separable mixed density matrix is

$$\rho = p_{00}F_0 \otimes G_0 + p_{01}F_0 \otimes G_1 + p_{10}F_1 \otimes G_0 + p_{11}F_1 \otimes G_1$$

Separability enables the expression of the event represented by P_{ij} as the product of two distinct events, thus it allows us to express the fact that a four-event set is the product of two binary event sets, that is, $\{00, 01, 10, 11\}$ where the first bit refers to the first event set and the second bit refers to the second event set. Let's consider the co-occurrence of two terms such that the occurrence of the first term corresponds to an event set and the occurrence of the other term corresponds to another event set; for example, $|01\rangle$ would represent the occurrence of a term while the other term does not occur. A separable density matrix may be

$$\mu = p_{00}|00\rangle\langle 00| + p_{01}|01\rangle\langle 01| + p_{10}|10\rangle\langle 10| + p_{11}|11\rangle\langle 11| \qquad (6.13)$$

Since $|ij\rangle\langle ij| = |i\rangle\langle i| \otimes |j\rangle\langle j|$, it follows that

$$\mu = p_{00}|0\rangle\langle 0| \otimes |0\rangle\langle 0| + p_{01}|0\rangle\langle 0| \otimes |1\rangle\langle 1| + p_{10}|1\rangle\langle 1| \otimes |0\rangle\langle 0| + p_{11}|1\rangle\langle 1| \otimes |1\rangle\langle 1|$$

The possibility of expressing term co-occurrence as tensor product does not imply that the terms are uncorrelated, indeed, $P_{ij} = F_i \otimes G_j$ does not imply that $p_{ij} = f_i g_j$. Hence, co-occurrence and correlation are two distinct properties. For example, the mixed density matrix

$$\mu = \frac{1}{2}|00\rangle\langle 00| + \frac{1}{2}|11\rangle\langle 11|$$

is separable and correlated, while every $|ij\rangle\langle ij|$ is separable and uncorrelated since it is pure.

A mixed density matrix is *entangled* if it is not separable. Entanglement does not allow the event represented by P_{ij} to be expressed as the product of two distinct events. For example, if P_{ij} is entangled, one cannot say whether a term does or does not occur while the other term does or does not occur. As P_{ij} represents an event, entanglement means that event cannot be reduced as a series of other simple events combined through the classical logical operators. For example, the Bell vectors

$$|\phi_1\rangle = \frac{|00\rangle + |11\rangle}{\sqrt{2}}$$

$$|\phi_2\rangle = \frac{|00\rangle - |11\rangle}{\sqrt{2}}$$

$$|\phi_3\rangle = \frac{|10\rangle + |01\rangle}{\sqrt{2}}$$

$$|\phi_4\rangle = \frac{|01\rangle - |10\rangle}{\sqrt{2}}$$

and the corresponding projectors $|\phi_i\rangle\langle\phi_i|$'s represent four mutually exclusive events and are not separable. Since $|\phi_1\rangle\langle\phi_1|$ is entangled, it cannot be separated in two projectors $|\phi_a\rangle\langle\phi_a|$ and $|\phi_b\rangle\langle\phi_b|$ where $|\phi_1\rangle\langle\phi_1| = |\phi_a\rangle\langle\phi_a| \otimes |\phi_b\rangle\langle\phi_b|$, $|\phi_a\rangle = a_0|0\rangle + a_1|1\rangle$ and $|\phi_b\rangle = b_0|0\rangle + b_1|1\rangle$. The same holds for the other Bell vectors.

Entanglement does not imply that the mixed density matrix is correlated; for example,

$$\mu = f_0 g_0 P_{00} + f_0 g_1 P_{01} + f_1 g_0 P_{10} + f_1 g_1 P_{11}$$

is entangled because the projectors cannot be separated, but is uncorrelated because $p_{ij} = f_i g_j$. Indeed, $\text{tr}(\mu P_{ij}) = f_i g_j$.

In quantum probability, pure uncorrelated density matrices can be entangled; for example, (6.14) is pure, uncorrelated and entangled. Indeed, the spectral theorem tells us that there is only one eigenvalue 1, but (6.14) cannot be written as the tensor product of marginal density matrices.

$$|\phi_1\rangle\langle\phi_1| = \begin{pmatrix} \frac{1}{2} & 0 & 0 & \frac{1}{2} \\ 0 & 0 & 0 & 0 \\ 0 & 0 & 0 & 0 \\ \frac{1}{2} & 0 & 0 & \frac{1}{2} \end{pmatrix} \tag{6.14}$$

Let's consider the special case of classical probability. In this case the density matrices are diagonal. When a mixed diagonal density matrix is uncorrelated, it can be expressed as a tensor product of two diagonal density matrices which represent the marginals. That is, if a mixed diagonal density matrix is uncorrelated, it is also separable. For example, if μ is uncorrelated, then

$$\mu = f_0 g_0 |00\rangle\langle00| + f_0 g_1 |10\rangle\langle10| + f_1 g_0 |01\rangle\langle01| + f_1 g_1 |11\rangle\langle11| \tag{6.15}$$

As $|ij\rangle\langle ij|$ is also separable (i.e., $|ij\rangle\langle ij| = |i\rangle\langle i| \otimes |j\rangle\langle j|$), μ is separable and uncorrelated, that is,

$$\mu = \mu_F \otimes \mu_G \quad \mu_F = f_0 |0\rangle\langle0| + f_1 |1\rangle\langle1| \quad \mu_G = g_0 |0\rangle\langle0| + g_1 |1\rangle\langle1| \tag{6.16}$$

Therefore, when the probability space is classical (i.e., the density matrix is diagonal), a density matrix is separable if all the correlations arise from its being a classical mixture of uncorrelated, pure density matrices. In classical probability, entanglement does not exist and the unique source of "correlation" is the probability distribution given by the mixture weights (Rieffel 2007).

In constrast, in quantum probability, there are two sources of "correlation". One source is the probability distribution given by the mixture weights, the other source is the non-separability of the projectors.

The difference between entanglement and correlation in IR when quantum probability is adopted has an impact on prediction. Consider the following example. Suppose that two binary event sets with the same elements are defined, that is, $\{|s_0\rangle, |s_1\rangle\}$ (e.g., "system" occurrence) and $\{|r_0\rangle, |r_1\rangle\}$ (e.g., "retrieval" occurrence). The event $|s_i r_j\rangle$ represents one of the four possibilities. The first bit of the event $|s_i r_j\rangle$ refers to the occurrence of "system". For example $|r_1 s_1\rangle\langle r_1 s_1|$ can represent the co-occurrence of "system" and "retrieval". When the density matrix is (6.13), one can easily check that $p_{ij} = \text{tr}(\mu|s_i r_j\rangle\langle s_i r_j|)$ and that it is separable, yet may be correlated as happens in classical probability or when term co-occurrence is considered in IR. The unique source of correlation is the probability distribution given by the mixture weights.

The occurrence of "retrieval system" is different from the co-occurrence of "system" and "retrieval" and another projector has to be defined. Let the projector of the occurrence of "retrieval system" be the entangled projector $|\phi_1\rangle\langle\phi_1|$ defined in a four-dimensional Hilbert space. Suppose the following density matrix is defined:

$$\rho = |\phi_1\rangle\langle\phi_1|$$

This density matrix can be regarded as a special case of (6.15) such that $f_1 g_1 = 1$ and $P_{11} = |\phi_1\rangle\langle\phi_1|$. Since $f_1 g_1 = 1$, "system" and "retrieval" are uncorrelated. Moreover, the probability that "retrieval system" occurs is

$$\text{tr}(\rho P_{11}) = 1$$

while the probabililty that "system" and "retrieval" co-occurs is

$$\text{tr}(\rho|11\rangle\langle11|) = \frac{1}{2}$$

Furthermore, whereas the occurrence of "retrieval system" implies the occurrence of "system" and "retrieval" in classical probability, the implication does not hold in Quantum Probability because P_{11} cannot be expressed as tensor product.

6.4 Quantum Probability and Information Retrieval

The literature which has appeared since the publication of the book by van Rijsbergen (van Rijsbergen 2004) and relevant to QM and IR can in this work be classified according to the following aims:

1. To investigate the Hilbert spaces for representing models, techniques or new perspectives, but without concentrating on the analogies of quantum-like phenomena or on the modeling of the key notions of QM in IR.
   This group includes the *ante litteram* work by Deerwester et al. devoted to Latent Semantic Analysis in the 1990s, the work by Widdows devoted to finding a geometry of word meaning, and the work by Melucci devoted to defining an abstract vector space model of contextual IR.
2. To use at least one of the key notions of QM (i.e. superposition, interference and entanglement) for modeling some IR issues such as semantics, document ranking, word ambiguity.
   This group includes a variety of contributions:
   a. The use of the key notions of QM for describing semantic spaces (e.g., concepts and context).
   b. The use of the key notions of QM for document representation and ranking.
   c. Testing the presence of quantum phenomena using datasets or user studies.

6.4.1 Abstract Vector Spaces

6.4.1.1 Latent Semantic Analysis

The researchers who proposed the Latent Semantic Analysis (LSA) model started from experimental studies on the use and ambiguity of words. Afterwards, they refined LSA for IR purposes and proposed Latent Semantic Indexing (LSI). A recent account of LSA and its applications is (Landauer 2007) where the initial illustration can be found in (Deerwester et al. 1990). In this section, a description is provided in connection with the QM concepts illustrated in Sects. 6.2 and 6.3.

Suppose a vector $|x\rangle$ is defined as follows:

$$|x\rangle = \begin{pmatrix} \frac{1}{\sqrt{2}} \\ \frac{1}{\sqrt{2}} \end{pmatrix}$$

such that the components are term weights, that is, the measures of the contribution of two terms for describing something more complex (e.g., a document, a query or another term). Note that the weights are equal, thus the terms contribute equally.

We here propose another way of looking at weights: They measure the association between rather the *uses* than the semantics of terms. Whenever a term is used for describing something more complex, the other term is used to the same degree (or with the same probability). In a sense, the *uses* of the two terms are perfectly and mutually associated yet the semantics can be mutually independent.

The vector is expressed with the canonical basis as follows:

$$|x\rangle = \frac{1}{\sqrt{2}}|1\rangle + \frac{1}{\sqrt{2}}|0\rangle \quad |1\rangle = \begin{pmatrix} 1 \\ 0 \end{pmatrix} \quad |0\rangle = \begin{pmatrix} 0 \\ 1 \end{pmatrix}$$

where the basis vectors correspond to simpler terms than that represented by $|x\rangle$. As the basis vectors are mutually is orthogonal and have length 1, they represent unrelated simple terms, namely, terms which are by definition independent. Nevertheless, the uses of these simple terms is perfectly associated (i.e., when a simple term is used, the other is used too). Of course, the perfect association may disappear when the terms are used in another object. In general, as the use happens in the context of an object, the degree to which the uses are associated may vary. If the perfect association were observed in every object, one of the two terms would be useless and a more compact representation of the objects could be obtained. This more compact representation is another basis through which the object is represented by one vector only as depicted in Fig. 6.2. Indeed,

$$|x\rangle = 1|v\rangle + 0|\bar{v}\rangle = |v\rangle \quad |v\rangle = \begin{pmatrix} +\frac{1}{\sqrt{2}} \\ +\frac{1}{\sqrt{2}} \end{pmatrix} \quad |\bar{v}\rangle = \begin{pmatrix} +\frac{1}{\sqrt{2}} \\ -\frac{1}{\sqrt{2}} \end{pmatrix} .$$

This is quite an extreme case. Actually, the presence of objects in which the association is not perfect is the most likely. Suppose, for example, that another object $|y\rangle$ is represented using the canonical basis as follows:

$$|y\rangle = \begin{pmatrix} \frac{2}{\sqrt{13}} \\ \frac{3}{\sqrt{13}} \end{pmatrix} = \frac{2}{\sqrt{13}}|1\rangle + \frac{3}{\sqrt{13}}|0\rangle$$

Fig. 6.2 Two bases for one object

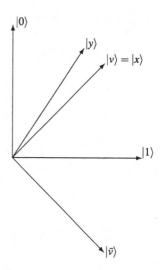

while it is represented using the alternative basis as follows:

$$|y\rangle = \begin{pmatrix} +\frac{5}{\sqrt{26}} \\ -\frac{1}{\sqrt{26}} \end{pmatrix} = \frac{5}{\sqrt{26}}|v\rangle - \frac{1}{\sqrt{26}}|\bar{v}\rangle$$

The probability that $|v\rangle$ is observed in $|y\rangle$ is high, that is, $\mathrm{tr}(|y\rangle\langle y||v\rangle\langle v|) = |\langle y|v\rangle|^2 = \left(\frac{5}{\sqrt{26}}\right)^2 = \frac{25}{26}$ where $\langle y|v\rangle = \frac{5}{\sqrt{26}}$. When a collection includes x, y, the vector $|v\rangle$ is a good approximation and one of the two terms (represented by the canonical basis vectors) can be left out.

In practice, the perfect association between two terms does not exist when a quite large collection of documents is considered, albeit the association may be stronger in some documents than in others. When the association is strong enough across the collection, it is nonetheless useful to find an alternative basis to the canonical basis such that the alternative basis vectors are as close to the object vectors as possible.

The key point is the distance function used to measure how close the object vectors are to the alternative basis vectors. When the distance function is the Frobenius norm, the closest alternative basis is provided by the Singular Value Decomposition (SVD) of a rectangular matrix consisting of the object (column) vectors. Suppose that there are n vectors of a k-dimensional complex space arranged in a $k \times n$ matrix A. The SVD theorem assures that there are three matrices U, D, V such that $A = UDV'$ where U is $k \times k$ and orthonormal, D is $k \times n$ and pseudo-diagonal and V is $n \times k$ and orthonormal.

The SVD is linked to the spectral theorem since the density matrix can be computed as the matrix of association between the row vectors of A corresponding to the k terms, divided by k. The division by k makes the trace of the matrix 1. It follows that the projectors resulting from the spectral theorem correspond to the column vectors of U and the eigenvalues placed along the diagonal of D are the probabilities. For example, consider the object vectors $|a_i\rangle$'s arranged as columns of A and

Fig. 6.3 Four object vectors
in the space

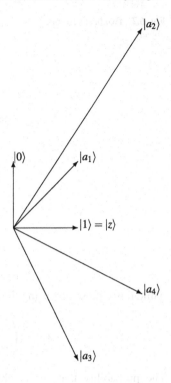

displayed in Fig. 6.3.

$$A = \begin{pmatrix} 1 & 2 & 1 & 2 \\ 1 & 3 & -2 & -1 \end{pmatrix}$$

Let's compute the correlation matrix C between the $|a_i\rangle$'s:

$$C \approx \begin{pmatrix} 1 & \frac{7}{10} \\ \frac{7}{10} & 1 \end{pmatrix} \qquad \rho = \begin{pmatrix} \frac{1}{2} & \frac{7}{20} \\ \frac{7}{20} & \frac{1}{2} \end{pmatrix}$$

The spectral theorem applied to ρ says that the projectors are $|v\rangle\langle v|$ and $|\bar{v}\rangle\langle\bar{v}|$

$$|v\rangle\langle v| = \begin{pmatrix} \frac{1}{2} & \frac{1}{2} \\ \frac{1}{2} & \frac{1}{2} \end{pmatrix} \qquad |\bar{v}\rangle\langle\bar{v}| = \begin{pmatrix} \frac{1}{2} & -\frac{1}{2} \\ -\frac{1}{2} & \frac{1}{2} \end{pmatrix}$$

The first projector represents the event that the uses of the two terms are perfectly associated. The second projector represents the opposite event. The probabilities are approximatively $\frac{7}{10}$ and $\frac{3}{10}$, respectively, such that

$$\rho = \frac{7}{10}|v\rangle\langle v| + \frac{3}{10}|\bar{v}\rangle\langle\bar{v}|$$

The interpretation of the probability space stemming from the association matrix and from the SVD depends on how the density matrix is computed. When LSI is considered, the density matrix is the normalized association matrix of which the minimization function returns the eigenvectors. If another algorithm is adopted to compute the density matrix or another function is minimized, the interpretationn of the probability space changes.

6.4.1.2 The Geometry of Word Meaning

Widdows (2004), Widdows and Peters (2003) observed that the vector space model for IR lacks a logic like the Boolean model. It is therefore difficult to combine words using Boolean operators, that is, AND, OR, NOT. Although the percentage of the users of a search engine who use the logical operators is small, Boolean are nonetheless crucial because some tasks, e.g., filtering or personalization require more advanced search methods than a basic bag-of-words method. Thus, it is useful to investigate how the Boolean operators map to the Hilbert spaces. Moreover, if a search for a logic for the vector space model is successful, one will have a powerful tool to combine vectors and logic in a elegant and mathematically sound way.

How the vector space model and logics are related is explained in van Rijsbergen (2004, Chap. 5). Widdows (2004), Widdows and Peters (2003) includes the formalism for quantum logic illustrated by Birkhoff and von Neumann (1936) in the classical vector space model defined over the complex field. Widdows (2004), Widdows and Peters (2003) describe how words are related, thus defining a geometry of word meaning. A brief account is given in the rest of this section with reference to the formalism of Sects. 6.2 and 6.3.

The vector space model for IR describes information objects as vectors. A vector $|x\rangle$ of a complex vector space represents such an object and the ith element x_i is the weight of descriptor i in relation to the object. Note that the vector space model is usually defined over the real field so as to compute real inner products, which are required for ranking objects. The peculiarity of the vector space model is that it assumes that there is a unique basis and that every vector is generated by that basis. Moreover, that basis spans the whole space, i.e., $n = k$, or the number of basis vectors is the number of dimensions of the vector space. In particular, the canonical basis[4] is often assumed as the unique basis and then a document or query vector is given by the set of weights.

The way the documents (or information objects) are represented by the vector space model is based on the linear combination of basis vectors representing the words. The number of basis vectors linearly combined is the dimension of the vector space in which the documents (and the words) are placed. When the basis is orthonormal, the linear combination is the implementation of disjunction in the logics defined within quantum mechanics, that is, the disjunction of quantum mechanics is

---

[4]The canonical basis vector $|e_i\rangle$ of a vector space with n dimensions is $(0, \ldots, 1, \ldots, 0)^\top$ such that 1 occurs at the i-th position.

not the union of the subspaces spanned by the basis vectors, it is instead given by the linear combination of these basis vectors. The result of this linear combination is also called "span". Hence, the quantum disjunction is larger than the Boolean disjunction because it includes the basis vectors and all the linear combinations of the these two. The coefficients of this linear combination are probability amplitudes; see (6.9). The result of quantum disjunction is a subspace from which the distances of other subspaces can be computed. The distance between two subspaces is computed by using the trace-based function of probability where the density operator is the projector of a subspace.

Boolean logic allows one to use the negation operator for expressing, for example, that documents about a keyword, but not about another keyword, are wanted. Negation was not introduced in the original vector-space model because the aim of this model is to overcome the Boolean model's limitations in ranking and to rank the documents by vector distance or closeness.

The geometry of word meaning by Widdows (2004), Widdows and Peters (2003) proposes an elegant way for representing word negation in the vector space which is based on the notion of orthogonality. Orthogonality is used to represent irrelevance, thus for example the vector representing "river" would be orthogonal to the vector representing "NOT river", or the projector (i.e. subspace) representing relevance would be orthogonal to the projector representing non-relevance. Suppose that, for example, the vectors $|e_1\rangle, |e_2\rangle, |e_3\rangle$ are basis vectors of a three-dimensional vector space. Two vectors $|x_1\rangle, |x_2\rangle$ can be defined with respect to that basis and therefore are vectors of the same space. If $|x_1\rangle, |x_2\rangle$ represents terms (e.g., "bank", "river"), the projectors $|x_1\rangle\langle x_1|, |x_2\rangle\langle x_2|$ represents the events that term x_1, x_2 occurs, respectively. Suppose that the event "bank NOT river" has to be represented where "bank" is represented by $|x_1\rangle$ and "river" is represented by $|x_2\rangle$. Such an event would be represented by a one-dimensional projector $|y\rangle\langle y|$ such that $|y\rangle$ is orthogonal to $|x_2\rangle$. It can be shown that

$$|y\rangle = |x_1\rangle - \lambda|x_2\rangle \quad \lambda = \frac{\langle x_1|x_2\rangle}{|\langle x_2|x_2\rangle|^2} \tag{6.17}$$

Let us consider a numerical example where the basis vectors represent senses and are, by definition, mutually orthogonal and, in particular, are the canonical vectors. The vectors $|x_1\rangle, |x_2\rangle, |x_3\rangle$ may represent ambiguous words (e.g., "bank", "river", "finance", respectively) and thus be about more than one sense if defined as:

$$|x_1\rangle = \frac{1}{\sqrt{2}}|e_1\rangle + \frac{1}{\sqrt{2}}|e_2\rangle \quad |x_2\rangle = |e_2\rangle \quad |x_3\rangle = |e_3\rangle$$

If "bank" needs to be disambiguated, the expression "bank NOT river" can be represented with (6.17), that is,

$$\lambda = \frac{1}{\sqrt{2}} \quad |y\rangle = \frac{1}{\sqrt{2}}|e_1\rangle$$

Fig. 6.4 The difference
between subsets and
subspaces

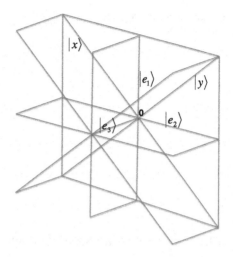

Vector negation resembles negative relevance feedback when the vectors represent
documents and queries, and the canonical basis vectors represent index terms. Indeed, negative relevance feedback aims at computing a new query vector by sub-
stracting some irrelevant document vectors from the original query vector. In the
vector space model, the coefficients of relevance feedback are set after experimental
tuning while in vector negation the coefficients (i.e., λ) are defined in a principled
way.

The most glaring difference between Boolean logic and quantum logic is the
same as the difference between subsets of a set and subspaces of a vector space.
While the distributive law is valid in the Boolean logic, it is no longer valid in the
quantum logic. This difference is due to the definition of disjunction in the two
logics. A useful example is in (Hughes 1989, p. 190) and reproduced in Fig. 6.4.
The three-dimensional vector space is generated by $|e_1\rangle, |e_2\rangle, |e_3\rangle$. The ray (i.e.,
one-dimensional subspace) L_x is generated by $|x\rangle$, the plane (i.e., two-dimensional
subspace) $L_{x,y}$ is generated by $|x\rangle, |y\rangle$. Note that $L_{e_1,e_2} = L_{x,y} = L_{e_1,y}$ and so
on. According to Hughes (1989, p. 191), consider the subspace $L_{e_2} \wedge (L_y \vee L_x)$
where $\wedge$ means "intersection" and $\vee$ means "span" (and not set union). Since
$L_y \vee L_x = L_{x,y} = L_{e_1,e_2}$, it follows that $L_{e_2} \wedge (L_y \vee L_x) = L_{e_2} \wedge L_{e_1,e_2} = L_{e_2}$.
However, since $L_{e_2} \wedge L_y = 0$ and $L_{e_2} \wedge L_x = 0$, it follows that $(L_{e_2} \wedge L_y) \vee$
$(L_{e_2} \wedge L_x) = 0$, therefore

$$L_{e_2} \wedge (L_y \vee L_x) \neq (L_{e_2} \wedge L_y) \vee (L_{e_2} \wedge L_x)$$

thus meaning that the distributive law does not hold. If these vectors and the corresponding projectors represent the events usually considered in IR, such as relevance,
aboutness or term occurrence, the use of the logic of subspaces is radically different
from the logic of subsets (van Rijsbergen 2004).

Fig. 6.5 Modeling context
using subspaces

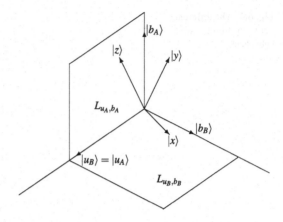

6.4.1.3 Abstract Vector Spaces of Contextual Information Retrieval

IR is intrinsically context-dependent—what is relevant to one user in one place at one time can no longer be relevant to another user, in another place or at another time. In principle, an IR system should be context-aware. Recently, search engines have been capturing some search environment features exploited at retrieval-time; examples are location or search history. A principled way to address contextual IR has been proposed by Melucci (2008).

Suppose somebody has decided which dimensions are deemed to be important for building a representation of context. The term "contextual factor" may be used for signifying one of the possible values of a contextual dimension. Let us assume that there are two contextual dimensions. One dimension is the user, whereas the other dimension is the meaning of the term "bank"—in a given context A, the meaning of "bank" is represented by the vector $|b_A\rangle$ and the user is represented by the vector $|u_A\rangle$. In another context, say, B, the meaning of "bank" is represented by $|b_B\rangle$ and the user is represented by $|u_B\rangle$. The vectors $|b_A\rangle$ and $|b_B\rangle$ are mutually exclusive as they are factors of the same contextual dimension. The vector $|b_B\rangle$ cannot be derived from $|u_B\rangle$ through any linear combination, i.e., these two vectors are mutually independent. If $|b_B\rangle$ and $|u_B\rangle$ are independent, they are elements of a basis B. Another basis A includes $|b_A\rangle$ and $|u_A\rangle$. In this way a distinct context yields a distinct basis. Since every basis spans a subspace, a context corresponds to a subspace. An example is depicted in Fig. 6.5.

A subspace includes all the vectors generated by a basis of that subspace; for example, the vector $|x\rangle$ of Fig. 6.5 belongs to L_{u_B,b_B}. Beside contextual dimensions and factors, the subspaces generated by the linear combination of basis vectors can also describe documents, queries or other information objects. The uniform description of objects and contextual factors as elements of a vector space is one of the strengths of the model proposed and an essential feature which distinguishes this model from other vector-based approaches proposed in the past, such as clustering or relevance feedback.

Given an object y, the event that a contextual factor of A or B is observed is an uncertain event—this uncertainty is the analogue of the uncertainty of the event "relevance" of the probabilistic model for IR. A question involving a factor of context takes the form of "Is factor i occurring in object y?"; for example, "Is document y useful to user John?", "Is document y introductory?" or "Is document y relevant to a query about information retrieval?" More complex questions like "Are factors i and j occurring in object y?" can also be answered by linearly combining the subspaces which describe i and j and thus obtaining another subspace; for example, "Is an introductory document y useful to user John?". In Quantum Mechanics, the concepts of contextual dimension and contextual factors refer to observable and value, respectively.

To decide whether such a factor exists in the object a measure of probability is needed. Therefore, the question is, what is the probability that a contextual factor of A, B or any other basis is observed given an object represented by $|y\rangle$? For example, if $|y\rangle$ describes a document, what is the probability that the said document has been generated in the context corresponding to $|b_A\rangle$ and $|u_A\rangle$? The solution to this question would enable documents to be ranked with respect to a query by taking context into account. A vector $|y\rangle$ simultaneously assigns probabilities to all questions involving contextual factors. The way the probabilities are assigned causes these probabilities to vary when object y varies, that is, the distribution of probability is dependent on the object y. As a consequence, two objects give different probabilities to one question involving some contextual factors. These two objects can then be ranked, thus answering questions like "In which object is a factor i more likely to occur?" with the most probable object being presented first.

Gleason's Theorem assures that, whatever the measure used for assigning the probabilities to the questions involving some factors of context in relation to an object, a unique description in terms of subspaces or combinations thereof exists in the vector space for the object, such that the probabilities can be computed as one single function of the subspaces describing the contextual factors and the object. For instance, if a measure were to be used for assigning a probability for each question like "Is factor i occurring in object y?" for all the i's, then a unique description of y in the vector space exists, such that all the probabilities can be expressed as values of a function of the subspaces which describe i and y.

6.4.1.4 Quantum Probability and Contextual Information Retrieval

In Sect. 6.4.1.3, it was argued that the basis of an abstract vector space can be an effective formalism for representing context in IR. In particular, in (Melucci 2008), the hypothesis that the fact that information objects (e.g., documents and queries) and operators (e.g., relevance and aboutness) are placed in a context can be represented as vectors placed in an abstract vector space defined through a basis was investigated. In other words, the basis was proposed as the formalism for representing and processing the context. This means that the basis vectors and their implementation represents the semantics of contextual dimensions—for example, if the documents are represented as vectors defined through a basis and the basis vectors represent terms, the implementation of the basis vectors is a representation of the semantics of the index terms.

The fact that the basis vectors and their implementation represents the semantics of contextual dimensions would also entail that the evolution of context can be represented as a linear transformation of the basis vectors—that is, if the context evolves and the contextual dimensions change their own semantics, the basis vectors which represent the contextual dimensions will also change.

When quantum probability and the framework based on Hilbert spaces is adopted for measuring the uncertainty of events, the conditionalization rule can no longer be that of Bayes' postulate (Hughes 1989). That rule says that the probability of an event conditioned to another event is still a trace-based function, yet the density operator is a transformation of the density operator of the trace-based function for the non-conditioned event (see Sect. 6.2).

We show that the Lüder rule corresponds to a change of basis and an evolution of context. Indeed, suppose Y is observed inducing the change of the density matrix from D to D_Y as ruled by Lüder. Suppose that P_X is a rank-one projector (that is, it corresponds to a one-dimensional space), thus $P_X = |x\rangle\langle x|$. Hence,

$$\text{tr}(D_Y P_X) = \langle x|D_Y|x\rangle = \langle x|P_Y D P_Y|x\rangle = \langle z|D|z\rangle \qquad (6.18)$$

where $|z\rangle = P_Y|x\rangle$. As $|x\rangle$ can be spanned by a basis B, that is, $|x\rangle = x_1|b_1\rangle + \cdots + x_k|b_k\rangle$, it follows that $|z\rangle = x_1|e_1\rangle + \cdots + x_k|e_k\rangle$ where the new basis vectors are defined as $|e_i\rangle = P_Y|b_i\rangle$, that is, the new basis vectors have been obtained after projecting the previous basis vectors to the subspace corresponding to the conditioning event.

The correspondence between the Lüder condizionalization rule and the change of basis used to express the vector representing an information object or an operator establishes a connection, in general, between conditional probability and context evolution and, in particular, between conditional quantum probability and context evolution. On the one hand, whenever context evolves, the probability of an event may change since the degree of belief that the event occurs depends on the contextual dimensions along which the belief is expressed. On the other, the conditional probability rules are the means to formalize the change of degree of belief in an event since these are the rules for incorporating the additional knowledge (i.e., the context) about the event. Furthermore, the Lüder rule establishes a clear connection between the conditional probability and the geometry of space since the former can be expressed in terms of change of a density matrix to another.

The connection between the conditional probability and the geometry of space established by the Lüder rule and the use of subspaces for representing contextual dimensions suggests another connection between the relevance feedback algorithms used in the vector space model and in the probabilistic models. The relevance feedback algorithm proposed with the vector-space model for IR, also known as Rocchio's method, can be expressed as a change of the basis used for representing the query vector (Melucci 2005)—vector negation is an instance of vector space-based relevance feedback (see Sect. 6.4.1.2). As the change of basis corresponds to a change of density matrix, and hence of probability distribution, the connection between the relevance feedback algorithm proposed with the vector-space model for IR and the change of basis corresponds to a connection to a change of density matrix, and hence of probability distribution. As a consequence, the Rocchio method comes up to be a probabilistic method for relevance feedback, thus posing the question if the relevance feedback mechanism of the probabilistic models (e.g., the Binary Independence model) subsume a single theoretical framework.

6.4.2 Using Quantum Mechanics in Information Retrieval

6.4.2.1 Semantic Spaces

Semantic spaces and QM were especially investigated in human cognition and natural language processing which are naturally related to IR due to the relevance of the natural language issues (Aerts and Gabora 2005; Bruza and Cole 2005; Bruza et al. 2010; Hou and Song 2009; Widdows 2004; Melucci and Sitbon 2011). A semantic space of a word w is implemented as a density matrix S_w. The density matrix which implements a semantic space is basically a word correlation matrix. Word correlation can be estimated using either a collection of texts or asking human subjects for assessments about word proximity. Using a collection of texts, for each occurrence of w within a text, all the windows centered around w are considered. A correlation measure[5] between the window words is used and a $n \times n$ correlation matrix is computed where n is the vocabulary dimension. After normalizing the correlation matrix, the density matrix is obtained. Asking human subjects to assess word proximity, words or word pairs are proposed to the subjects who are asked to associate another word which may have previously been seen.

The first intuition is that a word corresponds to a density matrix (i.e., a quantum state) and therefore to a probability distribution. The probabilities refer to events which are word senses and then are represented as projectors. In other words, if a word sense is represented as a projector, the probability that a word w has a given sense can be computed using the density matrix and the trace-based function. Suppose w is "bank", the words "river" and "finance" have been found in the text windows and the correlation matrix is

$$\rho = \begin{pmatrix} \frac{1}{3} & \frac{1}{6} & -\frac{1}{15} \\ \frac{1}{6} & \frac{1}{3} & \frac{1}{10} \\ -\frac{1}{15} & \frac{1}{10} & \frac{1}{3} \end{pmatrix}$$

After computing SVD, the eigenvectors and the corresponding eigenvalues are

$$V = \begin{pmatrix} \frac{13}{20} & \frac{23}{50} & \frac{61}{100} \\ \frac{37}{50} & -\frac{19}{100} & -\frac{13}{20} \\ \frac{9}{50} & -\frac{87}{100} & \frac{23}{50} \end{pmatrix} \qquad \Lambda = \begin{pmatrix} \frac{1}{2} & 0 & 0 \\ 0 & \frac{2}{5} & 0 \\ 0 & 0 & \frac{1}{10} \end{pmatrix}$$

---

[5] "Statistical correlation" is meant.

The first eigenvector represents the first (and most probable) sense of "bank", indeed,

$$\text{tr}(\rho|v_1\rangle\langle v_1|) = \lambda_1 \quad |v_1\rangle = \begin{pmatrix} \frac{13}{20} \\ \frac{37}{50} \\ \frac{9}{50} \end{pmatrix} \quad \lambda_1 = \frac{1}{2}$$

The second intuition is that a density matrix is not necessarily a mixture like (6.6), but can also be a superposition like (6.9). Therefore, how the word senses are combined differs depending on the interpretation of word sense combination—superposition enables the modeling of interference and then the non-distributiveness with respect to w and its senses. Suppose that a new word vector is defined as the following superposition of the eigenvectors,

$$|v\rangle = \frac{1}{\sqrt{3}}|s_1\rangle + \frac{1}{\sqrt{3}}|s_2\rangle + \frac{1}{\sqrt{3}}|s_2\rangle$$

It follows that $\frac{1}{3}$ is the probability that the word has sense s_i for every i.

The third intuition is that compound terms or word senses can be modeled using entanglement (instead of superposition). For example, the semantic space associated to "pet fish" can be defined as an entangled density matrix which cannot be decomposed into the semantic space of "pet" and that of "fish". Suppose two Hilbert spaces are used to represent the semantics of "pet" and that of "fish", respectively. Also, suppose that $\{|\text{pet}_0\rangle, |\text{pet}_1\rangle\}$ and $\{|\text{fish}_0\rangle, |\text{fish}_1\rangle\}$ are the possible sense vectors of "pet" and that of "fish", respectively. It follows that $\{|\text{pet}_0\rangle \otimes |\text{fish}_0\rangle, |\text{pet}_1\rangle \otimes |\text{fish}_0\rangle, \{|\text{pet}_0\rangle \otimes |\text{fish}_1\rangle, |\text{pet}_1\rangle \otimes |\text{fish}_1\rangle\}$ is a basis of the product of the two spaces and represents the possible combined senses. If "pet fish" is represented by

$$|\text{petfish}\rangle = \frac{1}{\sqrt{2}}|\text{pet}_0\rangle \otimes |\text{fish}_0\rangle + \frac{1}{\sqrt{2}}|\text{pet}_1\rangle \otimes |\text{fish}_1\rangle$$

there are no vectors $|\text{pet}\rangle$, $|\text{fish}\rangle$ such that

$$|\text{pet}\rangle = a_0|\text{pet}_0\rangle + a_1|\text{pet}_1\rangle \qquad |\text{fish}\rangle = b_0|\text{fish}_0\rangle + b_1|\text{fish}_1\rangle$$

$$|\text{petfish}\rangle = |\text{pet}\rangle \otimes |\text{fish}\rangle$$

Melucci and Sitbon (2011) investigates the formalism of interference for modeling emergent associate words within compounds like "pet fish". They consider the situation that $b = b_1 b_2$ is a compound (e.g., "pet fish") and v is an associate word (e.g., "ocean"). Using classical probability, these events are sets and emergent associate words cannot be easily modeled. Using superposition, b is "pet fish", b_1 is "pet", b_2 is "fish", $\bar{b}_1$ and $\bar{b}_2$ are the corresponding negations. As the vectors lie in the same space, b can be represented as a superposition of "pet" and its negation or equivalently as a superposition of "fish" and its negation as follows:

$$|b\rangle = a_{ib}|b_i\rangle + \bar{a}_{ib}|\bar{b}_i\rangle \qquad |a_{ib}|^2 + |\bar{a}_{ib}|^2 = i \qquad \langle b_i|\bar{b}_i\rangle = 0 \qquad i = 1, 2$$

The $|a_{ij}|^2$'s are the probability that, say, "pet" occurs in "pet fish" and $|\bar{a}_{ij}|^2$ is the complement probability. The fact that b can be represented as a superposition is witnessed by the infinite number of ways of writing it as the sum of two other vectors which are not those corresponding to "pet" or to "fish". Using Quantum Probability,

$$|\langle v|b\rangle|^2 = |a_{ib}|^2|a_{iv}|^2 + |\bar{a}_{ib}|^2|\bar{a}_{iv}|^2 + 2I \qquad i = 1,2 \qquad (6.19)$$

where the sum of the first two terms of the right-hand side is the classical probability $P(v|b)$ and $I = |a_{ib}||a_{iv}||\bar{a}_{ib}||\bar{a}_{iv}|\cos\theta$ is the interference term. As $-1 \le I \le +1$, (6.19) can be lower or higher than $P(v|b)$ then it can be used for predicting emergent associates.

6.4.2.2 Document Representation and Ranking

The research in document representation and ranking using QM is characterized by the algebraic approach providing a uniform and general description of information object indexing, retrieval and ranking. While the general framework for a uniform and general description in IR is presented by van Rijsbergen (2004), some aspects are addressed by Piwowarski et al. (2010), Huertas-Rosero et al. (2008, 2009), Zuccon et al. (2009), Zuccon and Azzopardi (2010). Unlike the semantic spaces, this area of research in the use of QM in IR is more varied and has produced seemingly different contributions.

Starting from Melucci (2008), vector spaces are implemented by Piwowarski et al. (2010) for representing documents and information needs which are formally defined, respectively, as vectors or in general as subspaces spanned by vectors and as density matrices. Unlike other works, this representation is used for modeling an interaction framework in which the density matrices are updated thanks to user behavior and input, and the subspaces that represent the documents are events.

Something different is illustrated by Huertas-Rosero et al. (2008, 2009). An eraser is an operator which resembles a projector. Intuitively, an eraser transforms a text in a set of text windows centered around a word while the text outside the windows is removed. More formally, a set of erasers gives rise to a non-Boolean lattice in which distributiveness does not hold. Hence, erasers are like events of a non-classical probability space. Perhaps, the main contribution of erasers is a formal language for indexing and retrieval in a QM setting.

The assumption of the Probability Ranking Principle (PRP) that the relevance assessment of a document is independent of the relevance assessment of another document is addressed by Zuccon et al. (2009), Zuccon and Azzopardi (2010). In order to remove that assumption, the interaction between a user and the retrieved documents is revisited. The documents are no longer supposed to be presented one at a time. On the contrary, they are presented together. The relevance assessments are viewed as a photon passing through a double-slit, thus it produces interference. Therefore, the relevance assessment is modeled as a superposition of two vectors corresponding to the documents while the probability of relevance (i.e., the probability that the user stops studied by Zuccon et al. (2009)) is given by the squared sum of probability amplitudes rather that the sum of the probabilities of disjoint events. Hence, the Quantum PRP says that the documents should be ranked by the probability of relevance modified by the interference term (which has to be estimated).

6.4.2.3 Testing Quantum-Like Models

The study of the presence of quantum phenomena in IR and in general the evaluation of quantum-like models are still at the beginning. Nevertheless, there are already some efforts which may be classified into two main classes. The first class of experiments includes the classical experiments aiming at comparing the quantum-like models with the non-quantum-like ones which are used as baseline for measuring the difference in precision; examples of the first class can be found in (Huertas-Rosero et al. 2009; Zuccon and Azzopardi 2010). The second class of experiments includes the experiments designed for testing the hypothesis that quantum phenomena in processes of IR or of areas related to IR occurs. As regards the areas related to IR, the experiments have mainly addressed the presence of interference in human cognition and lexicon and have been based on user studies; examples are reported by Aerts and Gabora (2005), Busemeyer (2009), Hou and Song (2009). An experiment more directly related to IR is reported by Melucci (2010); it discusses a situation in which quantum probability arises naturally in IR, and reports that the best terms for query expansion have probabilities which do not admit classical probability but instead can be defined by a quantum probability function. Di Buccio et al. (2011) discusses the situation where the user's relevance state is modeled using quantum-like probability and the interference term is proposed so as to model the evolution of the state and the user's uncertainty about the assessment. The theoretical framework has been formulated and the results of an experimental user study based on a TREC test collection have been reported. Their hypothesis is that the superposition of relevance and non-relevance, which reflects the user's uncertainty about his assessment, affects the user's behavior and therefore the interaction features, thus making prediction performed by the system less precise and more prone to error. If the hypothesis is true, it can have important theoretical and practical implications. For example, if interference is detected, the system may support the user to clarify his state by suggesting example documents or by presenting the results in more effective way. Moreover, if there is interference, the system may infer that the initial query is difficult and therefore invite the user to add terms.

6.5 Conclusions

"But does it work? Well as always that is a matter for experimentation. [...] The great thing is that we now have a formalism that allows us to reason sensibly about that underlying mechanism and it applies to objects or documents in any media. It is not text specific. No assumptions are made about the vectors in the space other than that they participate in the geometry and that they can be observed for answers in the way I have been explaining" (van Rijsbergen 2004).

In this chapter, we argue that quantum probability is a crucial step to achieve a significant increase of retrieval performance accompanied by the understanding of the mechanism underlying the retrieval process. Since van Rijsbergen's book, further investigations and some preliminary experiments have been done by a very active research community trying to achieve that objective.

Acknowledgements   The work by Massimo Melucci has received funding from the European Union Seventh Framework Programme (FP7/2007-2013) under grant agreement N. 247590.

Chapter 7
Multimedia Resource Discovery

Stefan Rüger

Abstract This chapter examines the challenges and opportunities of Multimedia Information Retrieval and corresponding search engine applications. Computer technology has changed our access to information tremendously: We used to search authors or titles (which we had to know) in library cards in order to locate relevant books; now we can issue keyword searches within the full text of whole book repositories in order to identify authors, titles and locations of relevant books. What about the corresponding challenge of finding multimedia by fragments, examples and excerpts? Rather than asking for a music piece by artist and title, can we hum its tune to find it? Can doctors submit scans of a patient to identify medically similar images of diagnosed cases in a database? Can your mobile phone take a picture of a statue and tell you about its artist and significance via a service that it sends this picture to?

In an attempt to answer some of these questions we get to know basic concepts of multimedia resource discovery technologies for a number of different query and document types: piggy-back text search, i.e., reducing the multimedia to pseudo text documents; automated annotation of visual components; content-based retrieval where the query is an image; and fingerprinting to match near duplicates.

Some of the research challenges are given by the semantic gap between the simple pixel properties computers can readily index and high-level human concepts; related to this is an inherent technological limitation of automated annotation of images from pixels alone. Other challenges are given by polysemy, i.e., the many meanings and interpretations that are inherent in visual material and the corresponding wide range of a user's information need.

This book chapter is an updated re-print of Rüger (2009), Multimedia resource discovery, in Göker and Davies (eds), Information Retrieval: Searching in the 21st Century, pp. 39–62, Wiley, with excerpts from Rüger (2010), Multimedia information retrieval, Lecture notes in the series Synthesis Lectures on Information Concepts, Retrieval, and Services, Morgan and Claypool Publishers, http://dx.doi.org/10.2200/S00244ED1V01Y200912ICR010.

S. Rüger (✉)
Knowledge Media Institute, The Open University, Milton Keynes, MK7 6AA, United Kingdom
e-mail: s.rueger@open.ac.uk
url: http://people.kmi.open.ac.uk/stefan

M. Melucci, R. Baeza-Yates (eds.), *Advanced Topics in Information Retrieval*,
The Information Retrieval Series 33,
DOI 10.1007/978-3-642-20946-8_7, © Springer-Verlag Berlin Heidelberg 2011

157

This chapter demonstrates how these challenges can be tackled by automated processing and machine learning and by utilising the skills of the user, for example through browsing or through a process that is called relevance feedback, thus putting the user at centre stage. The latter is made easier by "added value" technologies, exemplified here by summaries of complex multimedia objects such as TV news, information visualisation techniques for document clusters, visual search by example, and methods to create browsable structures within the collection.

7.1 Introduction

Resource discovery is more than just search: it is browsing, searching, selecting, assessing and evaluating, i.e., ultimately accessing information. Giving users access to collections is one of the defining tasks of a library. For thousands of years the traditional methods of resource discovery have been facilitated by librarians: they create reference cards with meta-data that are put into catalogues (nowadays, databases); they also place the objects in physical locations that follow certain classification schemes and they answer questions at the reference desk.

The advent of digital documents has radically changed the organisation principles; now it is possible to *automatically* index and search document collections as big as the Web *à la* Google and browse collections utilising author-inserted links. It is almost as if automated processing has turned the traditional library access paradigm upside down. Instead of searching meta-data catalogues in order to retrieve the document, web search engines search the full content of documents and retrieve their meta-data, i.e., the location where documents can be found. Not all manual intervention has been abandoned, though. For example, the Yahoo directory[1] is an edited classification scheme of submitted web sites that are put into a browsable directory structure akin to library classification schemes.

At its very core, multimedia information retrieval means the process of searching for and finding multimedia documents; the corresponding research field is concerned with building multimedia search engines. The intriguing bit about multimedia retrieval is that the query itself can be a multimedia excerpt: for example, if you walk around in pleasant Milton Keynes, you may stumble across the interesting building that is depicted in Fig. 7.1.

Would it not be nice if you could just take a picture with your mobile phone and send it to a service that matches your picture to their database and tells you more about the building? The service could reply with

"Built by the monks and nuns of the Nipponzan Myohoji, this was the first Peace Pagoda to be built in the western hemisphere and enshrines sacred relics of Lord Buddha. The Inau-

---

[1] See http://dir.yahoo.com/.

Fig. 7.1 Milton Keynes's Peace Pagoda

guration ceremony, on 21st September 1980, was presided over by the late most Venerable Nichidattsu Fujii, founder …"[2]

Given the much wider remit of multimedia search over just text search, and assuming we could perfectly search with queries that are "multimedia" itself, what could we do with multimedia search?

The previous example is an obvious application for tourism. There are also applications for advertising that so much seems to underpin the whole search industry: Snaptell Inc, is a startup company that specialises in mobile image search; their idea is that customers take pictures from print-media adverts, send them in and receive promotion or product information, vouchers and so on. For example, customers sending in a picture of the print poster that advertises a new movie receive an exclusive trailer, see showtimes of cinemas in the area and, in theory, could straight away phone to order tickets. One added benefit for advertisers is that they receive feedback as to where print adverts were noticed. Snaptell has since then specialised on recognising book, CD and DVD covers, from photographs that can then be bought with a few clicks.

Another considerable and obvious application is for medical image databases. When someone who suffers from shortness of breath consults doctors, they might wonder where they have seen the light shadow on the X-ray before. If computers were able to match significant, medically relevant patterns with those in the database, they could return data on these diagnosed cases, so the specialists

---

[2]See http://www.mkweb.co.uk/places_to_visit/displayarticle.asp?id=411 accessed Aug 2010.

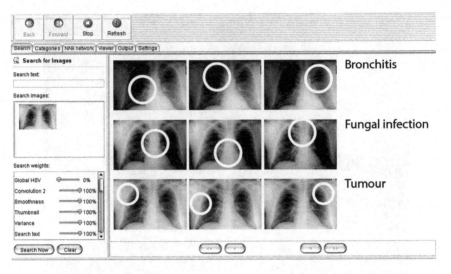

Fig. 7.2 Medical-image retrieval (mock-up)

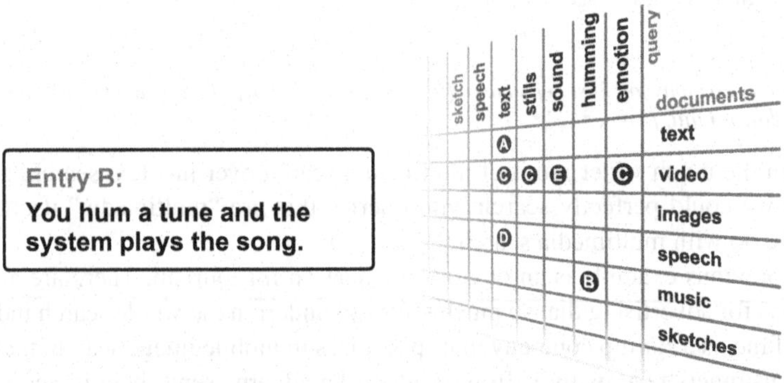

Entry B:
You hum a tune and the
system plays the song.

Fig. 7.3 New search engine types

can undertake an informed differential diagnosis using medical-image retrieval (Fig. 7.2).

The common factor of the previous examples was that documents and queries can consist of various different media. Figure 7.3 takes this observation radically forward by looking at the full matrix of combining different query modes (columns) with document repository types (rows). Entry A in this matrix corresponds to a traditional text search engine; this deploys a completely different technology than Entry B, a system that allows you to express musical queries by humming a tune and that then plays the corresponding song. The three C entries in Fig. 7.3 correspond to a multi-modal video search engine allowing search by emotion with example images and text queries, e.g., *find me video shots of "sad" scenes using an image of a dilapidated castle and the text "vampire".* In contrast to this, Entry D could be a search engine with a query text box that returns BBC Radio 4 discussions.

It is relatively easy to come up with a usage scenario for each of the matrix elements in Fig. 7.3: for example, the image input speech output matrix element might be "given an X-ray image of a patient's chest, retrieve dictaphone documents with a relevant spoken description of a matching diagnosis". However, creating satisfying retrieval solutions is highly non-trivial and the main subject of the multimedia information retrieval discipline. This chapter summarises different basic technologies involved in these multimedia search modes. Not all combinations are equally useful, desirable or well researched, though: Entry E might be a query where you roar like a lion and hope to retrieve a wildlife documentary.

Undoubtedly, it is the automated approaches that have made all the difference to the way the vast Web can be used. While the automated indexing of text documents has been successfully applied to collections as large as the Web for more than a decade now, multimedia indexing by content involves different, still less mature and less scalable technologies.

Multimedia collections pose their very own challenges; for example, images and videos don't often come with dedicated reference cards or meta-data, and when they do, as in museum collections, their creation will have been expensive and time-consuming. Section 7.3 explores the difficulties and limitations of automatically indexing, labelling and annotating image and video content. It briefly discusses the inherent challenges of the semantic gap, polysemy, fusion and responsiveness.

Even if all these challenges were solved, indexing sheer mass is no guarantee of a successful annotation either: While most of today's inter-library loan systems allow access to virtually any publication in the world—around 198M bibliographic records in OCLC's Worldcat database[3] in contrast to only 3M entries from Bowker's Books In Print that can be bought—students and researchers alike seem to be reluctant to actually make use of this facility. On the other hand, the much smaller catalogue offered by the online bookseller Amazon appears to be very popular, presumably owing to added services such as subject categories; fault tolerant search tools; personalised services telling the customer what's new in a subject area or what other people with a similar profile bought; pictures of book covers; media and customer reviews; access to the table of contents, to selections of the text and to the full-text index of popular books; and the perception of fast delivery. In the multimedia context Sect. 7.4 argues that automated added services such as visual queries, relevance feedback and summaries can prove useful for resource discovery in multimedia digital libraries. Section 7.4.1 is about summarising techniques for videos, Sect. 7.4.2 exemplifies visualisation of search results, while Sect. 7.4.3 discusses content-based visual search modes such as query-by-example and relevance feedback.

Finally, Sect. 7.5 promotes browsing as resource discovery mode and looks at underlying techniques to automatically structure the document collection to support browsing.

---

[3] See http://www.oclc.org/worldcat/statistics accessed Aug 2010.

7.2 Basic Multimedia Search Technologies

The current best practice to index multimedia collections is via the generation of a library card, i.e., a dedicated database entry of meta-data such as author, title, publication year and keywords. Depending on the concrete implementation these can be found with SQL queries, text-search engines or XML query language, but all these search modes are based on text descriptions of some form and are agnostic to the structure of the actual objects they refer to, be it books, CDs, videos, newspaper articles, paintings, sculptures, web pages, consumer products etc.

The text column of the matrix of Fig. 7.3 is underpinned by text search technology and requires the textual representation of the multimedia objects, an approach that I like to call *piggy-back text retrieval*. Other approaches are based on an automatic classification of multimedia objects and on assigning words from a fixed vocabulary. This can be a certain camera motion that can be detected in a video (zoom, pan, tilt, roll, dolly in and out, truck left and right, pedestal up and down, crane boom, swing boom etc.); a genre for music pieces such as jazz, classics; a generic scene description in images such as inside/outside, people, vegetation, landscape, grass, city-view etc. or specific object detection like faces and cars etc. These approaches are known as *feature classification* or *automated annotation*.

The type of search that is most commonly associated with multimedia is *content-based*: The basic idea is that still images, music extracts, video clips themselves can be used as queries and that the retrieval system is expected to return 'similar' database entries. This technology differs most radically from the thousands-year-old library card paradigm in that there is no necessity for meta-data at all. In certain searches there is the desire to match not only the general type of scene or music that the query represents, but instead one and only one exact multimedia object. For example, you take a picture of a painting in a gallery and submit this as a query to the gallery's catalogue in the hope of receiving the whole database record about this particular painting, and not a variant or otherwise similar exhibit. This is sometimes called *fingerprinting* or *known-item search*.

The rest of this section outlines these four basic multimedia search technologies.

7.2.1 Piggy-Back Text Retrieval

Amongst all media types, TV video streams arguably have the biggest scope for automatically extracting text strings in a number of ways: directly from closed-captions, teletext or subtitles; automated speech recognition on the audio and optical character recognition for text embedded in the frames of a video. Full text search of these strings is the way in which most video retrieval systems operate, including Google's TV search engine http://video.google.com or Blinkx-TV http://www.blinkx.tv. In contrast to television, for which legislation normally requires subtitles to assist the hearing impaired, videos stored on DVD do not usually have textual subtitles. They have *subpicture* channels for different languages instead, which are overlayed on the video stream. This requires the extra step of optical character recognition, which can be done with a relatively low error rate owing to good quality fonts and clear background/foreground separation in the subpictures. In general, teletext has a much lower word error rate than automated speech recognition. In practice, it turns out that this does not matter too much as query words often occur repeatedly in the audio—the retrieval performance degrades gracefully with increased word error rates.

Web pages afford some context information that can be used for indexing multimedia objects. For example, words in the anchor text of a link to an image, a video clip or a music track, the file name of the object itself, meta-data stored within the files and other context information such as captions. A subset of these sources for text snippets are normally used in web image search engines.

Some symbolic music representations allow the conversion of music into text, such as MIDI files which contain a music representation in terms of pitch, onset times and duration of notes. By representing differences of successive pitches as characters one can, for example, map monophonic music to one-dimensional strings. A large range of different text matching techniques can be deployed, for example the edit distance of database strings with a string representation of a query. The edit distance between two strings computes the smallest number of deletions, insertions or character replacements that is necessary to transform one string into the other. In the case of query-by-humming, where a pitch tracker can convert the hummed query into a MIDI-sequence (Birmingham et al. 2006), the edit distance is also able to deal gracefully with humming errors. Other techniques create fixed-length strings, so called n-grams, with windows that glide over the sequence of notes. The resulting strings can be indexed with a normal text search engine. This approach can also be extended to polyphonic music, where more than one note can be sounded at any one time (Doraisamy and Rüger 2003).

7.2.2 Automated Annotation

Two of the factors limiting the uptake of digital libraries for multimedia are the scarcity and the expense of metadata for digital media. Flickr,[4] a popular photo sharing site, lets users upload, organise and annotate their own photographs with tags. In order to search images in Flickr, little more than user tags are available with the effect that many photographs are difficult or impossible to find. The same is true for the video sharing site YouTube.[5] At the other end of the spectrum are commercial sites such as the digital multimedia store iTunes,[6] which sells music, movies, TV shows, audio-books, podcasts and games. They tend to have sufficiently many annotations as the commercial nature of iTunes makes it viable to supply

---

[4] See http://flickr.com.

[5] See http://www.youtube.com.

[6] See http://www.apple.com/itunes.

metadata to the required level of granularity. While personal photographs and videos do not come with much metadata except for the data that the camera provides (time-stamp and technical data such as aperture, exposure, sensitivity and focal length), a whole class of surveillance data carries even less incentive to create metadata manually: CCTV recordings, satellite images, audio recordings in the sea and other sensor data. The absence of labels and metadata is a real barrier for complex and high-level queries such as "what did the person with a red jumper look like who exited the car park during the last 6 hours in a black Volvo at high speed".

One way to generate useful tags and metadata for multimedia objects is to in-volve a community of people who carry out the tagging collaboratively. This process is also called folksonomy, social indexing or social tagging. Del.icio.us[7] is a social bookmarking system and a good example for folksonomies. Similarly, the ability of Flickr to annotate images of other people falls also into this category. von Ahn and Dabbish (2004) have invented a computer game that provides an incentive (competi-tion and points) for people to label randomly selected images. All these approaches tap into "human computing power" for a good cause: the structuring and labelling of multimedia objects. Research in this area is still in the beginning, and it is by no way clear how to best harness the social power of collaborative tagging to improve metadata for, and access to, digital museums and libraries.

Another way to bridge the semantic gap (see Sect. 7.3) is to try to assign simple words automatically to images solely based on their pixels. Methods attempting this task include dedicated machine vision models for particular words such as "people" or "aeroplane". These individual models for each of the words can quickly become very detailed and elaborate: Thomas Huang of the University of Illinois at Urbana Champaign once joked during his keynote speech at CIVR 2002 that in order to enable a system to annotate 1,000 words automatically, it was merely a case of supervising 1,000 corresponding PhD projects!

Automated annotation can be formulated in more general terms of machine trans-lation as seen in Fig. 7.4. The basic idea is to first dissect images into blobs of similar colour and then use these blobs as "words" of a visual vocabulary. Given a training set of annotated images a correlation between certain words and certain blobs can then be established in a similar way to correlations between corresponding words of two different languages using a parallel corpus (for example, the official records of

Fig. 7.4 Automated annotation as machine translation problem

the Canadian Parliament in French and English). Duygulu et al. (2002) created the first successful automated annotation mechanisms based on this idea.

However, the most popular and successful *generic* approaches are based on classification techniques. This normally requires a large training set of images that have annotations from which one can extract features and correlate these with the existing annotations of the training set. For example, images with tigers will have orange-black stripes and often green patches from surrounding vegetation, and their existence in an unseen image can in turn bring about the annotation "tiger". As with any machine learning method, it is important to work with a large set of training examples. Figure 7.5 shows randomly selected, royalty free images from the Corel's Gallery 380,000 product that were annotated with *sunset* (top) and *city* (bottom). Each of these images can have multiple annotations: there are pictures that are annotated with *both* sunset and city, and possibly other terms.

Automated algorithms build a model for the commonalities in the features of images, which can later be used for retrieval. One of the simplest machine learning algorithms is the Naïve Bayes formula,

$$P(w|i) = \frac{P(w,i)}{P(i)}$$
$$= \frac{\sum_j P(w,i|j)P(j)}{\sum_j P(i|j)P(j)}$$
$$= \frac{\sum_j P(i|w,j)P(w|j)P(j)}{\sum_j \sum_w P(i|w,j)P(w|j)P(j)},$$

where j are training images, w are word annotations and $P(w|i)$ is the probability of a word w given an (unseen) image i. The probability $P(w,j)$ that word w is used to annotate image j can be estimated from an empirical distribution of annotations in the training data.

Figure 7.6 shows an unseen image i for which the five words with the highest probabilities $P(w|i)$ according to above Naïve Bayes classification are all sensible and useful.

Yavlinsky et al. (2005) built models based on a similar idea for which the model for keywords appearance is derived from non-parametric density estimators with specialised kernels that utilise the Earth mover's distance. The assumption is that these kernels reflect the nature of the underlying features well. Yavlinsky built a corresponding search engine Behold,[8] where one could search for Flickr images using these detected terms. These algorithms all make errors as one can expect from fully automated systems. Figure 7.7 shows screenshots from an early version of behold. Clearly, not all words are predicted correctly, and the ugly examples from this figure might motivate to study methods that use external knowledge, for example, that stairs and icebergs normally do not go together.

Today, Makadia et al.'s (2008) recent work on the nearest neighbour label transfer provide a baseline for automatic image annotation using global low-level features

---

[8] See http://www.behold.cc.

Fig. 7.5 Machine learning training samples for *sunset* (*top*) and *city* images (*bottom*)

Fig. 7.6 Automated annotation results in *water*, *buildings*, *city*, *sunset* and *aerial*

and a straightforward label transfer from the 5 nearest neighbours. This approach is likely to work very well if enough images are available in a labelled set that are very close to the unlabelled application set. This may be the case, for example, in museums where images of groups of objects are taken in a batch fashion with the same lighting and background and only some of the objects in the group have received manual labels. Liu et al. (2009c) also use label transfer, albeit in a slightly different setting since they aim to segment and recognise scenes rather than assign global classification labels.

Automated annotation from pixels faces criticism not only owing to its current inability to model a large and useful vocabulary with high accuracy. Enser and Sandom (2002, 2003) argue that some of the vital information for significance and content of images *has* to come from metadata: it is virtually impossible to, e.g., compute the date or location of an image from its pixels. A real-world image query such as "Stirling Moss winning Kentish 100 Trophy at Brands Hatch, 30 August 1968" cannot be answered without metadata. They argue that pixel-based algorithms will never be able to compute *significance* of images such as "first public engagement of Prince Charles as a boy" or "the first ordination of a woman as bishop". Their UK-funded arts and humanities research project "Bridging the Semantic Gap in Visual Information Retrieval" (Hare et al. 2006; Enser and Sandom 2003) brought a new understanding about the role of the semantic gap in visual image retrieval.

Owing to these observations and also owing to their relatively large error rates, automated annotation methods seem to be more suitable in the context of browsing or in conjunction with other search methods. For example, if you want to "find shots

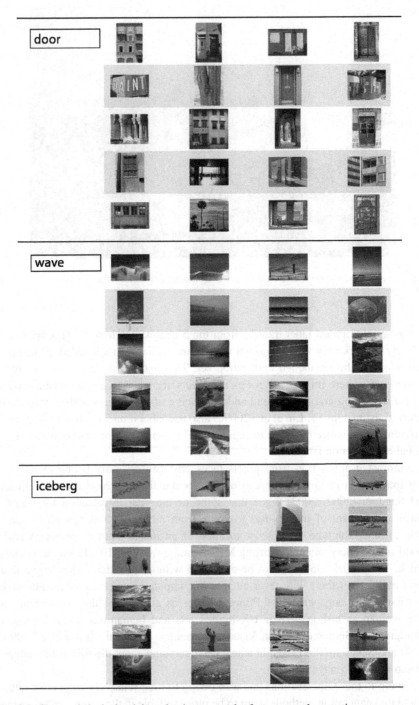

Fig. 7.7 The good, the bad and the ugly: three examples for automated annotation

of the front of the White House in the daytime with the fountain running",[9] then a query-by-example search in a large database may be solved quicker and better by emphasising those shots that were classified as "vegetation", "outside", "building" etc.—even though the individual classification may be wrong in a significant proportion of cases.

There is a host of research that supports the bridging of the semantic gap via automated annotation. Hare and Lewis (2004) use salient interest points and the concept of scale to the selection of salient regions in an image to describe the image characteristics in that region; they then extended this work (Hare and Lewis 2005) to model visual terms from a training set that can then be used to annotate unseen images. Magalhães and Rüger (2006) developed a clustering method that is more computationally efficient than the currently very effective method of non-parametric density estimation, which Magalhães and Rüger later 2007 integrated into a unique multimedia indexing model for heterogeneous data. Torralba and Oliva (2003) obtained relatively good results with simple scene-level statistics, while others deploy more complex models: Jeon et al. (2003) and Lavrenko et al. (2003) studied cross-lingual information retrieval models, while Metzler and Manmatha (2004) set up inference networks that connect image segments with words. Blei and Jordan (2003) carry out probabilistic modelling with latent Dirichlet allocation, while Feng et al. (2004) use Bernoulli distributions.

Machine learning methods for classification and annotation are not limited to images at all. For example, one can extract motion vectors from MPEG-encoded videos and use these to classify a video shot independently into categories such as object motion from left to right, zoom in, tilt, roll, dolly in and out, truck left and right, pedestal up and down, crane boom, swing boom etc. In contrast to the above classification tasks, the extracted motion vector features are much more closely correlated to the ensuing motion label than image features are to text labels, and the corresponding learning task should be much simpler a consequence.

The application area for classification can be rather diverse: Baillie and Jose (2004) use audio analysis of the crowd response in a football game to detect important events in the match; Cavallaro and Ebrahimi (2004) propose an interaction mechanism between the semantic and the region partitions, which allows to detect multiple simultaneous objects in videos.

On a higher level, Salway and Graham (2003) developed a method to extract information about emotions of characters in films and suggested that this information can help describe higher levels of multimedia semantics relating to narrative structures. Salway et al. (2005) contributed to the analysis and description of semantic video content by investigating what actions are important in films.

Musical genre classification can be carried out on extracted audio-features that represent a performance by its statistics of pitch content, rhythmic structure and timbre texture (Tzanetakis and Cook 2002): timbre texture features are normally computed using short-time Fourier transform and Mel-frequency cepstral coefficients that also play a vital role in speech recognition; the rhythmic structure of music

---

[9]Topic 124 of TRECVid 2003, see http://www-nlpir.nist.gov/projects/tv2003.

can be explored using discrete wavelet transforms that have a different time resolution for different frequencies; pitch detection, especially in polyphonic music, is more intricate and requires more elaborate algorithms. For details, see the work of Tolonen and Karjalainen (2000). Tzanetakis and Cook (2002) report correct classification rates of between 40% (rock) and 75% (jazz) in their experiments with 10 different genres.

7.2.3 Content-Based Retrieval

Content-based retrieval uses characteristics of the multimedia objects themselves, i.e., their content to search and find multimedia. Its main application is to find multimedia by examples, i.e., when the query consists not of words but of a similar example instance.

One of the difficulties of matching multimedia is that the parts the media are made from are not necessarily semantic units. Another difficulty comes about by the sheer amount of data with little apparent structure. Look at the black and white photograph of Fig. 7.8, for example. It literally consists of millions of pixels, and each of the pixels encodes an intensity (one number between $0 =$ black and $255 =$ white) or a colour (three numbers for the red, green and blue colour channel, say). One of the prime tasks in multimedia retrieval is to make sense out of this sea of numbers.

The key here is to condense the sheer amount of numbers into meaningful pieces of information, which we call *features*. One trivial example is to compute an inten-

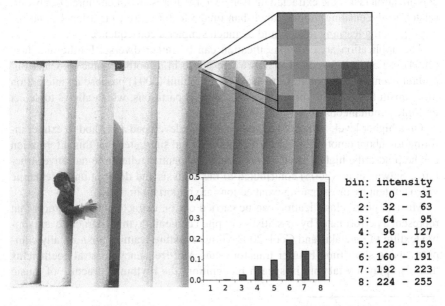

Fig. 7.8 Millions of pixels with intensity values and the corresponding intensity histogram

Fig. 7.9 Features and distances

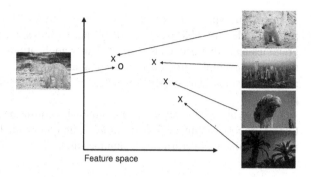

Feature space

sity histogram, i.e., count which proportion of the pixels falls into which intensity ranges. In Fig. 7.8 I have chosen 8 ranges, and the histogram of 8 numbers conveys a rough distribution of brightness in the image.

Figure 7.9 shows the main principle of *query-by-example*; in this case, the query is the image of an ice-bear on the left. This query image will have a representation as a certain point (O) in feature space. In the same way, every single image in the database has its own representation (X) in the same space. The images whose representations are closest to the representation of the query are ranked top by this process. The two key elements really are features and distances. Our choice of feature space and how to compute distances has a vital impact on how well visual search by example works.

Features and distances are a vital part of content-based retrieval and so is the ability to efficiently find nearest neighbours in high-dimensional spaces. Lew et al. (2006) and Datta et al. (2008) have published overview articles on content-based retrieval, and Rüger (2010) treats content-based retrieval including features and distances commonly used in depth.

The architecture presented here is a typical albeit basic one; there are many variations and some radically different approaches that have been published in the past. A whole research field has gathered around the area of video and image retrieval as exemplified by the annual International ACM Conferences on Video and Image Retrieval (CIVR), Multimedia (ACM MM) and Multimedia Information Retrieval (MIR) and the TREC video evaluation workshop TRECVid; there is another research field around music retrieval, see the annual International Conference on Music Information Retrieval (ISMIR).

7.2.4 Fingerprinting

Multimedia fingerprints are unique indices in a multimedia database. They are computed from the contents of the multimedia objects, are small, allow the fast, reliable and *unique* location of the database record and are robust against degradation or deliberate change of the multimedia document that do not alter their human perception. Audio fingerprints of music tracks are expected to distinguish even between different performances of the same song by the same artist at perhaps different concerts or studios.

Interesting applications include services that allow broadcast monitoring companies to identify what was played, so that royalties are fairly distributed or programmes and advertisements verified. Other applications uncover copyright violation or, for example, provide a service that allows you to locate the meta-data such as title, artist and date of performance from snippets recorded on a (noisy) mobile phone.

Cano et al. (2005) review some audio fingerprinting methods and Seo et al. (2004) proposes an image fingerprinting technique, while Rüger (2010) treats some audio and image fingerprinting techniques in depth.

7.3 Challenges of Automated Visual Indexing

There are a number of open issues with the content-based retrieval approach in multimedia. On a perceptual level, those low-level features do not necessarily correlate with any high-level meaning the images might have. This problem is known as the *semantic gap*: imagine a scene in which Bobby Moore, the captain of the English National Football team in 1966, receives the world cup trophy from Queen Elizabeth II; there is no obvious correlation between low-level colour, shape and texture descriptors and the high-level meaning of victory and triumph (or defeat and misery if you happened to support the West German team). Some of the computer vision methods go towards the bridging of the semantic gap, for example the ability to assign simple concrete labels to image parts such as "grass", "sky", "people", "plates". A consequent use of an ontology could explain the presence of higher-level concepts such as "barbecue" in terms of the simpler labels.

Even if the semantic gap could be bridged, there is still another challenge, namely *polysemy*: images usually convey a multitude of meanings so that the query-by-example approach is bound to under-specify the real information need. Users who submit an image such as the one in Fig. 7.8 could have a dozen different information needs in mind: "find other images with the same person", "find images of the same art scene", "find other bright art sculptures", "find images with gradual shadow transitions", ... It is these different interpretations that make further user feedback so important.

User feedback can change the weights of features in content-based retrieval scenarios; these weights represent the plasticity of the retrieval system. Hence, putting the user in the loop and designing a human-computer interaction that utilises the user's feedback has been one of the main approaches to tackle these perceptual issues. Amongst other methods there are those that seek to reformulate the query (Ishikawa et al. 1998) or those that weight the various features differently depending on the user's feedback. Weight adaptation methods include cluster analysis of the images (Wood et al. 1998); transposed files for feature selection (Squire et al. 2000); Bayesian network learning (Cox et al. 2000); statistical analysis of the feature distributions of relevant images and variance analysis (Rui et al. 1998); and analytic global optimisation (Heesch and Rüger 2003). Some approaches give the presentation and placement of images on screen much consideration to indicate similarity of images amongst themselves (Santini and Jain 2000; Rodden et al. 1999) or with respect to a visual query (Heesch and Rüger 2003).

On a practical level, the multitude of features assigned to images poses a *fusion problem*; how to combine possibly conflicting evidence of two images' similarity? There are many approaches to carry out fusion, some based on labelled training data and some based on user feedback for the current query (Aslam and Montague 2001; Bartell et al. 1994; Shaw and Fox 1994; Yavlinsky et al. 2004).

There is a *responsiveness problem*, too, in that the naïve comparison of query feature vectors to the database feature vectors requires a linear scan through the database. Although the scan is eminently scalable, the practicalities of doing this operation can mean an undesirable response time in the order of seconds rather than the 100 milli-seconds that can be achieved by text search engines. The problem is that high-dimensional tree structures tend to collapse to linear scans above a certain dimensionality (Weber et al. 1998). As a consequence, some approaches for fast nearest-neighbour search use compression techniques to speed up the disk access of linear scan as in (Weber et al. 1998) using VA-files; or they approximate the search (Nene and Nayar 1997; Beis and Lowe 1997); decompose the features componentwise (de Vries et al. 2002; Aggarwal and Yu 2000) saving access to unnecessary components; or deploy a combination of these (Müller and Henrich 2004; Howarth and Rüger 2005).

7.4 Added Services

7.4.1 Video Summaries

Even if the challenges of the previous section were all solved and if the automated methods of Sect. 7.2 enabled a retrieval process with high precision (proportion of the retrieved items that are relevant) and high recall (proportion of the relevant items that are retrieved) it would still be vital to present the retrieval results in a way so that the users can quickly decide to which degree those items are relevant to them.

Images are most naturally displayed as thumbnails, and their relevance can quickly be judged by users. Presenting and summarising videos is a bit more involved. The main metaphor used for this is that of a *storyboard* that contains *keyframes* with some text about the video. Several systems exist that summarise news stories in this way, most notably Informedia (Christel et al. 1999) and Físchlár (Smeaton et al. 2004). The Informedia system devotes much effort to added services such as face recognition and speaker voice identification allowing retrieval of the appearance of known people. Informedia also provides alternative modes of presentation, e.g., through film skims or by assembling 'collages' of images, text and other information (e.g., maps) sourced via references from the text (Christel and Warmack 2001). Físchlár's added value lies in the ability to personalise the content (with the user expressing like or dislike of stories) and in assembling lists of related stories and recommendations.

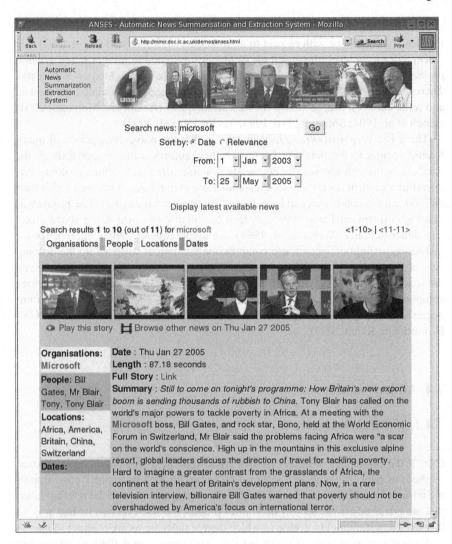

Fig. 7.10 News search engine interface

Our very own TV news search engine ANSES (Pickering et al. 2003; Pickering 2004) records the main BBC evening news along with the sub-titles, indexes
them, breaks the video stream into shots (defined as those video sequences that are
generated during a continuous operation of the camera), extracts one key-frame per
shot, automatically glues shots together to form news stories based on an overlap in
vocabulary in the sub-titles of adjacent shots (using lexical chains), and assembles
a story-board for each story. Stories can be browsed or retrieved via text searches.
Figure 7.10 shows the interface of ANSES. We used the natural language toolset
GATE (Cunningham 2002) for automated discovery of organisations, people, places
and dates; displaying these prominently as part of a storyboard as in Fig. 7.10 pro-

vides an instant indication of what the news story is about. ANSES also displays a short automated textual extraction summary, again using lexical chains to identify the most salient sentences. These summaries are never as informative as hand-made ones, but users of the system have found them crucial for judging whether or not they are interested in a particular returned search result.

Dissecting the video stream into shots and associating one keyframe along with text from subtitles to each shot has another advantage: A video collection can essentially be treated as an image collection, where each, possibly annotated image acts as entry point into the video.

7.4.2 New Paradigms in Information Visualisation

The 1990s have witnessed an explosion in interest in the field of information visualisation (Hemmje et al. 1994; Ankerst et al. 1996; Card 1996; Shneiderman et al. 2000; Börner 2000). Here we present three new visualisation paradigms, based on our earlier design studies (Au et al. 2000; Carey et al. 2003). These techniques all revolve around a representation of documents in the form of bag-of-words vectors, which can be clustered to form groups. We used a variant of the buckshot clustering algorithm for this. Basically, the top, say, 100 documents that were returned from a query are clustered via hierarchical clustering to initialise document centroids for k-means clustering that puts all documents returned by a query into groups. Another common element of our visualisations is the notion of *keywords* that are specific to the returned set of documents. The keywords are computed using a simple statistic; for details see (Carey et al. 2003). The new methods are:

Sammon Cluster View   This paradigm uses a Sammon map to generate a two dimensional screen location from a many-dimensional vector representing a cluster centroid. This map is computed using an iterative gradient search (Sammon 1969) while attempting to preserve the pairwise distances between the cluster centres. Clusters are thus arranged so that their mutual distances are indicative of their relationship. The idea is to create a visual landscape for navigation. Figure 7.11 shows an example of such an interface. The display has three panels, a scrolling table panel to the left, a graphic panel in the middle and a scrolling text panel to the right that contains the traditional list of returned documents as hotlinks and snippets. In the graphic panel each cluster is represented by a circle and is labelled with its two most frequent keywords. The radius of the circle represents the cluster size. The distance between any two circles in the graphic panel is an indication of the similarity of their respective clusters—the nearer the clusters, the more likely the documents contained within will be similar. When the mouse passes over the cluster circle a tool-tip box in the form of a pop-up menu appears that allows the user to select clusters and *drill down*, i.e., re-cluster and re-display only the documents in the selected clusters. The back button undoes this process and climbs up the hierarchy (*drill up*). The table of keywords includes box fields that can be selected. At the bottom of the table is a filter button that makes the scrolling text window display only the hot-links and snippets from documents that contain the selected keywords.

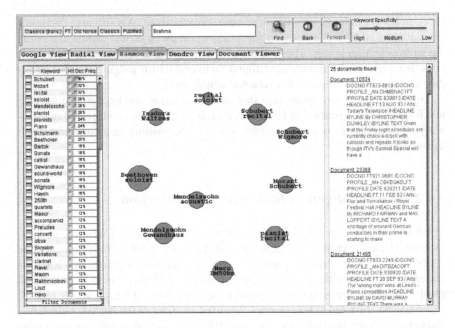

Fig. 7.11 Sammon map for cluster-guided search

Dendro Map Visualisation   The Dendro Map visualisation represents documents as leaf nodes of a binary tree that is output by the buckshot clustering algorithm. With its plane-spanning property and progressive shortening of branches towards the periphery, the Dendro Map mimics the result of a non-Euclidean transformation of the plane as used in hyperbolic maps without suffering from their computational load. Owing to spatial constraints, the visualisation depth is confined to five levels of the hierarchy with nodes of the lowest level representing either documents or subclusters. Different colours facilitate visual discrimination between individual documents and clusters. Each lowest level node is labelled with the most frequent keyword of the subcluster or document. This forms a key component of the Dendro Map as it gives the user the cues needed for navigating through the tree. As the user moves the mouse pointer over an internal node, the internal nodes and branches of the associated subcluster change colour from light blue to dark blue while the leaf nodes, i.e., document representations, turn bright red. As in the Sammon Map, a tool-tip window provides additional information about the cluster and can be used to display a table with a list of keywords associated with the cluster. The user may drill down on any internal node. The selected node will as a result replace the current root node at the center and the entire display is re-organised around the new root. The multi-level approach of the Dendro Map allows the user to gain a quick overview over the document collection and to identify promising subsets.

Radial Interactive Visualisation   Radial Visualisation (Fig. 7.13) is similar to VIBE (Korfhage 1991), to Radviz (Hoffman et al. 1999) and to Lyberworld (Hem-

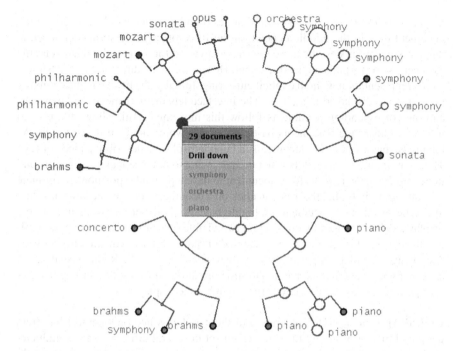

Fig. 7.12 Dendro Map—A plane-spanning binary tree (query "Beethoven")

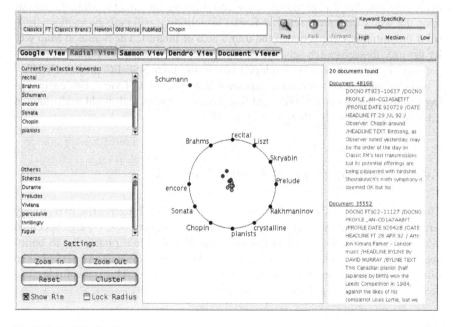

Fig. 7.13 Radial visualisation

mje et al. 1994). It places the keyword nodes round a circle, and the position of the document dots in the middle depend on the force of invisible springs connecting them to keyword nodes: the more relevant a keyword for a particular document, the stronger its spring pulls on the document. Hence, we made direct use of the bag-of-words representation without explicit clustering. Initially, the twelve highest ranking keywords are displayed in a circle. The interface lets the user move the keywords, and the corresponding documents follow this movement. This allows the user to manually cluster the documents based on the keywords they are interested in. As the mouse passes over the documents, a bubble displays a descriptive piece of text. The location of document dots is not unique owing to dimensionality reduction, and there may be many reasons for a document to have a particular position. To mitigate this ambiguity in Radial the user can click on a document dot, and the keywords that affect the location of document are highlighted. A choice of keywords used in the display can be exercised by clicking on two visible lists of words. Zoom buttons allow the degree of projection to be increased or reduced so as to distinguish between documents around the edges of the display or at the centre. The Radial visualisation appears to be a good interactive tool to structure the document set according to one's own preferences by shifting keywords around in the display.

Unified Approach   The integration of the paradigms into one application offers the possibility of browsing the same result set in several different ways simultaneously. The cluster-based visualisations give a broader overall picture of the result, while the Radial visualisation allows the user to focus on subsets of keywords. Also, as the clusters are approximations that highlight particular keywords, it may be useful to return to the Radial visualisation and examine the effect of these keywords upon the whole document set. The Radial visualisation will perhaps be more fruitful if the initial keywords match the user's area of interest. The Sammon Map will let the user dissect search sets and re-cluster subsets, gradually homing in on target sets. This interface was developed within the joint NSF-EC project CHLT;[10] it was evaluated from a human-computer-interaction point of view with encouraging results (Chawda et al. 2005) and has proven useful in real-world multi-lingual scholarly collections (Rydberg-Cox et al. 2004).

7.4.3 Visual Search and Relevance Feedback

The visual query-by-example paradigm discussed in Sect. 7.3 gives rise to relatively straightforward interfaces; an image is dragged into a query box, or, e.g., specified via a URL, and the best matching images are displayed in a ranked list to be inspected by the user, see Fig. 7.14(a). A natural extension of such an interface is to offer the selection of relevant results as new query elements. This type of relevance feedback, a.k.a. *query point moving*, is shown in Fig 7.14(b).

---

[10]See http://www.chlt.org.

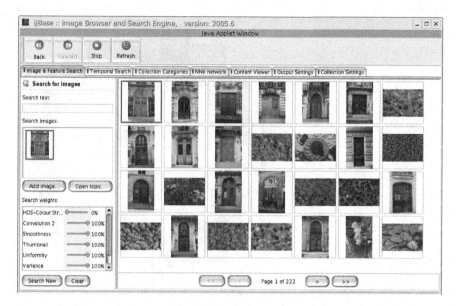

(a) Query by example (left panel) with initial results in the right panel

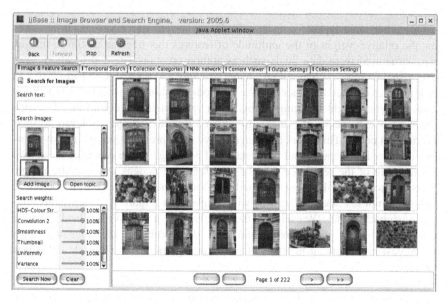

(b) A new query made of three images from (a) results in many more dark-door images

Fig. 7.14 Visual search for images of dark doors starting with a bright-door example

Fig. 7.15 A relevance
feedback

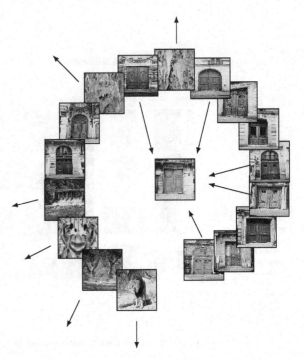

One other main type of relevance feedback, *weight space movement*, assumes
that the relative weight of the multitude of features that one can assign to images
(e.g., structured meta-data fields such as author, creation date and location; low-
level visual features such as colour, shape, structure and texture; free-form text) can
be learned from user feedback. Of the methods mentioned in Sect. 7.3 our group
chose analytic weight updating as this has a very small execution time. The idea
is that users can specify the degree to which a returned image is relevant to their
information needs. This is done by having a visual representation; the returned images are listed in a spiral, and the distance of an image to the centre of the screen
is a measure of the relevance that the search engine assigns to a specific image.
Users can now move the images around with the mouse or place them in the centre
with a left mouse click and far away with a right click. Figure 7.15 shows this relevance feedback model. We evaluated the effectiveness of negative feedback, positive
feedback and query point moving, and found that combining the latter two yields
the biggest improvement in terms of mean average precision (Heesch and Rüger
2003).

A new and relatively unexplored area of relevance feedback is the exploitation of
social context information. By looking not only at the behaviour and attributes of the
user, but also his past interactions and also the interactions of people he has some
form of social connection with could yield useful information when determining
whether search results are relevant or not. Browsing systems could recommend data
items based on the actions of a social network instead of just a single user, using
more data to yield better results.

The use of such social information is also becoming important for multimedia meta data generation, particular in the area of folksonomies where the feedback of users actively produces the terms and taxonomies used to describe the media in the system instead of using a predetermined, prescribed dictionary (Voss 2007). This can be seen being effectively used in online multimedia systems such as Flickr[11] and Delicious[12].

7.5 Browsing: Lateral and Geo-Temporal

The idea of representing text documents in a nearest-neighbour network was first presented by Croft and Parenty (1985), albeit, as an internal representation of the relationships between documents and terms, not for browsing. Document networks for interactive browsing were identified by Cox (1992 and 1995). Attempts to introduce the idea of browsing into content-based image retrieval include Campbell's work 2000; his ostensive model retains the basic mode of query based retrieval but in addition allows browsing through a dynamically created local tree structure. Santini and Jain's *El niño* system (2000) is another attempt to combine query-based search with browsing. The system tries to display configurations of images in feature space such that the mutual distances between images are preserved as well as possible. Feedback is given in the same spirit as in Fig. 7.15 by manually forming clusters of images that appear similar to the user. This in turn results in an altered configuration with potentially new images being displayed.

Other network structures that have increasingly been used for information visualisation and browsing are Pathfinder networks (Dearholt and Schvaneveldt 1990). They are constructed by removing redundant edges from a potentially much more complex network. Fowler et al. (1992) use Pathfinder networks to structure the relationships between terms from document abstracts, between document terms and between entire documents. The user interface supports access to the browsing structure through prominently marked high-connectivity nodes.

Our group (Heesch and Rüger 2004) determines the nearest neighbour for the image under consideration (which we call the *focal* image) for *every* combination of features. This results in a set of what we call *lateral neighbours*. By calculating the lateral neighbours of all database images, we generate a network that lends itself to browsing. Lateral neighbours share some properties of the focal image, but not necessarily all. For example, a lateral neighbour may share text annotations with the focal image, but no visual similarity with it at all, or it may have a very similar colour distribution, but no structural similarity, or it may be similar in all features except shape, etc. As a consequence, lateral neighbours are deemed to expose the polysemy of the focal image. Hence, when they are presented, the user may then follow one of them by making it the focal image and explore its lateral neighbours in turn. The user interaction is immediate, since the underlying network was computed offline.

---

[11] See http://www.flickr.com.

[12] See http://del.icio.us.

(a) Initial visual summary of the database (right panel) from which the user chooses the falcon, its nearest lateral neighbours are then displayed in the left panel.

(b) Clicking on any image will make it the centre of the nearest neighbours panel and display is associated lateral neighbours around it.

Fig. 7.16 Lateral browsing for an image "from behind the pitcher in a baseball game..."

We provide the user with entry points into the database by computing a representative set of images from the collection. We cluster high-connectivity nodes and their neighbours up to a certain depth using the Markov chain clustering algorithm (van Dongen 2000), which has robust convergence properties and allows one to specify the granularity of the clustering. The clustering result can be seen as an image database summary that shows highly-connected nodes with far-reaching connections. The right panel of Fig. 7.16(a) is such a summary for our TRECVid (2003) database. The user may select any of these images as an entry point into the network.

Starting with the football image (upper left) from the database overview, one of its lateral neighbours is an image of a lawn with a sprinkler; when this is made the focal image (upper right) there are already images from baseball scenes. Clicking on one of them (lower left) reveals that there are more of this kind; they can be enlarged and the corresponding video played in the "viewer tab" (lower right).

Fig. 7.17 Alternative ways to browse for images "from behind the pitcher ..."

Clicking on an image moves it into the centre around which the lateral neighbours are displayed, see the nearest-neighbour panel on the left side of Fig. 7.16(a). If the size of the lateral-neighbour set is above a certain threshold the actual number of images displayed is reduced to the most salient ones.

If a user wanted to find "video shots from behind the pitcher in a baseball game as he throws a ball that the batter swings at" (TRECVid 2003, topic102) then they might explore the database in Fig 7.16 by clicking on the falcon image. The hope is that the colour of a baseball field is not far off from the green colour of that image. The resulting lateral neighbours, displayed in the left panel of Fig. 7.16(a), do not contain the desired scene. However, there is an image of a sports field. Making that the focal image, as seen in the left part of Fig. 7.16(b), reveals it has the desired scene as a lateral neighbour. Clicking that will unearth a lot more images from baseball fields, see the right side of Fig. 7.16(b). The network structure, a bit of lateral thinking and three mouse clicks have brought the desired result.

In the same way, and again with only three clicks, one could have started from the football image in the database overview to find "video shots from behind the pitcher in a baseball game as he throws a ball that the batter swings at". Heesch (2005) has shown that this is no coincidence; lateral-neighbour networks computed in this way have the so-called *small world property* (Watts and Strogatz 1998) with only 3–4 degrees of separation even for the large (TRECVid 2003) database that contains keyframes from 32,000 video shots. Lateral browsing has proven eminently successful for similar queries (Heesch et al. 2003).

Geo-temporal browsing takes the idea of timelines and automatically generated maps, e.g., as offered in the Perseus Digital Library (Crane 2005), a step further. It integrates the idea of browsing in time and space with a selection of events through a text search box. In this way, a large newspaper or TV news collection can be made available through browsing based on what happened where and when as opposed to by keyword only.

The interface in Fig. 7.18 is a design study in our group that allows navigation within a large news event dataset along three dimensions: time, location and text subsets. The search term presents a text filter. The temporal distribution can be seen in lower part. The overview window establishes a frame of reference for the user's region of interest. In principle, this interface could implement new zooming techniques, e.g., speed-dependent automatic zooming (Cockburn and Savage 2003), and

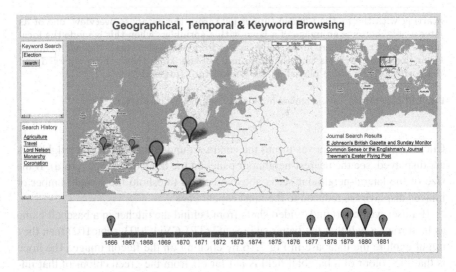

Fig. 7.18 Geo-temporal browsing in action

link to a server holding a large quantity of maps such as National Geographic's MapMachine[13] with street-level maps and aerial photos.

7.6 Conclusions

This chapter has introduced basic concepts of multimedia resource discovery technologies for a number of different query and document types; these were the piggy-back text search, automated annotation, content-based retrieval and fingerprinting. The paradigms we have discussed include summarising complex multimedia objects such as TV news, information visualisation techniques for document clusters, visual search by example, relevance feedback and methods to create browsable structures within the collection. These exploration modes share three common features: they are automatically generated, depend on visual senses and interact with the user of the multimedia collections.

Multimedia resource discovery has its very own challenges in the semantic gap, in polysemy inherently present in under-specified query-by-example scenarios, in the question how to combine possibly conflicting evidence and the responsiveness of the multimedia searches. In the last part of the chapter we have given some examples of user-centred methods that support resource discovery in multimedia digital libraries. Each of these methods can be seen as an alternative mode to the traditional digital library management tools of meta-data and classification. The new visual modes aim at generating a multi-faceted approach to present digital content: *video summaries* as succinct versions of media that otherwise would require a high bandwidth to display and considerable time by the user to assess; *information visualisation* techniques help the user to understand a large set of documents that match a query; *visual search* and *relevance feedback* afford the user novel ways to express their information need without taking recourse to verbal descriptions that are bound to be language-specific; alternative resource discovery modes such as *lateral browsing* and *geo-temporal browsing* will allow users to explore collections using lateral associations and geographic or temporal filters rather than following strict classification schemes that seem more suitable for trained librarians than the occasional user of multimedia collections. The cost for these novel approaches will be low, as they are automated rather than human-generated. It remains to be seen how best to integrate these services into traditional digital library designs and how much added value these services will bring about (Bainbridge et al. 2005).

My 2010 book provides further reading for content-based multimedia retrieval and complements the material of this chapter: Rüger (2010), Multimedia information retrieval, Lecture notes in the series Synthesis Lectures on Information Concepts, Retrieval, and Services, Morgan and Claypool Publishers, http://dx.doi.org/10.2200/S00244ED1V01Y200912ICR010.

In fact, this chapter utilised some excerpts and figures from this book.

---

[13] See http://plasma.nationalgeographic.com/map-machine/ as of January 2011.

Acknowledgements   Outlining the paradigms in this chapter and their implementations would not have been possible without the ingenuity, imagination and hard work of Paul Browne, Matthew Carey, Shyamala Doraisamy, Daniel Heesch, Peter Howarth, Suzanne Little, Haiming Liu, Ainhoa Llorente, João Magalhães, Alexander May, Simon Overell, Marcus Pickering, Adam Rae, Edward Schofield, Shalini Sewraz, Dawei Song, Lawrence Wong and Alexei Yavlinsky.

Credits   The photograph in Fig. 7.1 (Milton Keynes Peace pagoda) by Stefan Rüger, July 2007, was first published in Rüger (2010). Figure 7.2 is a mock-up based on the existing üBase search engine, see Fig. 7.14, with modifications by Peter Devine and was previously published in Rüger (2010). Figure 7.3 (new search engine types) was designed by Peter Devine and published in Rüger (2010). Figures 7.5, 7.6 and 7.9 use royalty-free images from Corel Gallery 380,000, © Corel Corporation, all rights reserved. Figure 7.7 (Behold) by Alexei Yavlinsky are screenshots from http://photo.beholdsearch.com, 19 July 2007, now http://www.behold.cc with thumbnails of creative-commons Flickr images. The photograph in Fig. 7.8 © by Stefan Rüger, taken May 1996 in the Nord Jyllands Kunstmuseum, Ålborg. Figures 7.8 and 7.9 were published in Rüger (2010). The screenshots in Figs. 7.10–7.14 and 7.16–7.18 are reproduced courtesy of © Imperial College London. The ANSES system in Fig. 7.10 was originally designed by Marcus Pickering and later modified by Lawrence Wong; the images and part of the text displayed in the screenshot of Fig. 7.10 were recorded from British Broadcasting Corporation (BBC), http://www.bbc.co.uk. The Sammon map in Fig. 7.11 and the radial visualisation in Fig. 7.13 were designed by Matthew Carey. The Dendro map in Fig. 7.12 was designed by Daniel Heesch. The üBase system depicted in the screenshots of Figs. 7.14(a), 7.14(b) and 7.16(a) was designed by Alexander May. The images used within the screenshot of Fig. 7.14 and within the illustration of Fig. 7.15 were reproduced from Corel Gallery 380,000, © Corel Corporation, all rights reserved. The images in the (partial) screenshots of Figs. 7.16 and 7.17 were reproduced from TREC Video Retrieval Evaluation 2003 (TRECVid), http://www-nlpir.nist.gov/projects. The geotemporal browsing screenshot in Fig. 7.18 was created by Simon Overell.

Chapter 8
Information Retrieval in Context

Ian Ruthven

Abstract The situations in which we search form a context: a complex set of variables describing our intentions, our personal characteristics, the data and systems available for searching, and our physical, social and organizational environments. Different contexts can mean that we want search systems to behave differently or to offer different responses. Creating search systems and search interfaces to be contextually sensitive raises many research challenges: what aspects of a searcher's context are useful to know about, how can we model context for use by retrieval systems and how do we evaluate search systems in context? In this chapter we will look at why differences in context can affect how we want search systems to operate and ways that we can use contextual information to help search systems behave more intelligently to our changing context. We will examine some new types of system that use different types of user context to learn about users, to adapt their response to different users or to help us make better search decisions.

8.1 Introduction

Context is a concept that has been discussed in Information Retrieval for several decades. Recently, through initiatives such as the IIiX conference series,[1] the HARD and ciQA tracks at TREC,[2] the IRIX workshops[3] and the recent monograph by Ingwersen and Järvelin (2005) we have seen a consolidation of activity in how contextual information can be used to design and evaluate information retrieval systems and interfaces. Indeed, as Finkelstein et al. noted in 2001

---

[1] See http://iiix2010.org/.

[2] See http://trec.nist.gov/.

[3] See http://ir.dcs.gla.ac.uk/context/.

I. Ruthven (✉)
Department of Computer and Information Sciences, University of Strathclyde, 26 Richmond Street, Glasgow, G1 1XH, United Kingdom
e-mail: ir@cis.strath.ac.uk

M. Melucci, R. Baeza-Yates (eds.), *Advanced Topics in Information Retrieval*,
The Information Retrieval Series 33,
DOI 10.1007/978-3-642-20946-8_8, © Springer-Verlag Berlin Heidelberg 2011

'A large number of recently proposed search enhancement tools have utilized the notion of context, making it one of the most abused terms in the field, referring to a diverse range of ideas from domain-specific search engines to personalization' Finkelstein et al. (2001).

In this chapter I seek to show why context is important to Information Retrieval; highlight some emerging trends from the discourse surrounding context; present some examples of systems that utilize contextual information; present the variety of uses to which we might put contextual information; and present some issues relating to the evaluation of contextual information retrieval systems. Contextual Information Retrieval covers a vast landscape of research. In this article I will only cover part of this landscape, considering only work on Information Retrieval systems. There is, however, a huge range of useful research from the related fields of information seeking, information behavior and relevance interaction which help us understand the human perspective of Information Retrieval. Good sources for reading in this area include Case (2002), Ingwersen and Järvelin (2005), Kelly (2009), Kelly and Ruthven (2010), Saracevic (2007), Spink and Cole (2005).

8.1.1 Contextual Information Seeking

Information seeking, the process by which humans find information, is a highly contextual activity. The field of Information Seeking (Case 2002) has demonstrated, repeatedly, and over decades of research, that how we request information, how we assess information and how we use information is affected by a set of complex, interrelated variables which describe a situation in which we search. Using a retrieval system is only one way in which we can access information but, even with this one mechanism, we have much evidence on the variables that can affect our information seeking activities. Major variables include our prior knowledge of a topic and resources available, our experience of searching for information, the purpose for which we want information, and a range of human factors including personality, cognitive abilities, age, gender, and learning styles.

Historically, however, the design of most retrieval systems has been largely context free. That is, most retrieval systems are designed to be used by any user for any retrieval task and using any data. Retrieval systems have largely ignored the difference between search contexts and search variables. Our use of retrieval systems, of course, is not context free and differences in our search context can change our expectations of searching. For example, if we frequently conduct the same search then a useful system response would be to show us new information on our search topic; a less useful response would be to repeatedly show us the same information. Or, if the person searching is a child then retrieving and displaying complex information is not an appropriate response; a better response is presenting information that is appropriate for the child's age and reading level.

The major claim for employing contextual approaches to Information Retrieval is that, if Information Retrieval systems are capable of recognizing and utilizing differences in search contexts, then they will provide a better match between how we search and the Information Retrieval tools that we use to search. Information Retrieval systems, therefore, will be intelligent at differentiating between different contexts, dynamic in altering their response to different contexts and adaptive to our needs and preferences. Or, at least, they will make it easier for us to make search decisions by providing us with more contextual information which we can use to operate the system more fluidly and effectively.

Understanding how contextual variables alter how we search will allow us as system designers and evaluators to design more appropriate search tools. This, of course, is a difficult challenge. As Suchman noted

> '[the] interaction between people and computers requires essentially the same interpretative work that characterizes interaction between people' Suchman (1988).

Which means that Contextual Information Retrieval is not a simple challenge. Before we consider in depth why Suchman's argument raises challenges for system designers, I want to consider some of the main elements of context that have been presented in the literature.

8.1.2 Elements of Context

Many contextual factors may affect how we use an Information Retrieval system and how we evaluate the system's performance. A number of researchers have tried to enumerate these factors. One useful example is the context model developed by Kofod-Petersen and Aamodt (2003) in the Ambisense project, Fig. 8.1, which was concerned with information seeking via mobile devices. This example is chosen primarily because it details with both system and user in one model; there are other useful models of context but this one illustrates the range of contextual factors which we might investigate.

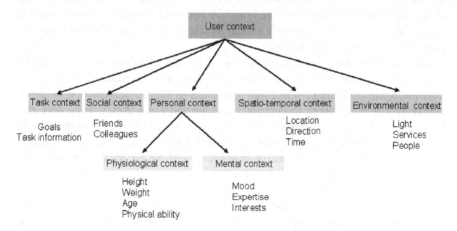

Fig. 8.1 Ambisense model of context

Task context is a major contextual variable for Information Retrieval (although perhaps less so for other fields which are interested in context). As noted by Vakkari (2003) task is an important concept in Information Retrieval and one that has many definitions. Here we take task to be the information problem, e.g. finding a holiday destination, writing an essay, giving a lecture, which promotes a need for information that leads, in turn, to using a retrieval system. The nature of the task can affect which information is useful in completing a task. For example a document that might be useful in writing an historical review on search interfaces may not be useful in writing a review on state-of-the-art search interfaces, even though the two tasks have the same topic. Tasks may be strictly defined before searching begins, and only specific information will be relevant, or they may less fixed, capable of being turned into a new task depending on what information has been encountered during the search.

Historically *social context* is a variable that has been overlooked by Information Retrieval research with most systems, at least implicitly, assuming that each person searches as an individual and for personal information needs. There are many situations in which this is true but often we do search for information that is to be used by other people, e.g. search for information for a family holiday, or where other people's preferences must be taken into account such as searching for a gift. There are also many situations, e.g. intellectual property searching (Tait 2008) or legal searching (Oard et al. 2008), where professionals search on information needs described by others. Therefore the professional's knowledge of the end-user and their understanding of the search request are important. Recently retrieval system designers have responded to challenges of searching within social and organizational contexts and the systems are designed to acknowledge other searcher's activities (Jameson and Smyth 2007).

Personal contexts have been the most commonly investigated use of context in Information Retrieval. Here the range of contextual factors that might be important is vast ranging from age, physical and cognitive ability (which may require altering the presentation of search results as well as the selection of results), learning styles, education level, or mood of searcher. The most common personal context investigated so far is the searcher's topical search interests, particularly through applications of information filtering.

In some situations, e.g. information retrieval through mobile devices, a searcher's *physical context* may be important to provide situationally relevant information. For example, their direction of travel may important to suggest information on destinations that they are about to encounter (Brown and Jones 2002). Time may also be an important variable: a query on restaurants issued at 11.30 AM might indicate the searcher is looking for suggestions for lunch whereas the same query issued at 7 PM would indicate suggestions for an evening meal. So far, location has been the most common physical contextual variable, partly due to the ease with which such information can be captured.

The *environmental context* in which information is being accessed may be important: some information may not be appropriate to show in public settings, some information is only appropriate for work, not personal, environments and so should only presented at appropriate times and what information is available to be retrieved may differ in different environments.

There is, then, a wide range of factors that may be used to improve the user's experience of Information Retrieval systems. Which ones are useful, and in which situations, provides the setting for a rich seam of research. In the next section we outline some of the practical uses for which we might adopt some of these contextual factors.

8.1.3 Practical Uses of Context

Contextual approaches to information retrieval have the potential to design very different types of systems from those we currently see available. Such systems could, for example:

- Learn what information we want by observing our reactions to information. This very practical, and commonly investigated, use of contextual information implies a system that tries to learn our regular information needs and provide additional, new material on similar topics to those in which we have expressed an interest. This use has been around for decades in the form of Information Filtering (Hanani et al. 2001) but is still a very common approach to use of context. It many cases, however, a weakness is that this context is poorly elucidated: are the regular information needs those that arise from personal interests or work requirements, are they time-limited requests or perennial ones? Too often such approaches do not describe or use the context beyond simple topical statements of areas of interest.
- Predict what information we need. Learning what we want and predicting what we want are two different functions of a system. In many cases we can say what we want but not what information would be useful to know about. Many information professionals, such as librarians, understand this and will provide contextual information to a person making a request as well as providing direct, relevant information. This contextual information may be on the accuracy of the information, the presence of conflicting information, and perhaps information on the use that others have made of the information provided.
- Learn how information should be displayed to the user. This can mean, at the simplest level, altering the presentation of search results to the device being used by the searcher. It could also mean altering the information itself, such as tailoring the information to the age of the reader (Belder and Moens 2010). Alternatively it could mean learning what a searcher wants to know about the information being interacted with, e.g. who else has used the information, how recent is the information, estimates of the quality of the information, and so on.
- Indicate how information relates to other information we have seen. We often use the same retrieval system, especial web search engines, heavily for similar information needs. Most retrieval systems provide little support for repeated searching

on the same needs or search tasks. A useful function of a contextual information retrieval system would be to remind us of information we have previously encountered, even if this information did not appear useful before.

- Decide who else should be informed about new information. As indicated above, context is not just a personal issue as we often work within groups or act within social settings. Learning who, within a group, should be made aware of information is a potentially powerful use of contextual information.

How these different uses of context manifest themselves within a system design depend very much on how contextual information can be used. In Sect. 8.2 present three views on the use of context within systems design.

8.2 Views of Context

Many authors have written about context and its potential role within interactive systems. Through this discourse two predominant lines of research have emerged. I loosely characterize these as being the *socio-technical systems* view and the *contextually sensitive systems* view. In Sect. 8.2.3 I introduce a third option, based on the level of *engagement* created by contextual information.

8.2.1 Socio-Technical Systems View

One view on context posits that contextual information is too rich and diverse to be captured and reasoned about by the current generation of computer systems. The argument goes that the range and complexity of contextual information, and the difficulty of being able to separate out which contextual aspects might be important for a given search decision, makes it unlikely that the correct contextual information can be reasoned about. That is, we cannot know which contextual information is the important contextual information for making individual system decisions. Partly, this is a representation issue: how do we represent contextual information within a system and how do we infer from it? However, the argument goes, even if computer systems cannot reason and predict about context they can still use contextual information to support intelligent searchers reasoning about their search interactions.

Contextual systems, therefore, can support searchers by either *explaining* how the systems operate (most Information Retrieval systems are still a black box), demonstrating some aspect of their *own* context (what data they have access to for example) or using other searchers' interactions to support search decisions. We see a number of such approaches already in use by Web Search systems. The figures below illustrate some of these as they occur in current web search engines.

Figure 8.2 shows a Google image search result for Warhol. The 'Related Searches' option offers two suggestions 'Andy Warhol' and 'Lichtenstein' both of

Google
warhol
SafeSearch is off
Showing: Extra Large images
Any content
Related searches: andy warhol lichtenstein

Fig. 8.2 Google's Related searches

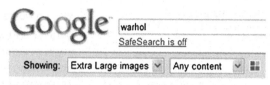

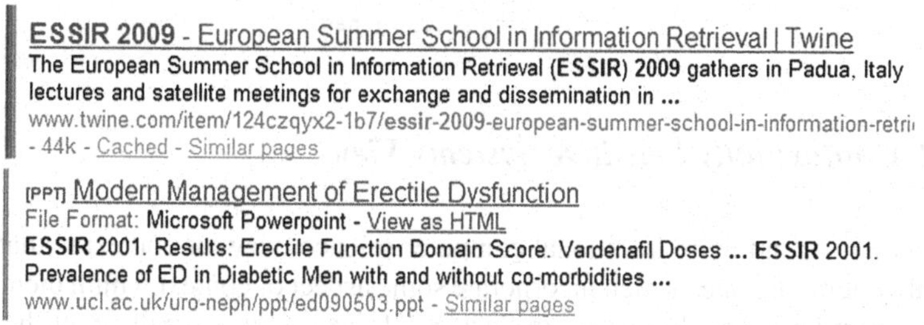

ESSIR 2009 - European Summer School in Information Retrieval | Twine
The European Summer School in Information Retrieval (ESSIR) 2009 gathers in Padua, Italy lectures and satellite meetings for exchange and dissemination in ...
www.twine.com/item/124czqyx2-1b7/essir-2009-european-summer-school-in-information-retri
- 44k - Cached - Similar pages
[PPT] Modern Management of Erectile Dysfunction
File Format: Microsoft Powerpoint - View as HTML
ESSIR 2001. Results: Erectile Function Domain Score. Vardenafil Doses ... ESSIR 2001. Prevalence of ED in Diabetic Men with and without co-morbidities ...
www.ucl.ac.uk/uro-neph/ppt/ed090503.ppt - Similar pages

Fig. 8.3 Keywords in context

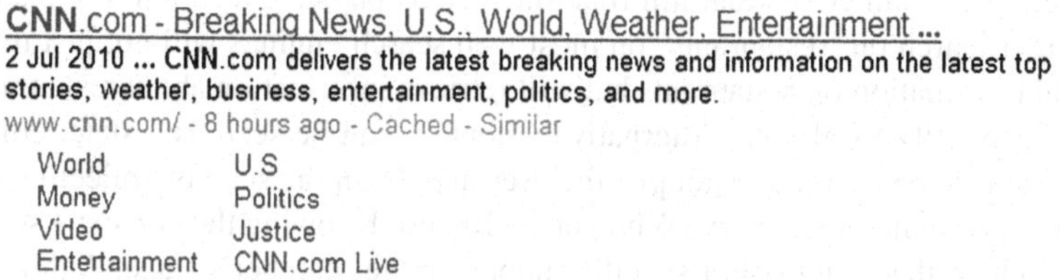

CNN.com - Breaking News, U.S., World, Weather, Entertainment ...
2 Jul 2010 ... CNN.com delivers the latest breaking news and information on the latest top stories, weather, business, entertainment, politics, and more.
www.cnn.com/ - 8 hours ago - Cached - Similar
World
U.S
Money
Politics
Video
Justice
Entertainment
CNN.com Live

Fig. 8.4 Website structure

which are statistically-motivated suggestions that provide semantically related suggestions for creating a better query. Figure 8.3 shows two search results for the query 'ESSIR' which show fragments of text taken from the retrieved pages with the query term shown in bold. This keyword-in-context approach shows how the query term has been used in the context of the original documents so that searchers can see immediately if the web page is likely to contain the correct sense of the query terms and which page is more likely to be useful. Figure 8.4 shows a Google search result for the query 'CNN' which shows popular sub-domains of the main CNN site, giving an indication of the major components of the website and thereby indicating something of the organizational context of the information contained within the website. Figure 8.5 shows Bing's query suggestion tool, which gives the contexts (in this case queries) within which the user's query terms have already been used. Such systems give more information to allow us to make, hopefully, better interactive decisions.

Fig. 8.5 Bing query
suggestion tool

why do women

why do women **live longer than men**
why do women **have affairs**
why do women **have periods**
why do women **lie**
why do women **blush**
why do women **fall for the wrong men**
why do women **get angry when pregnant**
why do women **nag**

Turn off   Preferences   What's this?

8.2.2 Contextually Sensitive Systems View

An alternative, and more traditional computer science, view of context is that contextual systems are ones which incorporate some aspect of context within their functioning. Similar to the discussion in Sect. 8.1.1, such systems will adapt their operation based on a model of the world or part of the world. Within this view there have been many definitions of context. The most commonly used view of context is as an additional input factor: systems operate in same way but make more accurate decisions with contextual information such as physical location. For example, running a search on 'restaurants' on most web search engines will not just retrieve general information on restaurants but will retrieve information about restaurants in a geographically local area. Alternatively context can be seen as a state, either of the system or the user. For example, the user may be in the state of collecting information or formulating a query (White et al. 2005a). Knowing the context a searcher is in can help the system offer specific support to the searcher's stage. A third view of context that is becoming more common is to describe context as tasks (Toms et al. 2003). Such tasks may be information problems, such as writing an essay, or may be tasks which require certain types of information to fulfil. An example of the latter can be seen in Fig. 8.6 which shows the results for a search on the query 'Padua'. Google's response to a geographical query consists of information that may be contextually appropriate to a location search: maps, hotel and restaurant suggestions, and images of Padua, all of which might be useful for someone planning a visit.

Many researchers present systems that claim to respond to or utilize contextual information. Few actually define what is meant by contextual information in their work. However, we can draw some useful distinctions based on the published research. Below are some axes that can characterize work on context, the list is not exhaustive:

- Contextual information may be *objective* or *subjective*. Objective contextual information is information where there is a commonly agreed standard by which we may measure the value of the contextual variable (such as GPS signals to measure position) whereas subjective contextual information is information where there needs to be some reasoning, either on the part of the user or system, to

Padua Italy maps.google.co.uk

Hotels - Restaurants - Vicenza - Palazzo della Ragione - Cappella degli Scrovegni - Prato della Valle - Basilica Di Sant Antonio - Treviso

Fig. 8.6 Google's Related searches

gain a value. Such information could include mood, search experience, search expertise, domain knowledge, etc. This latter type of information is often more difficult to deal with as techniques for obtaining sufficiently good estimates for these variables are often weak.

- Contextual information may be *individual* or *group based* and so may be the purposes for which the contextual information are used. Many approaches to utilizing contextual information have aimed at improving retrieval performance or ease of use for individual users. Here contextual information is used for personalizing an individual's experience with a retrieval system using contextual information about that searcher. However, other approaches, such as those based on collaborative filtering, use group information to support individual searcher's decision-making. As noted earlier, many people may search for information that is relevant for a group of people and so tailoring systems simply to that individual may not be appropriate. A good summary of collaborative information seeking and retrieval can be found in Foster's ARIST article (Foster 2006).

- Contextual information may be *meaningful* or *incidental* (Bradley and Dunlop 2005). Meaningful context can be defined as contextual information that directly affects how a task is performed or how the task results are interpreted. Incidental context is contextual information that is present but does not significantly affect the task performance. In the case of this essay the language required by the editors is a meaningful contextual variable: it makes it easy for me to write the article whereas another language choice may make it impossible for me to perform. The length of the article and the topic are also meaningful. Incidental variables, for this purpose of this task, might include the colour the shirt I chose to wear whilst typing: it doesn't affect my ability to write the article. Which variables are meaningful and which are incidental change in different search situations. Sometimes, my lack of domain knowledge will be a meaningful variable, sometimes it may be my lack of motivation to find a good search result. For humans distinguishing between meaningful and incidental variables is often easy; for computers it is not and hence the argument that computers cannot deal with context.

- Contextual information may be *extrinsic* or *intrinsic*. That is the contextual information may be a necessary part of the objects which we deal (intrinsic properties such as document language) or they may be additional factors (extrinsic ones like knowledge of document use) which we may have access to or not.

- Systems may be *directed* or *passive* with respect to contextual information. That is they may recognize and use contextual information when it becomes available (passive) or they may actively seek out and resolve contextual information before processing (directed).
- The effects of contextual information may be *visible* or *invisible*. *Visibility* refers to the degree to which a system makes its capture and use of contextual information apparent to the user. Relevance Feedback is usually an invisible contextual device as the new query is often not shown to the user and the user has no idea how or why the query has been modified to obtain the new research results (Ruthven 2002). (White et al. 2007) present a visible contextual device which offers suggestions on useful web destinations based on a searcher's query and other searchers' browsing behavior.
- The mechanism by which contextual information are handled are often *rule-based* or *statistical*. Rule-based approaches were common in user-modeling approaches where rules may express contextual variables such as search experience or knowledge. Currently, statistical approaches based on data mining are far more common and there is a growing theoretical strand to modeling context, e.g. Melucci (2008)

8.2.3 Engagement View

A third view which I would like to propose is based on the work of anthropologist Edward T. Hall (1976). Hall was interested in cross-cultural communication and proposed two types of culture or situation: high and low context situations.

High context situations are ones in which there are lots of connections between participants, where the participants have long term relationships and where there is a high use of implicit behavior and knowledge such as facial expressions, humor, and body language. Low context situations are ones in which there are far looser connections between participants, where interaction is short-term, usually only occurs to fulfil a particular purpose and where there is a greater emphasis on direct, verbal and rule-based communication.

We can see similar metaphors in search interaction. Many search interfaces operate on a low context method of communication. An example is shown in Figs. 8.7 and 8.8 which show the advanced search interface of the ACM Digital Library. Figure 8.7 shows the advanced query interface and Fig. 8.8 shows the results of a search using the interface.

In Fig. 8.7 we see similar elements to a low context situation: the emphasis is on textual (verbal) descriptions of a need, and we are encouraged to put in as a complete need description as possible, the emphasis is on the single task of describing the required information, rather than exploring information for example, and the communication is effectively rule-based (*if* I want papers authored by Norbert Fuhr *then* I enter Norbert Fuhr in the name field). Similarly in Fig. 8.8 the results are

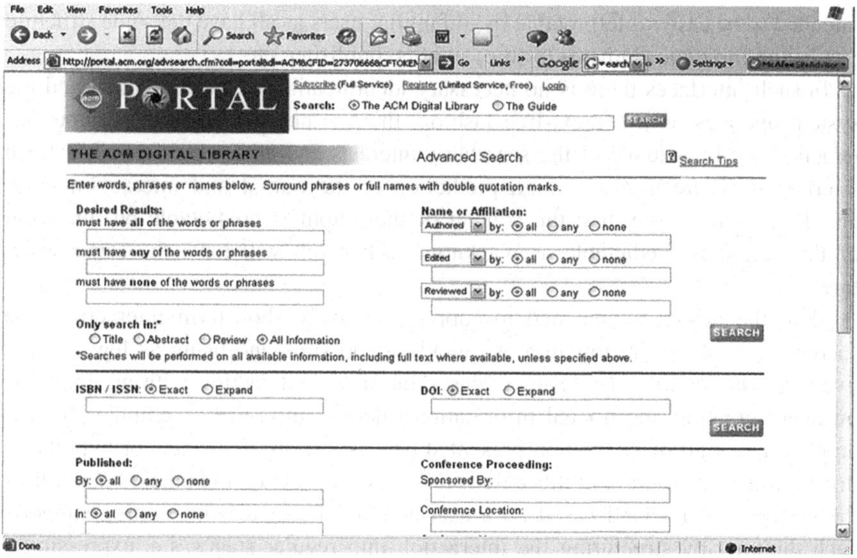

Fig. 8.7   Advanced search interface of the ACM Digital Library (querying)

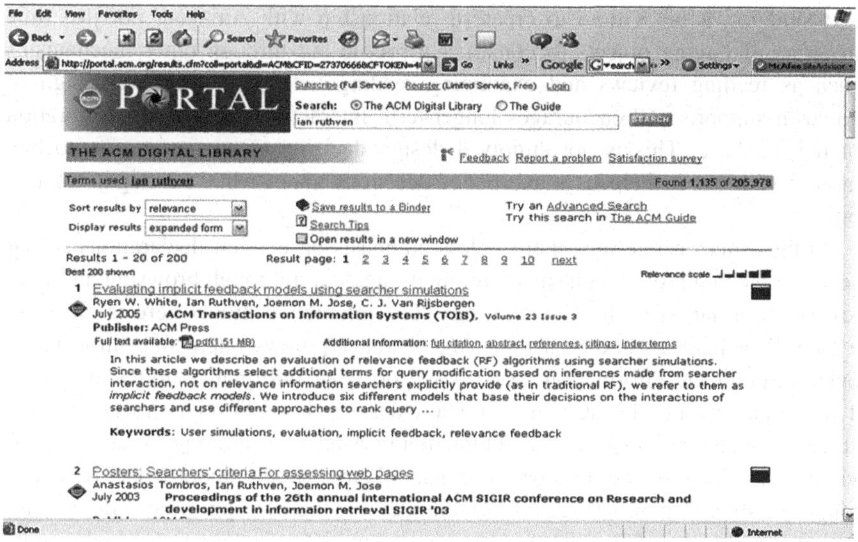

Fig. 8.8   Advanced search interface of the ACM Digital Library (results presentation)

intended to be easily interpretable by unfamiliar users as all have the same structure displaying the same elements of title, authors, publisher, etc.

In such interfaces there is no necessary identification of the individual and the system operates on a context-free fashion: there is no adaptation to previous interactions or knowledge of the searcher's interests and each interaction is a fresh interaction. There is also a high prediction of the output and interaction models. That is not to say that the content of the output is predictable but the form of the output is predictable as we know each result will have the same structure.

Here the design is intended to support relatively short-term interaction: the searcher can obtain information as quickly as possible and using as few interactive steps as possible. These interfaces value direct interaction with an emphasis on query creation and textual information (there is little use of graphics for example). The kind of interaction presented here is a form of 'linear', or hypothesis driven, logic. Interaction in this case follows user-generated hypotheses about how the system will respond based on a user action. The system interaction supports such thinking by structuring the interaction into regular stages, i.e. expressing a query, scanning results, selecting a result to investigate in further detail. This is not to say that the whole interface is context-free as the questions asked in the querying interface give some indication of what kind of data is available for searching and what information might be useful to specify what information is useful to provide in a query.

An alternative interaction style is that provided by systems like Amazon which are closer to Hall's high context situation. Figure 8.9 shows parts of the current Amazon.com interface. In interactive terms, who we are does matter as the initial information displayed is personalized to the individual. Like any high context situation it takes time to create a relationship with Amazon, not just time in terms of buying objects to construct a profile but through other mechanisms such as reading reviews and examining reading lists. The interface design of Amazon supports and encourages longer-term interaction and greater exploration of the database. This is not simply a design decision to encourage use to buy more books but to help us make better decisions about what we might want to buy.

In the Amazon interface there is less emphasis on explicit declarations of our search topic and more emphasis on implicit interaction through browsing and nontextual information such as star ratings. The interaction model here is closer to a 'spiral' or persuasion-driven logic: the searcher follows interesting information paths through the information space based on what information looks attractive. This is in contrast to the ACM model where the searcher follows a series of distinct stages to obtain information. The interaction in Amazon is more personal and individual. This is not to say it is better: Amazon's interaction model works best with long-term engagement whereas ACM's model may better support episodic and infrequent interaction. However they are distinct models of interaction which can be deployed for different types of use.

Ian, Welcome to Your Amazon.com (If you're not Ian Ruthven, click here.)

Today's Recommendations For You

Here's a daily sample of items recommended for you. Click here to see all recommendations.

Customers Who Bought This Item Also Bought

Fairy Godfather:
Straparola, Venice,
and... by Ruth B.

Fairy Tales: A New
History (Excelsior Edi...
by Ruth B. Bottigheimer

Giambattista Basile's
"The Tale of Tal... by
Giambattista Basile

First Sentence:
When it looked as if Christianity was taking hold in her native Cam
Key Phrases - Statistically Improbable Phrases (SIPs): (learn r
des quenouilles, magic donkey, fairytale writers, fairytale heroine,
Key Phrases - Capitalized Phrases (CAPs): (learn more)
Mother Goose, Saint Anne, Snow White, Les Evangiles, Little Merr
Antoine de La Sale, Arthur Rackham, Bruno Bettelheim, Dorothea \
New!
Books on Related Topics | Concordance | Text Stats
Browse Sample Pages:
Front Cover | First Pages | Index | Back Cover | Surprise Me!
Search Inside This Book:

Fig. 8.9   Elements from the Amazon.com interface

8.2.4 Summary

So far I have outlined different ways of exploiting context: either allowing searchers
to exploit their own context through better decision-making, allowing systems to exploit context through context-sensitive adaptation or creating systems that encourage a relationship with a system in the same way we develop a relationship with
other people. These are not mutually exclusive and some systems will incorporate
aspects of different views of context. These views are also not an exhaustive account and they are relatively broad-brush. In the next section I want to show some
examples of contextual approaches to Information Retrieval to give an outline of the
variety of work in this area.

8.3 Examples of Contextual Information Retrieval

In this section I will present some systems that can be classified as contextual approaches to Information Retrieval. There are many systems that I could have discussed so I have deliberately chosen very different approaches to show the range of research in this area. In Sect. 8.3.1 I will look at approaches for personal information management; in Sect. 8.3.2 social context; in Sect. 8.3.3 interaction context; and Sect. 8.3.4 task context.

8.3.1 Personal Context

Many contextual systems are ones that attempt to personalize a system towards an individual user, and indeed contextual approaches are often conflated with personalization. However, as we shall see, contextual approaches are often group based so contextual approaches cannot strictly be equated to personalization. In this case, however, we look at a very personal approach, namely personal information management or the study of how people manage their own information and how we can design systems to support people in this management and access.

Here, personal information can cover any information that we have experienced (such as webpages we have visited), information that we have received (such as email) or information that we have created (such as documents or images). Personal information is highly contextual. We have, for example, contextual information surrounding the original creation or obtaining of the information objects; contextual information about our use and re-use of the information; contextual information on our storage of the information objects (where has it been stored and within what type of information organization); and object specific contextual information. The latter covers attributes of the information objects themselves, e.g. who sent emails, did they have attachments, what type of document is being stored, what format is an image, etc. and attributes of the information, e.g. what information was contained within the email, who was in a photograph, who was the author of a document, etc. Elsweiler et al. (2009).

Contextual information is important in how we create information organizations, see Malone (1983) for example, but also in our needs from a system (Jones 2007). Searching personal information stores implies that we already have some idea of what we are looking for: we have experienced the information already and have some expectation that we have stored the information on our local information stores.

This is different from many Information Retrieval situations where we approach the system with a new information need and little knowledge of what we might expect to find. Information needs for new searches often contain contextual information about the situation that requires information, information needs for personal information management are rich in contextual information about the *object* to be

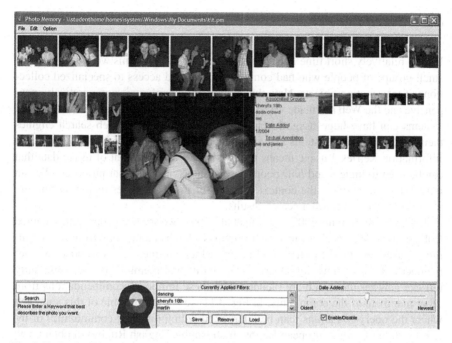

Fig. 8.10 Personal image search interface

found. Such an information need may look like "I need the photograph of Mark using the new interface, don't know where I put it but it was taken during that conference we attended last summer in Rome" which expresses information about the object type, what it contains and the fact that the object is specific. Unlike many searches personal information searches are ones where the user requires a specific information object rather than any information object that fulfills an information need.

Common approaches to personal information are similar to those for standard Information Retrieval, namely querying and browsing, but these approaches can be extended to help searchers use their contextual information within a search. Figure 8.10 shows an interface that mixes browsing and querying. This interface (Elsweiler et al. 2007) also provides *cues* that encourage searchers to remember and incorporate contextual information within a search: cues include the ability to use time as a search input, prompts on when the image was added to the collection and annotations on the content of the image.

The aim of such interfaces is to help the searcher remember the context in which they first saved the image (when did I have the image, how might I have annotated it, etc.) to help find it again. Iteratively remembering pieces of contextual information, which can be used as search criteria, leads to a form of 'retrieval journey' in which searchers navigate contextually to the information they want.

8.3.2 Social Context

Until a relatively short time ago, Information Retrieval systems were only used by small groups of people who had computer access and access to specialized collections of information objects. Now that computer technology is comparatively inexpensive and the Web has made vast amounts of data available, Information Retrieval systems can have huge usage levels. This is not just true of web search engines themselves but many systems that are made available on the Web. This increase in Information Retrieval usage means that we have a huge amount of usage data that can be used to understand *how* people use systems and for what purposes. We can mine this information—the context of use—for many purposes including filtering information to obtain better search results.

In Coyle and Smyth (2007), Freyne et al. (2007) we see such approaches, named Collaborative Web Search, in which previous search interactions from a community of users are used to filter good results which are then recommended to other members of the community. Queries from individual members of the community retrieve new results which are blended with these implicit recommendations from other members of the community. In Fig. 8.11 we see an example of this approach where the query '8 nations' can be interpreted within different communities of interest (Rugby Union, European Rugby, Irish Rugby, English Rugby) to obtain new information and information that has been selected as of interest by members of each community.

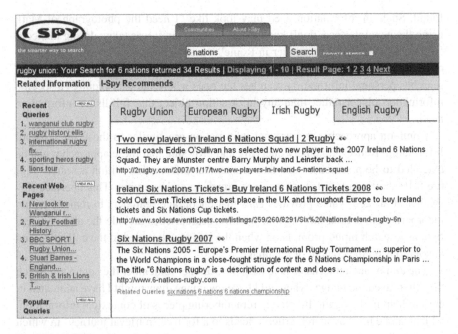

Fig. 8.11 Collaborative web search

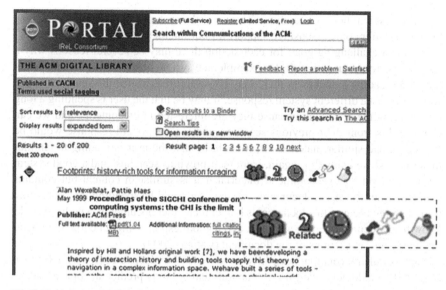

Fig. 8.12   Annotated collaborative web search

In Fig. 8.12 recommended results are annotated with icons to help interpret the result, the icons showing how relevant the result is to the community, how many queries would have retrieved the results, when the page was last visited by a member of the community, and so on. In these approaches we see a clever combination of system's use of context in deciding which results are of interest to a community with a socio-technical systems approach to context by displaying information to help a searcher evaluate the search results.

8.3.3   Interaction Context

A separate approach, but one which also uses searchers' interaction, is to react to the searcher's interaction context. Whilst searching on the Web we pass a lot of information to the search engine through our browser. Some of this information, such as our queries and the links we click, can be seen as direct indications of our interests. Other information, such as our scrolling behavior or the time we spend on pages, can be treated as implicit indications of our interests. That is, actions that may be used to infer our interests. In recent years there has been a wealth of activity in this type of behavioral modeling. Partly this is because such behavioral information does not require users to interrupt their normal searching activities to explicitly label items as relevant (as in relevance feedback), partly because it compensates for the lack of explicit relevance information in the form of queries, and partly because it gives information on more than just our interests. Watching our behavior may, for example, tell the system when we successfully conducting a search, and can be safely recommended new information, or when we are struggling to find useful information and may need system help in searching. That is, if the system can interpret our actions then it can offer context-sensitive support for our interaction.

This is a challenging goal: for each action there may be several reasons why a searcher performs an action. If, for example, the system observes that a user spent a long time reading a document there may be several reasons for this, each of which would suggest a different system response. It may be that the user is spending a long time reading the document because they are interested in its contents, and we can estimate this from their previous searches, and a good system response would be to recommend similar material. Or, it could be that the user is reading unfamiliar material, and we know this, again, from their previous searches, and a good system response might be to recommend material that is similar in content but contains simpler, easier to follow, documents. Or the user could be spending longer reading the document because the document is longer than other documents, which we could know from document length analyses, and a good response might be to recommend the most relevant sections of the document (Lalmas 2009).

Contextual information, seen here as a form of abductive reasoning (Ruthven et al. 2001) could help *interpret* user actions and possibly predict an appropriate response. However, as noted above, humans are often good at detecting which actions are meaningful but computers have to be told what is important.

One way in which we could determine which actions are important is by statistical data mining of interaction as in the work of Fox et al. (2005). In this study Fox et al. used a modified version of Internet Explorer to collect data on interaction with search engine results pages and search sessions (periods of web interaction separated by at least 10 minutes of inactivity) to gather information on user behaviors such as how long users spend reading a page, which links they clicked on, how quickly they left a results page and so on. At the same time they collected information on which pages a searcher found useful so that they could correlate which interactions were associated with successful information seeking and which were associated with a user being unsatisfied with the information they had encountered.

From their data they managed to statistically derive rules to predict when a searcher may be satisfied or not with the information they found. For example, a searcher who clicked on one of the first 3 results from a web search and did not return to the search engine was usually satisfied with the information they found whereas a searcher who clicked on a link further down the results page and quickly returns to the results was usually not satisfied with the information.

Such techniques give us useful information on the context of a search session which can be used to adapt search responses based on whether the user is interacting successfully or not. They also allow us to investigate how contextual variables affect interactive behavior. Do contextual variables such as task, search experience or search complexity lead to different interactive styles? Generally, the answer is yes and these statistical approaches can lead to useful ways to detect contextual differences within search. There is, of course, much still to be done here and there are basic questions that are not yet resolved such as which implicit features are useful, how should they be combined, and what are appropriate system responses to differences in a user's search context?

8.3.4 Task Context

A final example, and one that shows that contextual information can be incorporated in simple ways is the work of Liu and Chu (2007). Their work is based on medical information retrieval where medical retrieval is often based on scenarios such as diagnosis, prevention or treatment of a condition.

These diagnoses can be seen as *tasks* where the medical practitioner needs information for a specific medical task. Obvious terms to include in a query for each situation, such as 'treatment', are often too general to be of use in obtaining relevant information compared to task-specific terms such as 'lung excision', (Liu and Chu 2007). Liu and Chu's approach is to learn which terms are appropriate for which scenario and to expand the user's query with scenario-appropriate terms. So a query on preventing lung cancer may have the concept 'smoking reduction' added whereas a query on treating lung cancer would have terms such as 'radiotherapy' or 'chemotherapy' added. Such approaches performed favorably against standard statistical query expansion approaches and co-occurrence methods.

8.3.5 Summary

The systems described above are only a small set of approaches to Contextual Information Retrieval. However, I hope they show that there are many approaches to working with context; some involve system adaptation, some involve good interface design, others involve a mixture of both. All offer new ways of viewing the task of Information Retrieval systems and all raise evaluation challenges, the topic of the final section in this chapter.

8.4 Contextual Evaluation

How should we evaluate Contextual Information Retrieval systems? If we take a context-sensitive systems approach to contextual Information Retrieval then we immediately face the problem that evaluating adaptive systems implies evaluating a system whose goals are continually changing and where we have to measure the quality of adaptation as well as the final result.

Generally, in Contextual Information Retrieval there is no single definition of success; we might measure success by accuracy of retrieval results, increased reliability of the system, end-user satisfaction, more convenient systems to use or systems that increase our confidence in having found useful and appropriate information. Similarly the notion of failure is non-trivial: a contextual system may fail by making the wrong decisions, by making the right decisions at the wrong time, or by making too many decisions and hence reducing the user' ability to change the search. Systems may fail at the micro-level by, for example, adding the wrong terms to a user's query, or at the macro-level by simply being the wrong approach to utilizing contextual information.

Failure may also be caused by using the wrong contextual factors to make a decision, capturing insufficient contextual information and thereby having insufficient evidence to make a prediction or by having a poor understanding of how contextual information affects a user's task.

The basic question in contextual evaluations is often 'does a contextual approach work better than a non-contextual approach' and therefore the experimental comparison is simply a performance or experience comparison between two systems. However, what is much more useful in learning what works and why are deep evaluation techniques, often at the level of examining individual searches. This type of failure (or success) analysis was far more common in the early days of Information Retrieval. Now that the emphasis is on systems to support very large-scale Information Retrieval we often forget the value of examining systems in detail. A noticeable exception is the recent Reliable Information Access Workshop (Harman and Buckley 2009).

The most common Information Retrieval evaluation tool is the test collection, described in detail in Sanderson (2010). Depending on what we are testing it is possible to use test collections in Contextual Information Retrieval evaluation but they often only support a limited range of contextual factors.

In a paper discussing future of the TREC initiative (Spärck-Jones 2006), Karen Spärck Jones, one of the great supporters of TREC, characterized the relationship between context and test collections in this way:

> 'context is not embraced, but reluctantly and minimally acknowledged, like an awkward and difficult child. This applies even where explicit attempts have been made to include users (real or surrogate)'.

This argument was not against TREC but, rather, pointing out that the drive towards experimental control taken by Information Retrieval over several decades can lead to a lack of realism and that this realism is often contextual in nature. We should note that test collections are not context-free. Each test collection has a contextual background—why was the collection created, what were the assessment guidelines, who created the search requests and why were they important, etc. However, most of this useful contextual information is hidden and cannot be used for investigation.

A noticeable exception was the TREC HARD Track (Allan 2005), and its follow-on, the ciQA Track (Kelly and Lin 2007), which both allowed researchers limited interaction with the TREC assessors to better understand contextual factors involved in their topic and hence their process of assessment. Spärck Jones argued for a stronger contextual approach to evaluation, arguing

> 'However biologists know that you only get so far with studying creatures divorced from their ecologies. One might say now that we've learnt quite a lot about the retrieval system creature, and that we need some ecology study in order to design bigger and better bumble bees' Spärck-Jones (2006).

Many contextual approaches are user-centred evaluations. Here contextual approaches to evaluation can try to place experimental participants *within* a context

After your graduation you will be looking for a job in industry. You want information to help you focus your future job seeking. You know it pays to know the market. You would like to find some information about employment patterns in industry and what kind of qualifications employers will be looking for from future employees.

Fig. 8.13   Simulated work task situation

(Borlund 2003a). Borlund's simulated work task situations, discussed in detail in Ingwersen and Järvelin (2005), uses artificial tasks of the type shown below in Fig. 8.13. Although the tasks are artificially created they are based on realistic tasks of the type typically undertaken by a specific group who will participate in the evaluation. In this case the group are students and the task is a typical task for final year students. The task allows participants to incorporate their own contextual factors (what kind of discipline are they working in, what level of salary they might expect, etc.) to give more realistic searching behavior.

We can also manipulate search tasks used in experimental evaluations to investigate the effect of specific contextual variables within our evaluations. Bell and Ruthven (2004), for example, examined the role of search task complexity on searcher behavior and search satisfaction by experimentally manipulating artificial search tasks. Real tasks often incorporate contextual information. Elsweiler and Ruthven (2007) investigated using real search tasks, recorded at one point in time and reused later when investigating how to evaluate personal information management. However, there is still much to be done in the methodology of evaluating systems in context.

8.5 Conclusions

Whether we acknowledge the importance of the various contextual factors embedded within searching or not, contextual factors have been shown time and again to influence our use and evaluation of Information Retrieval systems. The more we know about what aspects of a searcher's context are important and why they are important then the better we can design more useful and successful Information Retrieval systems. This is not easy. However, as Alan Kay (2004) noted, in a slightly different context (no pun intended),

'Our game is more like art and sports than accounting, in that high percentages of failure are quite OK as long as enough larger processes succeed.'

Chapter 9
Digital Advertising: An Information Scientist's Perspective

James G. Shanahan and Goutham Kurra

Abstract Digital online advertising is a form of promotion that uses the Internet and Web for the express purpose of delivering marketing messages to attract customers. Examples of online advertising include text ads that appear on search engine results pages, banner ads, in-text ads, or Rich Media ads that appear on regular web pages, portals, or applications. Over the past 15 years online advertising, a $65 billion industry worldwide in 2009, has been pivotal to the success of the Web. That being said, the field of advertising has been equally revolutionized by the Internet, Web, and more recently, by the emergence of the social web, and mobile devices. This success has arisen largely from the transformation of the advertising industry from a low-tech, human intensive, "Mad Men" way of doing work to highly optimized, quantitative, mathematical, computer- and data-centric processes that enable highly targeted, personalized, performance-based advertising. This chapter provides a clear and detailed overview of the technologies and business models that are transforming the field of online advertising primarily from statistical machine learning and information science perspectives.

9.1 Introduction

Online advertising is a form of promotion that uses the Internet and Web for the express purpose of delivering marketing messages to attract customers. Since its fledgling beginning in 1994, online advertising has become a $65 billion dollar industry worldwide (in 2009) resulting in a double digit annual growth on average. It makes up almost 10% of the overall spending on advertising (across all media types such TV, radio, press, outdoor etc.). This success has arisen largely from the

J.G. Shanahan (✉)
Independent Consultant, 541 Duncan Street, San Francisco, CA 94131, USA
e-mail: James.Shanahan@gmail.com
url: http://churchandduncan.com/

G. Kurra
Turn Inc., 186 Liberty St., San Francisco, CA 94110, USA
e-mail: gkurra@gmail.com
url: http://kurra.net

M. Melucci, R. Baeza-Yates (eds.), *Advanced Topics in Information Retrieval*,
The Information Retrieval Series 33,
DOI 10.1007/978-3-642-20946-8_9, © Springer-Verlag Berlin Heidelberg 2011

transformation of the advertising industry from a low-tech, human intensive, "Mad Men"[1] way of doing work, that was common place for much of the 20th century and the early days of online advertising, to highly optimized, quantitative, mathematical, computer and data-centric processes (some of which have been adapted from Wall Street) that form the backbone of many current online advertising systems. More concretely, a modern day publisher and advertising system include modules for targeting, pricing, prediction, forecasting, and large scale storage and analytics. These components build on ideas from IR, machine learning, statistics, economic models, operations research, and distributed systems. This chapter focuses primarily on the information science aspects of online advertising. This is supplemented with background material on most aspects of a modern day online advertising system. Aspects of media planning and scheduling that mainly draw from operations research are beyond the scope of this chapter.

This chapter is structured as follows: Section 9.2 summarizes the key business concepts of online advertising; Section 9.3 presents sponsored search, reviewing key aspects of organic and sponsored search which highlighting active areas of research; Section 9.4 follows a similar structure focusing primarily on contextual advertising and display advertising; Section 9.5 reviews briefly auction models; Section 9.6 overviews new directions and issues, while Sect. 9.6 concludes the chapter.

9.2 Online Advertising Background

Traditionally, online advertising has been a formal relationship between the advertiser and the publisher. Each party in this relationship has a different objective. Advertisers want to convey a message to the consumer about a product or service to convince them to purchase or use that product or service; the more consumers that sign up the more revenue the advertiser makes. Often, advertisers are equally interested in latent effects, such as a positive branding experience. In short, advertisers see advertising as an investment for the growth of their sales and their brand, and wish to maximize their return on investment. On the other hand, publishers wish to generate revenue and, ultimately, a profit, be it from a news report written by a professional journalist, or from a blog entry or video created for free by a member of the public. This revenue can be offset against costs such as reporter salaries or online publishing fees and to potentially generating profits for the owners.

9.2.1 Purchase Funnel

From a marketing perspective, online advertising can be crudely categorized based on the primary objective of the advertising campaign: branding or direct market-

---

[1]"Mad men", as an expression, was coined in the late 1950s and refers to the people working on Madison Avenue, New York City in the advertising industry. It is also the name of a US AMC TV series that was first broadcast in 2007.

ing. This is more naturally framed in the field of marketing within the *advertising funnel* (also known as a *purchase funnel*). This funnel is divided into a sequence of phases organized around the following marketing objectives (ordered chronologically within a marketing campaign): category awareness, brand awareness, brand consideration, brand preference, purchase intent, purchase, customer retention, and customer advocacy. A marketing manager will select the parameters of an advertising campaign depending on the stage of marketing. These parameters will include the format of the ad (text, graphic, video), the message (purely informational or a call to action like a purchase or signup), and the desired reach (the reach refers to the total number of different people (unique users) or households exposed, at least once, to a medium during a given period of time). For example, for a product launch, a marketing manager may want to create product appeal through a broad reach ad campaign; this could be accomplished by reaching millions of people (with adequate frequency) through display advertising. Here, all online media sources can be leveraged, including contextual advertising around web pages (such as blogs and newswire), or online video, and sponsored search. Moving down through the funnel, ad formats such as rich media and online video can use their storytelling power to build favor toward the brand. Likewise, online sponsorships of unique content or events can push the middle funnel metrics. In addition, the advertiser website (specifically the landing page) will likely do great things for branding, provided the advertiser can get people there; search plays a critical role in driving traffic (be it organic search or sponsored search). The next stage in the marketing funnel is for the advertiser's site to do one or more of the following—close the sale there and then, push visitors to a retail dealer, or acquire an email address to continue the digital dialogue.

9.2.2 Types of Advertising

The advertiser message is generally embedded within an ad creative (be it text or graphic), which is subsequently embedded within a webpage that a consumer views via their web browser or application program. This page is commonly referred as the target page. Ad creatives are commonly hyperlinked to a landing page—a page on the advertiser's website that provides more details on the product or services advertised in the ad creative and how to obtain them. The landing page is rendered when the viewer clicks on the ad creative. Online creatives come in a huge variety of sizes and formats, ranging from text ads, to medium rectangle graphic ads (300 pixels wide by 250 pixels high), to skyscraper banners (728 pixels by 90 pixels), and from embedded ads (graphic, video) to pop-ups to overlays and interstitials. In the US, the Interactive Advertising Bureau (IAB), comprised of more than 460 leading media and technology companies who are responsible for selling 86% of online advertising in the United States, works with its member companies, evaluates and recommends standards and practices and fields critical research on interactive advertising (Broder et al. 2007a).

Embedding text ads within a search engine's results page (SERP) is referred to as *sponsored search*, while embedding text ads within publisher's online media such as a web pages, portals and online/mobile/offline applications is commonly referred to as *contextual advertising*. Embedding graphical/video ads within web pages or apps is referred to as *display advertising*. Other categories of advertising that take the form of text-ads or graphical ads include: classifieds and auctions (on newspaper sites, for example); local search; e-mail-based advertising; and sponsorship.

Other Types of Advertising   There are many other types of advertising that are summarized here. One of the bigger but less known categories is that of classifieds and auctions; this refers to advertisers who pay Internet companies to list specific products or services (e.g., online job boards and employment listings, real estate listings, automotive listings, auction-based listings, yellow pages). A good example is YellowPages.com, who provides a local search engine, where users can submit geographically constrained searches against a structured database of local business listings. Like sponsored, search some of the results page is sponsored, consisting of business/service listings that are paid for by the advertiser on a per impression-basis, or on a pay per transaction basis such as pay-per-call-basis (if a consumer calls a dedicated phone number then AT&T gets paid a negotiated fee in the case of YP.com). Other forms of advertising include lead generation, and email-based advertising.

9.2.3 Payment Models

From a business model perspective the field has adapted the traditional offline cost model (CPM), and also developed other custom built models for the online field. The CPM business model, *cost per mille* (corresponding to a thousand impressions), formed the core business model in the early days of online banner advertising (being directly adapted from traditional offline media such as newspaper). In this model, advertisers negotiate (or bid) a rate that will be paid for every thousand times the ad is displayed. This model is most often used when the placement of the ads (the sites and audience) is predetermined and when the value of the impressions is fairly uniform and known.

The CPM model imposes a large return on investment (ROI) risk on the advertiser as the ad impressions may not result in user engagement or purchases. The CPC model (*cost per click*) also known as PPC (pay per click) was first rolled out in 1997 by Goto.com (later acquired by Overture which was subsequently acquired by Yahoo!); CPC was originally created for advertising on SERPs. Google tweaked the CPC model in 2002 adding in an ad quality component (Edelman et al. 2005). CPC reduces the risk to the advertiser in that the advertiser does not pay for impressions that are not creating value. On the other hand, the publisher or intermediary now shares some of the risk. By using clicks as a proxy for user interest and engagement with the ads, the advertiser has some form of measuring and controlling the success of the campaign. However, not all clicks are valuable to advertisers as not all clicks convert to useful actions such as purchases. Furthermore, fraudulent clicks are easy to generate and pose an ROI risk to the advertiser.

In the CPA model, *cost per action* (sometimes known as Pay Per Action or PPA), the advertiser pays for each specified action (e.g., a purchase of a product, a lead form submission for a loan) linked to the advertisement. Since an action is usually the very thing that generates revenue for the advertiser, this is similar to sharing revenue with the publisher or intermediary. Actions can be defined as post-click or post-view and may have different values depending on the type. The CPA model is most common with ad networks which are intermediaries between publishers and advertisers. While CPA removes most of the advertiser's risk, it transfers all the business risk to the intermediary ad network or the publisher since users may not actually buy the advertiser's services or products despite a lot of advertising.

Hybrids of these models have also been constructed such as dCPM (dynamic CPM), where dCPM pricing optimizes an ad towards the users, sites and site sections that perform best for the advertiser, dynamically paying the most efficient CPM for the value of the inventory to the advertiser. dCPM ads are driven by two parameters, a maximum average CPM and a performance goal such as a CPA target. dCPM allows the risk of a campaign to be shared between the advertiser and the intermediary, typically, an ad network or demand-side platform (DSP) or ad exchange (defined subsequently).

9.2.4 Market Numbers and Trends

The field of online advertising was about $65 billion worldwide in 2009. This is broken down regionally as follows: Western Europe ad spending was $18 billion (€14.7 billion Euros) in 2009 or 27% of global online ad spending; the US revenue was $22.7 billion; Latin America ad revenue was $2 billion; China had a similar revenue of $2 billion; $2 billion in Latin America; and Russia accounted for $720 million (AdEx 2010). Looking more closely at these numbers trends are starting to emerge based on 2009 revenue numbers in the United States by the IAB (2009), which are largely echoed worldwide:

1. Sponsored search accounts for 47% of 2009 full year revenues ($10.7 billion);
2. Display-related advertising revenues totaled $8.0 billion;
3. Classifieds revenues (products such YellowPages.com) accounted for 10% or $2.3 billion;

9.3 Sponsored Search-Based Advertising

Abstractly, online advertising can be viewed as a supply and demand market economy. Demand in this context refers to how much (quantity) of ad slot inventory is desired by advertisers. Supply represents how much the market can offer. The quantity supplied refers to the amount of a certain ad inventory publishers are willing to supply when receiving a certain price. In this model, advertisers are demand-side entities and publishers are supply-side entities. In the early days the relationship between advertiser and publisher was direct and driven by large sales teams—it was inefficient and largely informal (by today's online advertising standards at least). This inefficient advertising market place left a lot to be desired by both the advertiser and the publisher. As a result lots of new models and marketplaces such as ad networks, ad exchanges, demand side trading platforms have been developed over the last four or five years (some of these marketplaces will be discussed below).

9.3.1 Sponsored Search Overview

Sponsored search, though one of the most innovative forms of advertising on the Internet, turns out to be one of most easily understood forms of online adverting. Here ads are embedded within the SERP, generally on the North and East ports of the SERP (corresponding to the top and right hand side of the SERP). Sponsored search is dominated by the CPC model. It is a direct relationship between the search engine and the advertiser or the advertiser agency. From a user's perspective, a search engine serves one key need: that of trying to satisfy a searcher's information need which is expressed via the searcher's query. This is accomplished by providing a ranked list of organic web pages and documents of various types (maps, videos, etc), sometimes known as hits (where each page is presented in terms of a title, snippet and corresponding URL), and a ranked list of sponsored results presented in the north and east sections of the SERP. Within the online advertiser world, the search engine plays the role of the publisher and the auctioneer. As auctioneer, the search engine gets to select which ads can participate in the auction, the ranking of these ads and the cost of a click (should the display of an ad result in a click). Viewed this way, the SERP can be simply broken into the organic set of results and the sponsored set of results generated by the organic search engine and the sponsored search engine respectively.

9.3.2 Organic Search Engine

An organic web search engine is designed to search for information on the web servers. A modern day organic search engine can be decomposed into the following core modules: crawler, webpage repository, document index, query processor, document ranker, logging, analytics, SERP generator and administrators console. Figure 9.1 presents these components and their relationship to each other. For completeness, a brief summary of these components is provided as many of them will be used in other online advertising ecosystems. A search engine operates in the following order:

1. web crawling;
2. indexing;
3. ranking documents for user search queries;
4. SERP generation.

Crawler   One of the core components of web search engines is the ability to retrieve and store the billions of pages available across the Web. The crawler sometimes, also known as a spider, is primarily responsible for retrieving these pages, and storing them locally. A web crawler is a computer program (or agent) that browses the Web in an automated manner. Web crawlers generally store a copy of all the visited pages for later processing by the featurization process and by the indexing process (that encodes the downloaded pages in an efficient data structure to provide fast retrieval). In general, a crawler is provided with an initial list of URLs to visit—called the seeds. As the crawler visits these URLs, it identifies all the hyperlinks in visited pages and adds them to the list of URLs to visit—called the crawl frontier. URLs from the frontier are recursively visited according to a set of crawling policies. Exclusions can be made by the use of `robots.txt` files. Policies include how deep to crawl, limits on how many pages are crawled from a site, and the order in which a URLs are visited.

Inverted Index and Scoring Process   The crawled web pages need to be stored in a manner that is computationally efficient (SERPs need to be generated in response to queries within 100s of milliseconds) and with minimum storage requirements (say 10–20% of the original raw page size). To enable this, web pages are stored in an inverted index data structure; this structure exploits the sparse nature of web documents. Within this framework, it is common to represent web pages in terms of the words, or phrases that occur in the titles, headings, body content, or other special HTML fields called meta-tags that occur in the raw HTML page. These words or phrases can be more generally referred to as features or characteristics of the webpage. An inverted index is an index data structure storing a key-value mapping from features, such as words or numbers, to their locations in a document or a set of documents. An everyday example of an inverted index is the index at the back any text book, where the index words are the keys, and the associated values are a list of pages where the corresponding word(s) occur. In web search the purpose of an inverted index is to allow fast full text searches, at a cost of increased processing when a document is added to the database.

Within the context of web search and, more broadly, digital advertising, one can generalize the use of inverted indexes beyond that of word-based keys. The key type in the inverted index mapping can be extended to any feature, f, that can be used to characterize a web page p (e.g., category of webpage, a word that occurs on the webpage, a postal code corresponding to the geographic area that had the highest density of visitors to this webpage in the past 3 days). The value associated with each key is generally referred to as the postings list. In this case, it could be a linked list of posting records. A posting could be simply a document identifier denoting that this feature occurred or is associated with this document and a corresponding payload.

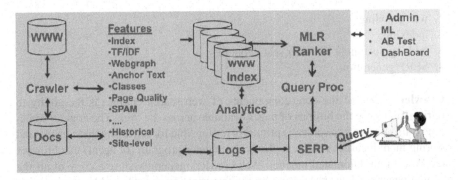

Fig. 9.1 Core components of a web search engine

The posting payload could be a number corresponding to the number of times a word occurred in a document (sometimes known as term frequency (TF) of a term in the document) and a list of numbers corresponding to the position of each word occurrence within a document. A posting is formally represented as tuple (ID, W), where ID is the page identifier (generally ranges from 1 to the number of unique pages N), and W, which is assumed for the purposes of ease of presentation to be limited to a number, known as a weight; e.g., this weight could be the term frequency of f within p. For efficiency of memory usage and query scoring time, each posting list is sorted in increasing order of *page* ID. As a result, there are numerous ways to encode postings lists to reduce memory requirements (Witten et al. 1999). Generally, since billions of documents are being indexed, the documents are divided into non-overlapping subsets where each subset is indexed separately on its own server; at query time responses from each server need to be merged.

Features The featurization step in Fig. 9.1 is concerned with representing each page in terms of features that summarize this page and distinguish it from other web pages. These features can be purely based on the textual content of the page (such as words and phrases). Values for these features can be simply frequency counts or normalized frequencies (frequency of word/total number of words). In addition, features can be based on the web graph of hyperlinked web pages such as PageRank (Brin and Page 1998) where the feature value corresponds to a probability that a web browser (user) who follows links randomly (with teleportation capabilities) for a long time will be at a particular page if polled randomly. This probability can provide a query-independent measure of the popularity (and quality) of the page. Another family of features could be behavioral/historical features, such as the number of times a page has been clicked on from a SERP. Many other features families are commonly used. In summary, an inverted index is used extensively within large web-scale systems such as organic web search, ad search, and in other sparse data problems such as user behavior problems.

Ranking Documents for user search queries Web search engine index sizes are in the order of tens of billions of web pages of pages. For example, the website, http://www.worldwidewebsize.com/,[2] estimates Google's index to be around 30 billion pages.[3] Typically, search engines need to process tens of thousands of queries per second (QPS).[4] This is generally a distributed, multistep process consisting of the following steps:

- query parsing,
- query featurization,
- scoring pages in the index and sorting them based on score, and
- generating a SERP.

Query parsing is concerned with splitting the query into words (tokenizing) and assigning a role to each word or sequence of words such as determining if a word is a proper noun, a determiner, a preposition, or a part of a phrase. This can be accomplished using part of speech taggers, lexicon lookup approaches, or Markov models, such as Hidden Markov Models (HMMs) or Conditional Random Fields (CRFs) (Rabiner 1989b).

Query featurization includes the features output by query parsing and possibly many other features. For example, the zip code from where the user typed the query, or the day of week, etc. At its simplest, this feature vector could just be a list of query words, as is the case in traditional information retrieval, or could be an augmented feature vector as briefly described above. Subsequently this query feature vector is taken and a join is performed over the pre-sorted feature posting lists in the index. One of the common approaches to performing this multi-way join is to use a document-at-a-time (DAAT) evaluation. Most of the DAAT algorithms in the literature are merge-joins with improved efficiency (Rabiner 1989a). To evaluate a query using a DAAT algorithm, a cursor is created for each feature f in the query vector, and is used to access f's posting list. During the join, the cursors are moved in a coordinated fashion forward over the posting lists. While traversing the posting list in this fashion one accumulates documents that have all the query features.

One can use these features to assign a relevance score (sometimes interpreted as a similarity) to each of the accumulated documents. This similarity score between page p and query vector q, can be as simple as summing contributions over all common features of the query vector and the document vector, and over all features that are local to the query and webpage as follows (this is commonly known as a dot product):

$$\text{Score}(p, q) = \sum_{f \in p \cap q} w_q w_p + \sum_{f \in q_0} w_q + \sum_{f \in p_0} w_p \tag{9.1}$$

where the weights w_p and w_q measure the importance of the feature f on the query side and on the page side respectively, and q_0 and p_0 denote features on the query side only and page side only.

---

[2] Visited on February 15, 2011.

[3] Editor's note: Section 2.1 reports that the indexed Web is estimated to contain *at least* 16.3 billion pages on the same date, thus, there is no contradiction.

[4] Section 2.4 uses "query processing throughput".

In reality, scoring each document as described above is impractical (due to millisecond time constraints on query turnaround time). As a result, various approaches have been proposed to address this constraint resulting, typically, in a multi-phase retrieval process. This multi-phase process can consist of two or three phases, where each phase can be functionally similar to the scoring process described above with the later phases consisting of more features (with some of these features being dependent on the distribution of the results set to-date). It is common to use a two-phase process using an operator such as the Weighted AND (WAND) operator in the first phase to improve first phase efficiency (Broder et al. 2003a).

SERP Generation   The organic SERP consists of a list of snippets of text extracted from each of the resultant web pages. This snippet serves the same role as an ad creative and needs to be carefully crafted (automatically).

Evaluation   Relevance is core to evaluation in IR. Here, relevance typically denotes how well a retrieved document or set of documents meets the information need of the user. *Relevance* is often viewed as multifaceted. One core facet of relevance relates to *topical* relevance or *aboutness* (Croft et al. 2009), i.e., to what extent the topic of a result matches the topic of the query or information need. Another facet of relevance is based on user perception, sometimes referred to as *user* relevance; it encompasses *topical* relevance and possibly other concerns of the user such as timeliness, authority or novelty of the result. Depending on the query yet another facet of relevance comes into play that of geographical aboutness, i.e., to what extent the location of a result, say in the case of a business listing, matches the location of the query or information need. Performance of systems is generally captured by relevance-centered metrics such as Discounted Cumulative Gain (DCG) (Järvelin and Kekäläinen 2002) or precision at specific ranks (say up rank 5) (Manning et al. 2008b). For example, DCG is defined here up until rank r as follows:

$$\text{DCG} @ r = \text{rel}_i + \sum_{i=2}^{r} \frac{\text{rel}_i}{\log_2 i} \tag{9.2}$$

The constants rel_i are the relevance scores generally provided by human assessors. Human assessors typically judge documents with respect a query on an ordinal scale, with labels such as "Perfect", "Excellent", "Good", "Fair", and "Bad". These are then mapped to a numeric scale. Though relevance is generally provided by a team of professional assessors, it is sometimes obtained via crowd sourcing services such as the Amazon Mechanical Turk (Manning et al. 2008a).

Machine Learnt Ranking Functions   Recent work on applying machine learning approaches to optimizing ranking functions has led to huge gains over hand-tuned expert systems. The field is commonly known as learning to rank or machine-learned ranking (MLR) and is a type of supervised or semi-supervised machine learning problem in which the goal is to automatically construct a ranking function from training data. Training data generally consists of query, webpage, and associated relevance triples $(q, p, RELEVANCE)$ with some partial order specified between web pages associated with the same query. This score or label may be provided manually by human assessors (or editors), who judge the relevance for each selected $(QUERY, PAGE)$ pair. It is not feasible to check relevance of all query document pairs, so typically a technique called top-k pooling is used—only top few documents, retrieved by some existing ranking models are checked (Manning et al. 2008b). Alternatively, training data labels may be derived automatically by analyzing click-through logs (i.e. search results which received clicks from users) (Joachims and Radlinski 2007). Training data is used by a learning algorithm to produce a ranking model, which can then be used to compute a relevance score for a document with respect to a given query. MLR problems can be reformulated as optimization problems with respect to evaluation metrics (such as DCG). This has lead to the development of a plethora of very powerful pair-wise and list-wise learning algorithms (Cao and Liu 2007).

9.3.3 Sponsored Search Engine

Sponsored search, unlike organic search, is concerned with selecting and presenting text ads in response to a searcher's query with the express goal of satisfying the searcher's information need while in parallel delivering the advertiser's message; these text ads are embedded along with organic search results on the SERP. This can be viewed as *"not seeing advertising as entertainment or an art form, but as a medium of information . . . "* (Ogilvy 1983).

Sponsored search system strongly parallels the functionality of organic web search but differs in subtle ways that make the automatic targeting of ads much more challenging. One could frame the problem of targeting ads as a web search or IR problem. Here the organic user query, q, and user, u, become the query vector (as is the case in web search) but the index differs to that in web search; it is created from features extracted from the ad creative, the keywords associated with the ad (for targeting), and sometimes the text of the corresponding landing pages. An ad search engine operates in a similar way to an organic search engine; it consists of the following core steps:

1. landing page crawling;
2. indexing;
3. ranking ads for user search queries;
4. presentation of ads within SERP.

In paid search, the crawler crawls the landing page associated with an ad creative; this is generally a much simpler and focused crawling process than for web search. Indexing uses, in addition to the features used in web search, a set of features specialized for advertising. An ad can be viewed as consisting of terms (unigram or n-gram) taken from the ad creative, or terms generated from the keywords that the advertiser associated with the ad, or terms extracted from the landing page. In addition, these n-gram terms can be further qualified by the zone in which they occur. For example, an n-gram term, such as, "ipod case", extracted from the creative title might be featurized as "ipod case:adTitle". These and other features will be discussed in detail below. Ranking of ads can be based on a hand-coded scoring function or based on a machine learning optimization strategy like those described in the MLR section above.

ECPM-Based Ranking of Ads   For a search engine (publisher) to show an advertiser's ad, the advertiser or their representative, e.g., search engine marketer (SEM)[5]:

- must create a text ad creative;
- select the key search words or phrases that they would like their ad to appear alongside (specifying exact match or a broader syntactic and semantic match);
- set other targeting constraints such as geo-constraints (e.g., show my ad in the San Francisco area only); and
- set budgeting and delivery constraints.

For the latter point, more concretely advertisers must set the following: their budget or total advertising spend for this ad campaign or overall; the start and end times for their ad campaigns and their maximum CPC, which is the maximum amount an advertiser is willing to spend to have one searcher click on the ad and be transferred to the advertiser's website. All of this information is known only by the advertiser and the publisher.

One of the biggest challenges for the search engine is to establish how much a click is worth such that the search engine makes money at a fair market value and that all advertisers are getting a good ROI. This type of decision-making falls squarely in the field of economics where recent work in auction theory combined with game-theoretic analyses of auctions can be leveraged to create marketplace mechanisms, i.e., auctions (rules for bidding, and pricing), that enable both the search engine and advertisers to operate collectively to maximize the social welfare of the marketplace. In other words, it is necessary to create an auction mechanism such that the advertiser pays up to one's maximum value of the impression/click without remorse (for paying too much or missing opportunities) and by doing so the search engine earns optimal revenue. Initial auction models for sponsored search operated as follows: When a searcher inputs a search query, the search engine conducts a sealed auction across all ads with keywords matching the query (corresponding to a partial match, or as an exact match of the keywords associated with an ad). This auction both induces a ranking of ads and establishes a price per click on the winning ad(s). This induced ranking and pricing scheme can take many forms depending on the type of auction used. For example, it could be based exclusively on the bid price associated with the triggered keyword(s). The pricing for this model could be based upon second pricing where the advertiser is charged the bid associated with the ad in second place. For multi-slot SERPs, ads are selected based upon bid price and

---

[5]SEMs are advertising agencies that manage the search ad campaigns of large companies.

charged for clicks based upon the bid price of the ad in the next rank down in the ranked list; this is known as a Generalized Second Price (GSP) auction (Edelman et al. 2005). This was the ranking strategy adapted by Goto.com/Overture when they introduced the first CPC-based cost model for online advertising back in 1997 (Edelman et al. 2005). This approach can be easily gamed by unscrupulous advertisers leading to many issues ranging from spamming-like behaviors to revenue reduction (due to active gaming-like behaviors that lead to reduced CPCs). For example, an advertiser could associate one's ads with a broad spectrum of keywords (possibly keywords that have nothing to do with the ads being targeted) and bid at high levels to insure impressions. Within this ranking model these ads would be shown to searchers thus leading to spam-like behavior (i.e., showing ads that have nothing to do with the information need or intent of the user's search). Ultimately, this type of activity would lead to reduced revenue (since there would be fewer clicks) and annoyed searchers. To overcome these limitations with bid-based ranking while maintaining keyword-based targeting Google developed a yield-based ranking model that optimized both revenue (via higher CPCs) and ad relevance. This ranking is based on a product of the advertiser bid price for that keyword and an ad quality score corresponding to the expected user behavior in terms of clicks on that ad. This product score is known as the expected CPM (ECPM) and is defined as follows:

$$ECPM(a) = P(\text{Click}(a)|p, a, u)\text{CPCBid}_a \times 1{,}000 \qquad (9.3)$$

where p, a and u denote the context of the impression in terms of the target page (where the ad is shown; the can be simply the organic search query or the organic part of the resulting SERP), the ad, and the user respectively; and CPCBid_a corresponds to the bid price that the advertiser has agreed to pay for a click on this ad in the case of a first price auction. This $P(\text{Click}(a)|p, a, u)$ component is generally referred to as a quality score and can be viewed as a proxy for the click-through rate (CTR) of an ad shown in the context of a target page, user and ad. The $1{,}000$ multiplier in the above ECPM equation corresponds to $1{,}000$ impressions (presentations of the ad to users). The ECPM-based scores induce a ranking and thereby determine the placement of ads on the search engine page with the top-ranked ad being placed in the top slot, and second ranking in the second slot, and so on. Pricing for this ranking model can take many forms. For now let's assume a second price auction mechanism whereby the advertiser is charged as follows for a click. The cost per click corresponds to the minimum it takes for an ad to maintain its position in the ECPM-based rank. For example, let's assume two ads ad_1 and ad_2 with corresponding bid prices Bid_1 and Bid_2 and quality scores Q_1 and Q_2 respectively. Let's assume that the rank scores for ad_1 is greater than ad_2. This is more succinctly stated as follows:

$$\text{Bid}_1 \times Q_1 > \text{Bid}_2 \times Q_2 \qquad (9.4)$$

For ad_1 to maintain its current rank (using some basic algebra on the above equation) then Bid_1 needs to be at least:

$$\text{Bid}_1 \geq \frac{\text{Bid}_2 \times Q_2}{Q_1} \qquad (9.5)$$

For a click on ad ad_1 the search charges the advertiser this minimum (plus an arbitrary small amount, say, one penny) to maintain its current ranking. This can be more naturally written in terms of CPC notation as follows:

$$CPC_1 = \frac{Bid_2 \times Q_2}{Q_1} \qquad (9.6)$$

where the advertiser pays a cost per click of CPC_1 for a click on ad_1. The GSP auction is used by most major search engines despite provable imperfections that will be discussed in Sect. 9.5. In its simplest form, if all click-through rates are equal, an advertiser's payment per click is the bid of the next-highest bidder. Since the context is implicit below for a given expression the notation $P(\text{click}(a)|p, a, u)$ is simplified to $P(\text{click})$.

Sponsored Search versus Organic Search   Ranking for organic search can be reduced to generating the best rank ordering for a set of webpages with respect to a *query* (based on, say, *topical* relevance). Sponsored search differs in that it needs to balance the need of selecting and presenting text ads that satisfy the searcher's information need while in parallel delivering the advertiser's message. This joint objective is optimized by ECPM-based ranking (also known as revenue-based ranking). Estimating $P(\text{Click})$ accurately is key to creating an optimal ranking and pricing. For ads that have been shown many times in the context of an organic SERP, p (here the user, u is marginalized), the estimate for $P(\text{Click})$ is the binomial maximum likelihood estimate; this is then simply the number of observed successes divided by the number of trials, i.e. clicks/impressions, or CTR. However this data requirement is generally very difficult to meet. Like most web distributions, the distribution of impressions and clicks follows a power law curve where the short head corresponds to ads with a high frequency of impressions and clicks on keywords and a long tail corresponds to rare events where an ad gets a small number of impressions and clicks on different keywords. In addition, since click rates for ads are generally very low (Burns (2010) reported a CTR of 2.6% for ads on SERPs) these estimates tend to have high variance. For example, if the true CTR for an ad is 2.6% then it must be shown 1,000 times before one can be 95% confident that this estimate is within 1% (about 40% relative error) of the estimated CTR, i.e., in the range [1.6%, 3.6%]. This interval is narrowed down to [2.3%, 2.9%] after 10,000 impressions. To converge on confident estimates of CTR can represent a significant investment by the publisher (in this case the search engine). For example, it could cost $40 to converge on the 95% interval of 2.6%±1% if the CPC were $1.60 or $400 for the tighter interval of 2.6%±0.3%. Errors in these estimates can be detrimental to the search engine as it might lead to a loss in revenue (under charge due to higher estimates of $P(\text{Click})$) or missed opportunities for advertisers (who are priced out by a low estimate for CTR). The CTR rates on an overall SERP basis is 25% (Khan 2010) corresponding about 3% CTR on any ad slot; most ads, however, will exhibit a CTR of less than 1% resulting in hugely rare events. This challenge is further compounded by a non-stationary marketplace: Sponsored search is a non-stationary market place consisting of hundreds of millions of ads, with a significant portion of new ads and advertisers entering (and leaving) the marketplace on a daily basis. Additionally, the constraints associated with current ads (such as keywords, geo, demographics) may also change. As a result there is a significant portion of ads for which there is limited or no information on P(Click) estimates.

Generally one is dealing with hundreds of millions of ads (order of 10^8) and billions of SERPs and over a billion users. The cross product of these three large dimensional variables yields a massive event space (10^{26}) most of which is unexplored (cannot possibly observe user interactions for most (QUERY, AD) pairs as there are not enough SERPs to do this and it would come at a very heavy cost to the publisher (the search engine) and user. This type of phenomenon is commonly known as the curse of dimensionality (Bellman 2003) and is well lamented in the field of machine learning. More concretely, with an estimated trillion (10^{12}) queries issued worldwide in 2009 by about 1.3 billion people issuing about 700 queries per year, one can only hope to see 10^{22} events or about one hundredth of one percent of the possible events (Khan 2010). Finally, scalability is a challenge, paralleled only by organic search. In 2009, an estimated trillion (10^{12}) queries were issued worldwide by about 1.3 billion people corresponding to about 700 queries per user per year or throughput of 34,000 queries per second globally. This is an extremely large number of SERPs. As a result of these key differences between organic search and sponsored search, many research opportunities have opened up that push the limits of areas such as machine learning, IR, statistics, and large scale computing. Some challenges and current work in these areas are reviewed next.

9.3.4 Research Challenges and Opportunities

Characterizing ad Selection and Pricing as an Online Learning Problem
Most of the major search engines (Bing, Google, Yahoo!, Yandex) rank ads and price clicks using ECPM or yield-based ranking. Inaccurate estimates of the P(Click) can have adverse effects on user satisfaction and on advertiser ROI, which, ultimately, effects the revenue of the search engine. Consequently, search engines are very motivated to accurately model P(Click). To simplify the problem of ad selection and pricing based upon ECPM, one can assume that all ads have the same bid without losing generality. Framed like this the problem reduces to accurate estimation of P(Click) for a huge variety of ad contexts (user, publisher, and ad combinations). As was presented previously, this problem suffers from the curse of dimensionality with little or no data about most possible contexts where an ad could be served. To overcome this problem various commercial entities have bootstrapped ad selection (i.e., accurately estimate P(Click)) in different ways leveraging both domain expertise and more statistically principled approaches. These schemes typically combine an exploit strategy that focuses on the short term and immediate revenue gains based upon accurate estimates of P(Click), generally for a small subset of possible events, with an explore strategy, where a small portion of query traffic is devoted to exploration that tends to be more speculative in nature. The goal of exploration is to

discover other ad contexts where an ad can deliver high ROI for the advertiser and high revenue for the search engine. In addition, recent studies such as (Broder et al. 2008) and (Shanahan and den Poel 2010a) have also started to look at lifetime value of users as opposed to the one-shot nature of the explore/exploit approaches discussed here; this is not discussed further here. Typically, one can frame all explore and exploit approaches as a form of online learning or sequence learning. Online learning is a model of induction that learns one instance at a time (Cesa-Bianchi and Lugosi 2006). The goal in online learning is to predict values for instances, i.e., here, the P(Click) on ad in a given context. The key defining characteristic of online learning is that soon after a prediction is made, a more accurate estimate is discovered. This information can then be used to refine the prediction system using learning. The goal of learning is to make predictions that are close to the true values. More formally, an online algorithm proceeds as a sequence of trials. Each trial can be decomposed into the following steps. First the algorithm generates an estimate of P(Click), say, in terms of its mean and variance values. Then the algorithm receives feedback via a click or lack of click on an ad in a specific context. The third stage is the most crucial as the learning algorithm can use this user feedback to update its hypothesis for future trials. The ultimate goal of the learning algorithm in the context of ad serving could be to maximize short-term revenue while balancing the need to learn about unknown ad behaviors. Because online learning algorithms continually receive feedback, the algorithms are able to adapt and learn in difficult situations.

Online learning algorithms have been studied extensively leading to many theoretical findings on learnability that help guide exploration and exploitation dilemma, even, in an ad serving setting. To aid with understanding it useful to cast the problem of ad serving as a multi-arm bandit problem (a slot machine with multiple arms) where each arm corresponds to an ad with an unknown P(Click) and where each machine corresponds to a (USER, TARGETPAGE) context. Let's assume one machine (corresponding to one ad context). When an arm is pulled it generates a revenue equivalent to the bid with a probability P(Click). The goal of online learning is to generate a finite series of arm pulls (ad servings) that maximizes the total expected revenue (this is often referred to reward in the online learning literature). This arm selection rule is often referred to as a policy.

A bandit policy or allocation rule is an adaptive sampling process that provides a mechanism to select an arm at any given time instant based on all previous pulls and their outcomes. These series of arm pulls (ad servings) could be based upon a random policy (selecting an arm at random) or based on an exploit policy where an arm is selected based upon it expected revenue (based on its most current estimates). Thus, an arm with a worse empirical mean but high variance might be preferred to an arm with a better mean but low variance (exploration). After the sampling is continued for a while the online learning algorithm should learn enough to sample the arm that will provide the highest payoff (exploitation). A good sampling scheme should reach this point as efficiently as possible.

A popular metric to measure the performance of a policy is called *regret*, which is the difference between the expected reward obtained by playing the best arm and the expected reward given by the policy under consideration (Lai and Robbins 1985); it corresponds to the number of mistakes made (i.e. a mistake is when a suboptimal arm/ad is selected). A large body of online learning literature has considered the problem of constructing policies that achieve tight upper bounds on regret as a function of the time horizon (which is modeled as the total number of arm pulls) for all possible values of the expected revenues. This work has culminated in the following key finding: assume that each arm is assigned a priority function which is a sum of the current empirical payoff plus a factor that depends on the estimated variability (as opposed to a function of the expected revenue and its variance) (Auer et al. 1985). Sampling the arm with the highest priority at any point in time, one explores arms with little information and exploits arms which are known to be good based on accumulated empirical evidence. With increasing sampling size, the sampling variability reduces and one ends up converging to the optimal arm. Consequently one cannot construct a variance adjustment factor to make the regret (or number of mistakes) better than $\log N$, thereby providing a benchmark for evaluating policies.

Though online learning provides a very nice framework to analyze ad selection behavior it has many practical limitations. For example, the current framework assumes just one winner, whereas most ad contexts have the ability to show multiple ads. In addition, as a result of the curse of dimensionality, it is not possible to explore and then exploit all possibilities. To address this shortcoming Pandey et al. (2007) developed an approximation using a hierarchical model with a multi-stage sample strategy combined with a Bayesian model to do online learning at different levels of resolution. Shrinkage and other back-off strategies can also be applied. Agarwal et al. (2009) report an interesting hierarchical Bayesian model that address some of the idiosyncrasies of online advertising such as short lifetimes, delayed feedback and non-stationary rewards with compelling results. They also provide a good review of recent literature in this area. Yet another alternative approximation is based upon building regression models to predict click behavior as function of ad, user and target page characteristics. This can be accomplished using commodity learning frameworks such as logistic regression, though care has to be taken in training set construction as will be highlighted below to avoid biases that can provide misleading probability estimates. This latter approach and variations thereof are commonly used in practice.

Predicting P(Click)   Reported studies on modeling $P(\text{Click})$ fall into a number of categories: collaborative filtering approaches; predictive approaches; and evaluation approaches. All approaches leverage user click behavior (that can be harvested from log files) to model the $P(\text{Click})$ estimates; this can be viewed as a form of implicit relevance modeling. In addition, hybrid models have been developed where predicted CTRs are combined with empirical data counts using, say, Beta updating. This is in contrast to modeling ranking functions for organic search, where the objective is to model topical (and sometimes user) relevance and use such models to rank documents with respect to user information needs as expressed through queries; in this context, it is common to obtain explicit relevance judgments from human labeler(s) though some recent studies (Chapelle et al. 2009) have shown that learnt ranking models from implicit judgments give performances that are within 4% (in terms of normalized DCG) of models built using explicit relevance judgments. In addition, to this stricter predictive (scoring) requirement, relevance needs to be modeled beyond users' topical needs and the commercial intent, and commercial opportunity also needs to be considered.

Previous studies (Vestergaard and Schroder 1985) have shown that advertising relevance involves complex inference processes that go beyond surface-form semantic models commonly used in traditional IR and organic web search (typically unigram modeling with limited semantics such as the role of the n-gram in the query or sentence, e.g., a city or person's name). It can involve a complex interplay between the message contained in the ad creative (words, images, video), the target audience, the pitch level of the ad (to produce increases in brand awareness or to achieve other marketing objectives such as product sales), and user modeling. For example, if a consumer has already purchased a product they may not need further brand-based advertising. Understanding and modeling some of these interplays is a very fruitful area of research and product development that cuts across all aspects of digital advertising. It is an area largely unexplored with few theoretical models and where guidance is often achieved via empirical studies.

An example of such a study is reported by Richardson et al. (2007), where they tackled the problem of estimating $P(\text{Click})$ for sponsored search ads from impression and click event log data using a logistic regression model:

$$P(\text{Click}) = \frac{1}{1 + \exp(-\sum_{i=1}^{n} w_i x_i)} \tag{9.7}$$

The problem of predicting $P(\text{Click})$ was modeled using training data of the form $(\text{AD}, \text{TERM}, \text{CTR})$ where Ad is the ad being potentially embedded in the SERP, Term is the search term (some or all of the query terms) input by the searcher, and CTR is the binomial maximum likelihood estimate of the CTR. Each Ad contains the following information: bid terms; creative title and body; display URL; landing page and the number of times the ad was presented and clicked in the context of the keyword Term. Note: advertisers may specify whether an ad is displayed under the rules of exact match, or broad match. In the exact match case, the searcher query must exactly match the bid terms. In the broad match case, the bid terms can be related more loosely, such as being a subset of the query words.

Richardson et al. used both exact match and broad match examples in their study. The dataset consisted of 10,000 advertisers, and one million example triples $(\text{AD}, \text{TERM}, \text{CTR})$. The following is a list of some of the key feature families used in this study and represent common practice:

1. Historical data: a smoothed CTR estimate for (AD, TERM) based on other ads with this keyword Term;
2. Appearance: features that describe the appearance of the ad creative such as the number of words in title or body; the presence of capitalization; the presence of punctuation; word length statistics;
3. Presence of certain call to action words such as "buy", "join", etc.;

4. Reputation based on URL: number of page-views and in-links; does the URL have a .com, etc.;
5. Landing page quality: is it WC3 compliant? etc.
6. Text Relevance: does the keyword match with ad title? Ad body? What is the fraction of match?

The learnt logistic regression models yields 29% improvement of mean squared error (MSE) over the baseline model (of always predicting the average click through rate of the training dataset). Though the paper focused on predicting the click-though rate for new ads, a similar model could be used for ads displayed repeatedly. Alternatively, data permitting, a P(Click) could be estimated empirically via maximum likelihood or using a hybrid of both approaches.

An alternative approach to predicting P(Click) for new (AD, TERM) pairs is based upon hierarchical clustering using keyword-advertiser matrix where the matrix entries correspond to the empirical CTR for ad (AD, TERM) pair (Regelson and Fain 2006). This can be seen as a type of collaborative filtering. Their approach to estimating the CTR for low-volume or novel terms builds on the hypothesis that the more closely terms are related, the closer their CTRs. Following clustering, each node in the hierarchy is characterized by the average CTR for that node. Subsequently, predictions for the CTR of (AD, TERM) were based upon a variety of strategies: backoff strategies (analogous to the back-off method used for smoothing n-gram probabilities in language models (Katz 1987)) that backed-off or smoothed the CTR estimates across parent, and grand parent nodes in the derived hierarchy; based on historical data (where available) such as average CTR of the entire (AD, TERM) dataset and the CTR of the (AD, TERM) in a previous time period. Regelson and Fain (2006) show that the clustering-derived back-off model yields the most accurate predictions (of the examined models). Despite this, this approach is susceptible to huge variances for a keyword (e.g., the CTR for the keyword "surgery" has a huge variance across all the ads with which it is associated; the max CTR for (AD, surgery) is 5 times the average (Regelson and Fain 2006)), which can be compounded even more when borrowing strength (smoothed) from clusters of keywords.

Ciaramita et al. (2008) explore a number of machine learning approaches for ranking ads (as opposed to predicting CTR) where ranking models were generated and evaluated using click logs. They use click behavioral data from a large scale commercial web search engine (Yahoo!). They formulate the problem of ranking a set of ads given a query as a learning task and investigate three learning methods of increasing complexity based on the perceptron algorithm: a binary linear classifier, a linear ranking model and a multilayer perceptron, or artificial neural net. To generate labeled data from the click logs, they adapt Joachims' blocking strategy (2002). This implicit labeling approach makes a conservative assumption that a click can only serve as an indication that an ad is more relevant than the ads ranked higher but not clicked, but not as an absolute indication of the ad relevance. As such the clicks on the top ranked ad do not carry any information, because the top ranked ad cannot be ranked any higher. Clicks at rank one are dropped from training and evaluation. For each clicked ad, they create a block which consists of the clicked ad and the non-clicked ads that ranked higher (lower in the SERP), yielding a total of 123,798 blocks in their study. In each block, they assign a score of $+1$ to the clicked ad and -1 to the ads that were ranked higher but were not clicked. Their results show that it is possible to learn and evaluate directly on click data encoding pair-wise preferences following simple and conservative assumptions. They considered the following feature families: word overlap between the query and ad creative; cosine similarity of the query and various aspects of the ad (such as ad title, ad description, and bid terms); and correlation features such as pointwise mutual information between terms of the query q and the bidded terms of an ad measured over queries in the Yahoo search query logs. They report that metrics, such as precision at 1 and mean reciprocal rank, increase with the complexity of the model with the online multilayer perceptron learning performing the best for the reported experiments.

Bias Correction   Though machine learning approaches like those reported in Richardson et al. (2007) provide very encouraging results, they suffer from a number of biases such as training data composition and highly correlated features. For example, in the case of Naïve Bayes where features are assumed to be conditional independent, the presence of correlated features will lead to over prediction. In other cases, datasets may be down-sampled to improve discrimination in the learnt model. Consequently, the probabilities predicted by supervised learning algorithms can be under or over estimated. Previous research (Niculescu-mizil and Caruana 2005; Zadrozny and Elkan 2001) generates de-biased (corrected) probability estimates from supervised learning algorithms (such as support vector machines, Naïve Bayes, etc. using a variety of approaches such as (Platt 1999) scaling (a sigmoidal-based maximum likelihood approach), isotonic regression (Härdle et al. 1989), and smoothing probabilistic estimates within decision tree leaf nodes. Calibration significantly improves the performance of most of these learning algorithms on a variety of learning problems.

Keyword Suggestion   When an advertiser creates an ad campaign one of the most important steps is setting up the keyword targeting constraints. i.e., on which queries should the ad been shown to the searcher. Many automatic approaches to keyword suggestion that have been developed and deployed have generally borrowed and extended ideas from IR and NLP. Various starting points can be adapted:

• Start with some seed keywords and suggest;
• Start with landing page (and URL) and suggest;
• Start with the ad creative, landing page and keywords and suggest.

Starting with seed keywords, Wu et al. (2009) compared a pseudo-relevance feedback system with an active learning approach. As a starting point for each keyword phrase they generated a corresponding characteristic or SERP-400 document. This document contained retrieved snippets from the top 400 search-hits; stop-words were removed and words were stemmed. The top 400 terms, weighted by TFIDF, in each seed's characteristic document are selected as candidate suggestion terms (inverse document frequency, IDF, is based upon a corpus of characteristic documents).

Three approaches were primarily compared by Wu et al. (2009):

- A baseline based on the TFIDF ranking of suggested keyword unigrams;
- An approach based on pseudo-relevance feedback where the top five candidate terms (based upon TFIDF) and the bottom five terms are used to expand the original query using an approach such as (Rocchio 1971) for query expansion; an active learning approach.

The active learning approach used the following feature set for each (*SEEDPHRASE, CANDIDATEUNIGRAM*) pair as predictor variables:

1. Candidate-TF and Candidate-TFIDF corresponding to the TF and TFIDF of the candidate unigram in the seed phrase's SERP-400 document and the overall SERP-400 corpus respectively;
2. Seed-TF: the frequency of the seed in the search snippets document of the candidate unigram (SERP-400 of the candidate unigram);
3. SERP similarity: the similarity of the seed-phrase's SERP and the candidate's SERP;
4. URL overlap: the number of common URLs between the seed-phrase's SERP and the candidate's SERP.

The learning algorithm used by Yu et al. (2006) is based upon Transductive Experimental Design (TED), which tends to select candidates (for labeling and training) that are hard-to-predict and representative for unlabeled candidates with a core learning algorithm based upon regularized linear regression with Gaussian kernels. Overall, the active learning approach outperforms all reported approaches on an evaluation set of 100 seed phrases (based on average precision); these seed keyword phrase were based on popular category names. Though Wu et al. focus on unigram suggestion their approach could be extended to consider multiword phrases (using, for example, a language model approach discussed next).

Ravi et al. (2010) tackle the problem of keyword suggestion starting from a landing page perspective. They explore a number of approaches: a cosine similarity-based model; support vector machines; and hybrid approach based on a language model combined with a translation model. Reviewing the latter approach only, to find good quality phrases, Ravi et al. used a bigram language model (i.e., using bigrams with back-off to unigrams) that was constructed from 76M queries taken from a web search engine query log. Scoring bid-phrases was accomplished using a translation model over a (*BIDPHRASE, LANDINGPAGE*) parallel corpus based on the IBM Model 1 translation model. A sample of 10,000 pages was used for testing purposes. In this study for evaluation purposes, ROUGE, a commonly used translation and summarization metric (based upon measuring the unordered overlap between terms in the suggested bid phrase and terms in all gold bid phrases), and a normalized edit distance were used. Overall, the combination of bigram language model and translation outperformed all other systems. Other approaches to keyword suggestion not covered in here include query expansion to provide enhanced ad matching; Broder et al. (2007b) report such a study using a taxonomy of 6,000 categories to enhance ad selection with compelling results. This will be indirectly covered later in the behavioral targeting section (Sect. 9.4.3).

Metrics   Evaluation is an important part of online advertising. While traditional IR measures such as precision, recall, mean reciprocal rank, fbeta etc. (Croft et al. 2009) and standard machine learning measures (such as mean squared error, MSE (Rabiner 1989b)) can be used, studies have highlighted weaknesses in these measures for ranking tasks. This has lead to the development of highly customized metrics and evaluation methods such as expected reciprocal rank (ERR) (Chapelle et al. 2009); and the replay-match method (Li et al. 2010). Lots more domain dependant metrics are called for to provide better model discriminating power while also minimizing experimental costs during live AB-testing similar in spirit of those approaches proposed by Carterette et al. (2010b) for IR metrics.

Borrowing from Direct Marketing   Online advertising targeting problems have many similarities with direct marketing systems and can borrow a lot from almost 70 years of experiences and ideas. Examples of such studies include (Hill et al. 2006) and (Larose 2004).

Forecasting   Forecasting is a key component of online advertising. This component can be used by an advertiser to predict how many impressions and potential clicks an ad (ad creative, keywords, bids, and budget) will generate. This forecasting feedback can then be used to refine a campaign's constraints. Wang et al. present a very innovative way to do ad impression forecasting using an IR framework for contextual advertising (Wang et al. 2009).

9.4 Contextual and Display Advertising

Embedding text ads within publisher's online media such as a web pages, portals and online/mobile/offline applications is commonly referred to as *contextual advertising*. This is also known as *content match*. Here the page where the ad is embedded is also known as the target page. Targeting of ads is largely based on the content of the target page, geographical constraints and demographic constraints. In terms of systems architecture, contextual advertising and sponsored search overlap to a large degree. Contextual advertising is generally provided to advertisers via ad networks whose key function is the aggregation of ad space *supply* from publishers and matching it with advertiser *demand*.

9.4.1 Research Challenges and Opportunities in Contextual Advertising

Contextual advertising presents many of the same challenges as that of sponsored search. For example, it parallels sponsored search with regard to estimating quality and ranking. However, contextual advertising is a lot more challenging as the user information needs and interests are not as crisply defined. For example, the intent, think commercial intent, of the user reading a target page is less clear than when a user types an information need into a search engine. A user may be less open to ads, whereas in sponsored search a searcher is in an information gathering mode and ads may well satisfy the information need (and not be ignored). As a result users are more prone to click on sponsored search ads. On average, CTRs for contextual ads is ten times less than that of sponsored search ads. With an order of magnitude lesser training data, campaigns suffer from bootstrap issues. In short, targeting ads in contextual advertising is much more challenging and goes beyond the traditional IR notion of topical relevance and geographical relevance; these are much more aligned with demand and preference studies (Menzel 1966).

In an attempt to characterize these user preferences and intent, a number of studies have focused on characterizing human propensity to buy online, examining the effects of factors such as gender, age, and trust of online vendors (see Levin et al. 2005; Zhou et al. 2007 for more details). In addition, various studies have examined the language and format of advertising (explicit call to action via words such as buy now and subliminal messages). This notion of user relevance and interest closely aligns with an online marketer's perspective, where the goal is identify a well-defined target market or target audience. This is one of the first and key elements to a marketing strategy. Target markets are groups of people separated by distinguishable and noticeable aspects. Target markets can be separated into:

1. Geographic segmentations (user's location);
2. Demographic/socio-economic segmentation (gender, age, income occupation, education, sexual orientation, household size, and stage in the family life cycle);
3. Psychographic segmentation (similar attitudes, values, and lifestyles);
4. Behavioral segmentation (occasions, degree of loyalty);
5. Product-related segmentation (relationship to a product).

Several studies have tackled this notion of audience creation from an information need and interest perspective within contextual advertising. For example, Ribeiro-Neto et al. (2005) reported a pure IR approach based on topical relevance to ad ranking (targeting) in the context of a Brazilian online newspaper. Ads and landing pages were indexed using word tokens (unigrams) that occur in the text-based ad creative and corresponding landing page. Here the target page can be viewed as a query, albeit a potentially long query, that characterizes an information need for ads that are topically related to its content. In this spirit, Ribeiro-Neto et al. (2005) explore traditional IR techniques based on a TFIDF cosine similarity while also addressing the vocabulary mismatch between the language used in the target page and in the ad (i.e., the words in the ad creative, the associated keyword portfolio, and the corresponding landing page) using approaches such as query (i.e., target page) expansion. The reported study (though limited to one hundred queries) showed that query expansion combined with indexing of the ad keywords and terms extracted from the landing page outperformed other IR approaches.

Targeting is a two-way street, where the advertiser specifies constraints that characterize target online media or online audience and where the publisher provides characterizations of the media and audience available through the publisher media resources. One of the key challenges here is to abstract the target page to a level that connects with advertiser keyword and category constraints. Approaches to this can be organized as follows:

- Keyword extraction;
- Target page classification;
- Translation of target pages.

Targeting ads using keywords dominates sponsored search advertising and with no modification (on the advertiser's side) these ads can also be targeted at webpage level once the page is represented as a collection of keywords. Yih (2006) refer to this problem as harvesting keywords from web pages. They train a logistic regression model system using a set of positive and negative examples of the form (*KEYWORDN—GRAM, TARGETPAGE, LABEL*), where keyword n-grams of up to length five were considered in the context of a target page to determine if a work or multiword phrase represents the topical focus of the page. Candidate keyword examples (positive and negative) were manually extracted from a sample of webpages. Two types of models were trained: one where a keyword n-gram is classified as a positive or negative phrase; and a more fine-grained model where each token was classified as B (beginning of a keyphrase, when the following word is also part of the keyphrase), I (inside a keyphrase, but not the first or last word), L (last word of a keyphrase), U (unique word of a keyword of length 1), and finally O (outside any keyword or keyphrase). The latter classifier requires a post processing step commonly known as the phrase-level inference step in information extraction (IE), where probabilities are assigned at the sequence level. This is commonly accomplished using Viterbi-like algorithms to find the most probable word label sequence assignment for each sentence (Rabiner 1989b). This work is closely related to (Grefenstette and Shanahan 2005) where keyword extraction was accomplished using a combination of part of speech tagging, phrase chunking and lexicon-based approaches and (Goodman and Carvalho 2005) where a machine learning-based approach was used for keyword extraction in emails (Goodman and Carvalho 2005). On the advertising front, suggesting keywords for advertisers to associate (and bid) with their ads is also a fundamental component of the contextual targeting system. This can be viewed as a keyword suggestion tool whereby keywords phrases related to already selected keywords (and bids) and to the keywords extracted from the ad creative and landing page can be used as a basis to find and suggest other keywords. Carrasco et al. (2003) tackle this problem by the clustering of a keyword-advertiser bi-partite graph (where each cell value in this connectivity matrix, corresponding to an edge in this graph, represents the keyword bid by an advertiser). They validated the generated clusters by measuring intra cluster similarity based upon semantic similarity (cosine similarity); this was accomplished using words associated with each bid phrase by human editors. High similarity measures were achieved using a top-down clustering approach.

Broder et al. (2007c) explore how to characterize a target page based upon a taxonomy of 6,000 topics in addition to the usual keyword characterization. Each node in this taxonomy is associated with a list of queries. In their study both target page and ad are assigned to topics using a nearest neighbor approach where the similarity measure is based on a TFIDF scoring between all query terms at a topic node and keywords associated with the target page or ad. They show that combining this topic-based (they refer to this as semantic) similarity and a cosine similarity measure between the keywords extracted from the target page and the ad leads to a 25% improvement for mid-range recalls of the combined model over the pure cosine (syntactic) model. The topic similarity score is a weighted product between every combination of page class and ad class category where the weight is the inverse distance of the pair of nodes in the taxonomy.

Predicting a quality score for an ad in the context of a target page presents similar challenges to scoring an ad for a SERP. Abstractly, similar approaches can be taken, however, there are differences that arise since the target page for contextual advertising is a web page (as opposed to a search engine results page consisting of 10 blue links and corresponding snippets) and the content of this page may not always be available for targeting at ad call time; since the ad selection engine has only a couple hundred of milliseconds available to select an ad thus preventing fetching and doing a text analysis of the target page content (for keyword extraction purposes). That being said, a number of studies have focused on using machine learning approaches to ranking ads for contextual advertising. For example, Lacerda et al. (2006) proposed to use a genetic programming algorithm to select a ranking function which maximizes the average precision on the training data. They show that the ranking functions selected in this way are 61% more accurate than the baseline proposed (a cosine TFIDF based ranker) in (Ribeiro-Neto et al. 2005). Murdock et al. (2007) explore a different ranking algorithm using support vector machines (SVM) with some novel input features that focus on the vocabulary mismatch between target pages and ads. Specifically, they use a ranking SVM approach which optimizes a function directly related to Kendall Tau (as opposed to margin-based objective functions that most traditional SVM learning algorithms follow). Kendall Tau directly uses the level of disagreement between an ideal query ranking (provided in this study by human editors) and a ranking induced by the ranking SVM (Joachims 2002) and serves as a lower bound on the average precision. In this study three categories of features are explored: traditional features based on cosine similarity and term overlap between the ad and the target page; features based on statistical machine translation; and features based on machine translation evaluation. Overall, this study showed that using both sets of translation-based features produce statistically significant improvements in precision at rank one compared to their baseline, a summed cosine similarity between the target page and each of the ad fields (title, keyword, summary, and landing page). Ciaramita et al. (2008) extend this work by looking at other novel features that capture semantic associations between the vocabularies of the ad and the web page. The examined features look at distributional co-occurrence patterns between lexical items in the ad and target page.

Serving ads for target pages in an advertising network has similar round trip requirements as in sponsored search. When a target page requests ads for the first time limited processing of the target page can be carried out due to latency and bandwidth constraints. Anagnostopoulos et al. (2007b) compare a number of alternative lightweight processing strategies of the target page such as page summarization that can be executed on the client-side. The resultant approaches yield targeting performances comparable with full-page processing.

9.4.2 Display Advertising

While contextual advertising is sometimes included within the larger realm of display advertising, the term is often reserved for graphical (as opposed to text ads). It includes all forms of advertising excluding text-based ads (i.e., excludes sponsored search, contextual and classifieds) and plays on a range of different online media. This type of advertisement ranges from traditional banner ads in a variety of size and shapes, to video ads, and can be positioned within a webpage or app or can be incorporated into pop-ups. In 2009 it made up 35% of online revenue in the US (IAB 2009). While in the past this form of advertising was primarily attractive to brand advertisers (due to the rich communication bandwidth afforded by images and video), today's display ads are often used for direct response as well. Recently, advertisers have begun to measure both brand and direct marketing effects of their display campaigns—this is called brand response. In a study conducted by the Atlas Institute (Anagnostopoulos et al. 2007a), users exposed to both search and display convert at an even higher rate—22 percent better than search alone and 400 percent better than display only.

One of the major differentiators of display advertising from a ranking and ad selection perspective is that images and video lack the kind of machine friendly features that text provides. Humans interpret and understand images and videos in ways that are not expressible by TFIDF type measures. To complicate things, display ads have one or two orders of magnitude smaller CTRs than search. Since many display ads are not easily clickable, advertisers also measure view-through conversions which are extremely rare events; with action rates typically in the range of $10e{-}5$, it makes learning and statistical aggregation extremely difficult. Ad selection and optimization in display advertising therefore revolves around making accurate predictions with efficient explore/exploit strategies. Due to the paucity of traditional machine learning features, collaborative filtering is an interesting alternative which is being explored (Agarwal and Chen 2010). A recent trend in display advertising is to target audiences rather than contexts. Users are segmented by data-driven modeling techniques into audiences that may be interested in the advertiser's products and therefore more likely to respond to the message. Display advertising is a large and growing field—however the scope of this chapter is simply to give an overview of the display landscape rather than an in-depth treatment.

9.4.3 Research Challenges and Opportunities in Display Advertising

Behavioral Targeting and Retargeting   One of the key technologies behind display advertising is behavioral targeting (BT) which is targeting of ads based on a user's browsing behavior. This is commonly used by e-commerce websites and has been more recently adapted en masse by companies providing sponsored search (Shanahan and den Poel 2010b) (e.g., expand user query by terms in previous queries), contextual advertising, and display advertising networks. In search, behavioral targeting can be accomplished using query expansion schemes such as (Rocchio 1971) to expand the original context with terms from recently browsed pages (or transactions) and then weighting these terms with contributions from the base context combined with weight from positive examples (e.g., clicked pages in user browse history), and weight from negative examples (skipped pages in browse history). See (Yan et al. 2009c) for a good example of a post-hoc study of IR approaches applied to BT and (Chen et al. 2009) who built a linear Poisson regression model from fine-grained user behavioral data to predict CTR from user history. Online learning techniques can also be use to model another aspect of BT by generating "Look-alike" models from users who exhibit positive behavior (e.g., purchase an advertiser's product) and from users who don't purchase. Exploration techniques can be used to generate interesting candidate users that could provide feedback to accelerate Look-alike learning. An alternative way to accomplish behavioral targeting is to perform offline categorization of a user based on one's browsing behavior and then constrain the ads results set based upon this categorization. This could be modeled using simple bag-of-word techniques or machine learning. Retargeting is a very high ROI model of advertising where users that have previously visited the advertiser's website but have not purchased, or may be likely to purchase again are targeted by the advertiser.

Economic Models of Online Advertising   One of core concepts in online advertising is the digital marketplace where publishers present their ad slots for sale to advertisers who wish to purchase these slots for the purpose of showing ads. In online advertising this price is established via a sealed auction. The goal is to create an auction that encourages bidders to bid their true value (known as an incentive compatible auction). Such an auction mechanism helps advertisers avoid buyer's remorse and enables publishers to get paid a fair market value. One such auction mechanism is the second price auction where in the case of a single item auction the winning advertiser (corresponding to the advertiser with the highest bid) pays the bid associated with the second ranking advertiser. Second price auctions were introduced by Nobel Laureate William Vickrey, who was one of the first people to use game theory to develop and study auction mechanisms. When multiple items are being auctioned in the same auction, the more general form of the second price auction can be used. This is commonly known as a generalized second price auction. Generalized second price auctions are commonly used in the online advertising world and have been demonstrated as an effective means of allocating ads to publishers slots at companies such as Google, Yahoo! and Turn (Edelman et al. 2005). Generalized second price auctions are not incentive compatible and as a result a new type of auction was developed that addresses this weakness. This is known as the Vickrey, Clarke, Groves (VCG) auction. Despite their lack of truth-telling, GSP auctions are the de facto standard for online auctions. This is primarily due to the ease of understanding of the auction mechanism (for both ranking and pricing) versus VCG. Both auction mechanism design (sometimes known as inverse game theory) and bidder design (analyzing effective bidding strategies) are very active areas of research within economics and online advertising with many conferences and journals devoted to the subject.

9.5 New Trends and Issues

This section is a highly condensed overview of new trends in online. Mobile advertising (advertising on cell-phones, be it SMS-based, application-based or browser-based) is one of the fastest growing segments in digital advertising and comes with its own challenges of performance and relevance measurements (e.g., clicks are uncommon in mobile). IP-based TV is a very new area that will transform a once broadcast advertising medium into a more personalized marketing experience. Real time bidded ad exchanges are fast-growing marketplaces where publishers bring their inventory to sell to advertisers who wish to advertise on that inventory. Individual ad impressions are auctioned off in real-time by publishers to buyers on the exchange. To take advantage of such real-time exchanges, demand side platforms (DSP), a new type of trading desk, empowers the advertiser or ad agency to make complex data driven decisions to evaluate, optimize, and purchase media and audiences across different media sources and exchanges via intuitive user interfaces. Challenges here include performing real-time bid optimization at an unprecedented scale of bid requests, each of which much be evaluated (in 2010 requests for bid is estimated to peak at 200,000 QPS across all exchanges for the US alone—compared to 34,000 QPS for search). Data exchanges are a relatively new entity in online advertising where third party suppliers and users of consumer intent and behavioral data congregate to sell and buy this data (in order to enhance targeting). The challenges here include mining user intent from hugely rare events sequences. Dynamic creatives refer to creatives constructed on the fly, typically based on the audience or context. Imagine an ad that shows a different image for a female user versus a male user—where the data about the gender of the user is either bought from a third party on a data exchange or algorithmically inferred based on the user's browsing patterns. Another major current topic of research and development concerns multiple touch points in the advertising chain (search, multiple display vendors, etc.) and how an advertiser can attribute conversions to individual ad impressions and thus to individual intermediaries in the advertising chain (this is also known as credit assignment). Social advertising leverages historically "offline" dynamics such as peer-pressure, recommendations, and other forms of social influence to target ads based an individual's social network or affinity network. This type of advertising, being very new, presents many algorithmic and computational challenges and opportunities to leverage recent work in social network analysis such as information diffusion.

Privacy and fraud (an estimated $2 billion problem in the US alone), though not discussed here, will continue to be important areas with big needs for technology solutions.

9.6 Conclusions

From an information science perspective the field of online advertising is very active in terms of research and development. This is fueled by an annual revenue stream of \$65 billion that continues to grow at a rate of 10% or more. In addition, as more of the traditional broadcast media sources (such as TV) move online, and the use of smart phones and handheld computers become more pervasive, the need for better ways to optimize the consumers advertising experience through personalization will become even greater. As was highlighted in this chapter information science will continue to be one of the cornerstones in making this happen.

References

Accardi L (1997) Urne e camaleonti. Il Saggiatore, in Italian

Accardi L, Fedullo A (1982) On the statistical meaning of complex numbers in quantum mechanics. Lettere al Nuovo Cimento 34:161–172

AdEx (2010) The definitive guide to the size and scale of European online advertising, 2009 report. http://www.iabeurope.eu, visited on December, 2010

Aerts D, Gabora L (2005) A theory of concepts and their combinations II: A Hilbert space representation. Kybernetes 34:176–205

Agarwal D, Chen B (2010) FLDA: Matrix factorization through latent Dirichlet allocation. In: Proceedings of the ACM Conference on Web Search and Data Mining. ACM Press, New York, NY, pp 91–100

Agarwal D, Chen B, Elango P (2009) Explore/exploit schemes for web content optimization. In: Proceedings of the International Conference on Data Mining, pp 1–10

Aggarwal C, Yu P (2000) The IGrid index: Reversing the dimensionality curse for similarity indexing in high dimensional space. In: Proceedings of the ACM Conference on Knowledge Discovery and Data Mining, pp 119–129

Agichtein E, Zheng Z (2006) Identifying "best bet" web search results by mining past user behavior. In: Proceedings of the ACM Conference on Knowledge Discovery and Data Mining, pp 902–908

Agosti M (1980) L'esperienza pilota dell'Istituto di Statistica dell'Università di Padova nel progetto BAC. In: Alcuni Problemi e Prospettive di Organizzazione e Diffusione Dell'informazione Bibliografica. CLEUP, Padova, Italy, pp 89–104

Agosti M (1996) An overview of hypertext. In: Information Retrieval and Hypertext. Springer, Berlin, pp 27–47

Agosti M (ed) (2008) Information Access Through Search Engines and Digital Libraries. Springer, Berlin

Agosti M, Ferro N (2003) Annotations: Enriching a digital library. In: Proceedings of the European Conference on Digital Libraries, pp 88–100

Agosti M, Ferro N (2005a) Annotations as context for searching documents. In: Proceedings of the Conference on Conceptions of Library and Information Science, pp 155–170

Agosti M, Ferro N (2005b) A system architecture as a support to a flexible annotation service. In: Proceedings of the DELOS Conference on Digital Libraries, pp 147–166

Agosti M, Ferro N (2006) Search strategies for finding annotations and annotated documents: The FAST service. In: Proceedings of the Conference on Flexible Query Answering Systems, pp 270–281

Agosti M, Ferro N (2008a) Adding advanced annotation functionalities to an existing digital library. In: Interdisciplinary Aspects of Information Systems Studies. Springer, Berlin, pp 279–286

Agosti M, Ferro N (2008b) A formal model of annotations of digital content. ACM Transactions on Information Systems 26(1):3–57

Agosti M, Ferro N (2009) Towards an evaluation infrastructure for DL performance evaluation. In: Tsakonas G, Papatheodorou C (eds) Evaluation of Digital Libraries: An Insight to Useful Applications and Methods. Chandos Publishing, Oxford, pp 93–120

Agosti M, Masotti M (1992a) Design and functions of DUO: The first Italian academic OPAC. In: Proceedings of the ACM Symposium on Applied Computing, pp 308–313

Agosti M, Masotti M (1992b) Design of an OPAC database to permit different subject searching accesses in a multi-disciplines universities library catalogue database. In: Proceedings of the ACM Conference on Research and Development in Information Retrieval. ACM Press, New York, NY, pp 245–255

Agosti M, Melucci M (2001) Information retrieval on the Web. In: Agosti M, Crestani F, Pasi G (eds) Lectures on Information Retrieval: Third European Summer-School. ESSIR 2000 (Revised Lectures). Springer, Berlin/Heidelberg, pp 242–285

Agosti M, Ronchi M (1979) Progetto BAC: La Biblioteca Automatica del CINECA. In: Atti del Congresso dell'Associazione Italiana per il Calcolo Automatico, Bari, Italy, pp 367–370

Agosti M, Caovilla E, Crescenti M, Lissandrini L, Rigoni A (1975) LINGEB—linguaggio gestione biblioteche. L'elaborazione Automatica 2(2):1–107

Agosti M, Bombi F, Melucci M, Mian G (1998) Towards a digital library for the venetian music of the eighteenth century (abstract). In: Proceedings of the International Conference on Digital Resources in the Humanities, the Humanities Advanced Technology and Information Institute, Glasgow, Scotland, pp 75–77

Agosti M, Ferro N, Frommholz I, Thiel U (2004) Annotations in digital libraries and collaboratories—facets, models and usage. In: Proceedings of the European Conference on Digital Libraries, pp 244–255

Agosti M, Berretti S, Brettlecker G, del Bimbo A, Ferro N, Fuhr N, Keim D, Klas CP, Lidy T, Milano D, Norrie M, Ranaldi P, Rauber A, Schek HJ, Schreck T, Schuldt H, Signer B, Springmann M (2007) DelosDLMS—the integrated DELOS digital library management system. In: Thanos C, Borri F, Candela L (eds) Proceedings of the DELOS Conference on Digital Libraries. Lecture Notes in Computer Science, vol 4877. Springer, Heidelberg, pp 36–45

Agosti M, Crivellari F, Di Nunzio G, Ioannidis Y, Stamatogiannakis E, Triantafyllidi M, Vayanou M (2009) Searching and browsing digital library catalogues: A combined log analysis for the European library. In: Proceedings of the Italian Research Conference on Digital Libraries, pp 120–135

Agrawal R, Gollapudi S, Halverson A, Ieong S (2009) Diversifying search results. In: Proceedings of the ACM Conference on Web Search and Data Mining. ACM Press, New York, NY, pp 5–14

Allan J (2005) High accuracy retrieval from documents (HARD) track overview. http://trec. nist.gov/, visited on February, 2011

Alonso O, Rose D, Stewart B (2008) Crowdsourcing for relevance evaluation. SIGIR Forum 42(2):9–15

Altingovde I, Ozcan R, Ulusoy O (2009) A cost-aware strategy for query result caching in web search engines. In: Boughanem M, Berrut C, Mothe J, Soule-Dupuy C (eds) Proceedings of the European Conference on Information Retrieval. Lecture Notes in Computer Science, vol 5478. Springer, Berlin/Heidelberg, pp 628–636

Anagnostopoulos A, Broder A, Gabrilovich E, Josifovski V, Riedel L (2007a) The combined impact of search and online display advertising—why advertisers should measure across channels. http://www.atlassolutions.com/uploadedFiles/Atlas/Atlas_Institute/Published_Content/ crosschanneldmi.pdf, visited on December, 2010

Anagnostopoulos A, Broder A, Gabrilovich E, Josifovski V, Riedel L (2007b) Just-in-time contextual advertising. In: Proceedings of the ACM Conference on Information and Knowledge Management. ACM Press, New York, NY, pp 331–340

Anh V, Moffat A (2004) Index compression using fixed binary codewords. In: Proceedings of the Australasian Database Conference. Australian Computer Society and Inc, Darlinghurst, pp 61–67

Anh V, Moffat A (2006a) Improved word-aligned binary compression for text indexing. IEEE Transactions on Knowledge and Data Engineering 18(6):857–861

Anh V, Moffat A (2006b) Pruned query evaluation using pre-computed impacts. In: Proceedings of the ACM Conference on Research and Development in Information Retrieval. ACM Press, New York, NY, pp 372–379

Anh V, de Kretser O, Moffat A (2001) Vector-space ranking with effective early termination. In: Proceedings of the ACM Conference on Research and Development in Information Retrieval. ACM Press, New York, NY, pp 35–42

Anick P (2003) Using terminological feedback for web search refinement: A log based study. In: Proceedings of the ACM Conference on Research and Development in Information Retrieval. ACM Press, New York, NY, pp 88–95

Ankerst M, Keim D, Kriegel H (1996) Circle segments: A technique for visually exploring large multidimensional data sets. http://nbn-resolving.de/urn:nbn:de:bsz:352-opus-70761, visited on February, 2011

Arasu A, Cho J, Garcia-Molina H, Paepcke A, Raghavan S (2001) Searching the Web. ACM Transactions on Internet Technology 1(1):2–43

Arguello J, Diaz F, Callan J, Crespo J (2009) Sources of evidence for vertical selection. In: Proceedings of the ACM Conference on Research and Development in Information Retrieval, pp 315–322

Arguello J, Diaz F, Paiement JF (2010) Vertical selection in presence of unlabeled verticals. In: Proceedings of the ACM Conference on Research and Development in Information Retrieval, pp 691–698

Aslam J, Montague M (2001) Models for metasearch. In: Proceedings of the ACM Conference on Research and Development in Information Retrieval. ACM Press, New York, NY, pp 276–284

Attenberg J, Suel T (2008) Cleaning search results using term distance features. In: Proceedings of the International Workshop on Adversarial Information Retrieval on the Web. AIRWeb '08. ACM Press, New York, NY, pp 21–24. http://doi.acm.org/10.1145/1451983.1451989, visited on December, 2010

Au P, Carey M, Sewraz S, Guo Y, Rüger S (2000) New paradigms in information visualisation. In: Proceedings of the ACM Conference on Research and Development in Information Retrieval. ACM Press, New York, NY, pp 307–309

Auer P, Cesa-Bianchi N, Fischer P (1985) Finite-time analysis of the multiarmed bandit problem. Machine Learning 47:235–256

Aula A, Rodden K (2009) Eye-tracking studies: more than meets the eye. http://googleblog. blogspot.com/2009/02/eye-tracking-studies-more-than-meets.html, visited on December, 2010

Backstrom L, Dwork C, Kleinberg JM (2007) Wherefore art thou r3579x?: Anonymized social networks and hidden patterns and structural steganography. In: Williamson CL, Zurko ME, Patel-Schneider PF, Shenoy PJ (eds) Proceedings of the International Conference on the World Wide Web. ACM Press, New York, NY, pp 181–190

Badue C, Baeza-Yates R, Ribeiro-Neto BA, Ziviani N (2001) Distributed query processing using partitioned inverted files. In: Proceedings of the International Symposium on String Processing and Information Retrieval, pp 10–20

Badue C, Baeza-Yates R, Ribeiro-Neto BA, Ziviani A, Ziviani N (2007) Analyzing imbalance among homogeneous index servers in a web search system. Information Processing and Management 43(3):592–608

Baeza-Yates R, Ribeiro-Neto B (1999) Modern Information Retrieval. ACM Press/Addison-Wesley, New York, NY

Baeza-Yates R, Ribeiro-Neto B (2010) Modern Information Retrieval, 2nd edn. Addison-Wesley, Reading, MA

Baeza-Yates R, Saint-Jean F (2003) A three level search engine index based in query log distribution. In: Nascimento M, de Moura E, Oliveira A (eds) Proceedings of the International Symposium on String Processing Information Retrieval. Lecture Notes in Computer Science, vol 2857. Springer, Berlin/Heidelberg, pp 56–65

Baeza-Yates R, Junqueira F, Plachouras V, Witschel H (2007a) Admission policies for caches of search engine results. In: Ziviani N, Baeza-Yates R (eds) Proceedings of the International Symposium on String Processing Information Retrieval. Lecture Notes in Computer Science, vol 4726. Springer, Berlin/Heidelberg, pp 74–85

Baeza-Yates R, Gionis A, Junqueira F, Murdock V, Plachouras V, Silvestri F (2007b) The impact of caching on search engines. In: Proceedings of the ACM Conference on Research and Development in Information Retrieval. ACM Press, New York, NY, pp 183–190

Baeza-Yates R, Castillo C, Junqueira F, Plachouras V, Silvestri F (2007c) Challenges in distributed information retrieval. In: Proceedings of the International Conference on Data Engineering. IEEE CS, New York, NY, pp 6–20

Baeza-Yates R, Gionis A, Junqueira F, Plachouras V, Telloli L (2009a) On the feasibility of multi-site web search engines. In: Proceedings of the ACM Conference on Information and Knowledge Management. ACM Press, New York, NY, pp 425–434

Baeza-Yates R, Murdock V, Hauff C (2009b) Efficiency trade-offs in two-tier web search systems. In: Proceedings of the ACM Conference on Research and Development in Information Retrieval. ACM Press, New York, NY, pp 163–170

Baillie M, Jose JM (2004) An audio-based sports video segmentation and event detection algorithm. In: Proceedings of the IEEE International Conference on Computer Vision and Pattern Recognition, pp 110–110

Bainbridge D, Browne P, Cairns P, Rüger S, Xu LQ (2005) Managing the growth of multimedia digital content. ERCIM News: special theme on Multimedia Informatics 16–17

Baldacci B, Sprugnoli R (1983) Informatica e Biblioteche: Automazione dei Sistemi Informativi Bibliotecari. NIS, Roma

Baldi P, Frasconi P, Smyth P (2003) Modeling the Internet and the Web: Probabilistic Methods and Algorithms. Wiley, Chichester

Banko M, Cafarella MJ, Soderland S, Broadhead M, Etzioni O (2007) Open information extraction from the Web. In: Veloso MM, Veloso MM (eds) Proceedings of the International Joint Conferences on Artificial Intelligence, pp 2670–2676

Barbaro M, Zeller T (2006) A face is exposed for AOL searcher No 4417749. http://www.nytimes.com/2006/08/09/technology/09aol.html, visited on December, 2010

Barroso L, Hölzle U (2009) The Datacenter as a Computer. Synthesis Lectures on Computer Architecture. Morgan & Claypool

Barroso L, Dean J, Hölzle U (2003) Web search for a planet: The Google cluster architecture. IEEE Micro 23(2):22–28

Barry CL (1994) User-defined relevance criteria: An exploratory study. Journal of the American Society for Information Science 45:149–159

Barry CL, Schamber L (1998) User's criteria for relevance evaluation: A cross situational comparison. Information Processing and Management 34(2/3):219–236

Bartell B, Cottrell G, Belew R (1994) Automatic combination of multiple ranked retrieval systems. In: Proceedings of the ACM Conference on Research and Development in Information Retrieval. ACM Press, New York, NY, pp 173–181

Barth A, Datta A, Mitchell JC, Nissenbaum H (2006) Privacy and contextual integrity: Framework and applications. In: Proceedings of the IEEE Symposium on Security and Privacy. IEEE Computer Society, Los Alamitos, pp 184–198

Baxter D, Shepard B, Siegel N, Gottesman B, Schneider D (2005) Interactive natural language explanations of Cyc inferences. http://www.cyc.com/doc/white_papers/ExACt2005.pdf, visited on February, 2011

Beaulieu M (1997) Experiments with interfaces to support query expansion. Journal of Documentation 53:8–19

Beaulieu M (2000) Interaction in information searching and retrieval. Journal of Documentation 431–439

Beaulieu M, Jones S (1998) Interactive searching and interface issues in the okapi best match probabilistic retrieval system. Interacting with Computers 10:237–248

Beis J, Lowe D (1997) Shape indexing using approximate nearest-neighbour search in high-dimensional spaces. In: Proceedings of the IEEE International Conference on Computer Vision and Pattern Recognition, pp 1000–1006

Belder J, Moens M (2010) Text simplification for children. In: Proceedings of the Workshop on Accessible Search Systems at the ACM Conference on Research and Development in Information Retrieval, pp 19–26

Belew R (2000) Finding out About: A Cognitive Perspective on Search Engine Technology and the WWW. Cambridge University Press, Cambridge

Belkin N, Vickery A (1985) Interaction in information systems. British Library, London

Belkin N, Oddy R, Brooks H (1982) Ask for information retrieval: Part 2. Journal of Documentation 38:145–164

Belkin N, Seeger T, Wersig G (1983) Distributed expert problem treatment as a model for information systems analysis and design. Journal of Information Science: Principles and Practice 5:153–167

Belkin N, Cool C, Croft W, Callan J (1993) The effect of multiple query representations on information retrieval performance. In: Proceedings of the ACM Conference on Research and Development in Information Retrieval. ACM Press, New York, NY, pp 339–346

Belkin N, Cool C, Koenemann J, Park S, Ng W (1996a) Information seeking behaviour in new searching environments. In: Ingwersen P, Pors N (eds) Proceedings of the Conference on Conceptions of Library and Information Science, pp 403–416

Belkin N, Cool C, Koenemann J, Ng W, Park S (1996b) Using relevance feedback and ranking in interactive searching. In: Harman D (ed) Proceedings of the Text Retrieval Conference, pp 181–210

Belkin N, Cool C, Kelly D, Lee HJ, Muresan G, Tang MC, Yuan XJ (2003) Query length in interactive information retrieval. In: Proceedings of the ACM Conference on Research and Development in Information Retrieval. ACM Press, New York, NY, pp 205–212

Bell D, Ruthven I (2004) Searchers' assessments of task complexity for Web. In: Proceedings of the European Conference on Information Retrieval. Lecture Notes in Computer Science, vol 2997, pp 57–71

Bellman R (2003) Dynamic Programming. Dover, New York, NY

Bellotti V, Ducheneaut N, Howard M, Smith I (2003) Taking email to task: The design and evaluation of a task management centered email tool. In: Proceedings of the ACM Conference on Human Factors in Computing Systems, pp 345–352

Berendt B (2007) Intelligent business intelligence and privacy: More knowledge through less data? In: Köppen, Müller R (eds) Business Intelligence: Methods and Applications. Verlag Dr. Kovač, Hamburg, pp 63–79

Berendt B (2008) You are a document too: Web mining and IR for next-generation information literacy. In: Macdonald C, Ounis I, Plachouras V, Ruthven I, White RW (eds) Proceedings of the European Conference on Information Retrieval. Lecture Notes in Computer Science, vol 4956. Springer, Berlin, p 3

Berendt B (2010) Text mining for news and blogs analysis. In: Sammut C, Webb G (eds) Encyclopedia of Machine Learning. Springer, Berlin, pp 968–972

Berendt B, Mobasher B, Nakagawa M, Spiliopoulou M (2002) The impact of site structure and user environment on session reconstruction in web usage analysis. In: Proceedings of the Workshop on Web Mining and Web Usage Analysis, pp 159–179

Berendt B, Krause B, Kolbe-Nusser S (2010) Intelligent scientific authoring tools: Interactive data mining for constructive uses of citation networks. Information Processing and Management 46(1):1–10

Berry M, Linoff G (2002) Mining the Web: Transforming customer data. Wiley, Hoboken, NJ

Berry M, Linoff G (2004) Data Mining Techniques. Wiley, Hoboken, NJ

Bharat K, Broder AZ (1999) Mirror, mirror on the Web: A study of host pairs with replicated content. In: Proceedings of the International Conference on the World Wide Web. Elsevier/North-Holland, New York, NY, pp 1579–1590

Bharat K, Broder A, Dean J, Henzinger M (2000) A comparison of techniques to find mirrored hosts on the WWW. Journal of the American Society for Information Science 51(12):1114–1122

Bilal D (2000) Children's use of the Yahooligans! web search engine: 1. Cognitive, physical, and affective behaviors on fact-based search tasks. Journal of the American Society for Information Science, pp 1170–1183

Bilal D (2002) Children's use of the Yahooligans! web search engine. III. Cognitive and physical behaviors on fully self-generated search tasks. Journal of the American Society for Information Science and Technology 53:1170–1183. http://portal.acm.org/citation.cfm?id=772458.772468, visited on December, 2010

Binding C, Brettlecker G, Catarci T, Christodoulakis S, Crecelius T, Gioldasis N, Jetter HC, Kacimi M, Milano D, Ranaldi P, Reiterer H, Santucci G, Schek HJ, Schuldt H, Tudhope D, Weikum G (2007) DelosDLMS: infrastructure and services for future digital library systems. http://hci.uni-konstanz.de/downloads/Paper_DelosDLMS_Infrastructure_and_Servcies.pdf, visited on February, 2011

Birkhoff G, von Neumann J (1936) The logics of quantum mechanics. The Annals of Mathematics 37:823–843

Birmingham W, Dannenberg R, Pardo B (2006) Query by humming with the VocalSearch system. Communications of the ACM 49:49–52

Bíró I, Szabó J, Benczúr AA (2008) Latent Dirichlet allocation in web spam filtering. In: Proceedings of the International Workshop on Adversarial Information Retrieval on the Web, pp 29–32

Bizer C, Heath T, Berners-Lee T (2009) Linked data—the story so far. International Journal of Semantic Web Information Systems 5(3):1–22

Blanco R, Barreiro A (2006) TSP and cluster-based solutions to the reassignment of document identifiers. Journal of Information Retrieval 9(4):499–517

Blanco R, Bortnikov E, Junqueira F, Lempel R, Telloli L, Zaragoza H (2010) Caching search engine results over incremental indices. In: Proceedings of the ACM Conference on Research and Development in Information Retrieval. ACM Press, New York, NY, pp 82–89

Blandford D, Blelloch G (2002) Index compression through document reordering. In: Proceedings of the Data Compression Conference. IEEE Computer Society, Washington, DC, pp 342–351

Blei DM, Jordan M (2003) Modeling annotated data. In: Proceedings of the ACM Conference on Research and Development in Information Retrieval. ACM Press, New York, NY, pp 127–134

Blei DM, Ng AY, Jordan MI (2003) Latent Dirichlet allocation. Journal of Machine Learning Research 3:993–1022

Boldi P, Codenotti B, Santini M, Vigna S (2004) UbiCrawler: a scalable fully distributed web crawler. Software: Practice and Experience 34(8):711–726

Boldi P, Bonchi F, Castillo C, Donato D, Gionis A, Vigna S (2008) The query-flow graph: Model and applications. In: Proceedings of the ACM Conference on Information and Knowledge Management. ACM Press, New York, NY, pp 609–618

Borlund P (2000) Experimental components for the evaluation of interactive information retrieval systems. Journal of Documentation 56:71–90

Borlund P (2003a) The IIR evaluation model: A framework for evaluation of interactive information retrieval systems. http://informationr.net/ir/8-3/paper152.html, visited on February, 2011

Borlund P (2003b) The concept of relevance in IR. Journal of the American Society for Information Science and Technology 54:913–925. http://portal.acm.org/citation.cfm?id=941240.941242, visited on December, 2010

Borlund P, Ingwersen P (1998) Measures of relative relevance and ranked half-life: performance indicators for interactive IR. In: Proceedings of the ACM Conference on Research and Development in Information Retrieval. ACM Press, New York, NY, pp 324–331. http://doi.acm.org/10.1145/290941.291019, visited on December, 2010

Börner K (2000) Visible threads: A smart VR interface to digital libraries. In: Proceedings of the International Symposium on Electronic Imaging: Visual Data Exploration and Analysis, pp 228–237

Bradley N, Dunlop M (2005) Toward a multidisciplinary model of context to support context-aware computing. Human-Computer Interaction 20:403–446

Brin S, Page L (1998) The anatomy of a large-scale hypertextual web search engine. Computer Networks and ISDN Systems 30(1–7):107–117

Broder A, Glassman S, Manasse M, Zweig G (1997) Syntactic clustering of the Web. Computer Networks and ISDN Systems 29:1157–1166

Broder A, Carmel D, Herscovici M, Soffer A, Zien J (2003a) Efficient query evaluation using a two-level retrieval process. In: Proceedings of the ACM Conference on Information and Knowledge Management. ACM Press, New York, NY, pp 426–434

Broder A, Najork M, Wiener J (2003b) Efficient URL caching for World Wide Web crawling. In: Proceedings of the International Conference on the World Wide Web. ACM Press, New York, NY, pp 679–689

Broder A, Fontoura M, Josifovski V, Riedel L (2007a) Internet advertising bureau. about the IAB. http://www.iab.net/about_the_iab, visited on December, 2010

Broder A, Fontoura M, Gabrilovich E, Joshi A, Josifovski V, Zhang T (2007b) Robust classification of rare queries using web knowledge. In: Proceedings of the ACM Conference on Research and Development in Information Retrieval. ACM Press, New York, NY, pp 231–238

Broder A, Fontoura M, Josifovski V, Riedel L (2007c) A semantic approach to contextual advertising. In: Proceedings of the ACM Conference on Research and Development in Information Retrieval. ACM Press, New York, NY, pp 559–566

Broder A, Ciaramita M, Fontoura M, Gabrilovich E, Josifovski V, Metzler D, Murdock V, Plachouras V (2008) To swing or not to swing: Learning when (not) to advertise. In: Proceedings of the ACM Conference on Information and Knowledge Management. ACM Press, New York, NY, pp 1003–1012

Brown E (1995) Fast evaluation of structured queries for information retrieval. In: Proceedings of the ACM Conference on Research and Development in Information Retrieval. ACM Press, New York, NY, pp 30–38

Brown P, Jones G (2002) Exploiting contextual change in context-aware retrieval. In: Proceedings of the ACM Symposium on Applied Computing. ACM Press, New York, NY, pp 650–656

Bruza P, Cole R (2005) Quantum logic of semantic space: An exploratory investigation of context effects in practical reasoning. In: We Will Show Them! Essays in Honour of Dov Gabbay, vol 1. College Publications, pp 339–362

Bruza P, Sofge D, Lawless W, van Rijsbergen C, Klusch M (eds) (2009) Proceedings of the Symposium on Quantum Interaction. Lecture Notes in Computer Science, vol 5494. Springer, Saarbrücken

Bruza P, Kitto K, Nelson D, McEvoy C (2010) Is there something quantum-like about the human mental lexicon? Journal of Mathematical Psychology 53:362–377

Buckland L, Voorhees E (eds) (2005) Proceedings of the Text Retrieval Conference. Government Printing Office, Washington, DC

Buckley C, Lewit A (1985) Optimization of inverted vector searches. In: Proceedings of the ACM Conference on Research and Development in Information Retrieval. ACM Press, New York, NY, pp 97–110

Buitelaar P, Cimiano P, Magnini B (2005) Ontology learning from text: An overview. In: Buitelaar P, Cimiano P, Magnini B (eds) Ontology Learning from Text: Methods, Evaluation and Applications/Frontiers in Artificial Intelligence and Applications, vol 7. IOS Press, pp 3–14

Burns E (2010) SEMs sees optimization PPC. http://www.clickz.com/showPage.html?page=3550881, visited on February, 2011

Busemeyer J (2009) Introduction to quantum probability for social and behavioral scientists. In: Bruza P, Sofge D, Lawless W, van Rijsbergen K, Klusch M (eds) Proceedings of the Symposium on Quantum Interaction. Lecture Notes in Computer Science, vol 5494. Springer, Berlin, pp 1–2

Büttcher S, Clarke C (2005) Indexing time vs query time: trade-offs in dynamic information retrieval systems. In: Proceedings of the ACM Conference on Information and Knowledge Management. ACM Press, New York, NY, pp 317–318

Büttcher S, Clarke C, Lushman B (2006a) Hybrid index maintenance for growing text collections. In: Proceedings of the ACM Conference on Research and Development in Information Retrieval. ACM Press, New York, NY, pp 356–363

Büttcher S, Clarke C, Lushman B (2006b) Term proximity scoring for ad-hoc retrieval on very large text collections. In: Proceedings of the ACM Conference on Research and Development in Information Retrieval. ACM Press, New York, NY, pp 621–622

Byström K, Järvelin K (1995) Task complexity affects information seeking and use. Information Processing and Management 31:191–213. http://portal.acm.org/citation.cfm?id=208327.208360, visited on December, 2010

Cacheda F, Carneiro V, Plachouras V, Ounis I (2007) Performance analysis of distributed information retrieval architectures using an improved network simulation model. Information Processing and Management 43(1):204–224

Cafarella MJ (2009) Extracting and querying a comprehensive Web database. http://www-db.cs.wisc.edu/cidr/cidr2009/Paper_106.pdf, visited on February, 2011

Cahoon B, McKinley K, Lu Z (2000) Evaluating the performance of distributed architectures for information retrieval using a variety of workloads. ACM Transactions on Information Systems 18(1):1–43

Callan J (2000) Distributed information retrieval. In: Advances in Information Retrieval, pp 127–150

Callan J (2009) The ClueWeb09 dataset. http://boston.lti.cs.cmu.edu/Data/clueweb09/, visited on December, 2010

Callan J, Connell M (2001) Query-based sampling of text databases. ACM Transactions on Information Systems 19(2):97–130

Callan J, Lu Z, Croft WB (1995a) Searching distributed collections with inference networks. In: Proceedings of the ACM Conference on Research and Development in Information Retrieval. ACM Press, New York, NY, pp 21–28

Callan J, Lu Z, Croft W (1995b) Searching distributed collections with inference networks. In: Proceedings of the ACM Conference on Research and Development in Information Retrieval. ACM Press, New York, NY, pp 21–28

Cambazoglu B, Aykanat C (2006) Performance of query processing implementations in ranking-based text retrieval systems using inverted indices. Information Processing and Management 42(4):875–898

Cambazoglu B, Turk A, Aykanat C (2004) Data-parallel web crawling models. In: Proceedings of the Symposium on Computer and Information Sciences. Lecture Notes in Computer Science. Springer, Berlin/Heidelberg, pp 801–809

Cambazoglu B, Plachouras V, Junqueira F, Telloli L (2008) On the feasibility of geographically distributed web crawling. In: Proceedings of the International Conference on Scalable Information Systems. ICST (Institute for Computer Sciences and Social-Informatics and Telecommunications Engineering), ICST, Brussels, pp 1–10

Cambazoglu B, Plachouras V, Baeza-Yates R (2009) Quantifying performance and quality gains in distributed web search engines. In: Proceedings of the ACM Conference on Research and Development in Information Retrieval. ACM Press, New York, NY, pp 411–418

Cambazoglu B, Zaragoza H, Chapelle O, Chen J, Liao C, Zheng Z, Degenhardt J (2010a) Early exit optimizations for additive machine learned ranking systems. In: Proceedings of the ACM Conference on Web Search and Data Mining. ACM Press, New York, NY, pp 411–420

Cambazoglu B, Varol E, Kayaaslan E, Aykanat C, Baeza-Yates R (2010b) Query forwarding in geographically distributed search engines. In: Proceedings of the ACM Conference on Research and Development in Information Retrieval. ACM Press, New York, NY, pp 90–97

Cambazoglu B, Junqueira F, Plachouras V, Banachowski S, Cui B, Lim S, Bridge B (2010c) A refreshing perspective of search engine caching. In: Proceedings of the International Conference on the World Wide Web. ACM Press, New York, NY, pp 181–190

Campbell I (2000) Interactive evaluation of the ostensive model using a new test collection of images with multiple relevance assessments. Journal of Information Retrieval 2:89–114. http://portal.acm.org/citation.cfm?id=593954.593979, visited on December, 2010

Candela L, Castelli D, Ioannidis Y, Koutrika G, Pagano P, Ross S, Schek HJ, Schuldt H (2006) The digital library manifesto. http://www.delos.info/index.php?option=com_content&task=view&id=345&Itemid, visited on February, 2011

Candela L, Castelli D, Ferro N, Ioannidis Y, Koutrika G, Meghini C, Pagano P, Ross S, Soergel D, Agosti M, Dobreva M, Katifori V, Schuldt H (2007) The DELOS digital library reference model. Foundations for digital libraries. Version 0.98. http://www.delos.info/index.php?option=com_content&task=view&id=345&Itemid=#reference_model, visited on February, 2011

Cano P, Batlle E, Kalker T, Haitsma J (2005) A review of audio fingerprinting. Journal of VLSI Signal Processing 41:271–284

Cao Z, Liu T (2007) Learning to rank: From pairwise approach to listwise approach. In: Proceedings of the International Conference on Machine Learning, pp 129–136

Card S (1996) Visualizing retrieved information: A survey. IEEE Computer Graphics and Applications 16:63–67

Carey M, Heesch D, Rüger S (2003) Info navigator: A visualization interface for document searching and browsing. In: Proceedings of the International Conference on Distributed Multimedia Systems, pp 23–28

Carlson A, Betteridge J, Wang RC, Hruschka ER Jr, Mitchell TM (2010) Coupled semi-supervised learning for information extraction. In: Davison BD, Suel T, Craswell N, Liu B (eds) Proceedings of the ACM Conference on Web Search and Data Mining. ACM Press, New York, NY, pp 101–110

Carmel D, Cohen D, Fagin R, Farchi E, Herscovici M, Maarek Y, Soffer A (2001) Static index pruning for information retrieval systems. In: Proceedings of the ACM Conference on Research and Development in Information Retrieval. ACM Press, New York, NY, pp 43–50

Carrasco J, Fain D, Lang K, Zhukov L (2003) Clustering of bipartite advertiser-keyword graph. http://citeseerx.ist.psu.edu/viewdoc/download?doi=10.1.1.4.8969&rep=rep1&type=pdf, visited on February, 2011

Carterette B, Allan J, Sitaraman R (2006) Minimal test collections for retrieval evaluation. In: Proceedings of the ACM Conference on Research and Development in Information Retrieval, pp 268–275

Carterette B, Gabrilovich E, Metzler D (2010a) Measuring the reusability of test collections. In: Proceedings of the ACM Conference on Web Search and Data Mining. ACM Press, New York, NY, pp 231–240

Carterette B, Kanoulas E, Yilmaz E (2010b) Low cost evaluation in information retrieval. In: Proceedings of the ACM Conference on Research and Development in Information Retrieval. ACM Press, New York, NY, p 903

Case D (2002) Looking for Information: A Survey of Research on Information Seeking and Needs and Behavior. Academic Press, San Diego, CA

Castillo C (2003) Cooperation schemes between a web server and a web search engine. In: Proceedings of the Latin American Conference on World Wide Web. IEEE CS, New York, NY, pp 212–213

Cavallaro A, Ebrahimi T (2004) Interaction between high-level and low-level image analysis for semantic video object extraction. Journal on Applied Signal Processing 786–797

Cesa-Bianchi N, Lugosi G (2006) Prediction, Learning and Games. Cambridge University Press, New York, NY

Chakrabarti S (2003) Mining the Web. Morgan Kaufmann, San Francisco, CA

Chakrabarti S, van den Berg M, Dom B (1999) Focused crawling: A new approach to topic-specific web resource discovery. Computer Networks and ISDN Systems 31(11–16):1623–1640

Chapelle O, Metlzer D, Zhang Y, Grinspan P (2009) Expected reciprocal rank for graded relevance. In: Proceedings of the ACM Conference on Information and Knowledge Management. ACM Press, New York, NY, pp 621–630

Chawda B, Craft B, Cairns P, Rüger S, Heesch D (2005) Do "attractive things work better"? An exploration of search tool visualisations. In: Proceedings of the Australasian Database Interaction Conference, vol 2, pp 46–51

Chen Y, Pavlov D, Canny J (2009) Large-scale behavioral targeting. In: Proceedings of the ACM Conference on Knowledge Discovery and Data Mining. ACM Press, New York, NY, pp 209–218

Cho J, Garcia-Molina H (2000) The evolution of the Web and implications for an incremental crawler. In: Proceedings of the International Conference on Very Large Data Bases. Morgan Kaufmann, San Francisco, CA, pp 200–209

Cho J, Garcia-Molina H (2002) Parallel crawlers. In: Proceedings of the International Conference on the World Wide Web. ACM Press, New York, NY, pp 124–135

Cho J, Garcia-Molina H (2003) Effective page refresh policies for web crawlers. ACM Transactions on Database Systems 28(4):390–426

Cho J, Garcia-Molina H, Page L (1998) Efficient crawling through URL ordering. Computer Networks and ISDN Systems 30(1–7):161–172

Cho J, Shivakumar N, Garcia-Molina H (2000) Finding replicated web collections. ACM SIGMOD Record 29(2):355–366

Chowdhury A, Pass G (2003) Operational requirements for scalable search systems. In: Proceedings of the ACM Conference on Information and Knowledge Management. ACM Press, New York, NY, pp 435–442

Chowdhury A, Frieder O, Grossman D, McCabe M (2002) Collection statistics for fast duplicate document detection. ACM Transactions on Information Systems 20(2):171–191

Christel M, Warmack A (2001) The effect of text in storyboards for video navigation. In: Proceedings of the IEEE International Conference on Acoustics, Speech and Signal Processing, pp 1409–1412

Christel M, Hauptmann A, Warmack A, Crosby S (1999) Adjustable filmstrips and skims as abstractions for a digital video library. In: Proceedings of the IEEE Forum on Research and Technology Advances in Digital Libraries, pp 98–104

Chung C, Clarke CA (2002) Topic-oriented collaborative crawling. In: Proceedings of the ACM Conference on Information and Knowledge Management. ACM Press, New York, NY, pp 34–42

Ciaramita M, Murdock V, Plachouras V (2008) Online learning from click data for sponsored search. In: Proceedings of the International Conference on the World Wide Web. ACM Press, New York, NY, pp 227–236

Clarke CA, Cormack G, Burkowski F (1994) Fast inverted indexes with on-line update. Tech Rep CS-94-40, University of Waterloo

Clarke CA, Agichtein E, Dumais S, White R (2007) The influence of caption features on click-through patterns in web search. In: Proceedings of the ACM Conference on Research and Development in Information Retrieval. ACM Press, New York, NY, pp 135–142

Clarke CA, Kolla M, Cormack G, Vechtomova O, Ashkan A, Buttcher S, MacKinnon I (2008) Novelty and diversity in information retrieval evaluation. In: Proceedings of the ACM Conference on Research and Development in Information Retrieval, pp 659–666

Clarke CA, Craswell N, Soboroff I (2009) Overview of the TREC 2009 Web track. http://trec.nist.gov/, visited on February, 2011

CLEF (2010) Cross-language evaluation forum. http://www.clef-campaign.org/, visited on February, 2011

Cleverdon C (1991) The significance of the Cranfield tests on index languages. In: Proceedings of the ACM Conference on Research and Development in Information Retrieval, pp 3–12

Cockburn A, Savage J (2003) Comparing speed-dependent automatic zooming with traditional scroll and pan and zoom methods. In: Proceedings of the Australasian Database Interaction Conference, pp 87–102

Cooper J, Coden A, Brown E (2002) Detecting similar documents using salient terms. In: Proceedings of the ACM Conference on Information and Knowledge Management. ACM Press, New York, NY, pp 245–251

Cosijn E, Ingwersen P (2000) Dimensions of relevance. Information Processing and Management 36:533–550. http://portal.acm.org/citation.cfm?id=348834.348836, visited on December, 2010

Cothey V (2002) A longitudinal study of world wide web users' information-searching behavior. Journal of the American Society for Information Science and Technology 53:67–78. http://portal.acm.org/citation.cfm?id=506072.506073, visited on December, 2010

Cox K (1992) Information retrieval by browsing. In: Proceedings of the International Conference on New Information Technology, pp 69–80

Cox K (1995) Searching through browsing. PhD thesis, University of Canberra

Cox I, Miller M, Minka T, Papathomas T, Yianilos P (2000) The Bayesian image retrieval system and PicHunter. IEEE Transactions on Image Processing 9:20–38

Coyle M, Smyth B (2007) On the community-based explanation of search results. In: Proceedings of the International Conference on Intelligent User Interfaces, pp 282–285

Crane G (2005) Perseus digital library project. Tech rep, Tufts University. http://www.perseus.tufts.edu, visited on December, 2010

Croft B, Parenty T (1985) A comparison of a network structure and a database system used for document retrieval. Information Systems 10:377–390

Croft W, Thompson R (1987) I3r: a new approach to the design of document retrieval systems. Journal of the American Society for Information Science 38(6):389–404

Croft B, Metzler D, Strohman T (2009) Search Engines: Information Retrieval in Practice. Addison-Wesley, Reading, MA

Cunningham H (2002) GATE: a general architecture for text engineering. Computers and the Humanities 36:223–254

Cutting D, Pedersen J (1990) Optimization for dynamic inverted index maintenance. In: Proceedings of the ACM Conference on Research and Development in Information Retrieval. ACM Press, New York, NY, pp 405–411

Cycorp (2001) Foundations of knowledge representation in Cyc: Microtheories. http://www.cyc.com/doc/tut/DnLoad/Microtheories.pdf, visited on December, 2010

Czerwinski M, Horvitz E, Cutrell E (2001) Subjective duration assessment: An implicit probe for software usability. In: Proceedings of the Conference on Interaction Homme-Machine and Human-Computer Interaction, pp 167–170

Dasgupta A, Ghosh A, Kumar R, Olston C, Pandey S, Tomkins A (2007) The discoverability of the Web. In: Proceedings of the International Conference on the World Wide Web. ACM Press, New York, NY, pp 421–430

Datta R, Joshi D, Li J, Wang J (2008) Image retrieval: Ideas, influences and trends of the new age. ACM Computing Surveys 40:1–60

Davenport T, Beck J (2001) The Attention Economy: Understanding the New Currency of Business. Harvard Business School Press, Cambridge, MA

de Kretser O, Moffat A, Shimmin T, Zobel J (1998) Methodologies for distributed information retrieval. In: Proceedings of the International Conference on Distributed Computing Systems. IEEE Computer Society, Washington, DC, p 66

de Vries A, Mamoulis N, Nes N, Kersten M (2002) Efficient k-nn search on vertically decomposed data. In: Proceedings of the ACM Conference on Management of Data, pp 322–333

Dean J, Ghemawat S (2008) MapReduce: simplified data processing on large clusters. Communications of the ACM 51(1)):107–113

Dearholt D, Schvaneveldt R (1990) Properties of Pathfinder networks. In: Schvaneveldt R (ed) Pathfinder Associative Networks: Studies in Knowledge Organization. Norwood, pp 1–30

Deerwester SC, Dumais S, Furnas G, Landauer T, Harshman R (1990) Indexing by latent semantic analysis. Journal of the American Society for Information Science 41:391–407

Dennis S, Bruza P, McArthur R (2002) Web searching: a process-oriented experimental study of three interactive search paradigms. Journal of the American Society for Information Science and Technology 53:120–133. http://portal.acm.org/citation.cfm?id=506072.506077, visited on December, 2010

Di Buccio E, Melucci M, Song D (2011) Towards predicting relevance using a quantum-like framework. In: Proceedings of the European Conference on Information Retrieval Research (ECIR)

Di Nunzio G, Ferro N (2005) DIRECT: A system for evaluating information access components of digital libraries. In: Proceedings of the European Conference on Digital Libraries, pp 483–484

Diaz F (2009) Integration of news content into web results. In: Proceedings of the ACM Conference on Web Search and Data Mining. ACM Press, New York, NY, pp 182–191

Diaz F, Arguello J (2009) Adaptation of offline selection predictions in presence of user feedback. In: Proceedings of the ACM Conference on Research and Development in Information Retrieval, pp 323–330

Diaz F, Lalmas M, Shokouhi M (2010) From federated to aggregated search. In: Proceedings of the ACM Conference on Research and Development in Information Retrieval, p 910

Diligenti M, Coetzee F, Lawrence S, Giles C, Gori M (2000) Focused crawling using context graphs. In: Proceedings of the International Conference on Very Large Data Bases. Morgan Kaufmann, San Francisco, CA, pp 527–534

Ding S, Attenberg J, Suel T (2010) Scalable techniques for document identifier assignment in inverted indexes. In: Proceedings of the International Conference on the World Wide Web. ACM Press, New York, NY, pp 311–320

Domingo-Ferrer J (2007) A three-dimensional conceptual framework for database privacy. In: Secure Data Management. Lecture Notes in Computer Science, vol 4721. Springer, Berlin, pp 193–202

Doraisamy S, Rüger S (2003) Robust polyphonic music retrieval with n-grams. Journal of Intelligent Information Systems 21:53–70

Drost I, Scheffer T (2005) Thwarting the nigritude ultramarine: Learning to identify link spam. In: João Gama RC, Brazdil P, Jorge A, Torgo L (eds) Proceedings of the European Conference on Machine Learning and Principles and Practice of Knowledge Discovery. Lecture Notes in Computer Science, vol 3720. Springer, Berlin, pp 96–107

D'Souza D, Thom J, Zobel J (2004) Collection selection for managed distributed document databases. Information Processing and Management 40(3):527–546

Dumais S, Cutrell E, Cadiz J, Jancke G, Sarin R, Robbins D (2003) Stuff i've seen: A system for personal information retrieval and re-use. In: Proceedings of the ACM Conference on Research and Development in Information Retrieval. ACM Press, New York, NY, pp 72–79

Dussin M, Ferro N (2009) DIRECT: Applying the DIKW hierarchy to large-scale evaluation campaigns. In: Larsen R, Paepcke A, Borbinha J, Naaman M (eds) Proceedings of the ACM/IEEE-CS Joint Conference on Digital Libraries. ACM Press, New York, NY, p 424

Duygulu P, Barnard K, de Freitas N, Forsyth D (2002) Object recognition as machine translation: Learning a lexicon for a fixed image vocabulary. In: Proceedings of the European Conference on Computer Vision. Lecture Notes in Computer Science, vol 2353. Springer, Berlin, pp 349–354

Edelman B, Ostrovsky M, Schwarz M (2005) Internet advertising and the generalized second price auction: Selling billions of dollars worth of keywords. http://www.aeaweb.org/articles.php?doi=10.1257/aer.97.1.242, visited on February, 2011

Edwards J, McCurley K, Tomlin J (2001) An adaptive model for optimizing performance of an incremental web crawler. In: Proceedings of the International Conference on the World Wide Web. ACM Press, New York, NY, pp 106–113

Efron M (2009) Using multiple query aspects to build test collections without human relevance judgments. In: Proceedings of the European Conference on Information Retrieval. Springer, Heidelberg, pp 276–287

Efthimiadis E (1993) A user-centered evaluation of ranking algorithms for interactive query expansion. In: Proceedings of the ACM Conference on Research and Development in Information Retrieval. ACM Press, New York, NY, pp 146–156

Eichmann D (1995) Ethical web agents. Computer Networks and ISDN Systems 28(1–2):127–136

Elsweiler D, Ruthven I (2007) Towards task-based personal information management evaluations. In: Proceedings of the ACM Conference on Research and Development in Information Retrieval. ACM Press, New York, NY, pp 23–30

Elsweiler D, Ruthven I, Jones C (2007) Towards memory supporting personal information management tools. Journal of the American Society for Information Science and Technology 58:924–946

Elsweiler D, Baillie M, Ruthven I (2009) On understanding the relationship between recollection and refinding. http://journals.tdl.org/jodi/article/view/436/542, visited on February, 2011

Enser P, Sandom C (2002) Retrieval of archival moving imagery—CBIR outside the frame? In: Proceedings of the International Conference on Image and Video Retrieval. Lecture Notes in Computer Science, vol 2383. Springer, Berlin, pp 85–106

Enser P, Sandom C (2003) Towards a comprehensive survey of the semantic gap in visual image retrieval. In: Proceedings of the International Conference on Image and Video Retrieval. Lecture Notes in Computer Science, vol 2728. Springer, Berlin, pp 163–168

Ericsson K, Simon H (1996) Protocol Analysis: Verbal Reports as Data. MIT Press, Cambridge, MA

Etzioni O, Cafarella MJ, Downey D, Popescu AM, Tal Shaked SS, Weld DS, Yates A (2004) Methods for domain-independent information extraction from the Web: An experimental comparison. In: Proceedings of the National Conference on Artificial Intelligence, pp 391–398

Exposto J, Macedo J, Pina A, Alves A, Rufino J (2005) Geographical partition for distributed web crawling. In: Proceedings of the Workshop on Geographic Information Retrieval. ACM Press, New York, NY, pp 55–60

Exposto J, Macedo J, Pina A, Alves A, Rufino J (2008) Efficient partitioning strategies for distributed web crawling. In: Proceedings of the International Conference on Information Networking: Towards Ubiquitous Networking and Services. Lecture Notes in Computer Science. Springer, Berlin/Heidelberg, pp 544–553

Fagni T, Perego R, Silvestri F, Orlando S (2006) Boosting the performance of web search engines: Caching and prefetching query results by exploiting historical usage data. ACM Transactions on Information Systems 24(1):51–78

Fayyad U, Piatetsky-Shapiro G, Smyth P (1996) From data mining to knowledge discovery. In: Fayyad M, G Piatetsky-Shapiro PS, Uthurusamy R (eds) Advances in Knowledge Discovery and Data Mining. AAAI/MIT Press, Cambridge, MA, pp 1–34

Feldman R, Sanger J (2007) The Text Mining Handbook. Advanced Approaches in Analyzing Unstructured Data. Cambridge University Press, Cambridge

Fellbaum C (1998) Wordnet: An Electronic Lexical Database. MIT Press, Cambridge, MA

Feng S, Manmatha R, Lavrenko V (2004) Multiple Bernoulli relevance models for image and video annotation. In: Proceedings of the IEEE International Conference on Computer Vision and Pattern Recognition, pp 1002–1009

Ferro N (2005) Design choices for a flexible annotation service. In: Proceedings of the Italian Research Conference on Digital Libraries, pp 101–110

Fetterly D, Manasse M, Najork M, Wiener J (2004) A large-scale study of the evolution of web pages. Software: Practice and Experience 34(2):213–237

Fetterly D, Craswell N, Vinay V (2009) The impact of crawl policy on web search effectiveness. In: Proceedings of the ACM Conference on Research and Development in Information Retrieval. ACM Press, New York, NY, pp 580–587

Feynman R, Leighton R, Sands M (1965) The Feynman Lectures on Physics. Addison-Wesley, Reading, MA

Fidel R (1993) Qualitative methods in information retrieval research. Library and Information Science Research 15:219–247

Fidel R, Soergel D (1983) Factors affecting online bibliographic retrieval: A conceptual framework for research. Journal of the American Society for Information Science 34:163–180

Fidel R, Davies RK, Douglass MH, Holder JK, Hopkins CJ, Kushner EJ, Miyagishima BK, Toney CD (1999) A visit to the information mall: Web searching behavior of high school students. Journal of the American Society for Information Science 50:24–37

Finkelstein L, Gabrilovich E, Matias Y, Rivlin E, Solan Z, Wolfman G, Ruppin E (2001) Placing search in context: The concept revisited. In: Proceedings of the International Conference on the World Wide Web, pp 406–414

Ford N, Miller D, Moss N (2001) The role of individual differences in internet searching: An empirical study. Journal of the American Society for Information Science and Technology 52:1049–1066

Fortuna B, Grobelnik M, Mladenic D (2005) Visualization of text document corpus. Informatica (Slovenia) 29(4):497–504

Fortuna B, Mladenic D, Grobelnik M (2006) Semi-automatic construction of topic ontologies. In: Ackermann M (ed) Proceedings of the Semantics, Web and Mining Workshops at the European Conference on Machine Learning and Principles and Practice of Knowledge Discovery. Lecture Notes in Computer Science, vol 4289. Springer, Berlin, pp 121–131

Fortuna B, Galleguillos C, Cristianini N (2009) Detecting the bias in media with statistical learning methods. In: Text Mining: Classification, Clustering and Applications. Chapman & Hall/CRC Press, New York, NY, pp 27–50

Foster J (2006) Collaborative information seeking and retrieval. Annual Review of Information Science and Technology 40:242–255

Fowler R, Wilson B, Fowler W (1992) Information navigator: An information system using associative networks for display and retrieval. Tech Rep NAG9-551, 92-1, Department of Computer Science and University of Texas

Fox E, Lee W (1991) FAST-INV: A fast algorithm for building large inverted files. Tech Rep 91–10, Virginia Polytechnic Institute and State University

Fox S, Karnawat K, Mydland M, Dumais S, White T (2005) Evaluating implicit measures to improve web search. ACM Transactions on Information Systems 23:147–168

Frankfort-Nachmias C, Nachmias D (2000) Research Methods in the Social Sciences. Worth Publishers, New York

Frankowski D, Cosley D, Sen S, Terveen LG, Riedl J (2006) You are what you say: Privacy risks of public mentions. In: Efthimiadis EN, Dumais ST, Hawking D, Järvelin K (eds) Proceedings of the ACM Conference on Research and Development in Information Retrieval. ACM Press, New York, NY, pp 565–572

Freyne J, Farzan R, Brusilovsky P, Smyth B, Coyle M (2007) Collecting community wisdom: Integrating social search & social navigation. In: Proceedings of the International Conference on Intelligent User Interfaces, pp 52–61

Frokjaer E, Hertzum M, Hormbaek K (2000) Measuring usability: Are effectiveness and efficiency and satisfaction really correlated? In: Proceedings of the ACM Conference on Human Factors in Computing Systems, pp 345–352

Frommholz I, Larson RR (2007) Report on the INEX 2006 heterogeneous collection track. SIGIR Forum 41(1):75–78

Fuhr N, Tsakonas G, Aalberg T, Agosti M, Hansen P, Kapidakis S, Klas CP, Kovács L, Landoni M, Micsik A, Papatheodorou C, Peters C, Sølvberg S (2007) Evaluation of digital libraries. International Journal on Digital Libraries 8(1):21–38

Gan Q, Suel T (2009) Improved techniques for result caching in web search engines. In: Proceedings of the International Conference on the World Wide Web. ACM Press, New York, NY, pp 431–440

Gao W, Lee H, Miao Y (2006) Geographically focused collaborative crawling. In: Proceedings of the International Conference on the World Wide Web. ACM Press, New York, NY, pp 287–296

Goodman J, Carvalho V (2005) Implicit queries for email. http://research.microsoft.com/en-us/um/people/joshuago/ceas05-fixed.pdf, visited on February, 2011

Goodman E, Feldblum E (2010) Blended search and the new rules of engagement. http://www.comscore.com/Press_Events/Presentations_Whitepapers/2010/Blended_Search_and_the_New_Rules_of_Engagement, visited on February, 2011

Gordon DF, des Jardins M (1995) Evaluation and selection of biases in machine learning. Machine Learning 20(1–2):5–22

Gradmann S (2007) Interoperability: A key concept for large scale, persistent digital libraries. http://www.digitalpreservationeurope.eu/publications/briefs/interoperability.pdf, visited on February, 2011

Gravano L, Garcia-Molina H (1995) Generalizing GlOSS to vector-space databases and broker hierarchies. In: Proceedings of the International Conference on Very Large Data Bases. Morgan Kaufmann, San Francisco, CA, pp 78–89

Gravano L, Chang C, Garcia-Molina H, Paepcke A (1997) STARTS: Stanford proposal for internet metasearching. In: Proceedings of the ACM Conference on Management of Data, pp 207–218

Grefenstette G, Shanahan J (2005) Document souls: Joining personalities to documents to produce proactive documents engaged in contextualized, independent search. http://ftp.informatik.rwth-aachen.de/Publications/CEUR-WS/Vol-151/CIR-05_2.pdf, visited on February, 2011

Guan Z, Cutrell E (2007) An eye tracking study of the effect of target rank on web search. In: Proceedings of the ACM Conference on Human Factors in Computing Systems, pp 417–420

Guerrini M, Sardo L (2003) Authority Control. Associazione Italiana Biblioteche, Roma

Gürses FS (2010) Multilateral privacy requirements analysis in online social network services. PhD thesis, KU Leuven and Dept of Computer Science

Gürses FS, Berendt B (2010) The social Web and privacy: Practices, reciprocity and conflict detection in social networks. In: Ferrari E, Bonchi F (eds) Privacy-Aware Knowledge Discovery. Chapman & Hall/CRC Press, New York, NY, pp 395–432

Gyöngyi Z, Garcia-Molina H (2005a) Link spam alliances. In: Proceedings of the International Conference on Very Large Data Bases. VLDB Endowment, pp 517–528

Gyöngyi Z, Garcia-Molina H (2005b) Web spam taxonomy. http://airweb.cse.lehigh.edu/2005/gyongyi.pdf, visited on February, 2011

Gyöngyi Z, Garcia-Molina H, Pedersen J (2004) Combating web spam with TrustRank. In: Proceedings of the International Conference on Very Large Data Bases. VLDB Endowment, pp 576–587

Hall E (1976) Beyond Culture. Anchor Books/Doubleday

Halmos P (1987) Finite-Dimensional Vector Spaces. Undergraduate Texts in Mathematics. Springer, Berlin

Hanani U, Shapira B, Shoval P (2001) Information filtering: Overview of issues, research and systems. User Modeling and User-Adapted Interaction 11:203–259

Hand DJ, Smyth P, Mannila H (2001) Principles of Data Mining. MIT Press, Cambridge, MA

Hare J, Lewis P (2004) Salient regions for query by image content. In: Proceedings of the International Conference on Image and Video Retrieval. Lecture Notes in Computer Science, vol 3115. Springer, Berlin, pp 264–268

Hare J, Lewis P (2005) Saliency-based models of image content and their application to auto-annotation by semantic propagation. http://eprints.ecs.soton.ac.uk/id/eprint/10954, visited on February, 2011

Hare J, Lewis P, Enser P, Sandom C (2006) Mind the gap: Another look at the problem of the semantic gap in image retrieval. In: Multimedia Content Analysis and Management and Retrieval. Lecture Notes in Computer Science, vol 6073, Springer, Berlin, pp 1–12

Harman D (ed) (1996) Proceedings of the Text Retrieval Conference. Government Printing Office, Washington, DC

Harman D, Buckley C (2009) Overview of the reliable information access workshop. Journal of Information Retrieval 12:615–641

Harman D, Candela G (1990) Retrieving records from a gigabyte of text on a mini-computer using statistical ranking. Journal of the American Society for Information Science 41(8):581–589

Harman D, Baeza-Yates R, Fox E, Lee W (1992) Inverted files. In: Baeza-Yates WBFR (ed) Information Retrieval: Data Structures and Algorithms. Prentice-Hall, Upper Saddle River, NJ, pp 28–43

Harper D, Koychev I, Sun Y, Pirie I (2004) Within-document retrieval: A user-centred evaluation of relevance profiling. Journal of Information Retrieval 7:265–290

Hartig O (2009) Provenance information in the Web of data. http://www.dbis.informatik.hu-berlin.de/fileadmin/research/papers/conferences/2009-ldow-hartig.pdf, visited on December, 2010

Hawking D (1997) Scalable text retrieval for large digital libraries. In: Proceedings of the European Conference on Digital Libraries. Springer, London, pp 127–145

Hawking D, Voorhees EM, Craswell N, Bailey P (1999) Overview of the TREC Web track. http://trec.nist.gov/, visited on February, 2011

Hawking D, Voorhees E, Craswell N, Bailey P (2000) Overview of the TREC web track. In: Voorhees E, Harman D (eds) Proceedings of the Text Retrieval Conference, pp 131–150

Hayes P (2009) Blogic. http://www.slideshare.net/PatHayes/blogic-iswc-2009-invited-talk, visited on December, 2010

Hearst MA (1992) Automatic acquisition of hyponyms from large text corpora. In: Proceedings of the Conference on Computational Linguistics, pp 539–545

Heesch D (2005) The NN^k technique for image searching and browsing. PhD thesis, Imperial College. London

Heesch D, Rüger S (2003) Relevance feedback for content-based image retrieval: What can three mouse clicks achieve? In: Proceedings of the European Conference on Information Retrieval. Lecture Notes in Computer Science, vol 2633. Springer, Berlin, pp 363–376

Heesch D, Rüger S (2004) Approaching the problem of multi-lingual information retrieval and visualization in Greek and Latin and Old Norse texts. In: Proceedings of the European Conference on Information Retrieval. Lecture Notes in Computer Science, vol 2997. Springer, Berlin, pp 253–266

Heesch D, Pickering M, Rüger S, Yavlinsky A (2003) Video retrieval using search and browsing with key frames. http://www-nlpir.nist.gov/projects/tvpubs/tvpapers04/imperial.pdf, visited on February, 2011

Heinz S, Zobel J (2003) Efficient single-pass index construction for text databases. Journal of the American Society for Information Science 54(8):713–729

Hemmje M, Kunkel C, Willet A (1994) LyberWorld—a visualization user interface supporting fulltext retrieval. In: Proceedings of the ACM Conference on Research and Development in Information Retrieval. ACM Press, New York, NY, pp 249–259

Henzinger M (2006) Finding near-duplicate web pages: A large-scale evaluation of algorithms. In: Proceedings of the ACM Conference on Research and Development in Information Retrieval. ACM Press, New York, NY, pp 284–291

Hersh W, Pentecost J, Hickam D (1996) A task oriented approach to information retrieval evaluation. Journal of the American Society for Information Science 47:50–56

Heydon A, Najork M (1999) Mercator: a scalable, extensible web crawler. World Wide Web 2(4):219–229

Hildreth C (1985) Online public access catalogs. Annual Review of Information Science and Technology 20:233–285

Hildreth C (ed) (1989) The Online Catalogue: Developments and Directions. Library Association, London

Hill S, Provost F, Volinsky C (2006) Network-based marketing: Identifying likely adopters via consumer networks. Statistical Science 22:256–276

Hirai J, Raghavan S, Garcia-Molina H, Paepcke A (2000) WebBase: a repository of web pages. In: Proceedings of the International Conference on the World Wide Web. North-Holland, Amsterdam, pp 277–293

Hirsh S (1999) Children's relevance criteria and information-seeking on electronic resources. Journal of the American Society for Information Science 50:1265–1283

Hodge G (2000) Systems of knowledge organization for digital libraries: Beyond traditional authority files. Tech rep, Council on Library and Information Resources (CLIR). http://www.clir.org/pubs/reports/pub91/contents.html, visited on December, 2010

Hoffman P, Grinstein G, Pinkney D (1999) Dimensional anchors: A graphic primitive for multidimensional multivariate information visualizations. In: Proceedings of the New Paradigms in Information Visualisation and Manipulation Workshop at ACM Conference on Information and Knowledge Management, pp 9–16

Hornbaek K (2006) Current practice in measuring usability: Challenges to usability studies and research. International Journal of Human-Computer Studies 64:79–102

Hotchkiss G (2007) Eye tracking on universal and personalized search. http://searchengineland.com/eye-tracking-on-universal-and-personalized-search-12233, visited on December, 2010

Hou Y, Song D (2009) Characterizing pure high-order entanglements in lexical semantic spaces via information geometry. In: Bruza P, Sofge D, Lawless W, van Rijsbergen C, Klusch M (eds) Proceedings of the Symposium on Quantum Interaction. Lecture Notes in Computer Science, vol 5494. Springer, Saarbrücken, pp 237–250

Howarth P, Rüger S (2005) Trading precision for speed: Localised similarity functions. In: Proceedings of the International Conference on Image and Video Retrieval. Lecture Notes in Computer Science, vol 3568. Springer, Berlin, pp 415–424

Hsieh-Yee I (1998) Search tactics of web users in searching for texts, graphics, known items and subjects: A search simulation study. Reference Librarian 60:61–85

Hu M, Liu B (2004) Mining opinion features in customer reviews. In: Proceedings of the National Conference on Artificial Intelligence, pp 755–760

Hu J, Zeng HJ, Li H, Niu C, Chen Z (2007) Demographic prediction based on user's browsing behavior. In: Proceedings of the International Conference on the World Wide Web. ACM Press, New York, NY, pp 151–160

Huertas-Rosero A, Azzopardi L, van Rijsbergen K (2008) Characterising through erasing: A theoretical framework for representing documents inspired by quantum theory. http://arxiv.org/abs/0802.1738, visited on February, 2011

Huertas-Rosero A, Azzopardi L, van Rijsbergen K (2009) Eraser lattices and semantic contents: An exploration of the semantic contents in order relations between erasers. In: Bruza P, Sofge D, Lawless W, van Rijsbergen C, Klusch M (eds) Proceedings of the Symposium on Quantum Interaction. Lecture Notes in Computer Science, vol 5494. Springer, Saarbrücken, pp 266–275

Hughes R (1989) The Structure and Interpretation of Quantum Mechanics. Harvard University Press, Harvard

IAB (2009) Internet Advertising Revenue Report. Pricewaterhouse Coopers LLP. http://www.iab.net/insights_research/947883/adrevenuereport, visited on December, 2010

Ingwersen P (1992) Information Retrieval Interaction. Taylor Graham, London

Ingwersen P, Järvelin K (2005) The Turn: Integration of Information Seeking and Retrieval in Context. Springer, Berlin

Ingwersen P, Järvelin K (2007) On the holistic cognitive theory for information retrieval: Drifting outside the cave of the laboratory framework. In: Dominich S, Kisss F (eds) Studies in Theory of Information Retrieval. Foundation for Information Society, pp 135–147

Ingwersen P, Willett P (1995) An introduction to algorithmic and cognitive approaches for information retrieval. Libri 45:160–177

Ioannidis Y, Maier D, Abiteboul S, Buneman P, Davidson S, Fox E, Halevy A, Knoblock C, Rabitti F, Schek HJ, Weikum G (2005) Digital library information-technology infrastructures. International Journal on Digital Libraries 5(4):266–274

Ioannidis Y, Milano D, Schek HJ, Schuldt H (2008) DelosDLMS from the DELOS vision to the implementation of a future digital library management system. International Journal on Digital Libraries 9:101–114

iProspect (2008) iProspect blended search results study. http://www.iprospect.com/about/researchstudy_2008_blendedsearchresults.htm, visited on December, 2010

Ishikawa Y, Subramanya R, Faloutsos C (1998) MindReader: Querying databases through multiple examples. In: Proceedings of the International Conference on Very Large Databases, pp 218–227

Jameson A, Smyth B (2007) Recommendation to groups. The Adaptive Web 596–627

Järvelin K (2007) An analysis of two approaches in information retrieval: From frameworks to study designs. Journal of the American Society for Information Science and Technology 58:971–986

Järvelin K, Kekäläinen J (2000) IR evaluation methods for highly relevant documents. In: Belkin N, Ingwersen P, Leong MK (eds) Proceedings of the ACM Conference on Research and Development in Information Retrieval. ACM Press, New York, NY, pp 41–48

Järvelin K, Kekäläinen J (2002) Cumulated gain-based evaluation of IR techniques. ACM Transactions on Information Systems 20:422–446

Jeh G, Widom J (2003) Scaling personalized web search. In: Proceedings of the International Conference on the World Wide Web. ACM Press, New York, NY, pp 271–279

Jeon J, Lavrenko V, Manmatha R (2003) Automatic image annotation and retrieval using cross-media relevance models. In: Proceedings of the ACM Conference on Research and Development in Information Retrieval. ACM Press, New York, NY, pp 119–126

Jeong BS, Omiecinski E (1995) Inverted file partitioning schemes in multiple disk systems. IEEE Transactions on Parallel and Distributed Systems 6(2):142–153

Joachims T (2002) Optimizing search engines using clickthrough data. In: Proceedings of the ACM Conference on Knowledge Discovery and Data Mining. ACM Press, New York, NY, pp 133–142

Joachims T, Radlinski F (2007) Search engines that learn from implicit feedback. Computer 40:34–40

Joachims T, Granka L, Pan B, Hembrooke H, Gay G (2005a) Accurately interpreting click-through data as implicit feedback. In: Proceedings of the ACM Conference on Research and Development in Information Retrieval. ACM Press, New York, NY, pp 154–161

Joachims T, Granka L, Pan B, Hembrooke H, Gay G (2005b) Accurately interpreting clickthrough data as implicit feedback. In: Proceedings of the ACM Conference on Research and Development in Information Retrieval, pp 154–161

Jones W (2007) Keeping Found Things Found: The Study and Practice of Personal Information Management. Morgan Kaufmann, San Diego, CA

Jónsson B, Franklin M, Srivastava D (1998) Interaction of query evaluation and buffer management for information retrieval. ACM SIGMOD Record 27(2):118–129

Käki M (2004) Proportional search interface usability measures. In: Proceedings of the Nordic Forum for Human-Computer Interaction Research, pp 365–372

Katayama T, Utsuro T, Sato Y, Yoshinaka T, Kawada Y, Fukuhara T (2009) An empirical study on selective sampling in active learning for splog detection. In: Proceedings of the International Workshop on Adversarial Information Retrieval on the Web. ACM Press, New York, NY, pp 29–36

Katz S (1987) Estimation of probabilities from sparse data for the language model component of a speech recognizer. IEEE Transactions on Acoustics, Speech and Signal Processing 400–401

Kay A (2004) The power of the context. http://www.vpri.org/html/writings.htm, visited on December, 2010

Kayaaslan E, Cambazoglu B, Aykanat C (2010) Document replication strategies for geographically distributed Web search engines. To be submitted

Kazai G, Lalmas M, de Vries AP (2004) The overlap problem in content-oriented XML retrieval evaluation. In: Proceedings of the ACM Conference on Research and Development in Information Retrieval, pp 72–79

Keane MT, O'Brien M, Smyth B (2008) Are people biased in their use of search engines? Communications of the ACM 51(2):49–52

Kekäläinen J (2005) Binary and graded relevance in IR evaluations—comparison of the effects on ranking of IR systems. Information Processing and Management 41:1019–1033

Kekäläinen J, Järvelin K (2002b) Using graded relevance assessments in IR evaluation. Journal of the American Society for Information Science and Technology 53:1120–1129

Kekäläinen J, Järvelin K (2002a) User-oriented evaluation methods for information retrieval: A case study based on conceptual models for query expansion. In: Lakemeyer G, Nebel B (eds) Exploring Artificial Intelligence in the New Millennium. Morgan Kaufmann, San Diego, CA, pp 355–379

Kelly D (2009) Methods for evaluating interactive information retrieval systems with users. Foundations and Trends in Information Retrieval 3:1–224

Kelly D, Belkin N (2004) Display time as implicit feedback: Understanding task effects. In: Proceedings of the ACM Conference on Research and Development in Information Retrieval. ACM Press, New York, NY, pp 377–384

Kelly D, Fu X (2007) Eliciting better information need descriptions from users of information search systems. Information Processing and Management 43:30–46

Kelly D, Lin J (2007) Overview of the TREC ciQA task. ACM SIGIR Forum 41:107–116

Kelly D, Ruthven I (2010) Interactive Information Seeking and Behaviour and Retrieval. Facet Publishing

Kelly D, Dollu V, Fu X (2005) The loquacious user: A document-independent source of terms for query expansion. In: Proceedings of the ACM Conference on Research and Development in Information Retrieval. ACM Press, New York, NY, pp 457–464

Khan I (2010) Nothing but net. https://mm.jpmorgan.com/stp/t/c.do?i=3c571-1cf&u=a_p*d_254466.pdf*h_1v23jmle, visited on February, 2011

Klas C, Albrechtsen H, Hansen P, Kapidakis S, Kovacs L, Kriewel S, Micsik A, Papatheodorou C, Tsakonas G, Jacob E (2006) A logging scheme for comparative digital library evaluation. In: Proceedings of the European Conference on Digital Libraries, pp 17–22

Koenemann J, Belkin N (1996) A case for interaction: A study of interactive information retrieval behavior and effectiveness. In: Proceedings of the ACM Conference on Human Factors in Computing Systems, pp 205–212

Kofod-Petersen A, Aamodt A (2003) Case-based situation assessment in a mobile context-aware system. In: Krüger A, Malaka R (eds) Proceedings of the Artificial Intelligence in Mobile Systems Workshop, pp 41–49

Kolmogorov A (1956) Foundations of the Theory of Probability. Chelsea, New York, NY

Korfhage R (1991) To see or not to see—is that the query? In: Proceedings of the ACM Conference on Research and Development in Information Retrieval. ACM Press, New York, NY, pp 134–141

Kulkarni A, Callan J (2010) Topic-based index partitions for efficient and effective selective search. http://www.lsdsir.org/, visited on February, 2011

Kushmerick N, Weld DS, Doorenbos RB (1997) Wrapper induction for information extraction. In: Proceedings of the International Joint Conferences on Artificial Intelligence, pp 729–737

Lacerda A, Cristo M, Goncalves M, Fan W, Ziviani N, Ribeiro-Neto B (2006) Learning to advertise. In: Proceedings of the ACM Conference on Research and Development in Information Retrieval. ACM Press, New York, NY, pp 549–556

Lai T, Robbins H (1985) Asymptotically efficient adaptive allocation rules. Advances in Applied Mathematics 4–22

Lalmas M (2009) XML Retrieval. Synthesis Lectures on Information Concepts and Retrieval and Services. Morgan & Claypool

Lalmas M, Tombros A (2007) INEX: Understanding XML retrieval evaluation. In: Proceedings of the International Conference on Digital Libraries, pp 2002–2006

Landauer T (2007) Handbook of Latent Semantic Analysis. Lawrence Erlbaum

Larkey L, Connell M, Callan J (2000) Collection selection and results merging with topically organized US patents and TREC data. In: Proceedings of the ACM Conference on Information and Knowledge Management. ACM Press, New York, NY, pp 282–289

Larose D (2004) Discovering Knowledge in Data: An Introduction to Data Mining. Wiley, New York, NY

Larsen SM, Tombros A (2006) The interactive track at INEX. In: Fuhr N, Lalmas M, Malik S, Kazai G (eds) Proceedings of the Workshop of Initiative for the Evaluation of XML Retrieval. Springer, Berlin, pp 398–410

Lavrenko V, Manmatha R, Jeon J (2003) A model for learning the semantics of pictures. In: Neural Information Processing Systems, pp 553–560

Lawrence S, Giles C (2000) Accessibility of information on the Web. Intelligence 11(1):32–39

Lee HT, Leonard D, Wang X, Loguinov D (2008) IRLbot: Scaling to 6 billion pages and beyond. In: Proceedings of the International Conference on the World Wide Web. ACM Press, New York, NY, pp 427–436

Lempel R, Moran S (2003) Predictive caching and prefetching of query results in search engines. In: Proceedings of the International Conference on the World Wide Web. ACM Press, New York, NY, pp 19–28

Lester N, Zobel J, Williams H (2004) In-place versus re-build versus re-merge: Index maintenance strategies for text retrieval systems. In: Proceedings of the Australasian Database Conference. Australian Computer Society, Darlinghurst, pp 15–23

Lester N, Moffat A, Zobel J (2008) Efficient online index construction for text databases. ACM Transactions on Database Systems 33(3):1–33

Levin A, Levin I, Weller J (2005) A multi-attribute analysis of preferences for online and offline shopping: Differences across products and consumers and shopping stages. Journal of Electronic Commerce Research 281–290

Lew M, Sebe N, Djeraba C, Jain R (2006) Content-based multimedia information retrieval: State of the art and challenges. ACM Transactions on Multimedia Computing and Communications and Applications 2:1–19

Lewandowskii D (2008) A three-year study on the freshness of web search engine databases. Journal of Information Science 34(6):817–831

Li L, Chu W, Langford J (2010) An unbiased and data-driven, offline evaluation method of contextual bandit algorithms. Tech rep, CoRR. abs/1003.5956. http://arxiv.org/abs/1003.5956, visited on December, 2010

Lin WH, Xing EP, Hauptmann AG (2008) A joint topic and perspective model for ideological discourse. In: Daelemans W, Goethals B, Morik K (eds) Proceedings of the European Conference on Machine Learning and Principles and Practice of Knowledge Discovery. Lecture Notes in Computer Science, vol 5212. Springer, Berlin, pp 17–32

Liu B (2007) Web Data Mining. Exploring Hyperlinks and Contents and Usage Data. Springer, Berlin

Liu Z, Chu W (2007) Knowledge-based query expansion to support scenario-specific retrieval of medical free text. Journal of Information Retrieval 10:173–202

Liu X, Croft W (2004) Cluster-based retrieval using language models. In: Proceedings of the ACM Conference on Research and Development in Information Retrieval. ACM Press, New York, NY, pp 186–193

Liu H, Mihalcea R (2007) Of men and women and computers: Data-driven gender modeling for improved user interfaces. In: Proceedings of the International Conference on Weblogs Social Media, pp 121–128

Liu F, Yu C, Meng W (2002) Personalized web search by mapping user queries to categories. In: Proceedings of the ACM Conference on Information and Knowledge Management. ACM Press, New York, NY, pp 558–565

Liu N, Yan J, Chen Z (2009a) A probabilistic model based approach for blended search. In: Proceedings of the International Conference on World Wide Web, pp 1075–1076

Liu N, Yan J, Fan W, Yang Q, Chen Z (2009b) Identifying vertical search intention of query through social tagging propagation. http://www2009.org/proceedings/pdf/p1209.pdf, visited on February, 2011

Liu C, Yuen J, Torralba A (2009c) Nonparametric scene parsing: Label transfer via dense scene alignment. In: Proceedings of the IEEE International Conference on Computer Vision and Pattern Recognition, pp 1972–1979

Liverani R (2008) Web spam techniques. http://malerisch.net/docs/web_spam_techniques/web_spam_techniques.html, visited on December, 2010

Long X, Suel T (2005) Three-level caching for efficient query processing in large web search engines. In: Proceedings of the International Conference on the World Wide Web. ACM Press, New York, NY, pp 257–266

Lu Z, McKinley K (1999) Partial replica selection based on relevance for information retrieval. In: Proceedings of the ACM Conference on Research and Development in Information Retrieval. ACM Press, New York, NY, pp 97–104

Lu Z, McKinley K (2000) Partial collection replication versus caching for information retrieval systems. In: Proceedings of the ACM Conference on Research and Development in Information Retrieval. ACM Press, New York, NY, pp 248–255

Lucchese C, Orlando S, Perego R, Silvestri F (2007) Mining query logs to optimize index partitioning in parallel web search engines. In: Proceedings of the International Conference on Scalable Information Systems. ICST (Institute for Computer Sciences, Social-Informatics and Telecommunications Engineering), Brussels, Belgium, pp 1–9

Lun A (2001) Measuring usability with the use questionnaire. http://www.stcsig.org/usability/newsletter/0110_measuring_with_use.html, visited on February, 2011

Lykke M (2001) A framework for work task based thesaurus design. Journal of Documentation 57:774–797

Lykke M (2004) Task-based evaluation of associative thesaurus in real-life environment. In: Proceedings of the Meeting of the American Society for Information Science and Technology, pp 437–447

Lyon D (2007) Surveillance Studies: An Overview. Polity Press, Cambridge

MacFarlane A, McCann J, Robertson S (2000) Parallel search using partitioned inverted files. In: Proceedings of the International Symposium on String Processing Information Retrieval. IEEE Computer Society, Washington, DC, pp 209–220

Maedche A, Staab S (2001) Ontology learning for the semantic Web. IEEE Intelligent Systems 16(2):72–79

Magalhães J, Rüger S (2006) Logistic regression of semantic codebooks for semantic image retrieval. In: Proceedings of the International Conference on Image and Video Retrieval. Lecture Notes in Computer Science, vol 4071. Springer, Berlin, pp 41–50

Magalhães J, Rüger S (2007) Information-theoretic semantic multimedia indexing. In: Proceedings of the International Conference on Image and Video Retrieval, pp 619–626

Magennis M, van Rijsbergen K (1997) The potential and actual effectiveness of interactive query expansion. In: Belkin N, Narasimhalu A, Willett P (eds) Proceedings of the ACM Conference on Research and Development in Information Retrieval. ACM Press, New York, NY, pp 324–332

Maglaughlin K, Sonnenwald D (2002) User perspectives on relevance criteria: A comparison among relevant, partially relevant and not-relevant judgments. Journal of the American Society for Information Science and Technology 53:327–342

Makadia A, Pavlovic V, Kumar S (2008) A new baseline for image annotation. In: Proceedings of the European Conference on Computer Vision. Lecture Notes in Computer Science, vol 5304. Springer, Berlin, pp 316–329

Malone T (1983) How do people organize their desks? Implications for the design of office information systems. ACM Transactions on Information Systems 1:99–112

Manning C, Raghavan P, Schütze H (2008b) Introduction to Information Retrieval. Cambridge University Press, New York, NY

Manning C, Raghavan P, Schütze H (2008a) Amazon mechanical turk. https://www.mturk.com/mturk/welcome, visited on December, 2010

Markatos E (2001) On caching search engine query results. Computer Communications 24(2):137–143

Marshall C (1998) Toward an ecology of hypertext annotation. In: Proceedings of the Conference on Hypertext and Hypermedia, pp 40–49

Matuszek C, Witbrock MJ, Kahlert RC, Cabral J, Schneider D, Shah P, Lenat DB (2005) Searching for common sense: Populating Cyc from the Web. In: Veloso MM, Kambhampati S (eds) Proceedings of the National Conference on Artificial Intelligence. AAAI/MIT Press, Cambridge, MA, pp 1430–1435

McGarry K (2005) A survey of interestingness measures for knowledge discovery. Knowledge Engineering Review 20(1):39–61

Melnik S, Raghavan S, Yang B, Garcia-Molina H (2001) Building a distributed full-text index for the Web. ACM Transactions on Information Systems 19(3):217–241

Melucci M (2005) Context modeling and discovery using vector space bases. In: Proceedings of the ACM Conference on Information and Knowledge Management. ACM Press, New York, NY, pp 808–815

Melucci M (2008) A basis for information retrieval in context. ACM Transactions on Information Systems 26:1–41

Melucci M (2010) An investigation of quantum interference in information retrieval. In: Proceedings of the Information Retrieval Facility Conference. Lecture Notes in Computer Science, vol 6107. Springer, Berlin, pp 136–151

Melucci M, Sitbon L (2011) Modeling emergent associations of nominal compounds: Ongoing research and preliminary results. http://CEUR-WS.org/Vol-704/, visited on February, 2011

Menzel H (1966) Uses in science and technology. Annual Review of Information Science and Technology 1:41–69

Metadata-IFLA-WG (2005) Guidance on the nature, implementation and evaluation of metadata schemas in libraries. Final report of the IFLA cataloguing section working group on the use of metadata schemas. Tech rep, IFLA. For the Review and Approval of the IFLA Cataloguing Section

Metzler D, Manmatha R (2004) An inference network approach to image retrieval. In: Proceedings of the International Conference on Image and Video Retrieval. Lecture Notes in Computer Science, vol 3115. Springer, Berlin, pp 42–50

Mihalcea R, Liu H (2006) A corpus-based approach to finding happiness. http://www.aaai.org/Papers/Symposia/Spring/2006/SS-06-03/SS06-03-027.pdf, visited on February, 2011

Mladenic D (1998) Turning Yahoo! to automatic web-page classifier. In: Proceedings of the European Conference on Artificial Intelligence, pp 473–474

Mobasher B (2007) Web usage mining. In: Liu B (ed) Web Data Mining: Exploring Hyperlinks and Contents and Usage Data. Springer, Berlin, pp 449–484. Chap 12

Moffat A, Bell TH (1995) In situ generation of compressed inverted files. Journal of the American Society for Information Science 46(7):537–550

Moffat A, Stuiver L (2000) Binary interpolative coding for effective index compression. Journal of Information Retrieval 3(1):25–47

Moffat A, Zobel J (1996) Self-indexing inverted files for fast text retrieval. ACM Transactions on Information Systems 14(4):349–379

Moffat A, Webber W, Zobel J, Baeza-Yates R (2007) A pipelined architecture for distributed text query evaluation. Journal of Information Retrieval 10(3):205–231

Müller W, Henrich A (2004) Faster exact histogram intersection on large data collections using inverted VA-files. In: Proceedings of the International Conference on Image and Video Retrieval. Lecture Notes in Computer Science, vol 3115. Springer, Berlin, pp 455–463

Murdock V, Ciaramita M, Plachouras V (2007) A noisy-channel approach to contextual advertising. In: Proceedings of the International Workshop on Data Mining and Audience Intelligence for Advertising. ACM Press, New York, NY, pp 21–27

Najork M, Wiener J (2001) Breadth-first crawling yields high-quality pages. In: Proceedings of the International Conference on the World Wide Web. ACM Press, New York, NY, pp 114–118

Nakasaki H, Kawaba M, Yamazaki S, Utsuro T, Fukuhara T (2009) Visualizing cross-lingual/cross-cultural differences in concerns in multilingual blogs. http://www.aaai.org/ocs/index.php/ICWSM/09/paper/view/161/485, visited on December, 2010

Narayanan A, Shmatikov V (2008) Robust de-anonymization of large sparse datasets. In: Proceedings of the IEEE Symposium on Security and Privacy. IEEE Computer Society, Los Alamitos, pp 111–125

Nene S, Nayar S (1997) A simple algorithm for nearest neighbor search in high dimensions. IEEE Transactions on Pattern Analysis and Machine Intelligence 19:989–1003

Niculescu-mizil A, Caruana R (2005) Predicting good probabilities with supervised learning. In: Proceedings of the International Conference on Machine Learning, pp 625–632

Nielsen J (2003) Usability 101: Introduction to usability. http://www.useit.com/alertbox/20030825.html, visited on February, 2011

Nielsen J (2009) Eyetracking Web Usability. Kara Pernice

Nissenbaum H (2004) Privacy as contextual integrity. Washington Law Review 79(1):119–158

Nonaka I, Takeuchi H (1995) The Knowledge-Creating Company: How Japanese Companies Create the Dynamics of Innovation. Oxford University Press, New York

NTCIR (2010) Evaluation of information access technologies research infrastructure for comparative evaluation of information retrieval and access technologies. http://research.nii.ac.jp/ntcir/index-en.html, visited on December, 2010

Ntoulas A, Cho J (2007) Pruning policies for two-tiered inverted index with correctness guarantee. In: Proceedings of the ACM Conference on Research and Development in Information Retrieval. ACM Press, New York, NY, pp 191–198

Ntoulas A, Cho J, Olston C (2004) What's new on the Web?: The evolution of the Web from a search engine perspective. In: Proceedings of the International Conference on the World Wide Web. ACM Press, New York, NY, pp 1–12

Oard D, Hedin B, Tomlinson S, Baron J (2008) Overview of the TREC legal track. http://trec.nist.gov/, visited on February, 2011

Ogilvy D (1983) Ogilvy on Advertising. Orbis, London

Olston C, Pandey S (2008) Recrawl scheduling based on information longevity. In: Proceedings of the International Conference on the World Wide Web. ACM Press, New York, NY, pp 437–446

Owad T (2006) Data mining 101: Funding subversives with amazon wishlists. http://www.applefritter.com/bannedbooks, visited on December, 2010

Ozcan R, Altingovde I, Ulusoy O (2008) Static query result caching revisited. In: Proceedings of the International Conference on the World Wide Web. ACM Press, New York, NY, pp 1169–1170

Page L, Brin S, Motwani R, Winograd T (1999) The PageRank citation ranking: Bringing order to the Web. http://ilpubs.stanford.edu:8090/422/, visited on February, 2011

Palmquist R, Kim K (2000) Cognitive style and on line database search experience as predictors of web search performance. Journal of the American Society for Information Science 51:558–566

Pandey S, Olston C (2005) User-centric web crawling. In: Proceedings of the International Conference on the World Wide Web. ACM Press, New York, NY, pp 401–411

Pandey S, Olston C (2008) Crawl ordering by search impact. In: Proceedings of the ACM Conference on web Search and Data Mining. ACM Press, New York, NY, pp 3–14

Pandey S, Agarwal D, Chakrabarti D, Josifovski V (2007) Bandits for taxonomies: A model-based approach. http://www.siam.org/proceedings/datamining/2007/dm07_020pandey.pdf, visited on February, 2011

Pang B, Lee L (2008) Opinion mining and sentiment analysis. Foundations and Trends in Information Retrieval 2(1–2):1–135

Papaeconomou C, Zijlema AF, Ingwersen P (2008) Searchers' relevance judgments and criteria in evaluating web pages in a learning style perspective. In: Proceedings of the International Symposium on Information Interaction in Context. IIiX '08. ACM Press, New York, NY, pp 123–132. http://doi.acm.org/10.1145/1414694.1414722, visited on December, 2010

Parthasarathy K (1992) An Introduction to Quantum Stochastic Calculus. Birkhäuser, Basel

Persin M (1994) Document filtering for fast ranking. In: Proceedings of the ACM Conference on Research and Development in Information Retrieval. ACM Press, New York, NY, pp 339–348

Petrelli D, Beaulieu M, Sanderson G, Demetriou M, Herring P, Hansen P (2004) Observing users and designing clarity: A case study on the user-centered design of a cross-language information retrieval system. Journal of the American Society for Information Science and Technology 55:923–934

Phillips D (2004) Privacy policy and PETs: The influence of policy regimes on the development and social implications of privacy enhancing technologies. New Media and Society 6(6):691–706

Pickering M (2004) Video retrieval and summarisation. PhD thesis, Imperial College London

Pickering M, Wong L, Rüger S (2003) ANSES: Summarisation of news video. In: Proceedings of the International Conference on Image and Video Retrieval. Lecture Notes in Computer Science, vol 2728. Springer, Berlin, pp 481–486

Piskorski J, Sydow M, Weiss D (2008) Exploring linguistic features for web spam detection: A preliminary study. In: Proceedings of the International Workshop on Adversarial Information Retrieval on the Web, pp 25–28

Pitkow J, Schütze H, Cass T, Cooley R, Turnbull D, Edmonds A, Adar E, Breuel T (2002) Personalized search. Communications of the ACM 45(9):50–55

Piwowarski B, Frommholz I, Lalmas M, van Rijsbergen K (2010) Exploring a multidimensional representation of documents and queries. In: Acte de la Conférence sur la Recherche d'Information Assistée par Ordinateur, pp 57–60

Platt J (1999) Probabilistic outputs for support vector machines and comparisons to regularized likelihood methods. Advances in Large Margin Classifiers 61–74

Ponnuswami AK, Pattabiraman K, Wu Q, Gilad-Bachrach R, Kanungo T (2011) On composition of a federated web search result page: Using online users to provide pairwise preference for heterogeneous verticals. In: Proceedings of the ACM Conference on Web Search and Data Mining. ACM Press, New York, NY, pp 715–724

Popescu AM, Etzioni O (2005) Extracting product features and opinions from reviews. In: Proceedings of the Human Language Technology Conference and Conference on Empirical Methods in Natural Language Processing. The Association for Computational Linguistics, pp 339–346

Preibusch S (2006) Implementing privacy negotiations in e-commerce. In: Zhou X, Li J, Shen HT, Kitsuregawa M, Zhang Y (eds) Proceedings of the Asia-Pacific Web Conference. Lecture Notes in Computer Science, vol 3841. Springer, Berlin, pp 604–615

Puolamäki K, Salojärvi J, Savia E (2005) Combining eye movements and collaborative filtering for proactive information retrieval. In: Proceedings of the ACM Conference on Research and Development in Information Retrieval. ACM Press, New York, NY, pp 146–153

Puppin D, Silvestri F, Perego R, Baeza-Yates R (2010) Tuning the capacity of search engines: Load-driven routing and incremental caching to reduce and balance the load. ACM Transactions on Information Systems 28(2):1–36

Purves R, Chris J (2004) Workshop on geographic information retrieval. SIGIR Forum 38(2):53–56

Pyle D (1999) Data Preparation for Data Mining. Academic Press, San Diego, CA

Rabiner L (1989a) Sort-merge join. http://en.wikipedia.org/wiki/Sort-merge_join, visited on December, 2010

Rabiner L (1989b) A tutorial on hidden Markov models and selected applications in speech recognition. Proceedings of the IEEE 257–286

Radoslavov P, Govindan R, Estrin D (2002) Topology-informed Internet replica placement. Computer Communications 25(4):384–392

Rafiei D, Bharat K, Shukla A (2010) Diversifying web search results. In: Proceedings of the International Conference on the World Wide Web. ACM Press, New York, NY, pp 781–790

Raghavan S, Garcia-Molina H (2001) Crawling the hidden Web. In: Proceedings of the International Conference on Very Large Data Bases. Morgan Kaufmann, San Francisco, CA, pp 129–138

Rasolofo Y, Savoy J (2003) Term proximity scoring for keyword-based retrieval systems. In: Sebastiani F (ed) Proceedings of the European Conference on Information Retrieval. Lecture Notes in Computer Science, vol 2633. Springer, Berlin/Heidelberg, pp 79. doi:10.1007/3-540-36618-0_15, visited on December, 2010

Ravi S, Broder AZ, Gabrilovich E, Josifovski V, Pandey S, Pang B (2010) Automatic generation of bid phrases for online advertising. In: Proceedings of the ACM Conference on Web Search and Data Mining. ACM Press, New York, NY, pp 341–350

Regelson M, Fain D (2006) Predicting click-through rate using keyword clusters. http://web.archive.org/web/20060716120359/www.bus.ualberta.ca/kasdemir/ssa2/regelson_fain.pdf, visited on February, 2011

Ribeiro-Neto B, Barbosa R (1998) Query performance for tightly coupled distributed digital libraries. In: Proceedings of the ACM Conference on Digital Libraries. ACM Press, New York, NY, pp 182–190

Ribeiro-Neto B, Kitajima J, Navarro G, Sant'Ana C, Ziviani N (1998) Parallel generation of inverted files for distributed text collections. In: Proceedings of the Conference of the Chilean Computer Science Society. IEEE Computer Society, Washington, DC, pp 149–157

Ribeiro-Neto B, Moura E, Neubert M, Ziviani N (1999) Efficient distributed algorithms to build inverted files. In: Proceedings of the ACM Conference on Research and Development in Information Retrieval. ACM Press, New York, NY, pp 105–112

Ribeiro-Neto B, Cristo M, Golgher P, de Moura ES (2005) Impedance coupling in content-targeted advertising. In: Proceedings of the ACM Conference on Research and Development in Information Retrieval. ACM Press, New York, NY, pp 496–503

Richardson M, Dominowska E, Ragno R (2007) Predicting clicks: Estimating the click-through rate for new ads. In: Proceedings of the International Conference on the World Wide Web, pp 521–530

Rieffel E (2007) Certainty and uncertainty in quantum information processing. http://arxiv.org/abs/quant-ph/0702121, visited on February, 2011

Risvik K, Aasheim Y, Lidal M (2003) Multi-tier architecture for web search engines. In: Proceedings of the Latin American Conference on World Wide Web. IEEE Computer Society, Washington, DC, p 132

Robertson T, WrighT F, Dykstra R (1989) Order restricted statistical inference. Statistical Papers 30:316–316

Rocchio J (1971) Relevance feedback in Information Retrieval. In: Salton G (ed) The SMART Retrieval System. Prentice Hall/Englewood Cliffs, New York, NY, pp 313–323

Rodden K, Basalaj W, Sinclair D, Wood K (1999) Evaluating a visualization of image similarity. In: Proceedings of the ACM Conference on Research and Development in Information Retrieval. ACM Press, New York, NY, pp 36–43

Rüger S (2009) Multimedia resource discovery. In: Göker A, Davies J (eds) Information Retrieval: Searching in the 21st Century. Wiley, New York, NY, pp 39–62

Rüger S (2010) Multimedia Information Retrieval. Morgan & Claypool

Rui Y, Huang T, Mehrotra S (1998) Relevance feedback techniques in interactive content-based image retrieval. In: Multimedia Content Analysis and Management and Retrieval, pp 25–36

Ruthven I (2002) On the use of explanations as mediating device for relevance feedback. In: Proceedings of the European Conference on Digital Libraries, pp 338–345

Ruthven I, Lalmas M, van Rijsbergen K (2001) Empirical investigations on query modification using abductive explanations. In: Proceedings of the ACM Conference on Research and Development in Information Retrieval. ACM Press, New York, NY, pp 181–189

Ruthven I, Lalmas M, van Rijsbergen K (2002) Ranking expansion terms with partial and ostensive evidence. In: Proceedings of the Conference on Conceptions of Library and Information Science, pp 199–220

Ruthven I, Lalmas M, van Rijsbergen K (2003) Incorporating user search behaviour into relevance feedback. Journal of the American Society for Information Science and Technology 54:529–549

Rydberg-Cox J, Vetter L, Rüger S, Heesch D (2004) Approaching the problem of multi-lingual information retrieval and visualization in Greek and Latin and Old Norse texts. In: Proceedings of the European Conference on Digital Libraries. Lecture Notes in Computer Science, vol 3232. Springer, Berlin, pp 168–178

Salojärvi J, Kojo I, Simola J, Kaski S (2003) Can relevance be inferred from eye movements in information retrieval? In: Proceedings of the Workshop on Self-Organizing Maps, Kitakyushu, Japan, pp 261–266

Salton G, McGill M (1983) Introduction to Modern Information Retrieval. McGraw-Hill, New York, NY

Salway A, Graham M (2003) Extracting information about emotions in films. In: Proceedings of the ACM Conference on Multimedia, pp 299–302

Salway A, Vassiliou A, Ahmad K (2005) What happens in films? http://doi.ieeecomputersociety.org/10.1109/ICME.2005.1521357, visited on February, 2011

Sammon J (1969) A nonlinear mapping for data structure analysis. IEEE Transactions on Computers 18:401–409

Sanderson M (2010) Test collection based evaluation of information retrieval systems. Foundations and Trends in Information Retrieval 4:247–375

Sanderson M, Zobel J (2005) Information retrieval system evaluation: Effort, sensitivity and reliability. In: Proceedings of the ACM Conference on Research and Development in Information Retrieval. ACM Press, New York, NY, pp 162–169

Sanderson M, Tang J, Arni T, Clough P (2009) What else is there? Search diversity examined. In: Proceedings of the European Conference on Information Retrieval, pp 562–569

Santini S, Jain R (2000) Integrated browsing and querying for image databases. IEEE Multimedia 7:26–39

Saracevic T (2004) Evaluation of digital libraries: An overview. http://comminfo.rutgers.edu/~tefko/DL_evaluation_Delos.pdf, visited on February, 2011

Saracevic T (2007) Relevance: A review of the literature and a framework for thinking on the notion in information science. Part II: Nature and manifestations of relevance. Journal of the American Society for Information Science and Technology 58:1915–1933

Saracevic T, Kantor P (1988a) A study of information seeking and retrieving: II. Users, questions and effectiveness. Journal of the American Society for Information Science 39:177–196

Saracevic T, Kantor P (1988b) A study of information seeking and retrieving: III. Searchers, searches, and overlaps. Journal of the American Society for Information Science 39:197–216

Saracevic T, Kantor P, Chamis A, Trivison D (1988) A study of information seeking and retrieving: I. Background and methodology. Journal of the American Society for Information Science 39:161–176

Saraiva P, Silva de Moura E, Ziviani N, Meira W, Fonseca R, Riberio-Neto B (2001) Rank-preserving two-level caching for scalable search engines. In: Proceedings of the ACM Conference on Research and Development in Information Retrieval. ACM Press, New York, NY, pp 51–58

Sarigiannis C, Plachouras V, Baeza-Yates R (2009) A study of the impact of index updates on distributed query processing for web search. In: Proceedings of the European Conference on Information Retrieval. Springer, Berlin/Heidelberg, pp 595–602

Sarjant S, Legg C, Robinson M, Medelyan O (2009) All you can eat ontology-building: Feeding wikipedia to Cyc. Web Intelligence 341–348

Schek HJ, Schuldt H (2006) DelosDLMS—infrastructure for the next generation of digital management systems. ERCIM News: Special Issue on the European Digital Library 66:22–24

Schenkel R, Broschart A, Hwang S, Theobald M, Weikum G (2007) Efficient text proximity search. In: Proceedings of the International Symposium on String Processing Information Retrieval. Lecture Notes in Computer Science, vol 4726. Springer, Berlin/Heidelberg, pp 287–299

Scholer F, Williams H, Yiannis J, Zobel J (2002) Compression of inverted indexes for fast query evaluation. In: Proceedings of the ACM Conference on Research and Development in Information Retrieval. ACM Press, New York, NY, pp 222–229

Schurman E, Brutlag J (2009) Performance related changes and their user impact. http://velocityconference.blip.tv/file/2279751/, visited on February, 2011

Seo J, Haitsma J, Kalker T, Yoo C (2004) A robust image fingerprinting system using the radon transform. Signal Processing: Image Communication 19:325–339

Shanahan J, den Poel DV (2010a) Determining optimal advertisement frequency capping policy via Markov decision processes to maximize click through rates. http://research.microsoft.com/en-us/um/beijing/events/mload-2010/nips-mload-2010-poster-shanahan-camerareadyposter.pdf, visited on February, 2011

Shanahan J, den Poel DV (2010b) Google to offer ads based on interests. http://www.nytimes.com/2009/03/11/technology/internet/11google.html, visited on December, 2010

Shaw J, Fox E (1994) Combination of multiple searches. In: Proceedings of the Text Retrieval Conference, pp 243–252

Shearer C (2000) The CRISP-DM model: The new blueprint for data mining. Journal of Data Warehousing 5(4):13–22. http://www.crisp-dm.org, visited on December, 2010

Shieh WY, Chung CP (2005) A statistics-based approach to incrementally update inverted files. Information Processing and Management 41(2):275–288

Shieh WY, Chen TF, Shann J, Chung CP (2003) Inverted file compression through document identifier reassignment. Information Processing and Management 39(1):117–131

Shkapenyuk V, Suel T (2002) Design and implementation of a high-performance distributed web crawler. In: Proceedings of the International Conference on Data Engineering. IEEE Computer Society, Washington, DC, p 357

Shneiderman B, Feldman D, Rose A, Ferré Grau X (2000) Visualizing digital library search results with categorical and hierarchical axes. In: Proceedings of the ACM Conference on Digital Libraries, pp 57–66

Shokouhi M, Si L (2011) Federated information retrieval. Upcoming Issue

Shokouhi M, Zobel J, Tahaghoghi S, Scholer F (2007) Using query logs to establish vocabularies in distributed information retrieval. Information Processing and Management 43(1):169–180

Si L, Callan J (2003) Relevant document distribution estimation method for resource selection. In: Proceedings of the ACM Conference on Research and Development in Information Retrieval. ACM Press, New York, NY, pp 298–305

Si L, Jin R, Callan J, Ogilvie P (2002a) A language modeling framework for resource selection and results merging. In: Proceedings of the ACM Conference on Information and Knowledge Management. ACM Press, New York, NY, pp 391–397

Si L, Jin R, Callan J, Ogilvie P (2002b) A language modeling framework for resource selection and results merging. In: Proceedings of the ACM Conference on Information and Knowledge Management. ACM Press, New York, NY, pp 391–397

Silvestri F (2007) Sorting out the document identifier assignment problem. In: Amati G, Carpineto C, Romano G (eds) Proceedings of the European Conference on Information Retrieval. Lecture Notes in Computer Science, vol 4425. Springer, Berlin/Heidelberg, pp 101–112

Silvestri F, Orlando S, Perego R (2004) Assigning identifiers to documents to enhance the clustering property of fulltext indexes. In: Proceedings of the ACM Conference on Research and Development in Information Retrieval. ACM Press, New York, NY, pp 305–312

Skobeltsyn G, Junqueira F, Plachouras V, Baeza-Yates R (2008) ResIn: a combination of results caching and index pruning for high-performance web search engines. In: Proceedings of the ACM Conference on Research and Development in Information Retrieval. ACM Press, New York, NY, pp 131–138

Smeaton A, Gurrin C, Lee H, Mc Donald K, Murphy N, O'Connor N, O'Sullivan D, Smyth B, Wilson D (2004) The Físchlár-news-stories system: Personalised access to an archive of TV news. In: Acte de la Conférence sur la Recherche d'Information Assistée par Ordinateur, pp 3–17

Sormunen E (2002) Liberal relevance criteria of TREC—counting on negligible documents? In: Proceedings of the ACM Conference on Research and Development in Information Retrieval. ACM Press, New York, NY, pp 320–330

Spärck-Jones K (2006) What's the value of TREC: Is there a gap to jump or a chasm to bridge? ACM SIGIR Forum 40:10–20

Spink A, Cole C (2005) New Directions in Cognitive Information Retrieval. Springer, Berlin

Spink A, Greisdorf H, Bateman J (1998) From highly relevant to not relevant: Examining different regions of relevance. Information Processing and Management 34:599–621

Squire D, Müller W, Müller H, Pun T (2000) Content-based query of image databases: Inspirations from text retrieval. Pattern Recognition Letters 21:1193–1198

Strohman T, Turtle H, Croft W (2005) Optimization strategies for complex queries. In: Proceedings of the ACM Conference on Research and Development in Information Retrieval. ACM Press, New York, NY, pp 219–225

Stumme G, Hotho A, Berendt B (2006) Semantic web mining: State of the art and future directions. Journal of Web Semantics 4(2):124–143

Suchman L (1988) Representing practice in cognitive science. Human Studies 11:305–325

Sun JT, Zeng HJ, Liu H, Lu Y, Chen Z (2005) CubeSVD: a novel approach to personalized web search. In: Proceedings of the International Conference on the World Wide Web. ACM Press, New York, NY, pp 382–390

Sushmita S, Joho H, Lalmas M (2009) A task-based evaluation of an aggregated search interface. In: Proceedings of the International Symposium on String Processing and Information Retrieval, pp 322–333

Sushmita S, Joho H, Lalmas M, Villa R (2010b) Factors affecting click-through behavior in aggregated search interfaces. In: Proceedings of the ACM Conference in Information and Knowledge Management, pp 519–528

Sushmita S, Piwowarski B, Lalmas M (2010a) Dynamics of genre and domain intents. In: Cheng PJ, Kan MY, Lam W, Nakov P (eds) Proceedings of the Asian Information Retrieval Symposium. Lecture Notes in Computer Science, vol 6458, pp 399–409

Sweeney L (2002) K-anonymity: A model for protecting privacy. International Journal of Uncertainty, Fuzziness and Knowledge-Based Systems 10(5):557–570

Tague J, Schultz R (1988) Some measures and procedures for evaluation of the userinterface in an information retrieval system. In: Proceedings of the ACM Conference on Research and Development in Information Retrieval. ACM Press, New York, NY, pp 371–385

Tait J (ed) (2008) Proceedings of the ACM Workshop on Patent Information Retrieval. ACM Press, New York, NY

Tan B, Shen X, Zhai C (2006) Mining long-term search history to improve search accuracy. In: Proceedings of the ACM Conference on Knowledge Discovery and Data Mining. ACM Press, New York, NY, pp 718–723

Tanenbaum A (1996) Computer Networks, 3rd edn. Prentice Hall, Upper Addle River, NJ

Tang J, Sanderson M (2010) Evaluation and user preference study on spatial diversity. In: Proceedings of the European Conference on Information Retrieval, pp 179–190

Teevan J, Alvarado C, Ackerman M, Karger D (2004) The perfect search engine is not enough: A study of orienteering behavior in directed search. In: Proceedings of the ACM Conference on Human Factors in Computing Systems, pp 415–422

Teevan J, Dumais S, Horvitz E (2005) Personalizing search via automated analysis of interests and activities. In: Proceedings of the ACM Conference on Research and Development in Information Retrieval. ACM Press, New York, NY, pp 449–456

Tian Y, Weiss GM, Ma Q (2007) A semi-supervised approach for web spam detection using combinatorial feature-fusion. In: Proceedings of the Graph Labelling Workshop and Web Spam Challenge at the European Conference on Machine Learning and Principles and Practice of Knowledge Discovery, pp 16–23. http://citeseerx.ist.psu.edu/viewdoc/summary?doi=10.1.1.70.9384, visited on December, 2010

Tolonen T, Karjalainen M (2000) A computationally efficient multi-pitch analysis model. IEEE Transactions on Speech and Audio Processing 8:708–716

Tomasic A, Garcia-Molina H (1993) Caching and database scaling in distributed shared-nothing information retrieval systems. ACM SIGMOD Record 22(2):129–138

Tomasic A, Garcia-Molina H, Shoens K (1994) Incremental updates of inverted lists for text document retrieval. In: Proceedings of the ACM Conference on Management of Data. ACM Press, New York, NY, pp 289–300

Tomasic A, Gravano L, Lue C, Schwarz P, Haas L (1997) Data structures for efficient broker implementation. ACM Transactions on Information Systems 15(3):223–253

Tombros A, Ruthven I, Jose J (2003) Searchers' criteria for assessing web pages. In: Proceedings of the ACM Conference on Research and Development in Information Retrieval. ACM Press, New York, NY, pp 96–104

Toms E, Freund L, Kopak R, Bartlett J (2003) The effect of task domain on search. In: Proceedings of the Conference of the Centre for Advanced Studies on Collaborative research. IBM Press, pp 303–312

Tonellotto N, Macdonald C, Ounis I (2010) Efficient dynamic pruning with proximity support. http://www.lsdsir.org/wp-content/uploads/2010/05/lsdsir10-5.pdf, visited on February, 2011

Torralba A, Oliva A (2003) Statistics of natural image categories. Network: Computation in Neural Systems 14:391–412

TRECVid (2003) TREC video retrieval evaluation. http://trecvid.nist.gov/, visited on December, 2010

Turpin A, Tsegay Y, Hawking D, Williams H (2007) Fast generation of result snippets in web search. In: Proceedings of the ACM Conference on Research and Development in Information Retrieval. ACM Press, New York, NY, pp 127–134

Turtle H, Flood J (1995) Query evaluation: Strategies and optimizations. Information Processing and Management 31(6):831–850

Tzanetakis G, Cook P (2002) Musical genre classification of audio signals. IEEE Transactions on Speech and Audio Processing 10:293–302

Urvoy T, Lavergne T, Filoche P (2006) Tracking web spam with hidden style similarity. In: Proceedings of the International Workshop on Adversarial Information Retrieval on the Web, pp 25–31

Vakkari P (2001) Changes in search tactics and relevance judgments in preparing a research proposal: A summary of findings of a longitudinal study. Journal of Information Retrieval 4(3/4):295–310

Vakkari P (2003) Task-based information searching. Annual Review of Information Science and Technology 37:413–464

Vakkari P, Hakala N (2000) Changes in relevance criteria and problem stages in task performance. Journal of Documentation 56:540–562

Vakkari P, Sormunen E (2004) The influence of relevance levels on the effectiveness of interactive information retrieval. Journal of the American Society for Information Science and Technology 55:963–969 van Dongen S (2000) A cluster algorithm for graphs. Tech Rep INS-R0010, National Research Institute for Mathematics and Computer Science in the Netherlands

van Rijsbergen K (2004) The Geometry of Information Retrieval. Cambridge University Press, Cambridge

van Veen T, Oldroyd B (2004) Search and retrieval in the European library. A new approach. http://www.dlib.org/dlib/february04/vanveen/02vanveen.html, visited on December, 2010

Varadarajan R, Hristidis V (2006) A system for query-specific document summarization. In: Proceedings of the ACM Conference on Information and Knowledge Management. ACM Press, New York, NY, pp 622–631

Vestergaard T, Schroder K (1985) The Language of Advertising. Blackwell

von Ahn L, Dabbish L (2004) Labeling images with a computer game. In: Proceedings of the ACM Conference on Human Factors in Computing Systems, pp 319–326

Voorhees E (1998) Variations in relevance judgments and the measurement of retrieval effectiveness. In: Proceedings of the ACM Conference on Research and Development in Information Retrieval. ACM Press, New York, NY, pp 315–323

Voorhees E, Harman D (2005) TREC: Experiments and Evaluation in Information Retrieval. MIT Press, New York, NY

Voss J (2007) Tagging, folksonomy & Co—Renaissance of manual indexing? Computing Research Repository abs/cs/0701072:1–12

W3C (2000) HTML techniques for Web content accessibility guidelines. http://www.w3.org/TR/WCAG10-HTML-TECHS/, visited on December, 2010

Wang P (1997) Users' information needs at different stages of a research project: a cognitive view. In: Proceedings of the International Conference on Information Seeking in Context. Taylor Graham, London, pp 307–318. http://portal.acm.org/citation.cfm?id=267190.267209, visited on December, 2010

Wang P, Hawk W, Tenopir C (2000) Users' interaction with World Wide Web resources: An exploratory study using a holistic approach. Information Processing and Management 36:229–251

Wang X, Broder AZ, Fontoura M, Josifovski V (2009) A search-based method for forecasting ad impression in contextual advertising. http://www2009.eprints.org/50/, visited on February, 2011

Wang L, Lin J, Metzler D (2010) Learning to efficiently rank. In: Proceedings of the ACM Conference on Research and Development in Information Retrieval. ACM Press, New York, NY, pp 138–145

Wardlow DL (1996) Theory, Practice and Research Issues in Marketing: Gays, Lesbians and Consumer Behavior. Haworth

Watts D, Strogatz S (1998) Collective dynamics of 'small-world' networks. Nature 393:440–442

Weber R, Stock H, Blott S (1998) A quantitative analysis and performance study for similarity search methods in high-dimensional space. In: Proceedings of the International Conference on Very Large Databases, pp 194–205

Weber R, Schuler C, Neukomm P, Schuldt H, Schek HJ (2003) Webservice composition with O'GRAPE and OSIRIS. In: Proceedings of the International Conference on Very Large Databases, pp 1081–1084

White R (2006) Using searcher simulations to redesign a polyrepresentative implicit feedback interface. Information Processing and Management 42:1185–1202

White R, Jose JM, Ruthven I (2003) A task-oriented study of the influencing effects of query-biased summarization in web searching. Information Processing and Management 39:707–733

White R, Ruthven I, Jose J (2005a) A study of factors affecting the utility of implicit relevance feedback. In: Proceedings of the ACM Conference on Research and Development in Information Retrieval. ACM Press, New York, NY, pp 35–42

White R, Ruthven I, Jose J, van Rijsbergen K (2005b) Evaluating implicit feedback models using searcher simulations. ACM Transactions on Information Systems 325–361

White R, Jose J, Ruthven I (2006) An implicit feedback approach for interactive information retrieval. Information Processing and Management 42:166–190

White R, Bilenko M, Cucerzan S (2007) Studying the use of popular destinations to enhance web search interaction. In: Proceedings of the ACM Conference on Research and Development in Information Retrieval. ACM Press, New York, NY, pp 159–166

Widdows D (2004) Geometry and Meaning. CSLI

Widdows D, Peters S (2003) Word vectors and quantum logic: Experiments with negation and dijunction. In: Oehrle RT, Rogers J (eds) Proceedings of the Mathematics of Language Conference, vol 8, pp 141–154

Williams G, Anand S (2009) Predicting the polarity strength of adjectives using wordnet. http://www.aaai.org/ocs/index.php/ICWSM/09/paper/download/214/541, visited on December, 2010

Witten I, Moffat A, Bell T (1999) Managing Gigabytes: Compressing and Indexing Documents and Images, 2nd edn. Morgan Kaufmann, San Francisco, CA

Wolf J, Squillante M, Yu P, Sethuraman J, Ozsen L (2002) Optimal crawling strategies for web search engines. In: Proceedings of the International Conference on the World Wide Web. ACM Press, New York, NY, pp 136–147

Wong WP, Lee D (1993) Implementations of partial document ranking using inverted files. Information Processing and Management 29(5):647–669

Wood M, Campbell N, Thomas B (1998) Iterative refinement by relevance feedback in content-based digital image retrieval. ACM Multimedia 13–20

Wu B, Davison BD (2005) Identifying link farm spam pages. In: Ellis A, Hagino T (eds) Proceedings of the International Conference on the World Wide Web. ACM Press, New York, NY, pp 820–829

Wu H, Qiu G, He X, Shi Y, Qu M, Shen J, Bu J, Chen C (2009) Advertising keyword generation using active learning. In: Proceedings of the International Conference on the World Wide Web, pp 1095–1096

Xu J, Callan J (1998) Effective retrieval with distributed collections. In: Proceedings of the ACM Conference on Research and Development in Information Retrieval. ACM Press, New York, NY, pp 112–120

Xu J, Croft W (1999) Cluster-based language models for distributed retrieval. In: Proceedings of the ACM Conference on Research and Development in Information Retrieval. ACM Press, New York, NY, pp 254–261

Yan H, Ding S, Suel T (2009a) Compressing term positions in web indexes. In: Proceedings of the ACM Conference on Research and Development in Information Retrieval. ACM Press, New York, NY, pp 147–154

Yan H, Ding S, Suel T (2009b) Inverted index compression and query processing with optimized document ordering. In: Proceedings of the International Conference on the World Wide Web. ACM Press, New York, NY, pp 401–410

Yan J, Liu N, Wang G, Zhang W, Jiang Y, Chen Z (2009c) How much can behavioral targeting help online advertising? In: Proceedings of the International Conference on the World Wide Web. ACM Press, New York, NY, pp 261–270

Yavlinsky A, Pickering M, Heesch D, Rüger S (2004) A comparative study of evidence combination strategies. In: Proceedings of the IEEE International Conference on Acoustics, Speech and Signal Processing, pp 1040–1043

Yavlinsky A, Schofield E, Rüger S (2005) Automated image annotation using global features and robust nonparametric density estimation. In: Proceedings of the International Conference on Image and Video Retrieval. Lecture Notes in Computer Science, vol 3568. Springer, Berlin, pp 507–517

Yih W (2006) Finding advertising keywords on web pages. In: Proceedings of the International Conference on the World Wide Web. ACM Press, New York, NY, pp 213–222

Yu K, Bi J, Tresp V (2006) Active learning via transductive experimental design. In: Proceedings of the International Conference on Machine Learning. ACM Press, New York, NY, pp 1081–1088

Yu F, Xie Y, Ke Q (2010) Sbotminer: Large scale search bot detection. In: Proceedings of the ACM Conference on web Search and Data Mining. ACM Press, New York, NY, pp 421–430

Yuwono B, Lee D (1997) Server ranking for distributed text retrieval systems on the Internet. In: Proceedings of the International Conference on Database Systems for Advanced Applications. World Scientific, Singapore, pp 41–50

Zadrozny B, Elkan C (2001) Obtaining calibrated probability estimates from decision trees and naive Bayesian classifiers. In: Proceedings of the International Conference on Machine Learning. Morgan Kaufmann, San Diego, CA, pp 609–616

Zaïane OR (1998) From resource discovery to knowledge discovery on the internet. Tech Rep TR 1998-13, Simon Fraser University

Zeinalipour-Yazti D, Dikaiakos M (2002) Design and implementation of a distributed crawler and filtering processor. In: Proceedings of the International Workshop on Next Generation Information Technologies and Systems. Springer, London, pp 58–74

Zhang J, Long X, Suel T (2008) Performance of compressed inverted list caching in search engines. In: Proceedings of the International Conference on the World Wide Web. ACM Press, New York, NY, pp 387–396

Zhou L, Dai L, Zhang D (2007) Online shopping acceptance model—a critical survey of consumer factors in online shopping. Journal of Electronic Commerce Research 8:41–61

Zhou K, Lalmas M, Cummins R (2010) Building a test collection for aggregated search. Tech rep, University of Glasgow

Zittrain J (2008) The Future of the Internet—and How to Stop It. Caravan Books. http://futureoftheinternet.org/, visited on December, 2010

Zobel J, Moffat A (2006) Inverted files for text search engines. ACM Computing Surveys 38(2):6

Zuccon G, Azzopardi L (2010) Using the quantum probability ranking principle to rank interdependent documents. In: Proceedings of the European Conference on Information Retrieval, pp 357–369

Zuccon G, Azzopardi L, van Rijsbergen K (2009) The quantum probability ranking principle for information retrieval. In: Proceedings of the International Conference on the Theory of Information Retrieval, pp 232–240

Index

M. Melucci, R. Baeza-Yates (eds.), *Advanced Topics in Information Retrieval*,
The Information Retrieval Series 33,
DOI 10.1007/978-3-642-20946-8, © Springer-Verlag Berlin Heidelberg 2011